THE
unofficial GUIDE®
ᵀᴼDisneyland®

2008

THE *unofficial* GUIDE®
TO Disneyland*

2008

BOB SEHLINGER

*Disneyland® is officially known as the Disneyland Resort®.

WILEY

Please note that prices fluctuate in the course of time and that travel information changes under the impact of many factors that influence the travel industry. We therefore suggest that you write or call ahead for confirmation when making your travel plans. Every effort has been made to ensure the accuracy of information throughout this book, and the contents of this publication are believed to be correct at the time of printing. Nevertheless, the publishers cannot accept responsibility for errors or omissions, for changes in details given in this guide, or for the consequences of any reliance on the information provided by the same. Assessments of attractions and so forth are based upon the author's own experience; therefore, descriptions given in this guide necessarily contain an element of subjective opinion, which may not reflect the publisher's opinion or dictate a reader's own experience on another occasion. Readers are invited to write the publisher with ideas, comments, and suggestions for future editions.

Published by:
John Wiley & Sons, Inc.
111 River Street
Hoboken, NJ 07030-5774

Produced by Menasha Ridge Press

Cover design by Michael J. Freeland

Interior design by Vertigo Design

Photo credit: Disneyland® Resort

For information on our other products and services or to obtain technical support, please contact our Customer Care Department within the United States at 800-762-2974, outside the United States at 317-572-3993, or by fax at 317-572-4002.

John Wiley & Sons, Inc., also publishes its books in a variety of electronic formats. Some content that appears in print may not be available in electronic formats.

ISBN 978-0-470-08961-3

Manufactured in the United States of America

5 4 3 2 1

CONTENTS

LIST *of* MAPS *and* ILLUSTRATIONS

ACKNOWLEDGMENTS

A BIG SALUTE TO OUR WHOLE *UNOFFICIAL* TEAM, who rendered a Herculean effort in what must have seemed like a fantasy version of Sartre's *No Exit* to the tune of "It's a Small World." We hope you all recover to tour another day.

Special thanks to dining critic Pete Johnson; Disney historian Jim Hill; cartoonist Tami Knight; *Unofficial Guide* research director Len Testa; child psychologist Karen Turnbow, PhD; *Unofficial Guide* statistician Fred Hazleton; "Unheralded Treasures" writer Lani Teshima; roving reporter Kim Keck; and *Unofficial* friends Mike Scopa and David Swanson.

Ritchey Halphen, Myra Merkle, and Annie Long all contributed energetically to shaping this latest edition. Much appreciation also to proofreader Susan Roberts, editorial/production manager Molly Merkle, cartographer Steve Jones, and indexer Galen Schroeder.

—*Bob Sehlinger*

THE *unofficial* GUIDE®
ᵀᴼDisneyland®

2008

INTRODUCTION

WHY "UNOFFICIAL"?

DECLARATION OF INDEPENDENCE

THE AUTHOR AND RESEARCHERS OF THIS GUIDE specifically and categorically declare that they are and always have been totally independent of the Walt Disney Company, Inc., of Disneyland, Inc., of Walt Disney World, Inc., and of any and all other members of the Disney corporate family.

The material in this guide originated with the authors and the researchers and has not been reviewed, edited, or in any way approved by the Walt Disney Company, Inc., Disneyland, Inc., or Walt Disney World, Inc.

This guidebook represents the first comprehensive *critical* appraisal of Disneyland. Its purpose is to provide the reader with the information necessary to tour the theme parks with the greatest efficiency and economy and with the least amount of hassle and standing in line. The researchers of this guide believe in the wondrous variety, joy, and excitement of the Disney attractions. At the same time, we realistically recognize that Disneyland is a business, with the same profit motivations as businesses all over the world.

With no obligation to toe the Disney line, we represent and serve you, the reader. The contents were researched and compiled by a team of evaluators who were, and are, completely independent of the Walt Disney Company, Inc. If a restaurant serves bad food, if a gift item is overpriced, or if a certain ride isn't worth the wait, we say so. And in the process, we hope to make your visit more fun, efficient, and economical.

DANCE TO THE MUSIC

A DANCE HAS A BEGINNING AND AN END. But when you're dancing you're not concerned about getting to the end or where on the dance floor you might wind up. In other words, you're totally in the moment. That's the way you should be on your Disneyland vacation.

You may feel a bit of pressure concerning your vacation. Vacations, after all, are very special events, and expensive ones to boot. So you work hard to make your vacation the best that it can be. Planning and organizing are essential to a successful Disneyland vacation, but if they become your focus, you won't be able to hear the music and enjoy the dance.

So think of us as your dancing coach. We'll teach you the steps to the dance in advance so that when you're on vacation and the music plays, you will dance with effortless grace and ease.

THE IMPORTANCE OF BEING GOOFY

WALT DISNEY WORLD'S OPERATIONS MANAGER is happily munching his way through a jar of Gummi Bears when he's interrupted by the director of casting.

"Ed, I need to talk to you about Wilbur Wafflebein. I've been getting calls every day from his psychiatrist."

"Sorry, Norm, I don't recall the name. Who is Wilbur Wafflebein?"

"Wilbur is an abominable snowman at the Matterhorn Bobsleds. You know, the lurking, shadowy beast who threatens guests on the roller coaster."

"His name's *Wilbur*?"

"Yep, but he goes by Willie. His therapist says he's been seriously miscast and as a result he's clinically depressed."

"What's he talking about? I've never seen anyone so perfect for a part. He's 18 feet tall, he's hairier than a herd of yaks, and he smells like a chemical plant."

"C'mon, Ed, Willie tries hard to play the part, but he's nothing at all like the character he plays. He's a really sweet guy, and he's fastidious about his appearance when he's off the clock. He showers and shampoos daily, trims his beard, and wears his fur in sort of a sculpted perm. Kind of gives him a friendly giant-poodle look. And those snaggle teeth are fake—he actually has lovely dentition. He's a very snazzy dresser, too."

"Hmmm, I think I may have run into him at church. . . . anyway, how are you handling this? I wouldn't think you could find anyone else suitable for the part."

"Well, we recruited his cousin, a Sasquatch from the Pacific Northwest, to take his place. As for his good points, he's mean as a snake and smells like a wet camel; on the minus side, he has a drinking problem. He kept sliding off the mountain, so we put him in a leather harness. Gives him a sort of S-and-M appearance, but at least he's not plopping off a cliff every time he moons the guests."

"He *moons the guests*?! *Very* un-Disney!"

"It's not as bad as you think. He's so hairy that from the rear he looks like a really big bush with attitude. Plus when he turns around, you can't smell the whiskey on his breath. On hot days he prefers beer and always manages to slosh some on the guests. They really love that. Makes 'em feel like they're getting something for free. He has the food-and-beverage department a little nervous though, so we're trying to teach him to slosh only on riders of legal drinking age."

"This doesn't sound good to me. Is there anything else?"

"When he's super-snockered, he belts out 'Born in the U.S.A.' at the top of his lungs. On his better days, he actually sounds like The Boss."

" 'Born in the U.S.A.' doesn't fit the theme! Can't he yodel or sing 'Edelweiss'?"

"I know. The writers are revising the story line to introduce an American Sasquatch who came to the Continent as an exchange student and . . . ."

"Enough! Send this guy back to Oregon. What will it take to get Wilbur back?"

"He says he'll come back only if he can be clean and coiffed. He wants a picture window with blue silk drapes in his cave and an accent wall. He would also appreciate a Bukhara carpet, a floral-print love seat, two gold-framed Monet prints, and a carved teakwood coffee table."

"Yikes! Is that all?"

"Not quite. You know that place on the ride where the tracks are torn up and the train stops? Well, he wants to welcome the riders and thank them for visiting his country. He's adamant that the Matterhorn Bobsleds not make Switzerland seem inhospitable."

"Um, that kinda takes the punch out of the attraction."

"Oh, glad you reminded me. He also wants to serve punch and canapés and . . . Ed! Who are you calling?"

"Willie. Maybe he can make some suggestions about improving the feng shui of my office."

And so it goes. . . .

The Death of Spontaneity

One of our all-time favorite letters is from a man in Chapel Hill, North Carolina. He writes:

> Your book reads like the operations plan for an amphibious landing: Go here, do this, proceed to Step 15. You must think that everyone is a hyperactive, type A theme-park commando. What happened to the satisfaction of self-discovery or the joy of spontaneity? Next you will be telling us when to empty our bladders.

As it happens, we at the *Unofficial Guide* are a pretty existential crew. We are big on self-discovery when walking in the woods or watching birds. Some of us are able to improvise jazz without reading music, while others can whip up a mean pot of chili without a recipe. When it comes to Disneyland, however, we all agree that you either need a good plan or a frontal lobotomy. The operational definition of self-discovery and spontaneity at Disneyland is the "pleasure" of heat prostration and the "joy" of standing in line.

It's easy to spot the free spirits at Disneyland Park and Disney's California Adventure, particularly at opening time. While everybody else is stampeding to Splash Mountain or Indiana Jones, they're the ones standing in a cloud of dust puzzling over the park map. Later, they're the folks running around like chickens in a thunderstorm trying to find an attraction with less than a 40-minute wait. Face it: Disneyland Resort is not a very existential place. In many ways it's the ultimate in mass-produced entertainment, the most planned and programmed environment imaginable. Spontaneity and self-discovery work about as well at Disneyland as they do on your tax return.

We're not saying you can't have a great time at Disneyland. Bowling isn't very spontaneous either, but lots of people love it. What we *are* saying is that you need a plan. You don't have to be inflexible about it, just think about what you want to do—before you go. Don't delude yourself by rationalizing that the information in this modest tome is only for the pathological and super-organized. Ask not for whom the tome tells, Bubba; it tells for thee.

HOW *this* GUIDE WAS RESEARCHED *and* WRITTEN

WHILE MUCH HAS BEEN WRITTEN CONCERNING Disneyland Resort, very little has been comparative or evaluative. In preparing this guide, nothing was taken for granted. The theme parks were visited at different times throughout the year by a team of trained observers who conducted detailed evaluations, rating the theme parks along with all of their component rides, shows, exhibits, services, and concessions according to a formal, pretested rating criteria. Interviews with attraction patrons were conducted to determine what tourists of all age groups enjoyed most and least during their Disneyland visit.

Although our observers are independent and impartial, we do not claim special expertise or scientific background relative to the types of exhibits, performances, or attractions viewed. Like you, we visit the Disneyland parks as tourists, noting our satisfaction or dissatisfaction. Disneyland offerings are marketed to the touring public, and it is as the public that we have experienced them.

The primary difference between the average tourist and the trained evaluator is that the latter approaches attractions equipped with professional skills in organization, preparation, and observation. The trained evaluator is responsible for much more than simply observing and cataloging. While the tourist is being entertained and delighted by the *Enchanted Tiki Room,* the professional evaluator seated nearby is rating the performance in terms of theme, pace, continuity, and originality. The evaluator also checks out the physical arrangements: Is the sound system clear and audible without being overpowering; is the audience shielded from the sun or rain; is seating adequate; can everyone in the audience clearly see the stage? Similarly, detailed and relevant checklists are prepared by observer teams and applied to rides, exhibits, concessions, and to the theme park in general. Finally, observations and evaluator ratings are integrated with audience reactions and the opinions of patrons to compile a comprehensive profile of each feature and service.

In compiling this guide, we recognize the fact that a tourist's age, gender, background, and interests will strongly influence his or her taste in Disneyland offerings and will account for his or her preference of one ride or feature over another. Given this fact, we make no attempt at comparing apples with oranges. How, indeed, could a meaningful comparison be made between the serenity and beauty of the Storybook Land Canal Boats and the wild roller-coaster ride of California Screamin'? Instead, our objective is to provide the reader with a critical evaluation and enough pertinent data to make knowledgeable decisions according to individual tastes.

The essence of this guide, then, consists of individual critiques and descriptions of each feature of the Disneyland parks, supplemented with some maps to help you get around and several detailed touring plans to help you avoid bottlenecks and crowds. Because so many Disneyland guests also visit Universal Studios Hollywood, we have included comprehensive coverage and a touring plan for that park as well.

A WORD TO OUR READERS ABOUT ANNUAL REVISIONS

SOME OF YOU WHO PURCHASE EACH NEW EDITION of the *Unofficial Guide* have chastised us for retaining examples, comments, and descriptions from previous years' editions. This letter from a Grand Rapids, Michigan, reader is typical:

> *Your guidebook still has the same little example stories. When I got my* [new] *book I expected a true update and new stuff, not the same-old same-old!*

First, the *Unofficial Guide* is a reference work. Though we are flattered that some readers read the guide from cover to cover, and that some of you find it entertaining, our objective is fairly straightforward: to provide information that enables you to have the best possible Disneyland vacation.

Each year during our revision research, we check every attraction, restaurant, hotel, shop, and entertainment offering. Although there are many changes, much remains the same from year to year. When we profile and critique an attraction, we try to provide the reader with the most insightful, relevant, and useful information, written in the clearest possible language. It is our opinion that if an attraction does not change, then it makes little sense to risk clarity and content for the sake of freshening up the prose. Disneyland guests who try the Mad Tea Party, the Haunted Mansion, or the Matterhorn Bobsleds today, for example, experience the same presentation as guests who visited Disneyland in 2007, 1990, or 1986. Moreover, according to our extensive patron surveys (about 1,000 each year), today's guests still respond to these attractions in the same way as prior-year patrons.

The bottom line: we believe that our readers are better served if we devote our time to that which is changing and new as opposed to that which remains the same. The success or failure of this *Unofficial Guide* is determined not by the style of the writing but by the accuracy of the information and, ultimately, whether you have a positive experience at Disneyland. Every change to the guide we make (or don't make) is evaluated in this context.

WE'VE GOT ATTITUDE

SOME READERS DISAGREE with our attitude toward Disney. One, a 30-something woman from Golden, Colorado, lambasted us, writing:

> I read your book cover to cover and felt you were way too hard on Disney. It's disappointing, when you're all enthused about going, to be slammed with all these criticisms and possible pitfalls.

A reader from Little Rock, Arkansas, also took us to task, commenting:

> Your book was quite complimentary of Disney, perhaps too complimentary. Maybe the free trips you travel writers get at Disneyland are chipping away at your objectivity.

And from a Williamsport, Pennsylvania, mother of three:

> Reading your book irritated me before we went because of all the warnings and cautions. I guess I'm used to having guidebooks pump me up about where I'm going. But once I arrived I found I was fully prepared and we had a great time. In retrospect, I have to admit you were right on the money. What I regarded as you being negative was just a good dose of reality.

A Vienna, Virginia, family chimed in with this:

> After being at Disney for three days at the height of tourist season, I laughed out loud at your "Death of Spontaneity" section. We are definitely free-spirit types who don't like to plan our days when we are on vacation. A friend warned us, and we got your guidebook. After skimming through it before we left, I was terrified that we had made a terrible mistake booking this vacation. Thanks to your book, we had a wonderful time. If it had not been for the book, we definitely would have been trampled by all the people stampeding to Space Mountain while we were standing there with our maps.

Finally, a reader from Phoenixville, Pennsylvania, prefers no opinions at all, writing:

Although each person has the right to his or her own opinion, I did not purchase the book for an opinion.

For the record, we've always paid our own way at Disneyland Resort: hotels, admissions, meals, the works. We don't dislike Disney, and we most definitely don't have an ax to grind. We're positive by nature and much prefer to praise than to criticize. Personally, we have enjoyed the Disney parks immensely over the years, both experiencing them and writing about them. Disney, however, as with all corporations (and all people, for that matter), is better at some things than others. Because our readers shell out big bucks to go to Disneyland, we believe they have the right to know in advance what's good and what's not. For those who think we're overly positive, please understand that *The Unofficial Guide to Disneyland* is a guidebook, not an exposé. Our overriding objective is for you to enjoy your visit. To that end we try to report fairly and objectively. When readers disagree with our opinions, we, in the interest of fairness and balance, publish their point of view right alongside ours. To the best of our knowledge, the *Unofficial Guides* are the only travel guides in print that do this.

THE SUM OF ALL FEARS

EVERY WRITER WHO EXPRESSES AN OPINION is quite accustomed to readers who strongly agree or disagree. It comes with the territory. Troubling in the extreme, however, is the possibility that our efforts to be objective have frightened some readers away from Disneyland, or stimulated in others a state of apprehension. For the record, if you enjoy theme parks, Disneyland and Walt Disney World are as good as it gets: absolute nirvana. They're upbeat, safe, fun, eye-popping, happy, and exciting. Even if you arrive knowing nothing about the place and make every possible touring mistake, chances are about 90% that you'll have a wonderful time anyway. In the end, guidebooks don't make or break great destinations. They are simply tools to help you enhance your experience and get the most vacation for your money.

As wonderful as Disneyland is, however, it is nevertheless a complex destination. Even so, it's certainly not nearly as challenging or difficult as visiting New York, San Francisco, Paris, Acapulco, or any other large city or destination. And, happily, there are numerous ways, if forewarned, to save money, minimize hassle, and make the most of your time. In large measure, that's what this guide is about: giving you a heads-up regarding potential problems or opportunities. Unfortunately, some folks reading the *Unofficial Guide* unconsciously add up the various warnings and critical advice and conclude that Disneyland is altogether too intimidating or, alternatively, too expensive or too much work. They lose track of the wonder of Disneyland and become focused instead on what might go wrong.

Our philosophy is that knowledge is power (and time, and money, too). You're free to follow our advice or not at your sole discretion.

But you'd be denied the opportunity to exercise that discretion if we failed to fairly present the issues.

With or without a guidebook, you'll have a great time at Disneyland. If you let us, we'll help you smooth the potential bumps. We are certain that we can help you turn a great vacation into an absolutely superb one. Either way, once there, you will get the feel of the place and quickly reach a comfort level that will allay your apprehensions and allow you to have a great experience.

THE *UNOFFICIAL GUIDE* PUBLISHING YEAR

WE RECEIVE MANY QUERIES EACH YEAR asking when the next edition of the *Unofficial Guide* will be available. Usually our new editions are published and available in the stores by late August or early September. Thus the 2009 edition will be on the shelves in the autumn of 2008.

WHERE'S THE INDEX?

TO ELIMINATE YOUR HAVING TO CARRY THIS TOME around the theme parks, we've created quite a few tear-out pages with maps, touring plans, survey forms, and more at the end of the book. Consequently, we've moved the index from its usual position as the last thing in the book to immediately precede the tear-out pages.

LETTERS, COMMENTS, AND QUESTIONS FROM READERS

MANY OF THOSE WHO USE *The Unofficial Guide to Disneyland* write to us, asking questions, making comments, or sharing their own strategies for visiting Disneyland. We appreciate all such input, both positive and critical, and encourage our readers to continue writing. Readers' comments and observations are frequently used in revised editions of this *Unofficial Guide* and have contributed immeasurably to its improvement.

Reader Questionnaire

At the back of this guide is a short questionnaire you can use to express opinions about your Disneyland Resort visit. The questionnaire is designed to allow every member of your party, regardless of age, to tell us what he or she thinks. Clip the questionnaire on the dotted lines and mail it to:

Reader Survey
The Unofficial Guide to Disneyland
P.O. Box 43673
Birmingham, AL 35243

If you write us or return our reader-survey form, you can rest assured that we won't release your name and address to any mailing-list companies, direct-mail advertisers, or other third party. Unless you instruct us otherwise, we will assume that you do not object to being quoted in a future edition.

How to Contact the Author

Write to Bob Sehlinger, care of *The Unofficial Guide to Disneyland* at the above address, or e-mail **unofficialguides@menasharidge.com.**

When you write, put your address on both your letter and envelope; sometimes the two get separated. It is also a good idea to include your phone number and e-mail address. If you e-mail us, please tell us where you're from. Remember, as travel writers, we're often out of the office for long periods of time, so forgive us if our response is slow. *Unofficial Guide* e-mail is not forwarded to us when we're traveling, but we will respond as soon as possible when we return.

Questions from Readers

Questions frequently asked by readers are answered in an appendix at the end of this *Unofficial Guide.*

HEY, LOOK US OVER!

Did you know that the *Unofficial Guides* are a 70-book series consisting of travel guides, lifestyle guides (subjects such as investing in mutual funds, elder care, and buying a home), and technology guides? Check out all the *Unofficial Guides* at **www.theunofficialguides.com.**

DISNEYLAND RESORT: *an* OVERVIEW

IF YOU'VE NOT BEEN TO DISNEYLAND for a while, you'll hardly know the place.

First, of course, there is **Disneyland Park,** the original Disney theme park and the only one that Walt Disney saw completed in his lifetime. Much more than the Magic Kingdom at Walt Disney World, Disneyland Park embodies the quiet, charming spirit of nostalgia that so characterized Walt himself. The park is vast yet intimate, steeped in the tradition of its creator yet continually changing.

Disneyland was opened in 1955 on a 107-acre tract surrounded almost exclusively by orange groves, just west of the sleepy and little-known Southern California community of Anaheim. Constrained by finances and ultimately enveloped by the city it helped create, Disneyland operated on that same modest parcel of land until just recently.

Disneyland Park is a collection of adventures, rides, and shows symbolized by the Disney characters and Sleeping Beauty Castle. It's divided into eight subareas, or "lands," arranged around a central hub. First encountered is **Main Street, U.S.A.,** which connects the Disneyland entrance with the central hub. Moving clockwise around the hub, the other lands are **Adventureland, Frontierland, Fantasyland,** and **Tomorrowland.** Two major lands, **Critter Country** and **New Orleans Square,** are accessible via Adventureland and Frontierland but do not connect directly with the central hub. A newer land, **Mickey's Toontown,** connects to Fantasyland. All eight lands will be described in detail later.

Growth and change at Disneyland (until 1996) had been internal, in marked contrast to the ever-enlarging development of spacious Walt Disney World near Orlando, Florida. Until recently, when something new was added at Disneyland, something old had to go. The Disney engineers, to their credit, however, have never been shy about disturbing the status quo. Patrons of the park's earlier, modest years are amazed by the transformation. Gone are the days of the "magical little park" with the Monsanto House of the Future, flying saucer–style bumper cars, donkey riders, and Captain Hook's Pirate Ship. Substituted in a process of continuous evolution and modernization are state-of-the-art fourth-, fifth-, and sixth-generation attractions and entertainment. To paraphrase Walt Disney, Disneyland will never stop changing as long as there are new ideas to explore.

Disneyland Park was arguably Walt Disney's riskiest venture. It was developed on a shoestring budget and made possible only through Disney's relationship with ABC Television and a handful of brave corporate sponsors. The capital available was barely sufficient to acquire the property and build the park; there was nothing left over for the development of hotels or the acquisition and improvement of property adjoining the park. Even the Disneyland Hotel, connected to the theme park by monorail, was owned and operated by a third party until about a decade ago.

Disneyland's success spawned a wave of development that rapidly surrounded the theme park with whimsically themed mom-and-pop motels, souvenir stands, and fast-food restaurants. Disney, still deep in debt, looked on in abject shock, powerless to intervene. In fact, the Disneyland experience was etched so deeply into the Disney corporate consciousness that Walt purchased 27,500 acres and established his own autonomous development district in Florida (unaccountable to any local or county authority) when he was ready to launch Walt Disney World.

Though the Florida project gave Disney the opportunity to develop a destination resort in a totally controlled environment, the steady decline of the area encircling Disneyland continued to rankle him. After tolerating the blight for 30 years, the Walt Disney Company (finally flush with funds and ready for a good fight) set about putting Disneyland Park right. Quietly at first, then aggressively, Disney began buying up the mom-and-pop motels, as well as the few remaining orange and vegetable groves near the park.

In June 1993, the City of Anaheim adopted a Disney plan that called for the development of a new Disney destination resort, including a second theme park situated in what was once the Disneyland parking lot; a Disney-owned hotel district with 4,600 hotel rooms; two new parking facilities; and improvements, including extensive landscaping of the streets that provide access to the complex. City of Anaheim,

Orange County, and State of California infrastructure changes required to support the expanded Disney presence included widening Interstate 5, building new interchanges, moving a major power line, adding new sewer systems, and expanding utilities capacity.

By the end of 2000, all of the changes, modifications, and additions were finished, and Disneyland began the new century as a complete multi–theme park resort destination. The second and newest park, **Disney's California Adventure** (or DCA to the initiated), celebrated its grand opening on February 8, 2001.

DCA is an oddly shaped park built around a lagoon on one side and the Grand Californian Hotel on the other, with one of Disney's trademark mountains, **Grizzly Peak,** plopped down in the middle. An abbreviated entranceway leads to three "lands." Inside the front gate and to the left is **Hollywood Studios Backlot,** a diminutive version of the Disney-MGM Studios theme park at Walt Disney World. Then there's **Golden State,** a catch-all district that combines California's industry, cuisine, natural resources, people, and history. Next is **a bug's land,** with characters and attractions based on the Disney/Pixar film *a bug's life.* Finally, **Paradise Pier** recalls the grand old seaside amusement parks of the early 20th century. DCA is described in detail later in the guide.

The entrances to Disneyland Park and DCA face each other across a palm-studded pedestrian plaza called the **Esplanade,** which begins at Harbor Boulevard and runs west, between the parks, passing into **Downtown Disney,** a dining, shopping, entertainment, and nightlife venue. From Downtown Disney, the Esplanade continues via an overpass across Downtown Drive and past the new monorail station to the **Disneyland** and **Paradise Pier hotels.**

Sandwiched between the Esplanade and Downtown Disney on the north and DCA on the south is the 750-room **Grand Californian Hotel.** Designed in the image of rustic national-park lodges, the Grand Californian supplants the Disneyland Hotel as Disneyland's prestigious lodging property.

North of the hotels and across West Street from Disneyland Park is a huge multistory parking garage that can be accessed directly from Interstate 5. This is where most Disneyland guests park. Tram transport is provided from the garage, the adjacent oversized-vehicle lot, and outlying lots to the Esplanade. Kennels are located by the parking garage. Ticket booths are situated along the Esplanade.

SHOULD I GO TO DISNEYLAND PARK IF I'VE SEEN WALT DISNEY WORLD?

DISNEYLAND PARK IS ROUGHLY COMPARABLE to the Magic Kingdom theme park at Walt Disney World near Orlando, Florida. Both are arranged by "lands" accessible from a central hub and connected to the entrance by a main street. Both parks feature many rides and attractions of the same name: Space Mountain, Jungle Cruise, Pirates of the

Caribbean, It's a Small World, and Dumbo the Flying Elephant, to name a few. Interestingly, however, the same name does not necessarily connote the same experience. Pirates of the Caribbean at Disneyland Park is much longer and more elaborate than its Walt Disney World counterpart. Big Thunder Mountain is more elaborate in Florida, and Dumbo is about the same in both places.

Disneyland Park is more intimate than the Magic Kingdom, not having the room for expansion enjoyed by the Florida park. Pedestrian thoroughfares are narrower, and everything from Big Thunder Mountain to the Castle is scaled down somewhat. Large crowds are more taxing at Disneyland Park because there is less room for them to disperse. At Disneyland Park, however, there are dozens of little surprises, small unheralded attractions tucked away in crooks and corners of the park, which give Disneyland Park a special charm and variety that the Magic Kingdom lacks. And, of course, Disneyland Park has the stamp of Walt Disney's personal touch.

To allow for a meaningful comparison, we have provided a summary of those features found only at Disneyland Park (listed alphabetically below), followed by a critical look at the attractions found at both parks.

Attractions Found Only at Disneyland Park

ADVENTURELAND

Indiana Jones Adventure	Tarzan's Treehouse

FANTASYLAND

Pinocchio's Daring Journey	Casey Jr. Circus Train
Storybook Land Canal Boats	Alice in Wonderland
Mr. Toad's Wild Ride	Matterhorn Bobsleds

FRONTIERLAND

Sailing Ship *Columbia*	*Fantasmic!* (also at Disney-MGM Studios; seasonal)

MAIN STREET

Disneyland: The First 50 Years

MICKEY'S TOONTOWN

Roger Rabbit's Car Toon Spin	Goofy's Playhouse
Chip 'n' Dale's Treehouse	

TOMORROWLAND

Finding Nemo Submarine Voyage

Critical Comparison of Attractions Found at Both Parks*

ADVENTURELAND

Enchanted Tiki Room Better at the Magic Kingdom.

Jungle Cruise More-realistic audio-animatronic (robotic) animals and longer ride at Walt Disney World.

CRITTER COUNTRY

Splash Mountain Slower loading at Disneyland.

FANTASYLAND

Carousels About the same at both parks.

Castles Far larger and more beautiful at the Magic Kingdom.

Dumbo the Flying Elephant About the same at both parks.

It's a Small World Disneyland version renovated in 2006.

Mad Tea Party The same at both parks.

Peter Pan's Flight Better at Disneyland.

Snow White's Scary Adventures Magic Kingdom version is better.

FRONTIERLAND

Big Thunder Mountain Railroad About the same; sights and special effects are better at the Magic Kingdom.

Pirate's Lair on Tom Sawyer Island Comparable, but a little more elaborate and with a pirate theme at Disneyland.

Various river cruises (canoes, boats, and such) More-interesting sights at the Magic Kingdom, but only Disneyland offers canoes.

MAIN STREET, U.S.A.

WDW/Disneyland Railroad The Disneyland Railroad is far more entertaining by virtue of the Grand Canyon Diorama and the Primeval World components not found at the Magic Kingdom.

NEW ORLEANS SQUARE

The Haunted Mansion Slight edge to the Magic Kingdom version.

Pirates of the Caribbean Far superior at Disneyland.

TOMORROWLAND

Astro Orbiter About the same at both parks.

Buzz Lightyear About the same at both parks.

Autopia/Tomorrowland Speedway Disneyland version is superior.

Space Mountain Much better at Disneyland.

*It should be noted that several of the attractions at Disney's California Adventure, such as *The Twilight Zone* Tower of Terror, *Playhouse Disney*, *It's Tough to Be a Bug!*, and *Muppet Vision 3-D*, appeared first at one of the Walt Disney World theme parks. A version of Soarin' over California is the first DCA attraction exported to Walt Disney World. None of the remaining DCA attractions are found at Walt Disney World.

SURVEY: Which author do you prefer to write your guidebooks? (*Guess which one you got!*)

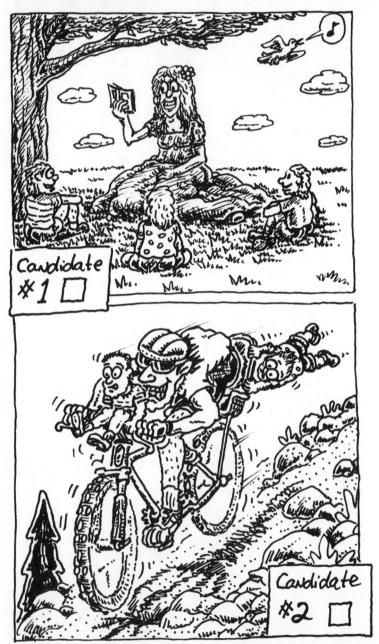

PART ONE

PLANNING *before* YOU LEAVE HOME

█ GATHERING INFORMATION

IN ADDITION TO THIS GUIDE, we recommend that you obtain copies of the following publications:

1. WALT DISNEY TRAVEL SALES CENTER CALIFORNIA BROCHURE This full-color booklet describes Disneyland in its entirety and lists rates for the Disneyland Hotel. Also described are Disneyland package vacations with lodging options at more than 25 nearby hotels. The brochure is available from most full-service travel agents, or it can be obtained by calling the Walt Disney Travel Sales Center at ☎ 714-520-7070. If you are in a hurry, a two-page faxed brochure is also available.

2. DISNEYLAND GUIDEBOOK FOR GUESTS WITH DISABILITIES If members of your party are sight- or hearing-impaired or partially or wholly non-ambulatory, you will find this small guide very helpful. Disney does not mail them, but copies are readily available at the park.

3. THE DISNEY CRUISE LINE BROCHURE AND DVD The Disney Cruise Line will operate seven-day cruises to the Mexican Riviera on the *Disney Magic* out of the port of Los Angeles in 2008. The brochure provides details on the cruises and on vacation packages that combine a cruise with a stay at Disneyland Resort. Disney Cruise Line also offers a free planning DVD that tells all you'd need to know about Disney cruises and then some. To obtain a copy, call ☎ 888-DCL-2500 or order online at **www.disneycruise.com.** (For more information, see page 68.)

4. CALIFORNIA TRAVELER DISCOUNT GUIDE Another good source of lodging, restaurant, and attraction discounts throughout the state of California, the California Traveler Discount Guide can be obtained by calling ☎ 352-371-3948, Monday through Friday, 8 a.m. to 5 p.m. EST. Published by Exit Information Guide, the Discount Guide is free, but you will be charged $3 for postage and handling. Similar guides to other states are available at the same number. You can also order online at **www.travelersdiscountguide.com** or by mail at 4205 NW Sixth Street, Gainesville, FL 32609.

Disneyland Main Information Address and Phone

The following address and phone numbers provide general information. Inquiries may be expedited by using addresses and phone numbers specific to the nature of the inquiry (other addresses and phone numbers are listed elsewhere in this chapter, under their relevant topics).

Disneyland Guest Relations
P.O. Box 3232
1313 South Harbor Boulevard
Anaheim, CA 92803-3232
☎ **714-781-4565 for recorded information**
☎ **714-781-7290 for live information**

The Phone from Hell

Sometimes it is virtually impossible to get through on the Disneyland information numbers listed above. When you get through, you will get a recording that offers various information options. If none of the recorded options answer your question, you will have to hold for a live person. Eat before you call—you may have a long wait. If, after repeated attempts, you get tired of a busy signal in your ear or, worse, 20 minutes' worth of singing mice warbling "Cinderellie" in alto falsettos while you wait on hold, call the Disneyland Hotel at ☎ 714-956-6425.

IMPORTANT DISNEYLAND RESORT PHONE NUMBERS	
Anaheim Travel Information	☎ 714-765-8888
Disney Cruise Line	☎ 888-DCL-2500
Disney Guided Tours	☎ 714-781-4400
Disneyland Hotel	☎ 714-778-6600
Disneyland Resort Hotel Reservations	☎ 714-956-6425
Disneyland Vacation Packages	☎ 714-520-7070
Foreign Language Assistance	☎ 714-781-7290
Grand Californian Hotel	☎ 714-635-2300
Guided Tours	☎ 714-781-4400
Fantasmic! Balcony Reservations	☎ 714-781-4400
Information: Live	☎ 714-781-7290
Information: Recorded	☎ 714-781-4565
Lost & Found	☎ 714-781-4765
Paradise Pier Hotel	☎ 714-999-0990
Priority Seating for Restaurants	☎ 714-781-3463, Option 4

RECOMMENDED WEB SITES

There are a number of good Disneyland information sources on the Web. The following are brief profiles of our favorites:

BEST OFFICIAL THEME PARK SITES The official Disneyland Web site, **disneyland.disney.go.com,** is so loaded with video, photos, special effects, and gimmicks that it's slow to load and cumbersome to search unless you have a very late-model computer and high-speed Internet access. For those who do, there's a ton of information to be had, but even so it usually takes a lot of clicks to find what you're looking for. As an example, we tried finding the phone number for restaurant reservations and searched for "dining" and "restaurants" and "restaurant reservations." Each search yielded 0 results. The Universal Studios official Web site is at **www.universalstudioshollywood.com.** Like the Disneyland site, it's complex with a lot of bells and whistles. As far as your computer's concerned, be new, be fast, or be gone.

BEST OFFICIAL AREA WEB SITE **www.anaheimoc.org** is the official Web site of the Anaheim–Orange County Visitors and Convention Authority. You'll find everything from hotels and restaurants to weather and driving instructions on this site.

BEST GENERAL UNOFFICIAL WEB SITES IntercotWest.com (The Internet Community of Tomorrow–West) is an active and friendly Web site filled with detailed information on every corner of the Disneyland Resort. Featured are frequent news updates and descriptions, reviews, and ratings of every attraction, restaurant, and shop at the resort. The site is also host to the largest Disney-related multimedia gallery on the Web, with thousands of photos chronicling the parks' recent history. Intercot West taps into the Internet's spirit of community via its interactive moderated discussion boards, a place where Disney fans convene to gain insightful trip-planning tips and make new friends. Intercot West is a part of Intercot (**www.intercot.com**), which features vacation-planning information for Walt Disney World.

MousePlanet.com is a comprehensive resource for Disneyland data, offering features and reviews by guest writers, information on the Disney theme parks, discussion groups, and news. The site includes an interactive Disney restaurant-and-hotel review page where users can voice opinions on their Disney dining and lodging experiences. Also available are trip reports by site contributors and users.

LaughingPlace.com features daily updated headlines and columns on all things Disney, including theme parks, films, TV, stage, merchandise, collectibles, and more. The free site specializes in current news on the Disney theme parks and resorts, with information such as hours, showtimes, events, and highlights of specific attractions. LaughingPlace offers interactive, user-rated attraction guides, lively discussion boards, and a customizable home page with a unique trip countdown feature and park info. The Web site, which distributes an informative daily newsletter via e-mail, is also the home of Laughing-Place Radio and The LaughingPlace Store.

BEST DISNEYLAND HISTORY WEB SITE At **Yesterland.com** you can visit the Disneyland of the past, where retired Disneyland attractions are brought back to life through vivid descriptions and historic photographs. Yesterland attraction descriptions relate what it was once like to experience the Flying Saucers, the Mine Train through Nature's Wonderland, the Tahitian Terrace, and dozens of other rides, shows, parades, and restaurants.

BEST WEB SITE FOR RUMORS AND THE INSIDE SCOOP www.jimhill media.com is perfectly attuned to what's going on behind the scenes—Jim Hill always has good gossip. He works with the *Unofficial Guides* as our resident historian and contributes sidebars and anecdotes to our Disney titles.

BEST MONEY-SAVING SITE MouseSavers.com specializes in finding you the deepest discounts on hotels, park admissions, and rental cars. MouseSavers does not actually sell travel, but rather unearths and publishes special discount codes that you can use to obtain the discounts. It's the first place we look for deals when we travel to Disneyland Resort.

BEST DISNEY DISCUSSION BOARDS The best online discussion of all things Disney can be found at **mousepad.mouseplanet.com** and **www .disboards.com.** With tens of thousands of members and millions of posts, they are the most active and popular discussion boards on the Web. For boards that feel more familiar than your neighborhood bar, try **disneyecho.emuck.com.**

BEST DISNEY PODCASTS Host Jeff Falvo (from Houston), who bills his show as "Consciousness from the Happiest Place on Earth," has a lot to say about what's happening at the parks, both in California and Florida. Access the Podcast and the Podcast Network Forum at **www.meanderingmouse.com.**

ADMISSION OPTIONS

THEME PARK ADMISSION OPTIONS ARE pretty straightforward at Disneyland Resort. You have only two things to decide:

1. How many days admission you'll need.
2. Whether you want to go to both Disneyland Park and Disney's California Adventure on the same day. This is known as "park hopping."

Park Hopper tickets expire 13 days from the day of first use, so you don't want to buy more days than you'll need. Needless to say, the Park Hopper tickets expire after you've used the number of days purchased even if the 13 days haven't passed yet.

All admissions can be purchased at the park entrance, at the Disneyland Resort hotels, from the Walt Disney Travel Sales Center, from Disneyland Ticket Mail Order, on the Disneyland Internet site, and at most Disney stores in the western United States. One- and two-year-olds are exempt from admission fees.

Admission Costs and Available Discounts

It's possible to obtain discounts on all multiday tickets, but only in the 1-to-7% range. One place to purchase admissions at a discount is **www.disneyland.com,** where Disney sells "Bonus" tickets. These tickets, in addition to the dollar discount, allow you to enter the theme park an hour earlier than the general public one time during your visit. The bonus feature is only offered on Three-, Four-, and Five-day Park Hopper tickets.

unofficial **TIP**
The money you can save makes researching Disney's dizzying array of ticket options worthwhile.

If you purchase tickets on the Disneyland Web site you can choose between "hard" tickets, which will be shipped to you, or e-tickets, which can be downloaded as PDF files and printed at home. E-tickets printed from your home computer are actual, valid admission passes, as opposed to vouchers to be exchanged later for real tickets. At the theme park, just take your print-at-home ticket directly to the turnstile, and you're good to go.

The deepest discounts we've found are available from **ARES Travel** (**www.arestravel.com**). ARES usually beats the Disney advance purchase price by $4 to $6 per ticket and also includes the early-entry bonus feature. ARES will send you the tickets by FedEx for a flat fee of $10 per order, plus a $1-per-ticket convenience fee. You can order online or call and speak with a warm body at ☎ 800-680-0977.

Military discounts are available for all Disney theme parks, usually in the 7-to-25% range. Check with your base MWR for info. Military ID may be required at the gate. Many readers, however, report buying military tickets for friends and relatives who used them without problems.

Admission prices, not unexpectedly, increase from time to time. For planning your budget, however, the following provides a fair estimate:

One-day, One-park Ticket

This pass is good for one day's admission at your choice of Disneyland Park or Disney's California Adventure. As the name implies, you cannot "hop" from park to park.

Park Hopper Tickets

These are good for one, two, three, four, or five days, respectively, and allow you to visit both parks on the same day. These multiday tickets do not have to be used on consecutive days, but they do expire 13 days after their first use.

The 13-day expiration is in marked contrast to similar passes sold at Walt Disney World for which you can purchase a No Expiration option. If you mistakenly bought multiday tickets because you were not aware of the 13-day expiration, call ☎ 714-781-7290 and ask to

ADMISSION OPTIONS

	AT THE GATE *ADULT | *CHILD	ADVANCE PURCHASE ADULT | CHILD
One-day, One-park Ticket with Tax	$63 | $63	$53 | $53
One-day Park Hopper	$83 | $83	$73 | $73
Two-day Park Hopper	$122 | $122	$102 | $102
Three-day Park Hopper	$179 | $159	$149 | $129
Four-day Park Hopper	$209 | $179	$179 | $149
Five-day Park Hopper	$229 | $189	$199 | $159
Deluxe Annual Passport (some blackout dates)	$239	$239
Premium Annual Passport (no blackout dates)	$359	$359

*Adult (age 10 and up) | *Child (ages 3–9)

be connected to Guest Communications, which has the authority to issue you a voucher for the unused days on your ticket. You must, however, that you return your expired passes.

Anytime before a pass expires, you can apply the value of unused days toward the cost of a higher-priced ticket. If you buy a Four-day Park Hopper Ticket, for example, and then decide you'd rather have an Annual Passport, you can apply the value of unused days on the former toward the purchase of the latter.

Annual Passports

The Disneyland Resort offers several Annual Passports. The Premium Annual Passport is good for an entire year with no blackout dates. The pass costs $359 and is good for admission to both parks (excluding arcades). Southern California Annual Passports, priced at $154, provide admission to both parks for a year, excluding 138 preselected blackout dates. These are available to residents in zip codes 90000 to 93599 and to Baja California residents in Mexico postal codes 21000 to 22999. Prices for children are the same as those for adults on all Annual Passports. All of these passes are a good idea if you plan to visit Disneyland parks five or more days in a year. If you purchase your Annual Passport in July of this year and schedule your visit next year for June, you'll cover two years' vacations with a single pass.

unofficial **TIP**
If you visit Disneyland three or more days each summer, an Annual Passport is a potential money saver.

Admission passes can be ordered through the mail by writing:

Disneyland Ticket Mail Order
P.O. Box 61061
Anaheim, CA 92803-6161

Disneyland Ticket Mail Order accepts personal checks and money orders. Mail orders take three to four weeks to process. To order tickets by telephone, call ☎ 714-781-4400.

In addition to Disneyland Ticket Mail Order and the Disneyland Web sites, Disneyland admissions can be purchased in advance from Disneyland Resort hotels; Disney Stores in the Western United States; and the Walt Disney Travel Sales Center, ☎ 800-854-3104.

Admission and Disneyland Hotel Discounts

For specials and time-limited discounts on Disneyland Resort admissions, visit **www.mousesavers.com.**

Rides and Shows Closed for Repairs or Maintenance

Rides and shows at Disneyland parks are sometimes closed for maintenance or repairs. If there is a certain attraction that is important to you, call ☎ 714-781-7290 before your visit to make sure it will be operating. A mother from Dover, Massachusetts, wrote us, lamenting:

> We were disappointed to find Space Mountain, Swiss Family Treehouse, and the Riverboat closed for repairs. We felt that a large chunk [of the park] was not working, yet the tickets were still full price and expensive!

HOW MUCH DOES IT COST TO GO TO DISNEYLAND FOR A DAY?

LET'S SAY WE HAVE A FAMILY OF FOUR—Mom and Dad, Tim (age 12) and Tami (age 8)—driving their own car. Since they plan to be in the area for a few days, they intend to buy the Three-day Park Hopper Tickets. A typical day would cost $417.64, excluding souvenirs, lodging, and transportation. See the chart below for a breakdown of expenses.

How Much Does a Day Cost?

Breakfast for four at Denny's with tax and tip	$28.00
Disneyland parking fee	$11.00
One day's admission on a Three-Day Park Hopper Passport	
Dad: Adult, Three-day = $179 divided by 3 (days)	$59.66
Mom: Adult, Three-day = $179 divided by 3 (days)	$59.66
Tim: Adult, Three-day = $179 divided by 3 (days)	$59.66
Tami: Child, Three-day = $149 divided by 3 (days)	$49.66
Morning break (soda or coffee)	$14.00
Fast-food lunch (burger, fries, soda), no tip	$36.00
Afternoon break (soda and popcorn)	$20.50
Dinner in park at counter-service restaurant with tax	$41.50
Souvenirs (Mickey T-shirts for Tim and Tami) with tax*	$38.00
One-day total (not including lodging and travel)	**$417.64**

Cheer up—you won't have to buy souvenirs every day.

TIMING *Your* VISIT

SELECTING THE TIME OF YEAR FOR YOUR VISIT

CROWDS ARE LARGEST at Disneyland during the summer (Memorial Day through Labor Day) and during specific holiday periods during the rest of the year. The busiest time of all is Christmas Day through New Year's Day. Thanksgiving weekend, the week of Washington's birthday, spring break for schools and colleges, and the two weeks around Easter are also extremely busy. To give you some idea of what *busy* means at Disneyland, more than 77,000 people have toured Disneyland Park on a single day! While this level of attendance is far from typical, the possibility of its occurrence should prevent all but the ignorant and the foolish from challenging this mega-attraction at its busiest periods. For the record, attendance at Disney's California Adventure Park runs about one-third that of Disneyland Park.

> **unofficial TIP**
> You can't pick a less crowded time to visit Disneyland than the period following Thanksgiving weekend and leading up to Christmas.

The least-busy time of all is from after Thanksgiving weekend until the week before Christmas. The next slowest times are September through the weekend preceding Thanksgiving, January 4 through the first week of March, and the week following Easter up to Memorial Day weekend. At the risk of being blasphemous, our research team was so impressed with the relative ease of touring in the fall and other "off" periods that we would rather take our children out of school for a few days than do battle with the summer crowds. Though we strongly recommend going to Disneyland in the fall or in the spring, it should be noted that there are certain trade-offs. The parks often close earlier on fall and spring days, sometimes early enough to eliminate evening parades and other live-entertainment offerings. Also, because these are slow times of the year at Disneyland, you can anticipate that some rides and attractions may be closed for maintenance or renovation. Finally, if the parks open late and close early, it's tough to see everything, even if the crowds are light.

> **unofficial TIP**
> In our opinion, the risk of encountering colder weather and closed attractions during an off-season visit to Disneyland is worth it.

Most readers who have tried Disney theme parks at varying times during the year agree. A gentleman from Ottawa, Ontario, who toured in early December, wrote:

> *It was the most enjoyable trip I have ever had, and I can't imagine going* [back to Disneyland] *when it is crowded. Even without the crowds we were still very tired by afternoon. Fighting crowds certainly would have made a hellish trip. We will never go again at any other time.*

Not to overstate the case: we want to emphasize that you can have a great time at the Disneyland parks regardless of the time of year or crowd level. In fact, a primary objective of this guide is to make the parks fun and manageable for those readers who visit during the busier times of year.

THE SPOILER

SO YOU CHOOSE YOUR OFF-SEASON DATES and then find it almost impossible to find a hotel room. What gives? In all probability you've been foiled by a mammoth convention or trade show at the Anaheim–Orange County Convention Center. One of the largest and busiest convention venues in the country, the convention center hosts meetings with as many as 75,000 attendees. The sheer numbers alone guarantee that hotel rooms will be hard to find. Compounding the problem is the fact that most business travelers don't have roommates. Thus a trade show with 8,000 people registered might suck up 13,000 rooms! The final straw as you might expect is that room rates climb into the stratosphere based on the high demand and scarcity of supply. In regard to increased crowds at the theme parks, it's estimated that less than 10% of attendees will find time to enjoy the parks. It's also true, however, that business travelers are more likely to bring their spouse and even kids to a convention held in Anaheim. The bottom line is that you don't want to schedule your vacation while a major event is ongoing at the convention center. To help you avoid major trade shows and conventions, we've created a calendar of meetings scheduled through December 31, 2008, showing the number of expected attendees of each (see pages 24 and 25).

SELECTING THE DAY OF THE WEEK FOR YOUR VISIT

THE CROWDS AT WALT DISNEY WORLD in Florida comprise mostly out-of-state visitors. Not necessarily so at Disneyland, which, along with

TOP TEN AMERICAN THEME PARKS

THEME PARK	ANNUAL ATTENDANCE	AVERAGE DAILY ATTENDANCE
Magic Kingdom	16.2 million	44,384
Disneyland Park	14.6 million	40,000
Epcot	9.9 million	27,123
Disney-MGM Studios	8.7 million	23,836
Animal Kingdom	8.2 million	22,466
Universal Studios Orlando	6.1 million	16,172
Islands of Adventure	5.8 million	15,890
Disney's California Adventure	5.8 million	15,890
SeaWorld Orlando	5.6 million	15,310
Universal Studios Hollywood	4.7 million	12,877

Source: *Amusement Business* magazine

Anaheim Convention and Special-event Calendar

DATES	CONVENTION/ EVENT	NUMBER OF ATTENDEES
2007		
Aug. 31–Sept. 2	SCRC Annual Convention	13,000
Sept. 24–30	State Bar of California	3,500
Oct. 3–7	LA Church of Christ	2,500
Oct. 4–6	Cystic Fibrosis Foundation	3,000
Oct. 8–11	California Assn. of Realtors	7,500
Oct. 13–17	Nat'l. Community Pharmacists Assn.	3,000
Oct. 20–25	American Assn. of Blood Banks	7,000
Oct. 31–Nov. 7	Int'l. Foundation of Employee Benefit Plans	7,500
Nov. 4–9	Reed Exhibitions Limited	3,500
Nov. 6–15	Society of Petroleum Engineers	9,000
Nov. 18–21	Assn. of Christian Schools Int'l.	10,000
2008		
Jan. 6–8	American Football Coaches Assn.	3,500
Jan. 17–20	Int'l. Music Products Assn.	75,000
Jan. 29–31	Canon Communications	45,000
Feb. 10–13	Craft and Hobby Assn.	22,000
Feb. 15–18	American Championships/Spirit Team	10,000
Feb. 22–25	Nat'l. Rural Electric Cooperative Assn.	11,500
Feb. 27–Mar. 2	Religious Education Congress	40,000
Feb. 27–Mar. 4	American Choral Directors Assn.	2,000
Mar. 11–16	Big West Conference	16,000
Mar. 12–16	Natural Products Expo West	50,000
Mar. 17–23	NCAA Basketball/Big West	18,000
Mar. 26–Apr. 5	AORN (Assn. of Perioperative Registered Nurses)	12,300
Mar. 28–29	Cal Events	3,000

DATES	CONVENTION/ EVENT	NUMBER OF ATTENDEES
2008 (CONTINUED)		
Apr. 27–29	California Assn. of School Business Officials	2,000
Apr. 28–May 6	California Dental Assn.	30,000
May 14–22	Nat'l. Postal Forum	8,000
May 15–17	Pri-Med	14,000
May 17–23	Ecobuild America	5,000
May 31–June 4	Public Risk Management Assn.	2,000
June 2–13	Design Automation Conference	10,000
June 20–30	Piano Technicians Guild	1,000
June 26–July 2	American Library Assn.	25,000
July 10–21	Nat'l. Model Railroad Assn.	2,200
July 18–20	Catholic Resource Center	7,000
July 20–27	Sunrider Int'l.	5,000
July 25–29	Int'l. Assn. of Assembly Managers	2,200
Aug. 2–5	American Accounting Assn.	3,000
Aug. 9–13	Academy of Management	5,500
Aug. 15–21	Institute of Transportation Engineers	2,000
Aug. 29–31	SCRC Annual Convention	12,000
Sept. 10–13	Applied Systems Client Network	2,200
Sept. 17–28	Nat'l. Safety Council	20,000
Oct. 2–25	American Academy of Optometry	4,000
Oct. 15–17	American Composites Manufacturers Assn.	5,000
Nov. 2–4	Irrigation Assn.	5,000
Nov. 6–8	Airlift Tanker Assn.	4,000
Nov. 15–22	Core Knowledge Foundation	2,300
Nov. 23–26	Assn. of Christian Schools Int'l.	10,000
Dec. 9–17	AARC	6,000

Six Flags Magic Mountain, serves as an often-frequented recreational resource for the greater Los Angeles and San Diego communities. To many Southern Californians, Disneyland Park and Disney's California Adventure are their private theme parks. Yearly passes are available at less cost than a year's membership to the YMCA, and the Disney management has intensified its efforts to appeal to the local market.

What all this means is that weekends are usually packed. Saturday is the busiest day of the week. Sunday, particularly Sunday morning, is the best bet if you have to go on a weekend, but it is also extremely busy.

During the summer, Monday and Friday are very busy; Tuesday and Wednesday are usually less so; and Thursday is normally the slowest day of all. During the "off-season" (September through May, holiday periods excepted) Thursday is usually the least crowded day, followed by Tuesday.

At Walt Disney World in Florida, there are four theme parks with a substantial daily variance in attendance from park to park. At Disneyland Resort, Disneyland Park usually hosts crowds three times larger than those at Disney's California Adventure, but because DCA is smaller, crowd conditions are comparable. Expressed differently, the most crowded and least crowded days are essentially the same for both Disneyland parks.

EARLY ENTRY

ANYONE WHO BUYS a three-or-more-day Park Hopper admission in advance (that is, not at the theme park) may enter Disneyland Park on one day an hour before the park is opened to the general public. You can exercise your early-entry privilege on Monday, Tuesday, Thursday, and Saturday. Only selected attractions in Fantasyland and Tomorrowland operate during early entry. Guests at the Paradise Pier, Grand Californian, and Disneyland Hotels are eligible to enter the park on all of the days listed above by showing their hotel ID card. If you buy a package vacation from the Walt Disney Travel Company, you can participate in Mickey's Toontown Morning Madness. In this program, package purchasers can enjoy the attractions in Mickey's Toontown one hour before the general public on Monday, Wednesday, Friday, and Saturday. Note that Mickey's Toontown opens one hour later than the rest of Disneyland Park. Thus, if the park opens at 8 a.m. and Mickey's Toontown opens at 9 a.m., you'll be eligible to enjoy Morning Madness from 8 to 9. Though you can enter Toontown early, you actually enter the park with the general public at official opening time. In practice, unless you're among the first to enter the park, it will take you so long to clear the turnstiles and walk back to Mickey's Toontown that you'll be fortunate if you arrive in time to enjoy more that 20 minutes or so of the event. For more information call ☎ 714-520-7070.

OPERATING HOURS

IT CANNOT BE SAID THAT THE DISNEY folks are inflexible when it comes to hours of operation for the parks. They run a dozen or more different operating schedules during the year, making it advisable to call ☎ 714-781-4565 the day before you arrive for exact hours of operation.

PACKED-PARK COMPENSATION PLAN

THE THOUGHT OF TEEMING, jostling throngs jockeying for position in endless lines under the baking Fourth of July sun is enough to wilt the will and ears of the most ardent Mouseketeer. Why would anyone go to Disneyland Park or DCA on a summer Saturday or during a major holiday period? Indeed, if you have never been to the parks, and you thought you would just drop in for a few rides and a little look-see on such a day, you might be better off shooting yourself in the foot. The Disney folks, however, being Disney folks, feel kind of bad about those interminably long lines and the basically impossible touring conditions on packed days and compensate their patrons with a no-less-than-incredible array of first-rate live entertainment and happenings.

unofficial **TIP**
If it's not your first trip to Disneyland and you must go during a crowded holiday weekend, you may have just as much fun enjoying Disney's fantastic array of shows, parades, and fireworks as you would riding the rides.

Throughout the day, the party goes on with shows, parades, concerts, and pageantry. In the evening, there is so much going on that you have to make some tough choices. Big-name musical groups perform on the River Stage in Frontierland and at the Fantasyland Theatre. Other concerts are produced concurrently at the Hyperion Theater at Disney's California Adventure. There are always parades and fireworks, and the Disney characters make frequent appearances. No question about it, you can go to the Disneyland parks on the Fourth of July (or any other crowded extended-hours day), never get on a ride, and still get your money's worth.

If you decide to go on one of the parks' "big" days, we suggest that you arrive an hour and 20 minutes before the stated opening time. Use the touring plan of your choice until about 1 p.m., and then take the monorail to Downtown Disney for lunch and relaxation. Southern Californian visitors often chip in and rent a room for the group (make reservations well in advance) at the Disneyland or Grand Californian hotels, thus affording a place to meet, relax, have a drink, or change clothes before enjoying the pools at the hotel. A comparable arrangement can be made at other nearby hotels as long as they furnish a shuttle service to and from the park. After an early dinner, return to the park for the evening's festivities, which really get cranked up at about 8 p.m.

GETTING THERE

INTERSTATE 5 HAS BEEN WIDENED, and improved interchanges allow Disney patrons to drive directly into and out of parking facilities without becoming enmeshed in surface street traffic.

To avoid traffic problems, we present the following list of recommendations:

1. Stay as close to Disneyland as possible. If you are within walking distance, leave your car at the hotel and walk to the park. If your hotel provides efficient shuttle service (that is, will get you to the parks at least a half hour before opening), use the shuttle.

2. If your hotel is more than five miles from Disneyland and you intend to drive your car, leave for the park extra-early, say an hour or more. If you get lucky and don't encounter too many problems, you can relax over breakfast at a restaurant near Disneyland while you wait for the parks to open.

3. If you must use the Santa Ana Freeway (I-5), give yourself lots of extra time.

4. Any time you leave the park just before, at, or just after closing time, you can expect considerable congestion in the parking lots and in the loading area for hotel shuttles. The easiest way to return to your hotel (if you do not have a car in the Disneyland Resort parking lot) is to take the monorail to the Disneyland Hotel, or walk to the Grand Californian Hotel, then take a cab to your own hotel. While cabs in Anaheim are a little pricey, they are usually available in ample numbers at the Disneyland hotels and at the pedestrian entrance on Harbor Boulevard. When you consider the alternatives of fighting your way onto a hotel shuttle or trudging back to your hotel on worn-out feet, spending a couple of bucks for a cab often sounds pretty reasonable.

5. If you walk or use a hotel shuttle to get to the parks and are then caught in a monsoon, the best way to return to your hotel without getting soaked is to take the monorail to the Disneyland Hotel and catch a taxi from there.

6. Finally, the Orange County Transit District provides very efficient bus service to Disneyland with three different long-distance lines. Running approximately every 30 minutes during the day and evening, service begins at 10 a.m. and concludes at midnight, depending on the season and your location. Buses drop off and pick up passengers at the Disneyland Hotel. From there, guests can take a Disney tram to the park entrance. Trams run approximately every six minutes. Bus fare is about $1.25, and the tram is free. For additional information, call ☎ 714-636-7433 or log on to **www.octa.net.** For public transportation in the immediate area surrounding Disneyland, see our discussion of the Anaheim Resort Transit (ART) system on page 33.

DISNEYLAND PARKING

DISNEYLAND HAS THREE PARKING AREAS. The main parking facility, the Mickey & Friends parking garage, can be accessed directly from I-5, Disneyland Drive, or Ball Road. One of the largest parking structures in the world, the garage is connected to Downtown Disney and the theme parks by Disney tram. If you have a noncollapsible stroller that's not permitted on the tram, the walking distance is just less than a mile.

A secondary parking lot is the Timon lot off Harbor Boulevard on the east side of Disneyland Resort. Timon can be reached by taking Harbor Boulevard south from I-5. Much more convenient than the main garage, Timon is the preferred lot of locals, though Annual Passport holders are not allowed to park there. After Timon is full, all vehicles are directed to the Mickey & Friends garage. Trams likewise serve the Timon lot. If you want to walk, the distance to the parks is about a half mile. The third parking lot, Pumbaa, is primarily a remote overflow-parking area. Parking fees for all lots are $11 for cars, $13 for RVs, and $18 for busses and oversized vehicles.

TAKING A TRAM OR SHUTTLE BUS FROM YOUR HOTEL

TRAMS AND SHUTTLE BUSES are provided by many hotels and motels in the vicinity of Disneyland. Usually without charge, they represent a fairly carefree means of getting to and from the theme parks, letting you off near the entrances and saving you the cost of parking. The rub is that they might not get you there as early as you desire (a critical point if you take our touring advice) or be available at the time you wish to return to your lodging. Also, some shuttles are direct to Disneyland, while others make stops at other motels and hotels in the vicinity. Each shuttle service is a little bit different, so check out the particulars before you book your hotel. If the shuttle provided by your hotel runs regularly throughout the day to and from Disneyland and if you have the flexibility to tour the parks over two or three days, the shuttle provides a wonderful opportunity to tour in the morning and return to your lodging for lunch, a swim, or perhaps a nap; then you can head back to Disneyland refreshed in the early evening for a little more fun.

Be forewarned that most hotel shuttle services do not add more vehicles at the parks' opening or closing times. In the mornings, your biggest problem is that you might not get a seat on the first shuttle. This occurs most frequently if your hotel is the last stop for a shuttle that serves several hotels. Because hotels that share a shuttle service are usually located close together, you can improve your chances of getting a seat by simply walking to the hotel preceding yours on the pick-up route. At closing time, and sometimes following a hard rain, you can expect a mass exodus from the parks. The worst-case scenario in this event is that more people will be waiting for the shuttle to your hotel than the bus will hold, and that some will be left. While most (but not all) hotel shuttles return for stranded guests, you may suffer a wait of 15 minutes to an hour. Our suggestion, if you are depending on hotel shuttles, is to exit the park at least 45 minutes before closing. If you stay in a park until closing and lack the energy to deal with the shuttle or hike back to your hotel, go to the Disneyland Hotel and catch a cab from there. There is also a cab stand adjacent to the

unofficial **TIP**
Warning: Most shuttles don't add vehicles at park-opening or -closing times. In the mornings, you may not get a seat.

southern california at a glance

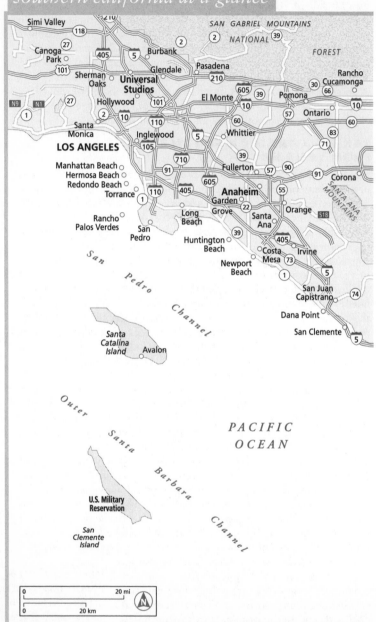

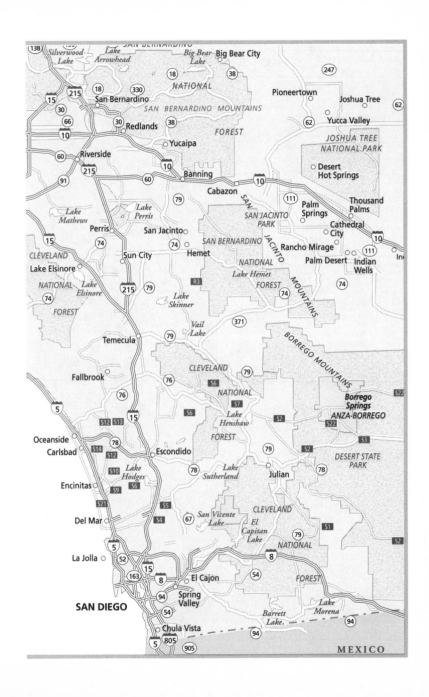

around disneyland

Harbor Boulevard pedestrian entrance and another at the Grand Californian Hotel.

The shuttle-loading area is located on the Harbor Boulevard side of the Disneyland Park's main entrances. The loading area connects to a pedestrian corridor that leads to the park entrances. Each hotel's shuttle bus is color-coded yellow, blue, red, silver, or white. Signs of like color designate where the shuttles load and unload.

Anaheim Resort Transit

Anaheim has undergone a renaissance, establishing the 1,100-acre area that surrounds Disneyland and the Anaheim Convention Center as a world-class destination known as The Anaheim Resort. Streets have been widened and attractively landscaped with towering palms as well as ornamental trees and plants. A score of new hotels and restaurants have opened, and many of the older hotels have expanded or remodeled.

To complete the Anaheim Resort package, a transit service was added to provide shuttle service to the Disneyland Parks, Downtown Disney, and the convention center. Called Anaheim Resort Transit (ART), the service operates 12 routes designated A through H plus J, K, L, and M. There are just two to six well-marked stops on each route, so a complete circuit on any given route only takes about 20 minutes. All of the routes originate and terminate at Disneyland. To continue on to the convention center, you must transfer at Disneyland to Route C, E, M, or N.

The shuttle vehicles themselves are little red trolleys similar to the trolleys in San Francisco (except on wheels) and are wheelchair accessible. They run every ten minutes on peak days during morning and evening periods, every 20 minutes during the less busy middle part of the day, and every 20 minutes all day long on nonpeak days. Service begins one hour before park opening and ends one half hour after park closing. If you commute to Disneyland on ART and then head to Downtown Disney after the parks close, you'll have to find your own way home if you stay at Downtown Disney more than half an hour. All shuttle vehicles and respective stops are clearly marked with the route designation (A through H and J, K, L, M, and N).

Hotels served by ART vending kiosks sell one-day, two-day, and three-day passes for $3, $6, and $8, respectively. A weekend-service unlimited-use pass is offered for $5. Children age 9 years and under ride free with a paying adult. Passes cannot be purchased from the driver. For more information, call ☎ 888-364-ARTS or check **www.rideart.org**. Passes are also available in advance or at ART's Web site.

A **WORD** *about* **LODGING**

WHILE THIS GUIDE IS NOT ABOUT LODGING, we have found lodging to be a primary concern of people visiting Disneyland. Traffic around Disneyland, and in the Anaheim–Los Angeles area in general, is so terrible that we advocate staying in accommodations within two or three miles of the park. Included in this radius are many expensive hotels as well as a considerable number of moderately priced establishments and a small number of bargain motels.

WALKING TO DISNEYLAND FROM NEARBY HOTELS

WHILE IT IS TRUE THAT MOST DISNEYLAND area hotels provide shuttle service, or are on the ART routes, it is equally true that an ever-increasing number of guests walk to the parks from their hotels. Shuttles are not always available when needed, and parking in the Disneyland lot has become pretty expensive. There is a pedestrian walkway from Harbor Boulevard that provides safe access to Disneyland for guests on foot. This pedestrian corridor extends from Harbor Boulevard all the way west to the Disneyland Hotel, connecting Disneyland Park, Disney's California Adventure, and all of the Disney entertainment and shopping venues.

Close proximity to the theme parks figures prominently in the choice of a hotel. Harbor Boulevard borders Disneyland Resort on the east, and Katella Avenue runs along the resort's southern boundary. The closest non-Disney hotels, and the only ones really within walking distance, are on Harbor Boulevard from just south of I-5 to the north to just south of the intersection of Katella Avenue, and along Katella Avenue near Harbor. Farther south on Harbor are some of the best hotels in the area, but they are a little far removed for commuting to the parks on foot. Additionally, these hotels are close to the Anaheim–Orange County Convention Center and tend to cater, though certainly not exclusively, to business travelers.

For families, a second important consideration is the quality of the hotel swimming pool. We mention this because, unfortunately, many of the non-Disney hotels closest to the theme parks have really crummy pools, sometimes just a tiny rectangle on a stark slab of concrete surrounded on four sides by a parking lot. To bring pool quality and proximity to the theme parks together, we've developed a chart (see right) that lists the hotels, both Disney and non-Disney, within walking distance of the theme parks.

The chart shows the walking time from each hotel to the theme-park entrances. The times provided are averages—a couple of fit adults might cover the distance in less time, and a family with small children will likely take longer. Also on the chart we rate the swimming areas of the hotels listed on a scale of 1 to 10, with 10 being best. As a rule of thumb, any pool with a rating less than 5 is not a place where most folks would want to spend much time. Any hotel not listed is, in our opinion, too far away for walking. Note that several non-Disney hotels are closer than the Disneyland Resort hotels, except for the Grand Californian.

Walking Times to the Theme-park Entrances; Swimming-pool Ratings

HOTEL	LOCATION	WALKING TIME	POOL RATING
Alpine Inn	Katella Avenue	13:00	2
America's Best Value Hotel	Katella Avenue	15:15	2
Anaheim Desert Inn & Suites	Harbor Boulevard	6:40	1
Anaheim Plaza Hotel	Harbor Boulevard	11:00	6
Best Western Anaheim Inn	Harbor Boulevard	7:15	2
Best Western Park Place	Harbor Boulevard	5:45	2
Camelot Inn & Suites	Harbor Boulevard	7:15	2
Candy Cane Inn	Harbor Boulevard	10:30	4
Carousel Inn & Suites	Harbor Boulevard	6:45	2
Castle Inn & Suites	Harbor Boulevard	12:30	1
Del Sol Hotel	Harbor Boulevard	7:00	3
Desert Palms Hotel & Suites	Katella Avenue	13:00	2
Disneyland Hotel, Bonita Tower	Disneyland Resort	12:00	10
Disneyland Hotel, Marina Tower	Disneyland Resort	10:00	10
Disneyland Hotel, Sierra Tower	Disneyland Resort	11:00	10
Fairfield Inn	Harbor Boulevard	9:30	4
Grand Californian Hotel	Disneyland Resort	4:00*	10
Holiday Inn Express	Katella Avenue	15:00	2
Howard Johnson Plaza Hotel	Harbor Boulevard	10:15	6
Jolly Roger Inn	Katella Avenue	16:30	4
Paradise Pier Hotel	Disneyland Resort	14:00	7
Park Vue Inn	Harbor Boulevard	6:30	4
Portofino Inn & Suites	Harbor Boulevard	16:30	7
Radisson Maingate Hotel	Harbor Boulevard	22:30	7
Ramada Maingate Hotel	Harbor Boulevard	9:15	6
Ramada Plaza Hotel	Katella Avenue	14:30	2
Sheraton Park Hotel	Harbor Boulevard	17:00	7
Super 8 Motel	Katella Avenue	15:30	2
Tropicana Inn & Suites	Harbor Boulevard	6:15	3

*To Disneyland Park. The Grand Californian has an on-site entrance to DCA.

The chart and the above discussion might lead you to wonder whether there's any real advantage to staying in a Disney-owned hotel. The Disney hotels, of course, are very expensive, but if you can handle the tariff, here are the primary benefits of staying in one:

1. You are eligible for early entry at Disneyland Park four days each week.
2. You have dozens of full- and counter-service restaurants within easy walking distance.
3. The Disney hotels offer the nicest rooms of any of the hotels within walking distance.
4. The Disney hotels offer the nicest swimming pools of any of the hotels within walking distance.
5. There are numerous entertainment and shopping options in Downtown Disney.
6. It's easy to retreat to your hotel for a meal, a nap, or a swim.
7. You don't need a car.

DISNEYLAND RESORT HOTELS

DISNEY OFFERS THREE ON-SITE HOTELS: the **Grand Californian,** the **Disneyland Hotel,** and the **Paradise Pier Hotel.** The Grand Californian, built in the rustic stone-and-timber style of the grand national-park lodges, is the flagship property. Newer, more elaborately themed, and closer to the theme parks and Downtown Disney than the other two on-property hotels, the Grand Californian is without a doubt the best place to stay . . . *if* you can afford it. Rooms at the Grand Californian start at about $340 and range up to $500 per night.

Next most convenient is the sprawling Disneyland Hotel, the oldest of the three. Comprising three guest-room towers, the hotel has no theme but is lushly landscaped and offers large, luxurious guest rooms. Walking from the hotel to the park entrances takes about 10 to 12 minutes. Walking time to the monorail station, with transportation to Disneyland Park, is about 3 to 6 minutes. Rates at the Disneyland Hotel run from $245 to $285 per night, depending on the season.

The east side of the third Disney hotel overlooks the Paradise Pier section of Disney's California Adventure theme park, hence the name Paradise Pier Hotel. Although there is a South Seas–island flavor, both in the guest rooms and in the public areas, the hotel is not themed. The guest rooms here are large. Walking to the theme-park entrances takes about 10 to 16 minutes, and to the monorail station and Downtown Disney about 5 to 10 minutes. Depending on season, room rates range from $225 to $255 per night.

Disney's Grand Californian Hotel & Spa

The Grand Californian Hotel is the flagship of Disneyland Resort's three hotels. With its shingle siding, rock foundations, cavernous hewn-beam lobby, polished hardwood floors, and cozy hearths, the hotel is a stately combination of elements from western national-park lodges. Designed by architect Peter Dominick (who also designed the Wilderness Lodge at Walt Disney World), the Grand Californian is rendered in the Arts and Crafts style of the early 20th century, with such classic features as "flying" roofs, projecting beams, massive buttresses, and an earth- and wood-tone color palette. Most reminiscent of the Ahwahnee Hotel at Yosemite National Park, the Grand Californian combines rugged craftsmanship and grand scale with functional design and intimate spaces. Pull up a vintage rocker in front of a blazing fire, and the bustling lobby instantly becomes a snug cabin.

The hotel's main entrance off Downtown Drive is primarily for vehicular traffic. Two pedestrian-only entrances open into Downtown Disney and DCA; this last makes it a cinch to return to the hotel from DCA for a nap or a swim or for lunch. Walking time to Disneyland Park is about five minutes.

The 745 guest rooms are livable but struggle to reconcile modern luxury with the hotel's signature rustic look. Pastel bedspreads and drapes seem much too feminine and delicate to live easily with the masculine polished-wood furniture. Room features we like include excellent light for reading in bed, more-than-adequate storage space, a two-sink vanity outside the toilet and bath, and, in some rooms, a private balcony. Views from the guest rooms overlook the pool area, Downtown Disney, or Disney's California Adventure theme park.

Ranging from about $280 to $550 per night, guest rooms are the most expensive at Disneyland Resort. And as if these rates aren't high enough, the Grand Californian charges an $11.50 daily resort fee to cover guest parking, use of the fitness center, local phone calls, Internet access, and a daily paper (weekdays only).

Inspired by Napa Valley cuisine, the Napa Rose Restaurant is the Disneyland Resort's flagship fine-dining venue. Situated in a stunning room overlooking DCA, Napa Rose is very expensive but still a very good value (see a full profile on page 189). Just a notch down in price and formality, but likewise located in an exceptionally lovely (albeit more rustic) room, is the Storytellers Cafe, which serves breakfast, lunch, and dinner (see a full profile on page 196). The restaurant's name is drawn from period murals depicting tall tales set in early California. The fare consists of house-specialty wood-fired pizza and hearty home-style comfort food.

The resort's pool complex, beautifully landscaped with rocks and conifers in a high Sierra theme, includes a lap pool, a Mickey-shaped pool, and a kids' pool with a 100-foot-long twisting slide. The on-site Mandara Spa is one of Disney's best, offering a wide selection of treatments and a state-of-the-art fitness facility. Rounding out the Grand Californian's amenity mix are two clubby lounges and a child-care center for children ages 5 to 12.

disneyland-area hotels

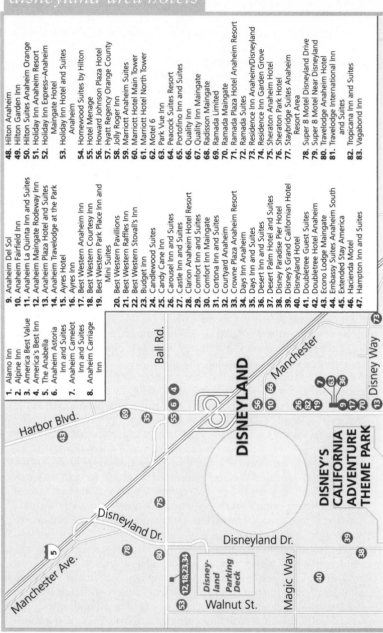

1. Alamo Inn
2. Alpine Inn
3. America Best Value
4. America's Best Inn
5. The Anabella
6. Anaheim Astoria Inn and Suites
7. Anaheim Camelot Inn and Suites
8. Anaheim Carriage Inn
9. Anaheim Del Sol
10. Anaheim Fairfield Inn
11. Anaheim La Quinta Inn and Suites
12. Anaheim Maingate Rodeway Inn
13. Anaheim Plaza Hotel and Suites
14. Anaheim Travelodge at the Park
15. Ayres Hotel
16. Ayres Inn
17. Best Western Anaheim Inn
18. Best Western Courtesy Inn
19. Best Western Park Place Inn and Mini Suites
20. Best Western Pavillions
21. Best Western Raffles Inn
22. Best Western Stovall's Inn
23. Budget Inn
24. Candlewood Suites
25. Candy Cane Inn
26. Carousel Inn and Suites
27. Castle Inn and Suites
28. Clarion Anaheim Hotel Resort
29. Comfort Inn and Suites
30. Comfort Inn Maingate
31. Cortona Inn and Suites
32. Courtyard Anaheim
33. Crowne Plaza Anaheim Resort
34. Days Inn Anaheim
35. Days Inn and Suites
36. Desert Inn and Suites
37. Desert Palm Hotel and Suites
38. Disney Paradise Pier Hotel
39. Disney's Grand Californian Hotel
40. Disneyland Hotel
41. Doubletree Guest Suites
42. Doubletree Hotel Anaheim
43. Econo Lodge Maingate
44. Embassy Suites Anaheim South
45. Extended Stay America
46. Hacienda Motel
47. Hampton Inn and Suites

48. Hilton Anaheim
49. Hilton Garden Inn
50. Hilton Suites Anaheim Orange
51. Holiday Inn Anaheim Resort
52. Holiday Inn Express–Anaheim Maingate Hotel
53. Holiday Inn Hotel and Suites Anaheim
54. Homewood Suites by Hilton
55. Hotel Menage
56. Howard Johnson Plaza Hotel
57. Hyatt Regency Orange County
58. Jolly Roger Inn
59. Marriott Anaheim Suites
60. Marriott Hotel Main Tower
61. Marriott Hotel North Tower
62. Motel 6
63. Park Vue Inn
64. Peacock Suites Resort
65. Portofino Inn and Suites
66. Quality Inn
67. Quality Inn Maingate
68. Radisson Maingate
69. Ramada Limited
70. Ramada Maingate
71. Ramada Plaza Hotel Anaheim Resort
72. Ramada Suites
73. Residence Inn Anaheim/Disneyland
74. Residence Inn Garden Grove
75. Sheraton Anaheim Hotel
76. Sheraton Park Hotel
77. Staybridge Suites Anaheim Resort Area
78. Super 8 Motel Disneyland Drive
79. Super 8 Motel Near Disneyland
80. Travelodge Anaheim Hotel
81. Travelodge International Inn and Suites
82. Tropicana Inn and Suites
83. Vagabond Inn

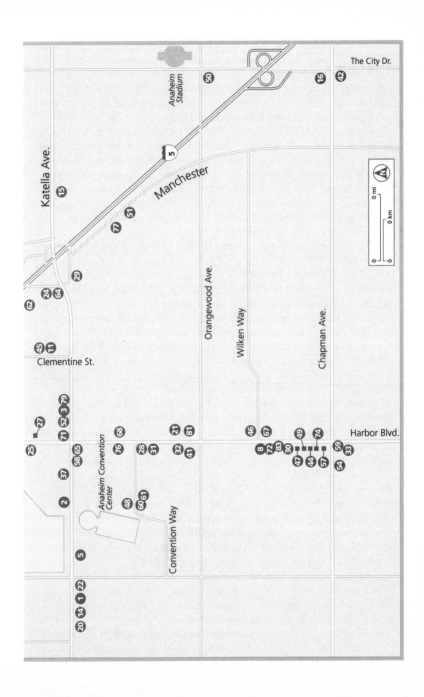

The Disneyland Hotel

Walt Disney barely managed to finance the construction of the Disneyland theme park. He certainly didn't have the funds to purchase adjacent property or build hotels, though on-site hotels were central to his overall concept. So he cut a deal with petroleum engineer and TV producer Jack Wrather to build and operate the Disneyland Hotel. The deal not only gave Wrather the rights to the Disneyland Hotel but also allowed him to build other Disneyland Hotels within the state of California until 2054. It always irked Walt that he didn't own the hotel that bore his name, but Wrather steadfastly refused to renegotiate the rights. After Jack Wrather died in 1984, the Walt Disney Company bought the entire Wrather Corporation, which among other things held the rights to the *Lone Ranger* and *Lassie* TV series and, improbably, the RMS *Queen Mary,* docked at Long Beach. By acquiring the whole corporation, the Walt Disney Company brought the Disneyland Hotel under Disney ownership in 1988.

The Disneyland Hotel consists of three hotel towers facing each other across a verdant landscaped plaza containing decorative pools, a swimming complex, restaurants, shops, and gardens. The hotel was originally connected to Disneyland Park by monorail, but the hotel station was demolished during the construction of DCA and relocated to Downtown Disney. Guest registration for all three towers is situated in the Marina Tower, which is connected to the Disneyland Convention Center and the Disneyland Hotel's self-parking garage. Though all three towers share restaurants, shopping, and recreational amenities, the Marina Tower is most conveniently located. It and the Sierra Tower are closest to Downtown Disney and the theme parks.

From the outside, the towers reflect a dated 1950s look, but the guest rooms inside have been renovated and updated many times over the years. Rack rates for the Disneyland Hotel range from around $210 for a "city view" in the off-season to more than $350 for a view of the inner pool and garden complex during holiday periods.

All rooms feature heavy blond furniture with inlays of Sleeping Beauty Castle and a map of Disneyland as it appeared in 1955. Earthtone soft goods likewise reflect a retro look. Unusual for hotels today, eight-foot sliding glass doors open onto a small balcony in most rooms. The best views can be had from the east/west-facing Sierra Tower, which overlooks the hotel's inner plaza and pool area on the west and Downtown Disney and the theme parks to the east. The most lackluster views are the north-facing vistas of the Marina Tower. High-speed Internet access is available in all guest rooms, and refrigerators are supplied in most.

The baths are small for an upscale hotel, but there is a double sink and vanity outside the bathrooms. As in most family hotels built in the 1950s and 60s, there is a connecting door, situated by the clothes closet and the aforementioned double sink, to an adjoining room. Soundproofing around the connecting doors is nonexistent, so be prepared to revel in the intimate sounds of your neighbors brushing their teeth, coping with indigestion, and arguing over what to wear. Fortunately, these sounds do not (except for especially enthusiastic gargling) carry into the sleeping area.

The swimming complex includes the Peter Pan–themed Never Land Pool, with its 100-foot waterslide. Adults, however usually gravitate to the nearby and quieter Cove Pools and beach. Fronting the Bonita Tower are tropical gardens, complete with walking paths, waterfalls, and koi ponds. Also in the inner plaza are the Lost Bar—with vaulted ceilings, tin roof, and wooden beams, and the intimate, rathskeller-like Wine Cellar pouring fine California wines by the glass. One of the hotel's better restaurants, Hook's Pointe, is located nearby. Other Disneyland Hotel restaurants include Steakhouse 55 (formerly Granville's) and Goofy's Kitchen, the hotel's character meal headquarters. (All Disneyland Hotel restaurants are profiled in full in Part Four.)

As concerns practical matters, parking is a royal pain at the Disneyland Hotel. The self-parking garage is convenient only to the Marina Tower, and even there you'll probably have a long walk. To reach the other two towers you must pass through the Marina Tower and navigate across the hotel's inner plaza and pool area. The Bonita Tower on the southern end of the property has a small parking lot to the rear accessible via Downtown Drive and Paradise Way. Unfortunately, many of the already limited spaces are reserved for the adjacent Disney Vacation Club time-share sales office. Even so, if you're staying at the Bonita Tower, it's your best bet. If there's no room in the Bonita lot, you're better off parking in the Paradise Pier Hotel's lot than in the Disneyland Hotel parking garage. The only valet parking is at the Marina Tower, so even if you valet park you'll still have to hoof to the other towers.

Like the Grand Californian, the Disneyland Hotel charges an $11.50-per-day resort fee that covers, among other things, the privilege of self-parking.

Paradise Pier Hotel

Disney acquired the independent Pan Pacific Hotel just south of the Disneyland Hotel in 1997 and changed its name to the Disneyland Pacific Hotel. Just before Disney's California Adventure opened in 2001, the hotel was rechristened as the Paradise Pier Hotel in recognition of the Paradise Pier district of DCA that the hotel overlooks.

The 489-room property has always had a South Seas theme and decor that extend to both public spaces and guest rooms. Guest rooms are furnished with blond faux-rattan furniture and the usual Disney-pastel soft goods, including bedspreads with a palm-tree pattern. Somewhat more whimsical than rooms at the Disneyland Hotel or the Grand Californian, Paradise Pier rooms include such accents as Mickey Mouse table lamps and confetti-patterned carpets. Guest-room picture windows on the hotel's east side offer the best vistas of any of the Disneyland Resort hotels with a perfect view of the lights and attractions of Paradise Pier inside DCA. From rooms on the other side of the hotel you can see, well, parking lots. Rates range from $225 to $255, depending on season and view.

Dining options include the informal PCH Grill, serving three meals daily including a character breakfast, and Yamabuki, a Japanese restaurant that has been trying to redefine itself as pan-Asian. Amenities include a fitness center and an often breezy rooftop pool complete with a waterslide (the view from the top of the slide is killer). Self-parking in Paradise Pier's on-site garage is fast and convenient. Somewhat isolated on the Disneyland Resort property, the hotel is a 15-minute hike to the theme park entrances, farther away than most non-Disney hotels lining Harbor Boulevard on the east side of the resort.

HOW TO GET DISCOUNTS ON LODGING AT DISNEYLAND RESORT HOTELS

THERE ARE SO MANY GUEST ROOMS in and around Disneyland Resort that competition is brisk, and everyone, including Disney, wheels and deals to keep them filled. This has led to a more flexible discount policy for Disneyland Resort hotels. Here are tips for getting price breaks:

1. SEASONAL SAVINGS You can save from $15 to $60 per night on a Disneyland Resort hotel room by scheduling your visit during the slower times of the year. Disney uses so many adjectives (*regular, holiday, peak, value,* and such) to describe its seasonal calendar, however, that it's hard to keep up without a scorecard. To confuse matters more, the dates for each season vary from hotel to hotel. Our advice: if you're set on staying at a Disney hotel, obtain a copy of the Walt Disney Travel Sales Center California Brochure, which is described on page 15.

If you have a hard time getting a copy of the brochure, forget trying to find the various seasonal dates on the Disneyland Resort Web site. Easier by far is to check them out on the independent-of-Disney **Mouse Savers.com** site described in tip 3 below.

Understand that Disney seasonal dates are not sequential like spring, summer, fall, and winter. That would be way too simple. For any specific resort, there are sometimes several seasonal changes in a month. This is important because your room rate per night will be determined by the season prevailing when you check in. Let's say that you checked into the Disneyland Hotel on April 19 for a five-night stay. April 19 is in the more expensive peak season that ends on April 20, followed by the less pricey regular season beginning on April 23. Because you arrived during peak season, the peak season rate will be applied during your entire stay, even though more than half of your stay will be in regular season. Your strategy, therefore, is to shift your dates (if possible) to arrive during a less expensive season.

2. ASK ABOUT SPECIALS When you talk to Disney reservationists, inquire specifically about special deals. Ask, for example, "What special rates or discounts are available at Disney hotels during the time of our visit?" Being specific and assertive paid off for an Illinois reader:

> *I called Disney's reservations number and asked for availability and rates. . . . [Because] of the* Unofficial Guide *warning about Disney reservationists answering only the questions posed, I specifically asked, "Are there any special rates or discounts for that room during the month of October?" She replied, "Yes, we have that room available at a special price. . . . " [For] the price of one phone call, I saved $440.*

Along similar lines, a Warren, New Jersey, dad chimed in with this:

> *Your tip about asking Disney employees about discounts was invaluable. They will not volunteer this information, but by asking we saved almost $500 on our hotel room using a AAA discount.*

3. LEARN ABOUT DEALS OFFERED TO SPECIFIC MARKETS The folks at **MouseSavers.com** keep an updated list of discounts and reservation codes for use at Disney resorts. The codes are separated into categories such as "for anyone," "for residents of certain states," "for Annual Passport holders," and so on. For example, the site listed a deal targeted to residents of the San Diego area published in an ad in a San Diego newspaper. Dozens of discounts are usually listed on the site, covering almost all Disneyland Resort hotels. Usually anyone calling the Disneyland Central Reservations Office (call ☎ 714-956-6425 and press 3 on the menu) can cite the referenced ad and get the discounted rate.

unofficial **TIP**
To enhance your chances of receiving a pin-code offer, you need to get your name and street or e-mail address into the Disney system.

You should be aware that Disney is trending away from room-discount codes that anyone can use. Instead, Disney is targeting people with pin codes in e-mails and direct mailings. Pin-code discounts are offered to specific individuals and are correlated with that person's name and address. Pin-code offers are nontransferable. When you try to make a reservation using the code, Disney will verify that the street or e-mail address to which the pin code was sent is yours.

To enhance your chances of receiving a pin-code offer, you need to get your name and street or e-mail address into the Disney system. One way is to call the Walt Disney Travel Company–Disneyland Reservation Center at ☎ 714-520-7070 and request that written info be sent to you. If you've been to Disneyland previously, your name and address will already be on record, but you won't be as likely to receive a pin-code offer as you would by calling and requesting to be sent information. The latter is regarded as new business. Or, expressed differently, if Disney smells blood they're more likely to come after you. On the Web, go to **www.disneyland.com** and sign up to have offers and news sent automatically to your e-mail address.

MouseSavers.com also features a great links page with short descriptions and URLs of the best Disney-related Web sites, and a current-year seasonal rates calendar.

4. EXPEDIA.COM Online travel seller Expedia has established an active market in discounting Disney hotels. Most discounts are in the 4 to 15% range but can go as deep as 25%.

5. DISNEYLAND RESORT WEB SITE Disney has become more aggressive about offering deals on its Web site. Go to **www.disneyland.com** and check the page for "Special Offers." When booking rooms on Disney's or any other site, be sure to click on "Terms and Conditions" and read the fine print *before* making reservations.

6. ANNUAL PASSPORT–HOLDER DISCOUNTS Annual Passport holders are eligible for a broad range of discounts on dining, shopping, and lodging. If you visit Disneyland Resort once a year or more, of if you plan on a visit of five or more days, you might save money overall by purchasing Annual Passes. During 2007, we saw resort discounts as deep as 30% offered to Annual Passport holders. It doesn't take long to recoup the extra bucks you spent on an Annual Passport when you're saving that kind of money on lodging. Discounts in the 10 to 15% range are more the norm.

7. TRAVEL AGENTS Travel agents are active players in the market and are particularly good sources of information on time-limited special programs and discounts. In our opinion, a good travel agent is the best friend a traveler can have. And though we at the *Unofficial Guide* know a thing or two about the travel industry, we always give our agent a chance to beat any deal we find. If our agent can't beat the deal, we let her book it if it's commissionable. In other words, we create a relationship that gives her plenty of incentive to really roll up her sleeves and work in our behalf.

As you might expect, some travel agents and agencies specialize, sometimes exclusively, in selling Disneyland and Walt Disney World. These agents have spent an incredible amount of time at both resorts and have completed extensive Disney education programs. They are usually the most Disney-knowledgeable agents in the travel industry. Most of these specialists and their agencies display the "Earmarked" logo indicating that they are Authorized Disney Vacation Planners.

8. ORGANIZATIONS AND AUTO CLUBS Eager to sell rooms, Disney has developed time-limited programs with some auto clubs and other organizations. Recently, for example, AAA members were offered 10-to-20% savings on Disney hotels and discounts on Disney package vacations. Such deals come and go, but the market suggests there will be more in the future. If you're a member of AARP, AAA, or any travel or auto club, ask whether the group has a program before shopping elsewhere.

9. ROOM UPGRADES Sometimes a room upgrade is as good as a discount. If you're visiting Disneyland Resort during a slower time, book the least expensive room your discounts will allow. Checking in, ask very politely about being upgraded to a "theme park" or "pool view" room. A fair percentage of the time, you will get one at no additional charge.

NON-DISNEY HOTELS

WHEN WALT DISNEY BUILT DISNEYLAND, he did not have the funding to include hotels or to purchase the property surrounding his theme park. Consequently, the area around the park developed in an essentially uncontrolled manner. Many of the hotels and motels near Disneyland were built in the early 1960s, and they are small and sometimes unattractive by today's standards. Quite a few motels adopted adventure or fantasy themes in emulation of Disneyland. As you might imagine, these themes from five decades ago seem hokey and irrelevant today. There is a disquieting (though rapidly diminishing) number of seedy hotels near Disneyland, and even some of the chain properties fail to live up to their national standards.

If you consider a non-Disney-owned hotel in Anaheim, check its quality as reported by a reliable independent rating system such as those offered by the *Unofficial Guides,* AAA Directories, Mobil Guides, or *Frommer's* guides. Also, before you book, ask how old the hotel is and when the guest rooms were last refurbished. Be aware that almost any hotel can be made to look good on a Web site, so don't depend on Web sites alone. Locate the hotel on our street map (pages 38–39) to verify its proximity to Disneyland. If you will not have a car, make sure the hotel has a shuttle service that will satisfy your needs.

GETTING A GOOD DEAL AT NON-DISNEY HOTELS

BELOW ARE SOME TIPS AND STRATEGIES for getting a good deal on a hotel room near Disneyland. Though the following list may seem a bit intimidating and may refer to players in the travel market that are unfamiliar to you, acquainting yourself with the concepts and strategies will serve you well in the long run. Simply put, the tips we provide for getting a good deal near Disneyland will work equally well at just about any other place where you need a hotel. Once you have invested a little time and have experimented with these strategies, you will be able to routinely obtain rooms at the best hotels and at the lowest possible rates.

unofficial **TIP**
For the best rates and least crowded conditions, try to avoid visiting Disneyland Resort when a major convention or trade show is in progress.

Remember that Disneyland Resort is right across the street from the Anaheim–Orange County Convention Center, one of the largest and busiest convention centers in the country. Room availability, as well as rates, are affected significantly by trade shows and other events at the convention center. To determine whether such an event will be ongoing during your projected dates, check out the convention calendar on pages 24 and 25.

1. MOUSESAVERS.COM is a site dedicated to finding great deals on hotels, admissions, and more at Disneyland Resort and Walt Disney World. The site covers discounts on both Disney and non-Disney hotels and is especially effective at keeping track of time-limited deals and discounts offered in a select market—San Diego, for example. However, the site does not sell travel products.

2. TRAVELAXE.COM offers free software you can download on your PC (sorry, no Macs) that will scan the better hotel-discount sites and find the cheapest rate on the Internet for each of more than 80 Disneyland-area hotels. The site offers various filters, such as price, quality rating, and proximity to a specific location (such as Disneyland, the convention center, or airport), that allow you to tailor your search.

While a Travelaxe search is always useful, we've frequently been unable to obtain the best rate shown for a particular hotel. Finally, Expedia and Travelocity, two giants among Internet sellers, are not among the sites searched.

3. KAYAK.COM, like Travelaxe, is a travel search engine, but unlike Travelaxe, there's no application to download. Where Travelaxe searches the better hotel discounter sites, Kayak primarily searches chain and individual hotel Web sites. Web sites searched vary from destination to destination but do not include Expedia and Travelocity.

4. EXPEDIA.COM AND TRAVELOCITY.COM These two Web sites sometimes offer good discounts on area hotels. We find that Expedia offers the best deals if you're booking within two weeks of your visit. In fact, some of Expedia's last-minute deals are amazing, really rock-bottom rates. Travelocity frequently beats Expedia, however, if you reserve two weeks to three months out. Neither site offers anything to get excited about if you book more than three months from the time of your visit. If you use either site, be sure to take into consideration the demand for rooms during the season of your visit, and check to see if any big conventions or trade shows are scheduled for the convention center.

5. PRICELINE.COM At Priceline you can tender a bid for a room. You can't bid on a specific hotel but you can specify location ("Disneyland Vicinity") and the quality rating expressed in stars. If your bid is accepted, you will be assigned to a hotel consistent with your location and quality requirements, and your credit card will be charged in a non-refundable transaction for your entire stay. Notification of acceptance usually takes less than an hour. We recommend bidding $25 to $45 per night for a three-star hotel and $45 to $70 per night for a four-star property. To gauge your chances of success, check to see if any major conventions or trade shows are scheduled for the convention center during your preferred dates.

6. OTHER WEB TRAVEL SELLERS Ever wonder which sites offer the best deals, or whether you're missing some tiny boutique site offering amazing discounts? So do we. *Unofficial Guide* statistician Fred Hazleton has analyzed more than 380,000 rate quotes from dozens of Internet sellers for Disneyland Resort and Anaheim-area hotels. Fred discovered that the pricing competition for Disneyland area hotels is a lot greater than we see in the Walt Disney World area or at our other *Unofficial Guide* destinations. Fewer than 5% of the Disneyland searches produced a single quote while another 5% of the searches produced more than ten quotes! The quoted rates are more varied in Anaheim than we usually see at other destinations, with a broader range between the highest and lowest rates for a given hotel. For a number of hotels, as many as six or more different rates are quoted. Fred's research has also shown that about 66% of the time the hotel Web site or hotel front desk will match or beat the best Internet rate available. We've also observed that Expedia and Travelocity are often the best Web sites for last-minute bookings.

Following are the Web sites that most often produce the best rate quotes for Disneyland Resort area hotels. The percentage in parenthesis tells how often the site has the winning (read: best) quote. Having the lowest rate 42% of the time, as **ARestravel.com** does, may not sound like much, but consider that probably 50 other Internet travel sites are selling the same hotels.

ARestravel.com (42%)   **Travelworm.com (40%)**

Hotelkingdom.com (34%)   **Hotels.com (32%)**

Lodging.com (23%)

7. ENTERTAINMENT BOOKS These area-specific guides contain discount coupons for hotels, restaurants, entertainment, shopping, and even car washes. The Anaheim version sells for about $45 at the beginning of the year but is discounted if you buy with only part of the year remaining. Sometimes the books sell out before summer. Unless you live in Orange County, you won't be able to use a lot of the coupons, but sometimes the savings on your hotel and dining will more than justify the purchase. To buy, or for additional information, visit **www.entertainment.com** online.

8. EXIT INFORMATION GUIDE A company called EIG (Exit Information Guide) publishes a book of discount coupons for bargain rates at hotels throughout California. These books are available free of charge at many restaurants and motels along the main interstate highways in and leading to California. However, since most folks make reservations before leaving home, picking up the coupon book en route does not help much. But, for $3 ($5 Canadian) EIG will mail you a copy, allowing you to examine the discounts offered before you make your reservations. You can use a credit card or send a money order or check. The guide is free; the charge is for the postage. Write or call, or order online at **www.travelersdiscountguide.com:**

Exit Information Guide
4205 NW Sixth Street
Gainesville, FL 32609
☎ 352-371-3948

9. SPECIAL WEEKEND RATES If you are not averse to about an hour's drive to Disneyland, you can get a great weekend rate on rooms in downtown Los Angeles. Most hotels that cater to business, government, and convention travelers offer special weekend discounts that range from 15 to 40% below normal weekday rates. You can find out about weekend specials by calling the hotel or by consulting your travel agent.

10. WHOLESALERS, CONSOLIDATORS, AND RESERVATION SERVICES Wholesalers and consolidators buy rooms, or options on rooms (room blocks), from hotels at a low negotiated rate. They then resell the rooms at a profit through travel agents, through tour packagers, or directly to the public. Most wholesalers and consolidators have a provision for returning unsold rooms to participating hotels, but they are disinclined to do so. The wholesaler's or consolidator's relationship with any hotel is predicated on volume. If they return rooms unsold, the hotel might not make as many rooms available to them the next time around. Thus, wholesalers and consolidators often offer rooms at bargain rates, anywhere from 15 to 50% off rack, occasionally sacrificing their profit margin in the process, to avoid returning the rooms to the hotel unsold.

When wholesalers and consolidators deal directly with the public, they frequently represent themselves as "reservation services." When you call, you can ask for a rate quote for a particular hotel or, alternatively, ask for their best available deal in the area where you prefer to stay. If there is a maximum amount you are willing to pay, say so. Chances are the service will find something that will work for you, even if they have to shave a dollar or two off their own profit. Sometimes you will have to prepay for your room with your credit card when you make your reservation. Most often, you will pay when you check out. Listed below are two services that frequently offer substantial discounts in the Anaheim area.

ANAHEIM AREA WHOLESALERS AND CONSOLIDATORS

California Reservations	☎ 800-576-0003	**www.hotellocators.com**
Hotel Reservations Network	☎ 800-715-7666	**www.hoteldiscounts.com**

11. CLUBS AND ORGANIZATIONS If you belong to AAA, AARP, or a number of other organizations or clubs, you can obtain discounts on lodging. Usually the discounts are modest, in the 5 to 15% range, but occasionally higher.

12. IF YOU MAKE YOUR OWN RESERVATION As you poke around trying to find a good deal, there are several things you should know. First, always call the hotel in question as opposed to the hotel chain's national toll-free number. Quite often, the reservationists at the national numbers are unaware of local specials. Always ask about specials before you inquire about corporate rates. Do not be reluctant to bargain. If you are buying a hotel's weekend package, for example, and want to extend your stay into the following week, you can often obtain at least the corporate rate for the extra days. Do your bargaining before you check in, however, preferably when you make your reservations. Work far enough in advance to receive a faxed or mailed confirmation.

HOW TO GET THE ROOM YOU WANT

MOST HOTELS, INCLUDING DISNEY'S, won't guarantee a specific room when you book, but will post your request on your reservations record and try to accommodate you. Our experience indicates that if you give them your first, second, and third choices, you'll probably get one of the three.

When speaking to the reservationist or your travel agent, it's important to be specific. If you want a room overlooking the pool, say so. Similarly, be sure to clearly state such preferences as a particular floor, a corner room, a room close to restaurants, a room away from elevators and ice machines, a nonsmoking room, a room with a certain type of balcony, or any other preference. If you have a laundry list of preferences, type it up in order of importance, and e-mail, fax, or mail it to the hotel or to your travel agent. Be sure to include your own contact information and, if you've already booked, your reservation confirmation number. If it makes you feel better, call back in a couple of days to make sure your preferences were posted to your reservations record.

About Hotel Renovations

We have inspected almost 100 hotels in the Disneyland Resort area to compile the list of lodging choices presented in this *Unofficial Guide.* Each year we phone each hotel to verify contact information and to inquire about renovations or refurbishments. If a hotel has been renovated or has refurbished its guest rooms, we reinspect that hotel along with any new hotels for the next edition of this book. Hotels that report no improvements are checked out every two years.

Most hotels more than five years old refurbish 10 to 20% of their guest rooms each year. This incremental approach minimizes disruption of business but makes your room assignment a crap shoot. You might luck into a newly renovated room or be assigned a threadbare room. Disney resorts will not guarantee a recently renovated room but will note your request and try to accommodate you. Non-Disney hotels will often guarantee an updated room when you book.

Our hotel ratings are provided shortly in the section "Hotels and Motels: Rated and Ranked," starting on page 51.

TRAVEL PACKAGES

PACKAGE TOURS THAT INCLUDE lodging, park admission, and

other features are routinely available. Some packages are very good deals if you make use of the features you are paying for.

Finally, here's a helpful source of regional travel information:

Anaheim–Orange County Visitor and Convention Bureau
Department C
P.O. Box 4270
Anaheim, CA 92803
☎ 714-765-8888
www.anaheimoc.org

How to Evaluate a Disneyland Travel Package

Hundreds of Disneyland package vacations are offered to the public each year. Some are created by the Walt Disney Travel Sales Center, others by airline touring companies, and some by independent travel agents and wholesalers. Almost all Disneyland packages include lodging at or near Disneyland and theme-park admission. Packages offered by the airlines include air transportation.

Package prices vary seasonally, with mid-June to mid-August and holiday periods being most expensive. Off-season, forget packages; there are plenty of empty rooms, and you can negotiate great discounts (at non-Disney properties) yourself. Similarly, airfares and rental cars are cheaper at off-peak times.

Almost all package ads feature a headline stating "Disneyland for Three Days from $298" or some such wording. The key word in the ads is *from*. The rock-bottom package price connotes the least desirable hotel accommodations. If you want better or more conveniently located digs, you'll have to pay more, often much more.

At Disneyland, packages offer a wide selection of hotels. Some, like the Disney-owned hotels, are very good. Others, unfortunately, run the quality gamut. Packages with lodging in non-Disney hotels are much less expensive.

When considering a package, choose one that includes features you are sure to use. Whether you use all the features or not, you will most certainly pay for them. Second, if cost is of greater concern than convenience, make a few phone calls and see what the package would cost if you booked its individual components (such as airfare, rental car, and lodging) on your own. If the package price is less than the à la carte cost, the package is a good deal. If the costs are about the same, the package is probably worth it for the convenience.

If you buy a package from Disney, do not expect Disney reservationists to offer suggestions or help you sort out your options. As a rule they will not volunteer information, but will only respond to specific questions you pose, adroitly ducking any query that calls for an opinion. A reader from North Riverside, Illinois, wrote to the *Unofficial Guide,* complaining:

> I have received various pieces of literature from [Disney], and it is
> very confusing to try and figure everything out. My wife made two

telephone calls and the [Disney] representatives were very courteous. However, they only answered the questions posed and were not very eager to give advice on what might be most cost-effective. The [Disney] reps would not say if we would be better off doing one thing over the other. I feel a person could spend eight hours on the telephone with [Disney] reps and not have any more input than you get from reading the literature.

If you cannot get the information you need from the Disney people, try a good travel agent. Chances are the agent will be more forthcoming in helping you sort out your options.

Information Needed for Evaluation

For quick reference and to save on phone expenses, write or call the Walt Disney Travel Sales Center at ☎ 714-520-7070 and ask that they mail you a current Walt Disney Travel Sales Center California Brochure containing descriptions and room rates for all Disneyland lodging properties. Summarized information sheets on lodging are also available by fax. In addition, ask for a rate sheet listing admission options and prices for the theme parks. With this in hand, you are ready to evaluate any package that appeals to you. Remember that all packages are quoted on a per-person basis, two to a room (double occupancy). Good luck.

> **ONE MORE THING**
>
> If your travel plans include a stay in the area of more than two or three days, lodge near Disneyland Resort only just before and on the days you visit the parks. The same traffic you avoid by staying close to the park will eat you alive when you begin branching out to other Los Angeles–area attractions. Also, the area immediately around Disneyland is uninspiring, and there is a marked scarcity of decent restaurants.

HOTELS *and* MOTELS:
Rated and Ranked

WHAT'S IN A ROOM?

EXCEPT FOR CLEANLINESS, STATE OF REPAIR, and decor, most travelers do not pay much attention to hotel rooms. There is, of course, a discernible standard of quality and luxury that differentiates Motel 6 from Holiday Inn, Holiday Inn from Marriott, and so on. In general, however, hotel guests fail to appreciate that some rooms are better engineered than others.

Contrary to what you might suppose, designing a hotel room is (or should be) a lot more complex than picking a bedspread to match the carpet and drapes. Making the room usable to its occupants is an art, a planning discipline that combines both form and function.

Disney Lodging for Less

Mary Waring, *Webmaster at* **MouseSavers.com** *(see page 18), knows more about Disney hotel packages than anyone on the planet. Here are her money-saving suggestions.*

BOOK "ROOM-ONLY." It's frequently a better deal to book a room-only reservation instead of buying a vacation package. Disney likes to sell vacation packages because they're easy and profitable. When you buy a package, you're typically paying a premium for convenience. You can often save money by putting together your own package—just book room-only at a resort and buy passes, meals, and extras separately.

Disney now prices its standard packages at the same rates as if you had purchased individual components separately at full price. However, what Disney doesn't tell you is that components can usually be purchased separately at a discount—and those discounts are not reflected in the brochure prices of Disney's packages. (Sometimes you can get special-offer packages that do include discounts; see below.)

Keep in mind that Disney's packages often include extras you are unlikely to use. Also, packages require a $200 deposit and full payment 45 days in advance; plus, they have stringent change and cancellation policies. Generally, booking room-only requires a deposit of one night's room rate with the remainder due at check-in. Your reservation can be changed or canceled for any reason until five days before check-in.

Whether you decide to book a Disney vacation package or create your own, there are a number of ways to save:

• *Use discount codes to reduce your room-only rate.* Disney uses these codes to push unsold rooms at certain times of year. (In the past two years, however, these codes have become scarcer.) Check a Web site like **MouseSavers.com** to learn about codes that may be available for your vacation dates. Some codes are available to anyone, while others are just for Florida residents, Annual Passport holders, and so on.

Discount codes aren't always available for every hotel or every date, and they typically don't appear until two to six months in advance. The good news is that you can usually apply a code to an existing room-only reservation. Simply call the Disneyland Reservations

unofficial **TIP**
Request a renovated room at your hotel— these can be much nicer than the older rooms.

Decor and taste are important, certainly. No one wants to spend several days in a room where the decor is dated, garish, or even ugly. But beyond the decor, there are variables that determine how "livable" a hotel room is. In Anaheim,

Center at ☎ 714-956-6425 (or contact a Disney-savvy travel agent) and ask whether any rooms are available at your preferred hotel for your preferred dates using the code.

- *Use discount codes to reduce your vacation package rate.* Disney occasionally offers packages that include resort discounts or value-added features such as a free dining plan. For those who like the convenience of packages, these offers are well worth seeking out.

  You'll need to present a discount code to get the special package rates. Check a Web site like **MouseSavers.com** for more information.

  As with room-discount codes, package-discount codes aren't available for every hotel or every date, and they typically don't appear until two to six months in advance. You can usually apply a code to an existing package reservation. Again, call the Disneyland Reservations Center at ☎ 714-956-6425 (or contact a Disney-savvy travel agent) and ask whether any rooms are available at your preferred hotel for your preferred dates using the package code.

- *Be flexible.* Buying a room or package with a discount code is a little like shopping for clothes at a discount store: if you wear size XX-small or XXXX-large, or you like green when everyone else is wearing pink, you're a lot more likely to score a bargain. Likewise, resort discounts are available only when Disney has excess rooms. You're more likely to get a discount during less-popular times (such as value season) and at larger or less-popular resorts. Animal Kingdom Lodge and Old Key West seem to have discounted rooms available more often than the other resorts do.

- *Be persistent.* This is the most important tip. Disney allots a certain number of rooms to each discount; reportedly this averages 100 rooms per night per code. Once the discounted rooms are gone, you won't get that rate unless someone cancels. Fortunately, people change and cancel reservations all the time. If you can't get your preferred dates or hotel with one discount code, try another one (if available) or keep calling back first thing in the morning to check for cancellations—the system resets overnight, and any reservations with unpaid deposits are automatically released for resale.

for example, we have seen some beautifully appointed rooms that are simply not well designed for human habitation. The next time you stay in a hotel, pay attention to the details and design elements of your room. Even more than decor, these are the things that will make you feel comfortable and at home.

ROOM RATINGS

TO SEPARATE PROPERTIES ACCORDING to the relative quality, tastefulness, state of repair, cleanliness, and size of their standard rooms, we have grouped the hotels and motels into classifications denoted by stars. Star ratings in this guide apply to Anaheim properties only, and do not necessarily correspond to ratings awarded by Mobil, AAA, or other travel critics. Because stars have little relevance when awarded in the absence of commonly recognized standards of comparison, we have tied our ratings to expected levels of quality established by specific American hotel corporations.

Star ratings apply to *room quality only* and describe the property's standard accommodations. For most hotels and motels a "standard accommodation" is a hotel room with either one king bed or two queen beds. In an all-suite property, the standard accommodation is either a studio or one-bedroom suite. In addition to standard accommodations, many hotels offer luxury rooms and special suites that are not rated in this guide. Star ratings for rooms are assigned without regard to whether a property has a restaurant, recreational facilities, entertainment, or other extras.

OVERALL STAR RATINGS		
★★★★★	Superior rooms	Tasteful and luxurious by any standard
★★★★	Extremely nice rooms	What you would expect at a Hyatt Regency or Marriott
★★★	Nice rooms	Holiday Inn or comparable quality
★★	Adequate rooms	Clean, comfortable, and functional without frills—like a Motel 6
★	Budget rooms	Spartan, not aesthetically pleasing

In addition to stars (which delineate broad categories), we also employ a numerical rating system. Our rating scale is 0 to 100, with 100 as the best possible rating. Numerical ratings are presented to show the difference we perceive between one property and another. Rooms at the Homewood Suites and Howard Johnson Plaza Hotel are both rated as three and a half stars (★★★½). In the supplemental numerical ratings, the Homewood Suites is rated an 82 and the Howard Johnson a 75. This means that within the three-and-a-half-star category, the Homewood Suites has slightly nicer rooms than the Howard Johnson.

HOW THE HOTELS COMPARE

COST ESTIMATES ARE BASED ON THE HOTEL'S published rack rates for standard rooms. Each "$" represents $50. Thus, a cost symbol of "$$$" means a room (or suite) at that hotel will be about $150 a night (it may be less for weekdays or more on weekends).

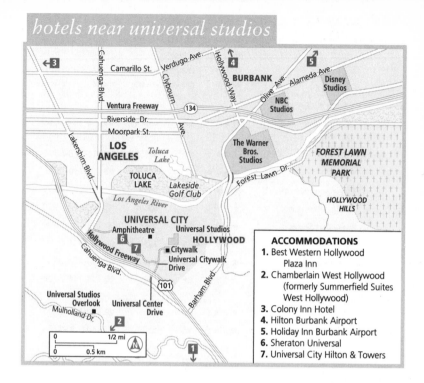

hotels near universal studios

ACCOMMODATIONS

1. Best Western Hollywood Plaza Inn
2. Chamberlain West Hollywood (formerly Summerfield Suites West Hollywood)
3. Colony Inn Hotel
4. Hilton Burbank Airport
5. Holiday Inn Burbank Airport
6. Sheraton Universal
7. Universal City Hilton & Towers

Following is a hit parade of the nicest rooms in town. We've focused strictly on room quality and have excluded any consideration of location, services, recreation, or amenities. In some instances, a one- or two-room suite can be had for the same price or less than that of a hotel room.

If you used an earlier edition of this guide, you will notice that many of the ratings and rankings have changed. In addition to the inclusion of new properties, these changes are occasioned by such positive developments as guest-room renovation or improved maintenance and housekeeping. A failure to properly maintain guest rooms or a lapse in housekeeping standards can negatively affect the ratings.

Finally, before you begin to shop for a hotel, take a hard look at this letter we received from a couple in Hot Springs, Arkansas:

We cancelled our room reservations to follow the advice in your book [and reserved a hotel highly ranked by the *Unofficial Guide*]. *We wanted inexpensive, but clean and cheerful. We got inexpensive, but dirty, grim, and depressing. I really felt disappointed in your advice and the room. It was the pits. That was the one real piece of information I needed from your book! The room spoiled the holiday for me aside from our touring.*

How the Hotels Compare

HOTEL	OVERALL-QUALITY RATING	ROOM-QUALITY RATING	COST ($ = $50)	PHONE
DISNEYLAND AREA				
Disney's Grand Californian Hotel and Spa	★★★★	90	$$$$$$$$–	☎ 714-635-2300
Disneyland Hotel	★★★★	89	$$$$$$–	☎ 714-778-6600
Courtyard Anaheim	★★★★	88	$$$$$+	☎ 714-740-2645
Crowne Plaza Anaheim Resort	★★★★	86	$$$+	☎ 714-867-5555
Disney Paradise Pier Hotel	★★★★	86	$$$$$	☎ 714-999-0990
Doubletree Guest Suites	★★★★	86	$$$$	☎ 714-750-3000
Hilton Suites Anaheim Orange	★★★★	86	$$$	☎ 714-938-1111
Peacock Suites Resort	★★★★	86	$$$$	☎ 714-535-8255
Staybridge Suites Anaheim Resort Area	★★★★	86	$$$+	☎ 714-748-7700
Ayres Hotel	★★★★	85	$$+	☎ 714-634-2106
Hyatt Regency Orange County	★★★★	85	$$$	☎ 714-750-1234
Marriott Hotel Main Tower	★★★★	85	$$$–	☎ 714-750-8000
Sheraton Park Hotel	★★★★	85	$$$$–	☎ 714-750-1811
Doubletree Hotel Anaheim	★★★★	84	$$$+	☎ 714-634-4500
The Anabella	★★★★	83	$$+	☎ 714-905-1050
Marriott Anaheim Suites	★★★★	83	$$$	☎ 714-750-1000
Sheraton Anaheim Hotel	★★★★	83	$$$+	☎ 714-778-1700
Candlewood Suites	★★★½	82	$$+	☎ 714-808-9000
Homewood Suites by Hilton	★★★½	82	$$$	☎ 714-740-1800
Marriott Hotel North Tower	★★★½	82	$$$	☎ 714-750-8000
Portofino Inn and Suites	★★★½	82	$$$+	☎ 714-782-7600
Residence Inn Garden Grove	★★★½	82	$$$$$–	☎ 714-591-4015
Embassy Suites Anaheim South	★★★½	81	$$$	☎ 714-539-3300
Hilton Anaheim	★★★½	81	$$	☎ 714-750-4321
Ramada Plaza Hotel Anaheim Resort	★★★½	81	$$+	☎ 714-991-6868
Residence Inn Anaheim/ Disneyland	★★★½	81	$$$–	☎ 714-533-3555

HOTEL	OVERALL-QUALITY RATING	ROOM-QUALITY RATING	COST ($ = $50)	PHONE
DISNEYLAND AREA (CONTINUED)				
Holiday Inn Anaheim Resort	★★★½	80	$$+	☎ 714-748-7777
Anaheim Camelot Inn and Suites	★★★½	79	$$$	☎ 714-635-7275
Desert Inn and Suites	★★★½	79	$$+	☎ 714-772-5050
Hilton Garden Inn	★★★½	79	$$$–	☎ 714-703-9100
Anaheim La Quinta Inn and Suites	★★★½	76	$$$–	☎ 714-635-5000
Howard Johnson Plaza Hotel	★★★½	75	$$$–	☎ 714-776-6120
Candy Cane Inn	★★★	74	$$$–	☎ 714-774-5284
Cortona Inn and Suites	★★★	73	$$	☎ 714-971-5000
Hampton Inn and Suites	★★★	73	$$$	☎ 714-703-8800
Holiday Inn Express-Anaheim Maingate Hotel	★★★	72	$$$	☎ 714-772-7755
Jolly Roger Inn	★★★	72	$$$–	☎ 714-782-7500
Ramada Suites	★★★	72	$$+	☎ 714-971-3553
Carousel Inn and Suites	★★★	70	$$+	☎ 714-758-0444
Clarion Anaheim Hotel Resort	★★★	70	$$+	☎ 714-750-3131
Radisson Maingate	★★★	70	$$$–	☎ 714-750-2801
Anaheim Fairfield Inn	★★★	69	$$$–	☎ 714-772-6777
Comfort Inn and Suites	★★★	69	$$	☎ 714-772-8713
Best Western Raffles Inn	★★★	67	$$+	☎ 714-750-6100
Ayres Inn	★★★	66	$$+	☎ 714-978-9168
Best Western Stovall's Inn	★★★	66	$$+	☎ 714-778-1880
Best Western Park Place Inn and Mini Suites	★★★	65	$$+	☎ 714-776-4800
Travelodge Anaheim Hotel	★★★	65	$$	☎ 714-774-7600
Castle Inn and Suites	★★½	64	$$	☎ 714-774-8111
Comfort Inn Maingate	★★½	64	$$	☎ 714-703-1220
Holiday Inn Hotel and Suites Anaheim	★★½	64	$$$$+	☎ 714-535-0300
Vagabond Inn	★★½	64	$+	☎ 714-971-5556

How the Hotels Compare (continued)

HOTEL	OVERALL-QUALITY RATING	ROOM-QUALITY RATING	COST ($ = $50)	PHONE
DISNEYLAND AREA (CONTINUED)				
Alpine Inn	★★½	63	$$−	☎ 714-535-2186
Anaheim Plaza Hotel and Suites	★★½	63	$$−	☎ 714-772-5900
Best Western Anaheim Inn	★★½	63	$$$−	☎ 714-774-1050
Best Western Pavilions	★★½	63	$$+	☎ 714-776-0140
Extended Stay America	★★½	63	$$−	☎ 714-502-9988
Hotel Menage	★★½	63	$$+	☎ 714-758-0900
Anaheim Astoria Inn and Suites	★★½	61	$$$$	☎ 714-774-3882
Days Inn Anaheim	★★½	61	$$−	☎ 714-520-0101
Desert Palms Hotel and Suites	★★½	61	$$$+	☎ 714-535-1133
Motel 6	★★½	61	$$−	☎ 714-520-9696
Ramada Limited	★★½	61	$$−	☎ 714-999-0684
Anaheim Carriage Inn	★★½	60	$$−	☎ 714-740-1440
Anaheim Del Sol	★★½	60	$$+	☎ 714-234-3411
Best Western Courtesy Inn	★★½	60	$$+	☎ 714-772-2470
Ramada Maingate	★★½	60	$$$	☎ 714-777-0440
Travelodge International Inn and Suites	★★½	59	$$	☎ 714-971-9393
America's Best Inn	★★½	58	$$−	☎ 714-533-2570
Quality Inn Maingate	★★½	58	$$	☎ 714-750-5211
Tropicana Inn and Suites	★★½	58	$$$	☎ 714-635-4082
Anaheim Maingate Rodeway Inn	★★½	57	$+	☎ 714-533-2500

Needless to say, this letter was as unsettling to us as the bad room was to our reader. Our integrity as travel journalists, after all, is based on the quality of the information we provide to our readers. Even with the best of intentions and the most conscientious research, however, we cannot inspect every room in every hotel. What we do, in statistical terms, is take a sample: we check out several rooms selected at random in each hotel and base our ratings and rankings on those rooms. The inspections are conducted anonymously and without the knowledge of the property's management. Although it would be unusual, it is certainly possible that the rooms we randomly

HOTEL	OVERALL-QUALITY RATING	ROOM-QUALITY RATING	COST ($ = $50)	PHONE
DISNEYLAND AREA (CONTINUED)				
Econo Lodge Maingate	★★½	57	$$	☎ 714-535-7878
Quality Inn and Suites Anaheim at the Resort	★★½	57	$$+	☎ 714-991-8100
Anaheim Travelodge at the Park	★★½	56	$$−	☎ 714-774-7817
Days Inn and Suites	★★½	56	$$−	☎ 714-533-8830
Park Vue Inn	★★	55	$$$−	☎ 714-772-3691
Super 8 Motel Disneyland Drive	★★	55	$$−	☎ 714-778-0350
Alamo Inn	★★	52	$+	☎ 714-635-8070
Super 8 Motel Near Disneyland	★★	51	$+	☎ 714-778-6900
Budget Inn	★★	50	$$−	☎ 714-535-5524
Hacienda Motel	★½	46	$+	☎ 714-750-2101
America Best Value	★½	41	$$−	☎ 714-776-2815
UNIVERSAL AREA				
Universal City Hilton and Towers	★★★★	87	$$$$$+	☎ 818-506-2500
Sheraton Universal	★★★★	85	$$$$$−	☎ 818-980-1212
Chamberlain West Hollywood	★★★½	81	$$$$$	☎ 310-657-7400
Hilton Burbank Airport	★★★½	80	$$$$	☎ 818-843-6000
Holiday Inn Burbank Media Center	★★★	68	$$$	☎ 818-841-4770
Best Western Hollywood Plaza Inn	★★½	62	$$$−	☎ 323-851-1800
Colony Inn Hotel	★★½	60	$$−	☎ 818-763-2787

inspect are not representative of the majority of rooms at a particular hotel. Another possibility is that the rooms we inspect in a given hotel are representative but that by bad luck a reader is assigned to an inferior room. When we rechecked the hotel our reader disliked so intensely, we discovered that our rating was correctly representative but that he and his wife had unfortunately been assigned to one of a small number of threadbare rooms scheduled for renovation.

The key to avoiding disappointment is to do some snooping around in advance. We recommend that you ask to get a photo of a hotel's standard guest room before you book, or at least a copy of the hotel's promotional brochure. Be forewarned, however, that some hotel chains

Top 30 Best Deals near Disneyland

HOTEL	OVERALL QUALITY RATING	ROOM-QUALITY RATING	COST ($ = $50)	PHONE
1. Hilton Anaheim	★★★½	81	$$	☎ 714-750-4321
2. The Anabella	★★★★	83	$$+	☎ 714-905-1050
3. Ayres Hotel	★★★★	85	$$+	☎ 714-634-2106
4. Marriott Hotel Main Tower	★★★★	85	$$$−	☎ 714-750-8000
5. Candlewood Suites	★★★½	82	$$+	☎ 714-808-9000
6. Ramada Plaza Hotel Anaheim Resort	★★★½	81	$$+	☎ 714-991-6868
7. Vagabond Inn	★★½	64	$+	☎ 714-971-5556
8. Hilton Suites Anaheim Orange	★★★★	86	$$$	☎ 714-938-1111
9. Desert Inn and Suites	★★★½	79	$$+	☎ 714-772-5050
10. Hyatt Regency Orange County	★★★★	85	$$$	☎ 714-750-1234
11. Cortona Inn and Suites	★★★	73	$$	☎ 714-971-5000
12. Holiday Inn Anaheim Resort	★★★½	80	$$+	☎ 714-748-7777
13. Hilton Garden Inn	★★★½	79	$$$−	☎ 714-703-9100
14. Travelodge Anaheim Hotel	★★★	65	$$	☎ 714-774-7600
15. Marriott Anaheim Suites	★★★★	83	$$$	☎ 714-750-1000

use the same guest-room photo in their promotional literature for all hotels in the chain, and that the guest room in a specific property may not resemble the photo in the brochure. When you or your travel agent call, ask how old the property is and when the guest room you are being assigned was last renovated. If you arrive and are assigned a room inferior to that which you had been led to expect, demand to be moved to another room.

THE TOP 30 BEST DEALS

HAVING LISTED THE BETTER ROOMS IN TOWN, let's take a look at the best combinations of quality and value in a room. As before, the rankings are made without consideration of location or the availability of restaurants, recreational facilities, entertainment, or amenities.

The Disneyland Hotel, you may notice, is not one of the best deals. This is because you can get more for your money at other properties.

HOTEL	OVERALL QUALITY RATING	ROOM-QUALITY RATING	COST ($ = $50)	PHONE
16. Staybridge Suites Anaheim Resort Area	★★★★	86	$$$+	☎714-748-7700
17. Residence Inn Anaheim/ Disneyland	★★★½	81	$$$–	☎714-533-3555
18. Crowne Plaza Anaheim Resort	★★★★	86	$$$+	☎ 714-867-5555
19. Sheraton Anaheim Hotel	★★★★	83	$$$+	☎ 714-778-1700
20. Extended Stay America	★★½	63	$$–	☎ 714-502-9988
21. Doubletree Hotel Anaheim	★★★★	84	$$$+	☎ 714-634-4500
22. Comfort Inn and Suites	★★★	69	$$	☎ 714-772-8713
23. Ramada Suites	★★★	72	$$+	☎ 714-971-3553
24. Howard Johnson Plaza Hotel	★★★½	75	$$$–	☎ 714-776-6120
25. Carousel Inn and Suites	★★★	70	$$+	☎ 714-758-0444
26. Homewood Suites by Hilton	★★★½	82	$$$	☎ 714-740-1800
27. Marriott Hotel North Tower	★★★½	82	$$$	☎ 714-750-8000
28. Anaheim La Quinta Inn and Suites	★★★½	76	$$$–	☎ 714-635-5000
29. Embassy Suites Anaheim South	★★★½	81	$$$	☎ 714-539-3300
30. Anaheim Maingate Rodeway Inn	★★★½	57	$+	☎ 714-533-2500

The Disneyland and Grand Californian Hotels, however, are two of the most popular hotels in the area, and many guests are willing to pay a higher rate for their convenience, service, and amenities.

We recently had a reader complain to us that he had booked one of our top-ranked rooms for value and had been very disappointed in the room. On checking we noticed that the room the reader occupied had a quality rating of ★★½. We would remind you that the value ratings are intended to give you some sense of value received for your lodging dollar spent. A ★★½ room at $35 may have the same value rating as a ★★★★ room at $85, but that does not mean the rooms will be of comparable quality. Regardless of whether it's a good deal or not, a ★★½ room is still a ★★½ room.

Listed above are the top 30 room buys for the money, regardless of location or star classification, based on rack rates. Note that sometimes a suite can cost less than a hotel room.

Hotel Information Chart

Alamo Inn ★★
1140 West Katella Avenue
Anaheim 92802
☎ 714-635-8070
FAX 714-778-3307
www.alamoinnandsuites.com

ROOM RATING	52
COST ($ = $50)	$+
POOL	•
ON-SITE DINING	—

Alpine Inn ★★½
715 West Katella Avenue
Anaheim 92802
☎ 714-535-2186
FAX 714-535-3714
www.alpineinnanaheim.com

ROOM RATING	63
COST ($ = $50)	$$—
POOL	•
ON-SITE DINING	—

America Best Value ★½
425 West Katella Avenue
Anaheim 92802
☎ 714-776-2815
FAX 714-533-4037
www.anaheimfantasyinn.com

ROOM RATING	41
COST ($ = $50)	$$—
POOL	•
ON-SITE DINING	—

Anaheim Camelot Inn and Suites ★★★½
1520 South Harbor Boulevard
Anaheim 92802
☎ 714-635-7275
FAX 714-635-7275
www.parkinn-anaheim.com

ROOM RATING	79
COST ($ = $50)	$$$
POOL	•
ON-SITE DINING	—

Anaheim Carriage Inn ★★½
2125 South Harbor Boulevard
Anaheim 92802
☎ 714-740-1440
FAX 714-971-5330
www.anaheimcarriageinn.com

ROOM RATING	60
COST ($ = $50)	$$—
POOL	•
ON-SITE DINING	—

Anaheim Del Sol ★★½
1604 South Harbor Boulevard
Anaheim 92802
☎ 714-234-3411
FAX 714-234-3422
www.delsolinn.com

ROOM RATING	60
COST ($ = $50)	$$+
POOL	•
ON-SITE DINING	—

Anaheim Plaza Hotel and Suites ★★½
1700 South Harbor Boulevard
Anaheim 92802
☎ 714-772-5900
FAX 714-772-8386
www.anaheimplazahotel.com

ROOM RATING	63
COST ($ = $50)	$$—
POOL	•
ON-SITE DINING	•

Anaheim Travelodge at the Park ★★½
1166 West Katella Avenue
Anaheim 92802
☎ 714-774-7817
FAX 714-774-7329
www.travelodge.com

ROOM RATING	56
COST ($ = $50)	$$—
POOL	•
ON-SITE DINING	—

Ayres Hotel ★★★★
2550 East Katella Avenue
Anaheim 92806
☎ 714-634-2106
FAX 714-634-2106
www.ayreshotels.com

ROOM RATING	85
COST ($ = $50)	$$+
POOL	•
ON-SITE DINING	—

Best Western Hollywood Plaza Inn ★★½
2011 North Highland Avenue
Hollywood 90068
☎ 323-851-1800
FAX 323-851-1836
www.bestwestern.com

ROOM RATING	62
COST ($ = $50)	$$$—
POOL	•
ON-SITE DINING	—

Best Western Park Place Inn and Mini Suites ★★★
1544 South Harbor Boulevard
Anaheim 92802
☎ 714-776-4800
FAX 714-758-1396
www.bestwestern.com

ROOM RATING	65
COST ($ = $50)	$$+
POOL	•
ON-SITE DINING	—

Best Western Pavilions ★★½
1176 West Katella Avenue
Anaheim 92802
☎ 714-776-0140
FAX 714-776-5801
www.bestwestern.com

ROOM RATING	63
COST ($ = $50)	$$+
POOL	•
ON-SITE DINING	—

Candlewood Suites ★★★½
1733 South Anaheim Boulevard
Anaheim 92805
☎ 714-808-9000
FAX 714-808-8989
www.candlewoodsuites.com

ROOM RATING	82
COST ($ = $50)	$$+
POOL	—
ON-SITE DINING	—

Candy Cane Inn ★★★
1747 South Harbor Boulevard
Anaheim 92802
☎ 714-774-5284
FAX 714-772-5462
www.candycaneinn.net

ROOM RATING	74
COST ($ = $50)	$$$—
POOL	•
ON-SITE DINING	—

Carousel Inn and Suites ★★★
1530 South Harbor Boulevard
Anaheim 92802
☎ 714-758-0444
FAX 714-772-9960
www.carouselinnandsuites.com

ROOM RATING	70
COST ($ = $50)	$$+
POOL	•
ON-SITE DINING	—

America's Best Inn ★★½
414 West Ball Road
Anaheim 92805
☎ 714-533-2570
FAX 714-635-3322
www.bestinnanaheim.com

ROOM RATING	58
COST ($ = $50)	$$−
POOL	•
ON-SITE DINING	—

The Anabella ★★★★
1030 West Katella Avenue
Anaheim 92802
☎ 714-905-1050
FAX 714-905-1055
www.anabellahotel.com

ROOM RATING	83
COST ($ = $50)	$$+
POOL	•
ON-SITE DINING	•

**Anaheim Astoria Inn
and Suites** ★★½
426 West Ball Road
Anaheim 92805
☎ 714-774-3882
FAX 714-234-2164
www.anaheimastoriainn.com

ROOM RATING	61
COST ($ = $50)	$$$$
POOL	•
ON-SITE DINING	—

Anaheim Fairfield Inn ★★★
1460 South Harbor Boulevard
Anaheim 92802
☎ 714-772-6777
FAX 714-999-1727
www.marriott.com

ROOM RATING	69
COST ($ = $50)	$$$−
POOL	•
ON-SITE DINING	•

**Anaheim La Quinta Inn
and Suites** ★★★½
1752 South Clementine Street
Anaheim 92802
☎ 714-635-5000
FAX 714-776-9073
www.laquinta.com

ROOM RATING	76
COST ($ = $50)	$$$−
POOL	—
ON-SITE DINING	—

**Anaheim Maingate
Rodeway Inn** ★★½
1211 West Place
Anaheim 92802
☎ 714-533-2500
FAX 714-398-8026
www.rodewayinn.com

ROOM RATING	57
COST ($ = $50)	$+
POOL	—
ON-SITE DINING	—

Ayres Inn ★★★
3737 West Chapman Avenue
Anaheim 92868
☎ 714-978-9168
FAX 714-978-9168
www.ayreshotels.com

ROOM RATING	66
COST ($ = $50)	$$+
POOL	•
ON-SITE DINING	—

Best Western Anaheim Inn ★★½
1630 South Harbor Boulevard
Anaheim 92802
☎ 714-774-1050
FAX 714-776-6305
www.bestwestern.com

ROOM RATING	63
COST ($ = $50)	$$$−
POOL	•
ON-SITE DINING	—

Best Western Courtesy Inn ★★½
1070 West Ball Road
Anaheim 92802
☎ 714-772-2470
FAX 714-774-3425
www.bestwestern.com

ROOM RATING	60
COST ($ = $50)	$$+
POOL	•
ON-SITE DINING	—

Best Western Raffles Inn ★★★
2040 South Harbor Boulevard
Anaheim 92802
☎ 714-750-6100
FAX 714-740-0639
www.bestwestern.com

ROOM RATING	67
COST ($ = $50)	$$+
POOL	•
ON-SITE DINING	—

Best Western Stovall's Inn ★★★
1110 West Katella Avenue
Anaheim 92802
☎ 714-778-1880
FAX 714-778-3805
www.bestwestern.com

ROOM RATING	66
COST ($ = $50)	$$+
POOL	•
ON-SITE DINING	•

Budget Inn ★★
1042 Ball Road
Anaheim 92802
☎ 714-535-5524
FAX 714-999-5900
www.anaheimbudgetinn.com

ROOM RATING	50
COST ($ = $50)	$$−
POOL	•
ON-SITE DINING	—

Castle Inn and Suites ★★½
1734 South Harbor Boulevard
Anaheim 92802
☎ 714-774-8111
FAX 714-956-4736
www.castleinn.com

ROOM RATING	64
COST ($ = $50)	$$
POOL	•
ON-SITE DINING	—

**Chamberlain
West Hollywood** ★★★½
1000 Westmount Drive
West Hollywood 90069
☎ 310-657-7400 FAX 310-657-1535
www.chamberlainwest
hollywood.com

ROOM RATING	81
COST ($ = $50)	$$$$$$
POOL	•
ON-SITE DINING	•

**Clarion Anaheim
Hotel Resort** ★★★
616 Convention Way
Anaheim 92802
☎ 714-750-3131
FAX 714-750-9027
www.chidirect.com

ROOM RATING	70
COST ($ = $50)	$$+
POOL	•
ON-SITE DINING	•

Hotel Information Chart (continued)

Colony Inn Hotel ★★½
4917 Vineland Avenue
North Hollywood 91601
☎ 818-763-2787
FAX 818-763-0909
www.colonyinn.com

ROOM RATING	60
COST ($ = $50)	$$–
POOL	–
ON-SITE DINING	–

Comfort Inn and Suites ★★★
300 East Katella Way
Anaheim 92802
☎ 714-772-8713 FAX 714-778-1235
www.comfortinnsuites
anaheim.com

ROOM RATING	69
COST ($ = $50)	$$
POOL	●
ON-SITE DINING	–

Comfort Inn Maingate ★★½
2171 South Harbor Boulevard
Anaheim 92802
☎ 714-703-1220
FAX 714-703-1401
www.choicehotels.com

ROOM RATING	64
COST ($ = $50)	$$
POOL	●
ON-SITE DINING	–

Days Inn Anaheim ★★½
1030 West Ball Road
Anaheim 92802
☎ 714-520-0101
FAX 714-758-9406
www.daysinn.com

ROOM RATING	61
COST ($ = $50)	$$–
POOL	●
ON-SITE DINING	–

Days Inn and Suites ★★½
1111 South Harbor Boulevard
Anaheim 92805
☎ 714-533-8830
FAX 714-778-0573
www.daysinn.com

ROOM RATING	56
COST ($ = $50)	$$–
POOL	●
ON-SITE DINING	–

Desert Inn and Suites ★★★½
1600 South Harbor Boulevard
Anaheim 92802
☎ 714-772-5050
FAX 714-778-2754
www.anaheimdesertinn.com

ROOM RATING	79
COST ($ = $50)	$$+
POOL	●
ON-SITE DINING	–

Disneyland Hotel ★★★★
1150 West Magic Way
Anaheim 92802
☎ 714-778-6600
FAX 714-520-6079
www.disneyland.com

ROOM RATING	89
COST ($ = $50)	$$$$$$–
POOL	●
ON-SITE DINING	●

Doubletree Guest Suites ★★★★
2085 South Harbor Boulevard
Anaheim 92802
☎ 714-750-3000
FAX 714-750-3002
www.hilton.com

ROOM RATING	86
COST ($ = $50)	$$$$
POOL	●
ON-SITE DINING	●

Doubletree Hotel Anaheim
★★★★
100 The City Drive
Orange 92868
☎ 714-634-4500
FAX 714-978-2370
www.doubletree.com

ROOM RATING	84
COST ($ = $50)	$$$+
POOL	●
ON-SITE DINING	●

Hacienda Motel ★½
2176 South Harbor Boulevard
Anaheim 92802
☎ 714-750-2101
FAX 714-971-1235

ROOM RATING	46
COST ($ = $50)	$+
POOL	–
ON-SITE DINING	–

Hampton Inn and Suites ★★★
11747 Harbor Boulevard
Garden Grove 92840
☎ 714-703-8800
FAX 714-703-8900
www.hamptoninn.com/hi/
anaheim

ROOM RATING	73
COST ($ = $50)	$$$
POOL	●
ON-SITE DINING	–

Hilton Anaheim ★★★½
777 Convention Way
Anaheim 92802
☎ 714-750-4321
FAX 714-740-4460
www.hilton.com

ROOM RATING	81
COST ($ = $50)	$$
POOL	●
ON-SITE DINING	●

Holiday Inn Anaheim Resort
★★★½
1915 South Manchester Avenue
Anaheim 92802
☎ 714-748-7777
FAX 714-748-7400
www.holiday-inn.com

ROOM RATING	80
COST ($ = $50)	$$+
POOL	●
ON-SITE DINING	●

**Holiday Inn Burbank
Media Center** ★★★
150 East Angeleno
Burbank 91502
☎ 818-841-4770
FAX 818-566-7886
www.ichotelsgroup.com

ROOM RATING	68
COST ($ = $50)	$$$
POOL	●
ON-SITE DINING	●

**Holiday Inn Express-Anaheim
Maingate Hotel** ★★★
435 West Katella Avenue
Anaheim 92802
☎ 714-772-7755
FAX 714-772-2727
www.holiday-anaheim.com

ROOM RATING	72
COST ($ = $50)	$$$
POOL	●
ON-SITE DINING	–

Cortona Inn and Suites ★★★
2029 South Harbor Boulevard
Anaheim 92802
☎ 714-971-5000
FAX 714-971-5001
www.cartonainnandsuites.com

ROOM RATING	73
COST ($ = $50)	$$
POOL	•
ON-SITE DINING	—

Courtyard Anaheim ★★★★
2045 South Harbor Boulevard
Anaheim 92802
☎ 714-740-2645
FAX 714-740-2646
www.courtyardanaheim.com

ROOM RATING	88
COST ($ = $50)	$$$$$+
POOL	•
ON-SITE DINING	•

**Crowne Plaza Anaheim
Resort** ★★★★
12021 Harbor Boulevard
Garden Grove 92840
☎ 714-867-5555
FAX 714-867-5123
www.anaheim.crowneplaza.com

ROOM RATING	86
COST ($ = $50)	$$$+
POOL	•
ON-SITE DINING	•

Desert Palms Hotel and Suites
★★½
631 West Katella Avenue
Anaheim 92802
☎ 714-535-1133
FAX 714-491-7409
www.desertpalmshotel.com

ROOM RATING	61
COST ($ = $50)	$$$+
POOL	•
ON-SITE DINING	•

Disney Paradise Pier Hotel
★★★★
1717 South Disneyland Drive
Anaheim 92802
☎ 714-999-0990
FAX 714-776-5763
www.disneyland.com

ROOM RATING	86
COST ($ = $50)	$$$$$
POOL	•
ON-SITE DINING	•

**Disney's Grand Californian
Hotel and Spa** ★★★★
1600 South Disneyland Drive
Anaheim 92802
☎ 714-635-2300
FAX 714-300-7300
www.disneyland.com

ROOM RATING	90
COST ($ = $50)	$$$$$$$$–
POOL	•
ON-SITE DINING	•

Econo Lodge Maingate ★★½
871 South Harbor Boulevard
Anaheim 92805
☎ 714-535-7878
FAX 714-535-8186
www.choicehotels.com

ROOM RATING	57
COST ($ = $50)	$$
POOL	•
ON-SITE DINING	—

**Embassy Suites
Anaheim South** ★★★½
11767 Harbor Boulevard
Garden Grove 92840
☎ 714-539-3300 FAX 714-539-4600
anaheimsouth.embassysuites.com

ROOM RATING	81
COST ($ = $50)	$$$
POOL	•
ON-SITE DINING	•

Extended Stay America ★★½
1742 South Clementine Street
Anaheim 92802
☎ 714-502-9988
FAX 714-502-9977
www.extendedstayamerica.com

ROOM RATING	63
COST ($ = $50)	$$–
POOL	•
ON-SITE DINING	—

Hilton Burbank Airport ★★★½
2500 Hollywood Way
Burbank 91505
☎ 818-843-6000
FAX 818-842-9720
www.hiltonburbank.com

ROOM RATING	80
COST ($ = $50)	$$$$
POOL	•
ON-SITE DINING	•

Hilton Garden Inn ★★★½
11777 Harbor Boulevard
Garden Grove 92840
☎ 714-703-9100
FAX 714-703-9200
www.hilton.com

ROOM RATING	79
COST ($ = $50)	$$$–
POOL	•
ON-SITE DINING	•

**Hilton Suites Anaheim
Orange** ★★★★
400 North State College Boulevard
Orange 92868
☎ 714-938-1111
FAX 714-938-0930
www.hilton.com

ROOM RATING	86
COST ($ = $50)	$$$
POOL	•
ON-SITE DINING	•

**Holiday Inn Hotel and Suites
Anaheim** ★★½
1240 South Walnut Avenue
Anaheim 92802
☎ 714-535-0300
FAX 714-491-8953
www.hianaheim.com

ROOM RATING	64
COST ($ = $50)	$$$$+
POOL	•
ON-SITE DINING	•

Homewood Suites by Hilton
★★★½
12005 Harbor Boulevard
Garden Grove 92840
☎ 714-740-1800
FAX 714-740-1867
www.homewoodsuites.com

ROOM RATING	82
COST ($ = $50)	$$$
POOL	•
ON-SITE DINING	—

Hotel Menage ★★½
1221 South Harbor Boulevard
Anaheim 92805
☎ 714-758-0900
FAX 714-533-1804
www.hotelmenage.com

ROOM RATING	63
COST ($ = $50)	$$+
POOL	•
ON-SITE DINING	•

Hotel Information Chart (continued)

Howard Johnson	
Plaza Hotel ★★★½	
1380 South Harbor Boulevard	
Anaheim 92802	
☎ 714-776-6120	
FAX 714-533-3578	
www.hojoanaheim.com	
ROOM RATING	75
COST ($ = $50)	$$$–
POOL	●
ON-SITE DINING	●

Hyatt Regency	
Orange County ★★★★	
11999 Harbor Boulevard	
Garden Grove 92840	
☎ 714-750-1234	
FAX 714-740-0465	
www.hyatt.com	
ROOM RATING	85
COST ($ = $50)	$$$
POOL	●
ON-SITE DINING	●

Jolly Roger Inn ★★★	
640 West Katella Avenue	
Anaheim 92802	
☎ 714-782-7500	
FAX 714-772-2308	
www.jollyrogerhotel.com	
ROOM RATING	72
COST ($ = $50)	$$$–
POOL	●
ON-SITE DINING	●

Motel 6 ★★½	
100 West Disney Way	
Anaheim 92802	
☎ 714-520-9696	
FAX 714-533-7539	
www.motel6.com	
ROOM RATING	61
COST ($ = $50)	$$–
POOL	●
ON-SITE DINING	—

Park Vue Inn ★★	
1570 South Harbor Boulevard	
Anaheim 92802	
☎ 714-772-3691	
FAX 714-635-5305	
www.parkvueinn.com	
ROOM RATING	55
COST ($ = $50)	$$$–
POOL	●
ON-SITE DINING	—

Peacock Suites Resort ★★★★	
1745 South Anaheim Boulevard	
Anaheim 92805	
☎ 714-535-8255	
FAX 714-535-8914	
www.peacocksuitesresort.com	
ROOM RATING	86
COST ($ = $50)	$$$$
POOL	●
ON-SITE DINING	—

Radisson Maingate ★★★	
1850 South Harbor Boulevard	
Anaheim 92802	
☎ 714-750-2801	
FAX 714-971-4754	
www.radisson.com	
ROOM RATING	70
COST ($ = $50)	$$$–
POOL	●
ON-SITE DINING	●

Ramada Limited ★★½	
921 South Harbor Boulevard	
Anaheim 92802	
☎ 714-999-0684	
FAX 714-956-8839	
www.ramada.com	
ROOM RATING	61
COST ($ = $50)	$$–
POOL	●
ON-SITE DINING	—

Ramada Maingate ★★½	
1650 South Harbor Boulevard	
Anaheim 92802	
☎ 714-772-0440	
FAX 714-991-8219	
www.ramada.com	
ROOM RATING	60
COST ($ = $50)	$$$
POOL	●
ON-SITE DINING	—

Residence Inn Garden Grove	
★★★½	
11931 Harbor Boulevard	
Garden Grove 92840	
☎ 714-591-4000	
www.marriott.com	
ROOM RATING	82
COST ($ = $50)	$$$$$–
POOL	●
ON-SITE DINING	—

Sheraton Anaheim Hotel ★★★★	
900 South Disneyland Drive	
Anaheim 92802	
☎ 714-778-1700	
FAX 714-535-3889	
www.sheraton.com	
ROOM RATING	83
COST ($ = $50)	$$$+
POOL	●
ON-SITE DINING	●

Sheraton Park Hotel ★★★★	
1855 South Harbor Boulevard	
Anaheim 92802	
☎ 714-750-1811	
FAX 714-971-4809	
www.sheratonparkanaheim.com	
ROOM RATING	85
COST ($ = $50)	$$$$–
POOL	●
ON-SITE DINING	●

Super 8 Motel Near Disneyland	
★★	
415 West Katella Avenue	
Anaheim 92802	
☎ 714-778-6900	
FAX 714-535-5659	
www.super8.com	
ROOM RATING	51
COST ($ = $50)	$+
POOL	●
ON-SITE DINING	

Travelodge Anaheim Hotel ★★★	
1057 West Ball Road	
Anaheim 92802	
☎ 714-774-7600	
FAX 714-535-6953	
www.travelodge.com	
ROOM RATING	65
COST ($ = $50)	$$
POOL	●
ON-SITE DINING	—

Travelodge International Inn	
and Suites ★★½	
2060 South Harbor Boulevard	
Anaheim 92802	
☎ 714-971-9393 FAX 714-971-2706	
www.anaheimresorttravelodge.com	
ROOM RATING	59
COST ($ = $50)	$$
POOL	●
ON-SITE DINING	—

Marriott Anaheim Suites ★★★★
12015 Harbor Boulevard
Anaheim 92802
☎ 714-750-1000
FAX 714-750-9000
www.marriott.com

ROOM RATING	83
COST ($ = $50)	$$$
POOL	•
ON-SITE DINING	•

Marriott Hotel Main Tower
★★★★
700 West Convention Way
Anaheim 92802
☎ 714-750-8000
FAX 714-750-9100
www.marriott.com

ROOM RATING	85
COST ($ = $50)	$$$–
POOL	•
ON-SITE DINING	•

Marriott Hotel North Tower
★★★½
700 West Convention Way
Anaheim 92802
☎ 714-750-8000
FAX 714-750-9100
www.marriott.com

ROOM RATING	82
COST ($ = $50)	$$$
POOL	•
ON-SITE DINING	•

Portofino Inn and Suites ★★★½
1831 South Harbor Boulevard
Anaheim 92802
☎ 714-782-7600
FAX 714-782-7619
www.portofinoinnanaheim.com

ROOM RATING	82
COST ($ = $50)	$$$+
POOL	•
ON-SITE DINING	—

Quality Inn and Suites Anaheim at the Resort ★★½
1441 South Manchester Avenue
Anaheim 92802
☎ 714-991-8100
FAX 714-533-6430
www.qualityinn.com

ROOM RATING	57
COST ($ = $50)	$$+
POOL	•
ON-SITE DINING	—

Quality Inn Maingate ★★½
2200 South Harbor Boulevard
Anaheim 92802
☎ 714-750-5211
FAX 714-750-2803
www.qualityinn.com

ROOM RATING	58
COST ($ = $50)	$$
POOL	•
ON-SITE DINING	—

Ramada Plaza Hotel Anaheim Resort ★★★½
515 West Katella Avenue
Anaheim 92802
☎ 714-991-6868
FAX 714-991-6565
www.ramadaplazadisney.com

ROOM RATING	81
COST ($ = $50)	$$+
POOL	•
ON-SITE DINING	•

Ramada Suites ★★★
2141 South Harbor Boulevard
Anaheim 92802
☎ 714-971-3553
FAX 714-971-4609
www.ramada.com

ROOM RATING	72
COST ($ = $50)	$$+
POOL	•
ON-SITE DINING	—

Residence Inn Anaheim/ Disneyland ★★★½
1700 South Clementine Street
Anaheim 92802
☎ 714-533-3555
FAX 714-535-7626
www.marriott.com

ROOM RATING	81
COST ($ = $50)	$$$–
POOL	•
ON-SITE DINING	•

Sheraton Universal ★★★★
333 Universal Hollywood Drive
Universal City 91608
☎ 818-980-1212
FAX 818-985-4980
www.starwoodhotels.com

ROOM RATING	85
COST ($ = $50)	$$$$$$–
POOL	•
ON-SITE DINING	•

Staybridge Suites Anaheim Resort Area ★★★★
1855 South Manchester Avenue
Anaheim 92802
☎ 714-748-7700
FAX 714-748-4700
www.staybridge.com

ROOM RATING	86
COST ($ = $50)	$$$+
POOL	•
ON-SITE DINING	—

Super 8 Motel Disneyland Drive ★★
915 South Disneyland Drive
Anaheim 92802
☎ 714-778-0350
FAX 714-778-3878
www.super8.com

ROOM RATING	55
COST ($ = $50)	$$–
POOL	•
ON-SITE DINING	—

Tropicana Inn and Suites ★★½
1540 South Harbor Boulevard
Anaheim 92802
☎ 714-635-4082
FAX 714-635-1535
www.tropicanainn-anaheim.com

ROOM RATING	58
COST ($ = $50)	$$$
POOL	•
ON-SITE DINING	—

Universal City Hilton and Towers ★★★★
555 Universal Hollywood Drive
Universal City 91608
☎ 818-506-2500
FAX 818-509-2058
www.hilton.com

ROOM RATING	87
COST ($ = $50)	$$$$$+
POOL	•
ON-SITE DINING	•

Vagabond Inn ★★½
2145 South Harbor Boulevard
Anaheim 92802
☎ 714-971-5556
FAX 714-971-5580
www.vagabondinn-anaheim-hotel.com

ROOM RATING	64
COST ($ = $50)	$+
POOL	•
ON-SITE DINING	—

The DISNEY CRUISE LINE

THE MOUSE AT SEA

THE WALT DISNEY COMPANY HAS BEEN in the cruise business with two almost identical ships, the *Disney Wonder* and the *Disney Magic,* since 1998. In the summer of 2008, the *Disney Magic* will be based in Los Angeles and will offer a seven-night itinerary to the Mexican Riviera.

unofficial **TIP**
Disney cruise itineraries can be bundled with a stay at Disneyland.

At the outset, Disney put together a team of respected cruise-industry veterans, dozens of the world's best-known ship designers, and Disney's own unrivaled creative talent. Together, they created the Disney ships, recognizing that every detail would be critical to the line's success. Their task was to design a product that makes every adult on board feel that the vacation is intended for him or her, while giving every child the same impression.

Disney Cruise Line Standard Features

Officers American and international

Staff Cabin and dining, multinational; cruise, American

Dining Three themed family restaurants with "rotation" dining; alternative adults-only restaurant; indoor-outdoor cafe for breakfast, lunch, snacks, and buffet dinner for children; pool bar–grill for burgers, pizza, and sandwiches; ice-cream bar

Special diets On request at the time of booking; health-conscious cuisine program

Room service 24 hours

Dress code Casual by day; casual and informal in the evenings

Cabin amenities Direct-dial telephone with voice mail; tub and shower; TV; safe; hair dryer; mini-fridge

Electrical outlets 110 A/C

Wheelchair access Yes

Smoking Only in designated areas

Disney-suggested tipping Dining-room server: $3–$4 per night. Assistant server: $3 per night. Dining-room head server: 3- and 4-night cruise, $3 and $4;. 7-night cruise, $7; 10-night cruise, $8. Stateroom host: $4 per night. Dining manager and room service: your discretion. A 15% service charge is added automatically to bar bills.

Credit cards For cruise payment and on-board charges, all major credit cards.

The first surprise is the *Magic* 's appearance: simultaneously classic and innovative. Exteriors are traditional, reminiscent of great ocean liners of the past, but you'll find a Disney twist or two nonetheless.

Inside, it's up-to-the-minute technologically, and full of novel ideas for dining, entertainment, and cabin design. When it comes to dining, each evening you dine in a different restaurant with a different motif, but your waiters and dining companions move with you.

Disney's plan has been to create a "seamless vacation package" by combining a stay at Disneyland with a cruise. Cruise passengers are met at the airport by Disney staff and transported to the port in easily identifiable Disney Cruise Line buses. During the ride, passengers watch a video preview of the cruise.

The company targets first-time cruisers, counting on Disney's reputation for quality, service, and entertainment to dispel noncruisers' doubts about cruise vacations. Much time and effort has been spent to ensure that the ships appeal to adults—with or without children—as much as to children and families. Adults are catered to in myriad ways and presented with an extensive menu of adult-oriented activities. For example, the ships have an adults-only alternative restaurant, swimming pool, and nightclub; entertainment ranges from family musicals to adults-only variety performances. Meanwhile, almost from sunrise to midnight, children are offered equally varied programs. Because all programs are offered à la carte, families can choose how much time to spend together or pursuing separate interests.

The children's programs are excellent. In fact, they're rated the best in the cruise industry in *The Unofficial Guide to Cruises,* by Kay Showker and Bob Sehlinger. Thus, it's no surprise that many parents see their kids only at breakfast and dinner. But while adults can easily get a breather from children, it's tougher to escape Disney's syrupy, wholesome, cuter-than-a-billion–Beanie Babies entertainment, which permeates every cruise. In other words, to enjoy a Disney cruise, you'd better love Disney.

Go Forth and Be Goofy: The Itinerary

The Disney Cruise Line will send the *Disney Magic* to Los Angeles to cruise the Mexican Riviera during the summer of 2008. The line

2008 *DISNEY MAGIC* WEST COAST ITINERARY	
SEVEN-NIGHT MEXICAN RIVIERA CRUISE	
Sunday	Port of Los Angeles
Monday	At sea
Tuesday	Cabo San Lucas
Wednesday	Mazatlán
Thursday	Puerto Vallarta
Friday	At sea
Saturday	At sea
Sunday	Port of Los Angeles

tested these waters in 2006 and sold out every cruise. Along with the cruises originating in Los Angeles, two 15-night repositioning cruises transit the Panama Canal, departing westbound May 10, 2008, and returning east on August 17.

In addition to the above, a handful of special cruises are offered each year. For more information see **www.disneycruise.com.**

THE *DISNEY MAGIC*

THIS MODERN CRUISE SHIP'S sleek lines, twin smokestacks, and nautical styling call to mind classic ocean liners, but with instantly recognizable Disney signatures. The colors—black, white, red, and yellow—and the famous face-and-ears silhouette on the stacks are clearly those of Mickey Mouse. Look closely, and you'll see that the *Magic*'s figurehead is a 15-foot Goofy swinging upside down from a boatswain's chair, "painting" the stern.

Interiors combine nautical themes with Art Deco inspiration. Disney images are everywhere, from Mickey's profile in the wrought-iron balustrades to the bronze statue of Helmsman Mickey at the center of the three-deck Grand Atrium. Disney art is on every wall and in every stairwell and corridor. A grand staircase sweeps from the atrium lobby to shops selling Disney Cruise Line–themed clothing, collectibles, jewelry, sundries, and more. (The shops are always full of eager buyers; some observers speculate that the cruise line will derive as much revenue here as other lines do from their casinos, which Disney ships don't have.)

The ship has two lower decks with cabins, three decks with dining rooms and show rooms, then three upper decks of cabins. Two sports and sun decks offer separate pools and facilities for families, and for adults without children. Signs point toward lounges and facilities, and all elevators are clearly marked forward, aft, or amidships.

unofficial **TIP**
If you want to see the sea on your Disney cruise, book a cabin with a private veranda.

Our main complaint concerning the ship's design is that outdoor public areas focus inward toward the pools instead of seaward, as if Disney wants you to forget you're on a cruise liner. There's no public place where you can curl up in the shade and watch the ocean (at least not without a Plexiglas wall between you and it).

Another predictable—and irritating—design characteristic is the extensive childproofing. There's enough Plexiglas on the *Magic* to build a subdivision of see-through homes. On the pool decks (Deck 9) especially, it feels as if the ship is hermetically sealed.

Cabins

Cabins and suites are spacious, with wood paneling throughout. About three-fourths are outside; almost half have private verandas. The 12 cabin categories range from standard to deluxe, deluxe with veranda, family suite, one- and two-bedroom suites, and royal suite.

Cabin design reveals Disney's finely tuned sense of the needs of families and children and offers a cruise-industry first: a split bathroom with a bathtub and shower combo and sink in one room, and toilet, sink, and vanity in another. This configuration, found in all but standard inside cabins, allows any family member to use the bathroom without monopolizing it. All bathrooms have tub and shower, except disabled rooms (shower only).

Decor includes such unusual features as bureaus designed to look like steamer trunks. Each cabin also has a direct-dial telephone with voice mail, TV, hair dryer, and mini-fridge. In some cabins, Murphy beds allow for extra daytime floor space. Storage is generous, with deep drawers and large closets.

The *Magic* has 256 inside cabins and 621 outside cabins. There are 8 one-bedroom suites and 80 family cabins. Of the outside cabins, 282 have private verandas. Fourteen cabins are wheelchair accessible. Most cabins accommodate three people, inside cabins up to four, deluxe cabins with verandas up to four, and family and one-bedroom suites up to five.

A Maylene, Alabama, reader offers this useful information about the cabins:

> A big difference between Walt Disney World and Disney Cruise Line is that when it comes to room capacity, infants are counted just like adults. So while a family of five can stay at a value resort (four adults on the double beds and an infant in a crib), that same family of five must either book a Category 4 (or above) cabin or book a pair of lower-category cabins.

Another question that keeps cropping up on the Disney message boards over and over is the question of children and cabins with a veranda. The two things parents need to know to put their minds at ease are that the railings are guarded by Plexiglas and that the veranda door has a two-part locking mechanism, with one of the mechanisms located six feet off the floor. Even many adults have problems trying to figure out how to operate these doors. The only way a child is going overboard is if an adult leaves a veranda door open and the child uses a piece of veranda furniture to climb over the railing.

SERVICES AND AMENITIES

PASSENGERS LAVISHLY PRAISE Disney cast members. They're among the most accommodating you'll ever encounter in travel, and they try hard to smooth your way from boarding to departure. *Unofficial Guides* cruise writer Kay Showker reports, "More than once when I stopped to get my bearings, a Disney cast member was there within seconds to help me."

You'll receive a *Disney Magic Passport,* a purse-size booklet covering about everything you need to know for your cruise. Daily in your cabin, you'll receive "Your Personal Navigator," listing entertainment and activities, with options for teens, children, adults, and families, as well as information on shore excursions.

Dining

Dining is Disney's most innovative area. The *Magic* has three family restaurants, plus an adults-only alternative eatery. Each night, passengers move to a different family restaurant, each with a different theme and menu. Their table companions and waitstaff move with them. In each restaurant, tableware, linens, menu covers, and waiters' uniforms fit the theme.

Lumière's, named for the candlestick character in *Beauty and the Beast,* is a handsome Art Deco venue serving Continental cuisine. A mural depicts *Beauty and the Beast.*

Parrot Cay dishes up Caribbean-accented food in a colorful, fun, tropical setting that reminds Disney veterans of the *Enchanted Tiki Room.* Parrot Cay is the most popular of the three restaurants for breakfast. Children particularly enjoy the decor and festivity, but the food, although adequate, is a notch below that of the other restaurants.

Animator's Palate reflects the creative genius of Disney animation and is the *Magic*'s dining pièce de résistance. Diners are given the impression that they have entered a black-and-white sketchbook. As the meal progresses, sketches on the walls are transformed through lighting, video, and fiber optics into a full-color extravaganza. Waiters change their costumes from black-and-white to color. A montage of appetizers is served on a palette-shaped plate, and dessert—a tasteless mousse shaped like Mickey—arrives with a parade of waiters bearing trays of colorful syrups—mango, chocolate, and strawberry—to decorate it. The food is less than inspired, and hot dishes are likely to arrive cold. But no one seems to care; they're too absorbed in watching Disney perform its magic. Conversation is often difficult, and the entertainment, though creative, is the ultimate in Disney cute (and totally inescapable). Children love it, but adults may find it overwhelming.

Palo, the casual Italian restaurant named for the pole that gondoliers use to navigate Venetian canals, is the intimate adults-only restaurant. It's the best on board and has its own kitchen. The sophisticated, semicircular room has soft lighting, Venetian glass, inlaid wood, and a backlit bar. Northern Italian cuisine is featured. Food and presentation are excellent. More than two dozen wines are available by the glass for $4.75 to $25. Cover charge is $10 per person, but no signs in the restaurant, on the menu, or in the ship's literature alert you. Service is attentive but leisurely, though it may just seem that way in comparison to the staccato pace in the other restaurants. Reservations are required; make them when you board or risk being shut out (Disney underestimated demand for this venue).

There are two seatings for dinner at Lumière's, Animator's Palate, and Parrot Cay. If your children are age 12 or younger and you plan to dine as a family, we recommend the early seating. If your kids are involved in programs where they dine with other children, go with your preference. All three restaurants offer special meals if your picky eaters can't find something they like on the menu.

On a seven-day cruise, your normal rotation will have you dining two nights each at Lumière's, Animator's Palate, and Parrot Cay, and one of the three will pop up a third time for the seventh night. If you book Palo (adults only), you'll skip the restaurant designated for that night on your rotation. Thus, you should choose your Palo night(s) carefully. We view Parrot Cay as the most expendable in the rotation. Shortly after boarding, you're given the opportunity to make Palo reservations (taken in the restaurant) and/or change your restaurant rotation.

Wondering what to do with your children while you dine at Palo? You have several options: make a late reservation, then keep your children company (but don't eat) while they dine at the regularly assigned restaurant (this works only if you eat at the first seating); enroll your children in a program where they'll eat with other kids; or take your children to **Pluto's Dog House** (poolside on Deck 9) for hot dogs and burgers.

BUFFET AND FAST FOOD   Other dining options include **Topsiders,** an indoor-outdoor cafe with a free soda fountain serving breakfast, lunch, snacks, and a buffet dinner for children; a pool bar and grill for hamburgers, hot dogs, and sandwiches; **Pinocchio's Pizzeria;** an ice-cream and frozen-yogurt bar; and 24-hour room service. Topsiders is the weakest; it's OK for breakfast but long on bulk and short on flavor for lunch. Pizza, dogs, burgers, yogurt, and ice cream are good.

Facilities and Entertainment

Nightly entertainment is unlike any other cruise line's. The 1,022-seat **Walt Disney Theater** stages a different show nightly, with talented actors, singers, and dancers. On par with Disney-park entertainment rather than Broadway, these family productions will probably appeal more to children than adults. Longer cruises present welcome-aboard and end-of-cruise shows in addition to the productions described below.

The **Pirates in the Caribbean** party transforms passengers into pirates for the evening and treats them to a special dinner. The meal is followed by a deck party with Disney characters dressed in pirate garb. The mood of the party changes as Captain Hook, Mr. Smee, and a gang of "bad" pirates take over the party. In the end Captain Mickey saves the day.

The Golden Mickeys is an Academy Awards–style tribute to the music and characters of Disney films over the decades.

Disney Dreams features virtually every Disney character and song ever heard. The thin plot has Mickey and the other characters helping a boy achieve his dream of becoming a seafaring captain. It's pure schmaltz, but audiences give it a standing ovation. At the late show, many kids doze off before the curtain falls.

Twice Charmed: An Original Twist on the Cinderella Story demonstrates that "living happily ever after" is not all that it's cracked up to be. Beginning where the original story ended, the musical introduces a wicked Fairy Godfather who sends the mean stepmother back in time to break Cinderella's glass slipper and thus destroy her chances of marrying the prince. It's a weird Disney version of *Back to the Future*, except that the stepmother doesn't travel in a DeLorean. The musical fields a cast of 21 performers in Disney's largest seagoing production to date. The low-budget production is *The Disney Trivia Game Show*. (Do you know Goofy's middle name? Or Daisy Duck's plastic surgeon?) The *Welcome Aboard Variety Show*, a magic show, and *Magical Farewell* complete the list.

unofficial **TIP**
Disney ships have no casinos or libraries.

First-run movies and classic Disney films are shown daily at the **Buena Vista Theater,** a 268-seat venue with full screen and Dolby sound and under the stars on Deck 5 on a jumbo 24- by 14-foot LED screen.

Studio Sea, modeled after a television- or film-production set, is a family-oriented nightclub offering dance music, cabaret acts, passenger game shows, karaoke, and multimedia entertainment. The Art Deco **Promenade Lounge** offers a haven for reading and relaxing by day, and enjoying cocktails and piano music by night. **Cove Cafe** is a quiet, secluded spot for reading over a designer coffee. **Beat Street,** an adult-oriented evening-entertainment district, comprises shops and three themed nightclubs: **Rockin' Bar D,** with live bands playing rock and roll, Top 40, and country music; **Diversions,** a sports pub offering group sing-alongs and karaoke in what Disney calls "a cross between a golf clubhouse and a local neighborhood bar" (running on empty in the theme department, eh?); and **Sessions,** a casual place to enjoy easy-listening music and jazz.

Children's Programs

Playrooms and other kids' facilities occupy more than 15,000 square feet. Age-specific programs, among the most extensive in cruising. include challenging interactive activities and play areas supervised by trained counselors. Age groups are 3 to 7, 8 to 12, and teens. Baby-sitting (ages 12 weeks to 3 years) is provided in the **Flounder's Reef** nursery 2 to 4 p.m. and 7 p.m. to midnight daily. Cost is $6 per child per hour, $5 per hour for each additional child.

The **Oceaneer's Adventure** program encompasses **Oceaneer's Club** (ages 3 to 7), themed to resemble Captain Hook's pirate ship, with plenty of activity space; and **Oceaneer's Lab** (ages 8 to 12), with video games, computers, lab equipment, and an area for listening to CDs. Kids wear ID bracelets, and parents receive pagers for staying in touch with them. Both parents and children give youth programs high marks. Children in the drop-off program eat dinner at Topsiders.

The Stack is a teen area with a coffee-bar theme, featuring a game arcade, videos, and a CD-listening lounge. Located in a nonfunctioning smokestack on the top deck, the spaces allow teens to rock out in arguably the most isolated part of the ship (chaperoned, of course). Activities (including nighttime volleyball) are supervised in a way that makes participants feel unfettered. For example, other than counselors, no adults are allowed in The Stack.

Sports, Fitness, and Beauty

Of three top-deck pools, one has a Mickey Mouse motif and water-slide and is intended for families; the second, a little less elaborate, is also set aside for families; the third is adults only. At night the pool area can be a stage for deck parties and dancing.

The 8,500-square-foot, ocean-view **Vista Spa and Salon** above the bridge offers Cybex exercise equipment, an aerobics room, exercise instruction, a thermal-bath area, saunas, and steam rooms. A qualified fitness director supervises. The spa, run by British-based Steiner, offers pricey beauty treatments plus a sales pitch for Steiner products. Nevertheless, it has proved to be very popular and is generally sold out within hours of embarkation. Passengers in concierge-level suites can have a private massage in their suite or veranda (50 minutes for about $109; prices vary).

The **Sports Deck** has a paddle tennis court, table tennis, basketball court, and shuffleboard. The full promenade deck lures walkers and joggers.

RATES

SHOP NON-DISNEY CRUISE-DISCOUNT AGENCIES. Some sell only cruises, but others sell the entire cruise and land package. However, we haven't seen a package that we couldn't beat by buying the components individually ourselves.

Once you've shopped and determined the lowest price available, give your travel agent the opportunity to match or beat it. For savings in addition to discounts offered by cruise sellers like those listed, book in advance to get early-bird discounts. If you prefer to buy directly from Disney, here's how to get in touch:

Disney Cruise Line
210 Celebration Place, Suite 400
Celebration, FL 34747-4600
☎ 800-951-6499 or 800-951-3532
FAX 407-566-7739
www.disneycruise.com

Disney Cruise Line offers a free planning DVD that tells all you need to know about Disney cruises and then some. To obtain a copy call ☎ 888-DCL-2500, or order online at **www.disneycruise.com.**

A FEW TIPS

1. If you opt for a package that includes the cruise and a Disneyland stay, go first to Disneyland. Cruising at the end of your vacation will ensure that you arrive home rested.

2. Board the ship as early as possible. Check your dining rotation, and change it if desired. Make Palo reservations as soon as the restaurant's reservations desk opens, usually at 2 p.m.

3. After making dining arrangements, register your children at Oceaneer Club (ages 3 to 7) and/or Oceaneer Lab (ages 8 to 12). If you board before 1:30 p.m., register your kids first, then arrange dining.

4. If you want spa services, sign up between 2 and 4 p.m. at the spa.

5. Disney requests that gentlemen wear jackets (no ties required) in the evening at Palo and Lumière's.

6. All cabins have a mini-fridge; bring your own snacks and beverages.

7. The Sessions (Cadillac Lounge) piano bar is one of the most relaxing and beautiful lounges we've seen on any cruise ship. Make a before- or after-dinner drink there part of your routine. It's on Deck 3, forward.

8. Don't miss the kids' programs.

MAKING *the* MOST *of* YOUR TIME

ALLOCATING TIME

THE DISNEY PEOPLE RECOMMEND SPENDING TWO to four full days at Disneyland Resort. While this may seem a little self-serving, it is not without basis. Disneyland Resort is *huge,* with something to see or do crammed into every conceivable space. In addition, there are now two parks, and touring requires a lot of walking, and often a lot of waiting in line. Moving in and among large crowds all day is exhausting, and often the unrelenting Southern California sun zaps even the most hardy, making tempers short.

During our many visits to Disneyland, we observed, particularly on hot summer days, a dramatic transition from happy, enthusiastic touring on arrival to almost zombielike plodding along later in the day. Visitors who began their day enjoying the wonders of Disney imagination ultimately lapsed into an exhausted production mentality ("We've got two more rides in Fantasyland; then we can go back to the hotel").

OPTIMUM TOURING SITUATION

WE DON'T BELIEVE THERE IS ONE IDEAL ITINERARY. Tastes, energy levels, and perspectives on what constitutes entertainment and relaxation vary. This understood, here are some considerations for developing your own ideal itinerary.

Optimum touring at Disneyland requires a good game plan, a minimum of three days on site (excluding travel time), and a fair amount of money. It also requires a fairly prodigious appetite for Disney entertainment. The essence of optimum touring is to see the attractions in a series of shorter, less-exhausting visits during the cooler, less-crowded times of day, with plenty of rest and relaxation between excursions.

Because optimum touring calls for leaving and returning to the theme parks, it makes sense to stay in one of the Disney hotels or in one of the non-Disney hotels within walking distance. If you visit Disneyland during busy times, you need to get up early to beat the crowds. Short lines and stress-free touring are incompatible with sleeping in. If you want to sleep in *and* enjoy your touring, visit Disneyland when attendance is lighter.

THE CARDINAL RULES FOR SUCCESSFUL TOURING

MANY VISITORS DON'T HAVE THREE DAYS to devote to Disneyland Resort. For these visitors, efficient touring is a must. Even the most time-effective plan, however, won't allow you to cover both Disney theme parks in one day. Plan to allocate at least an entire day to each park. If your schedule permits only one day of touring, concentrate on one theme park and save the other for another visit.

One-day Touring

A comprehensive one-day tour of Disneyland Park or Disney's California Adventure is possible, but it requires knowledge of the park, good planning, and plenty of energy and endurance. One-day touring doesn't leave much time for full-service meals, prolonged shopping, or lengthy breaks. One-day touring can be fun and rewarding, but allocating two days per park, especially for Disneyland Park, is always preferable.

Successful touring of Disneyland Park or Disney's California Adventure hinges on three rules:

1. DETERMINE IN ADVANCE WHAT YOU REALLY WANT TO SEE. What rides and attractions most appeal to you? Which additional rides and attractions would you like to experience if you have any time left? What are you willing to forgo?

To help you establish your touring priorities, we have described every attraction in detail. In each description, we include the author's critical evaluation of the attraction as well as the opinions of Disneyland Resort guests expressed as star ratings. Five stars is the highest (best) rating possible.

Finally, because Disneyland Resort attractions range in scope from midway-type rides and horse-drawn trolleys to colossal, high-tech extravaganzas spanning the equivalent of whole city blocks, we have developed a hierarchy of categories for attractions to give you some sense of their order of magnitude:

SUPER-HEADLINERS The best attractions the theme park has to offer. They are mind-boggling in size, scope, and imagination and represent the cutting edge of modern attraction technology and design.

HEADLINERS Full-blown, multimillion-dollar, full-scale, themed adventure experiences and theater presentations. They are modern in their technology and design and employ a full range of special effects.

MAJOR ATTRACTIONS Themed adventure experiences on a more modest scale but incorporating state-of-the-art technologies, or larger-scale attractions of older design.

MINOR ATTRACTIONS Midway-type rides, small-scale "dark rides" (spook-house-type rides), minor theater presentations, transportation rides, and elaborate walk-through attractions.

DIVERSIONS Exhibits, both passive and interactive. Also includes playgrounds, video arcades, and street theater.

Though not every attraction fits neatly into the above categories, the categories provide a relative comparison of attraction size and scope. Remember, however, that bigger and more elaborate does not always mean better. Peter Pan's Flight, a minor attraction, continues to be one of the park's most beloved rides. Likewise, for many small children, there is no attraction, regardless of size, that can surpass Dumbo.

2. ARRIVE EARLY! ARRIVE EARLY! ARRIVE EARLY! This is the single most important key to touring efficiently and avoiding long lines. With your admission pass in hand, be at the gate ready to go at least 30 minutes before the theme park's stated opening time. There are no lines and relatively few people first thing in the morning. The same four rides you can experience in one hour in the early morning will take more than three hours to see after 11 a.m. Have breakfast before you arrive so you will not have to waste prime touring time sitting in a restaurant.

3. AVOID BOTTLENECKS. Helping you avoid bottlenecks is what this guide is all about. Bottlenecks occur as a result of crowd concentrations and/or less-than-optimal traffic engineering. Concentrations of hungry people create bottlenecks at restaurants during the lunch and dinner hours; concentrations of people moving toward the exit near closing time create bottlenecks in the gift shops en route to the gate; concentrations of visitors at new and unusually popular rides create bottlenecks and long waiting lines; rides slow to load and unload passengers create bottlenecks and long waiting lines. Avoiding bottlenecks involves being able to predict where, when, and why they occur. To this end, we provide field-tested touring plans to keep you ahead of the crowd or out of its way (see discussion following). In addition, we provide critical data on all rides and shows that helps you estimate how long you may have to wait in line, compares rides in terms of their capacity to accommodate large crowds, and rates the rides according to our opinions and the opinions of other Disneyland visitors.

TOURING PLANS

OF UTMOST IMPORTANCE: READ THIS!

IN ANALYZING READER SURVEYS we were astonished by the percentage of readers who do not use our touring plans. Scientifically tested and proven, these plans can save you four entire hours or more of waiting in line. Four hours! Four fewer hours of standing, four hours freed up to do something fun. Our groundbreaking research that created the touring plans has been the subject of front-page articles in the *Dallas Morning News* and the *New York Times* and has been cited in numerous scholarly journals. So the question is, Why would you not use them?

We get a ton of mail from both our Disneyland and Walt Disney World readers—98% of it positive—commenting on our touring plans. First, from a family of four from West Chester, Pennsylvania:

> *This book and your touring plans, without a doubt, made the trip. We followed the adult one-day plans almost to the letter. Probably the longest line we stood in was maybe 30 minutes max during one of the [busiest] times of the year. The key was getting to the parks 30 minutes or so before opening. The plans also saved arguing over what to do next. We simply followed the guide. We are believers!*

A family from Stockton, California, descended on Disneyland Park over the Easter holiday:

> *We're not much for plans and regimentation so we winged it the first day. It was so awful that the next day we gave one of your itineraries a shot as sort of a last-ditch alternative. It worked so well that I was telling strangers about it that night like [I was] some kind of Bible thumper.*

A family from Waynesville, Ohio, visited Walt Disney World at one of the most crowded times of year:

> *We picked spring break week (week before Easter) to go and knew we had to have a game plan or it would be a terrible experience. I ordered two guides and used only one! The touring plans were a lifesaver, with the crowd levels being at 10 for almost the whole week. We planned our days according to your park recommendations and followed the plans. We were successful in EVERY park [reader's emphasis].*

From a New Albany, New York, reader:

> *[I had] only one full day in Disney, and I used the One-day Touring Plan for Adults. I was shocked by how well it worked. I even took about a three-hour break to go to Downtown Disney and I was still able to do everything on the plan. Incredible.*

A family of four from South Slocan, British Columbia, found they could easily customize the touring plans to meet their needs:

We amended your touring plans by taking out the attractions we didn't want to do and just doing the remainder in order. They worked great, and by arriving before the parks opened, we got to see everything we wanted, with virtually no waits! The best advice by far was "get there early"!

WHAT'S A QUEUE?

ALTHOUGH IT'S NOT COMMONLY used in the United States, *queue* (pronounced "cue") is the universal English word for a line, such as one in which you wait to cash a check at the bank or to board a ride at a theme park. There's a mathematical area of specialization within the field of operations research called queuing theory, which studies and models how lines work. Because the *Unofficial Guide* draws heavily on

this discipline, we use some of its terminology. In addition to the noun, the verb "to queue" means to get in line, and a "queuing area" is a waiting area that accommodates a line. When guests decline to join a queue because they perceive the wait to be too long, they are said to "balk."

TOURING PLANS: WHAT THEY ARE AND HOW THEY WORK

We followed your plans to the letter—which at times was troublesome to the dad in our party . . . somewhat akin to testing the strength of your marriage by wallpapering together!

—*Unofficial Guide* reader and mother of two
from Milford, Connecticut

WHEN WE INTERVIEWED DISNEYLAND VISITORS who toured the theme park(s) on slow days, they invariably waxed eloquent about the sheer delight of their experience. When we questioned visitors who toured on moderate or busy days, however, they talked at length about the jostling crowds and how much time they stood in line. What a shame, they said, that so much time and energy are spent fighting crowds in a place as special as Disneyland.

Given this complaint, our researchers descended on Disneyland to determine whether a touring plan could be devised that would liberate visitors from the traffic flow and allow them to see any theme park in one day with minimal waiting in line. On some of the busiest days of the year, our team monitored traffic into and through Disneyland Park, noting how it filled and how patrons were distributed among the attractions. We also observed which rides and attractions were most popular and where bottlenecks were most likely to occur.

After many years of collecting data, we devised preliminary touring plans, which we tested during one of the busiest weeks of the year. Each day, our researchers would tour the park using one of the preliminary plans, noting how long it took to walk from place to place and how long the wait in line was for each attraction. Combining the information gained on trial runs, we devised a master plan that we retested and fine-tuned. This plan, with very little variance from day to day, allowed us to experience all major rides and attractions and most lesser ones in one day, with an average wait in line of less than ten minutes at each.

From this master plan, we developed alternative plans that took into account the varying tastes and personal requirements of different Disneyland patrons. Each plan operated with the same logic as the master plan but addressed the special needs and preferences of its intended users.

unofficial **TIP**
By using our touring plans, you can save as much as four hours in line per day.

Finally, after all of the plans were tested by our staff, we selected (using convenience sampling) Disneyland visitors to test the plans. The only requisite for being chosen to test the plans was that the guests must have been visiting a Disney park for the first time. A second group of patrons was chosen for a "control group." These were first-time visitors who would tour the park according to their own plans but who would make notes about what they did and how much time they spent in lines.

When the two groups were compared, the results were amazing. On days when major theme-park attendance exceeded 42,000, visitors touring without our plans *averaged* 2.6 hours more waiting in line per day than the patrons touring with our plans, and they experienced 33% fewer attractions. In 2004, the application of a cutting-edge algorithm to our touring-plan software increased the waiting time saved to an average of four hours. We expect additional research to improve the performance of the touring plans again in next year's edition.

General Overview of the Touring Plans

Our touring plans are step-by-step guides for seeing as much as possible with a minimum of standing in line. They're designed to help you avoid crowds and bottlenecks on days of moderate-to-heavy attendance. On days of lighter attendance (see "Selecting the Time of Year for Your Visit," page 22), the plans still save time but aren't as critical to successful touring.

What You Can Realistically Expect from the Touring Plans

Though we present one-day touring plans for both of the theme parks, you should understand that Disneyland Park has more attractions than you can see in one day, even if you never wait in line. If you must cram your visit to Disneyland Park into a single day, the one-day touring plans will allow you to see as much as is humanly possible. Under certain circumstances you may not complete the plan, and you definitely won't be able to see everything. For Disneyland Park, the most comprehensive, efficient, and relaxing touring plans are the two-day plans. Although Disney's California Adventure will undoubtedly grow over the next few years, you should have no problem for the moment seeing everything in one day.

Variables That Will Affect the Success of the Touring Plans

How quickly you move from one ride to another; when and how many refreshment and restroom breaks you take; when, where, and how you eat meals; and your ability (or lack thereof) to find your way around will all have an impact on the success of the plans. Smaller groups almost always move faster than larger groups, and parties of adults generally can cover more ground than families with young children. Switching off (see page 152), among other things, prohibits families with little ones from moving expeditiously among attractions. Plus, some children simply cannot conform to the "early to rise" conditions of the touring plans.

A mom from Nutley, New Jersey, writes:

> [Although] the touring plans all advise getting to parks at opening, we just couldn't burn the candle at both ends. Our kids (10, 7, and 4) would not go to sleep early and couldn't be up at dawn and still stay relatively sane. It worked well for us to let them sleep a little later, go out and bring breakfast back to the room while they slept, and still get a relatively early start by not spending time on eating breakfast out. We managed to avoid long lines with an occasional early morning, and hitting popular attractions during parades, meal-times, and late evenings.

And a family from Centerville, Ohio, says:

The toughest thing about your tour plans was getting the rest of the family to stay with them, at least to some degree. Getting them to pass by attractions in order to hit something across the park was no easy task (sometimes impossible).

Finally, if you have young children in your party, be prepared for character encounters. The appearance of a Disney character is usually sufficient to stop a touring plan dead in its tracks. What's more, while some characters continue to stroll the parks, it is becoming more the rule to assemble characters in some specific venue (like at Mickey's Toontown) where families must queue up for photos of and autographs from Mickey. Meeting characters, posing for photos, and collecting autographs can burn hours of touring time. If your kids are into character-autograph collecting, you will need to anticipate these interruptions to the touring plan and negotiate some understanding with your children about when you will follow the plan and when you will collect autographs. Our advice is to either go with the flow or alternatively set aside a certain morning or afternoon for photos and autographs. Be aware, however, that queues for autographs, especially in Mickey's Toontown at Disneyland Park, are every bit as long as the queues for major attractions. The only time-efficient way to collect autographs is to line up at the character-greeting areas first thing in the morning. Because this is also the best time to experience the more popular attractions, you may have some tough decisions to make.

While we realize that following the touring plans is not always easy, we nevertheless recommend continuous, expeditious touring until around noon. After that hour, breaks and diversions won't affect the plans significantly.

Some variables that can profoundly affect the touring plans are beyond your control. Chief among these is the manner and timing of bringing a particular ride to capacity. For example, Big Thunder Mountain Railroad, a roller coaster in Disneyland Park, has five trains. On a given morning it may begin operation with two of the five, then add the other three if and when they are needed. If the waiting line builds rapidly before operators decide to go to full capacity, you could have a long wait, even in early morning.

Another variable relates to the time you arrive for a theater performance. Usually your wait will be the length of time from your arrival to the end of the presentation in progress. Thus, if the *Enchanted Tiki Room* show is 15 minutes long and you arrive 1 minute after a show has begun, your wait for the next show will be 14 minutes. Conversely, if you arrive as the show is wrapping up, your wait will be only a minute or two.

Clip-out Pocket Outlines of Touring Plans

For your convenience, we have prepared outlines of all the touring plans in this guide. These pocket versions present the same itineraries as the detailed plans, but with vastly abbreviated directions. Select the plan appropriate for your party, then familiarize yourself with the detailed version. Once you understand how the plan works, clip the pocket version from the back of this guide and carry it with you as a quick reference at the theme park.

Will the Plans Continue to Work Once the Secret Is Out?

Yes! First, all of the plans require that a patron be there when the theme parks open. Many Disneyland patrons simply refuse to get up early while on vacation. Second, less than one percent of any day's attendance has been exposed to the plans, too little to affect results. Last, most groups tailor the plans, skipping rides or shows according to personal taste.

How Frequently Are the Touring Plans Revised?

Because Disney is always adding new attractions and changing operations, we revise the touring plans every year. Most complaints we receive about them come from readers who are using out-of-date editions of the *Unofficial Guide*. Be prepared, however, for surprises. Opening procedures and showtimes, for example, may change, and you never know when an attraction might break down.

Tour Groups from Hell

We have discovered that tour groups of up to 200 people sometimes use our plans. Unless your party is as large as that tour group, this development shouldn't alarm you. Because tour groups are big, they move slowly and have to stop periodically to collect stragglers. The tour guide also has to accommodate the unpredictability of five dozen or so bladders. In short, you should have no problem passing a group after the initial encounter.

"Bouncing Around"

Many readers object to crisscrossing a theme park, as our touring plans sometimes require. A woman from Decatur, Georgia, said she "got dizzy from all the bouncing around" and that the "running back and forth reminded [her] of a scavenger hunt." We empathize, but here's the rub, park by park.

In Disneyland Park, the most popular attractions are positioned across the park from one another. This is no accident. It's good planning, a method of more equally distributing guests throughout the park. If you want to experience the most popular attractions in one day without long waits, you can arrive before the park fills and see those attractions first thing (which requires crisscrossing the park), or you can enjoy the main attractions on one side of the park first thing in the morning then use FASTPASS for the popular attractions on the other side. All other approaches will subject you to awesome waits at some attractions if you tour during busy times of year.

The best way to minimize "bouncing around" at Disneyland Park is to use one of our Two-day Touring Plans, which spread the more popular attractions over two mornings and work beautifully even when the park closes at 8 p.m. or earlier. Using FASTPASS will absolutely decrease your waiting time but will increase bouncing around because you must first go to the attraction to obtain your FASTPASS and then backtrack later to the same attraction to use your pass.

Disney's California Adventure is configured in a way that precludes an orderly approach to touring, or to a clockwise or counterclockwise rotation. Orderly touring is further frustrated by the limited guest capacity of the midway rides in the Paradise Pier district of the park. At DCA, therefore, you're stuck with "bouncing around," whether you use the touring plan or not, if you want to avoid horrendous waits.

We suggest you follow the touring plans religiously, especially in the mornings, if you're visiting Disneyland during busy, more crowded times. The consequence of touring spontaneity in peak season is hours of otherwise avoidable standing in line. During quieter times of year, there's no need to be compulsive about following the plans.

Touring-plan Rejection

We have discovered you can't implant a touring plan in certain personalities without rapid and often vehement rejection. Some folks just do not respond well to the regimentation. If you bump into this problem with someone in your party, it's best to roll with the punches, as did one couple from Maryland:

> The rest of the group was not receptive to the use of the touring plans. They all thought I was being a little too regimented about planning this vacation. Rather than argue, I left the touring plans behind as we ventured off for the parks. You can guess the outcome. We took our camcorder with us and when we returned home, watched the movies. About every five minutes there is a shot of us all gathered around a park map trying to decide what to do next.

Finally, as a Connecticut woman alleges, the touring plans are incompatible with some readers' bladders as well as their personalities:

> I want to know if next year when you write those "day" schedules if you could schedule bathroom breaks in there too. You expect us to be at a certain ride at a certain time and with no stops in between. In one of the letters in your book a guy writes, "You expect everyone to be theme-park commandos." When I read that I thought,

there is a man who really knows what a problem the schedules are if
you are a laid-back, slow-moving, careful detail-noticer. What were
you thinking when you made these schedules?

A Clamor for Customized Touring Plans

We're inundated by letters urging us to create additional touring plans. These include a plan for ninth- and tenth-graders, a plan for rainy days, a seniors' plan, a plan for folks who sleep late, a plan omitting rides that "bump, jerk, and clonk," a plan for gardening enthusiasts, and a plan for single women.

The touring plans in this book are intended to be flexible. Adapt them to your preferences. If you don't like rides that bump and jerk, skip them when they come up in a touring plan. If you want to sleep in and go to the park at noon, use the afternoon part of a plan. If you're a ninth-grader and want to ride Space Mountain three times in a row, do it. Will it decrease the touring plan's effectiveness? Sure, but the plan was created only to help you have fun. It's your day. Don't let the tail wag the dog.

WHAT TO EXPECT WHEN YOU ARRIVE AT THE PARKS

BECAUSE EACH TOURING PLAN IS BASED on being present when the theme park opens, you need to know a little about opening procedures. Disney transportation to the parks, and the respective theme-park parking lots, open an hour to two hours before official opening time.

Each park has an entrance plaza just outside the turnstiles. Usually you will be held outside the turnstiles until 30 minutes before official opening time. If you are admitted before the official opening time, what happens next depends on the season of the year and the anticipated crowds for that day.

1. MOST DAYS You will usually be held at the turnstiles or confined in a small section of the park until the official opening time. At Disneyland Park you might be admitted to Main Street, U.S.A.; at Disney's California Adventure to the Sunshine Plaza. If you proceed farther into a park, you will encounter a rope barrier manned by Disney cast members who will keep you from entering the remainder of the park. You will remain here until the "rope drop," when the rope barrier is removed and the park and all (or most) of its attractions are opened at the official opening time.

2. HIGH SEASON AND HOLIDAYS Sometimes, when large crowds are expected, you will be admitted through the turnstiles 30 minutes before the official opening time. This time, however, the entire park will be up and running and you will not encounter any rope barriers.

3. VARIATIONS Sometimes Disney will run a variation of the two opening procedures described above. In this situation, you will be permitted through the turnstiles and will find that one or several specific attractions are open early for your enjoyment.

A Word about the Rope Drop

Until recently, Disney cast members would dive for cover when the rope was dropped as thousands of adrenaline-charged guests stampeded to the most popular attractions. This practice occasioned the legendary Space Mountain Morning Mini-Marathon and the Splash Mountain Rapid Rampage at Disneyland Park.

Well, this scenario no longer exists—at least not in the crazed versions of years past. Recently, Disney has beefed up the number of cast members supervising the rope drop in order to suppress the mayhem. In some cases, the rope is not even "dropped." Instead, it's walked back. In other words, Disney cast members lead you with the rope at a fast walk toward the attraction you're straining to reach, forcing you (and everyone else) to maintain their pace. Not until they come within close proximity of the attraction do the cast members step aside.

So, here's the scoop. If Disney persists in walking the rope back, the only way you can gain an advantage over the rest of the crowd is to arrive early enough to be one of those up front close to the rope. Be alert, though; sometimes the Disney folks will step out of the way after about 50 yards or so. If this happens, you can fire up the afterburners and speed the remaining distance to your destination.

FASTPASS

IN 1999 DISNEY INITIATED A SYSTEM for moderating the waiting time for popular attractions. Called FASTPASS, it was originally tried at Walt Disney World and then subsequently expanded to cover attractions at all the American Disney parks. Here's how it works.

Your handout park map, as well as signage at respective attractions, will tell you which attractions are included. Attractions that use FASTPASS will have a regular line and a FASTPASS line. A sign at the entrance will tell you how long the wait is in the regular line. If the wait is acceptable, hop in line. If the wait seems too long, you can insert your park admission pass into a special FASTPASS turnstile and receive an appointment time (for sometime later in the day) to come back and ride. When you return at the appointed time, you will enter the FASTPASS line and proceed directly to the attraction's preshow or boarding area with no further wait. There is no extra charge to use FASTPASS, but you can get an appointment for only one attraction at a time. Interestingly, this procedure was pioneered by Universal Studios Hollywood many years ago and has been pretty much ignored by major theme parks until recently.

There has been a basic change made to the original FASTPASS program at the two Disneyland parks. Instead of having to return during the appointed time window printed on your FASTPASS, you can now return to ride anytime after the beginning of that window. If your return window is 10 to 11 a.m., for example, your FASTPASS is now good from 10 a.m. until the park closes. Thus the window on the FASTPASS represents only a recommended time to return.

FASTPASS works remarkably well, primarily because FASTPASS holders get amazingly preferential treatment.

The effort to accommodate FASTPASS holders makes anyone in the regular line feel like an illegal immigrant. As a telling indication of their status, Disney (borrowing a term from the airlines) refers to those in the regular line as "standby guests." Indeed, we watched guests in the regular line stand by and stand by, shifting despondently from foot to foot while dozens and sometimes hundreds of FASTPASS holders were ushered into the boarding area ahead of them. Clearly Disney is sending a message here, to wit: FASTPASS is heaven, anything else is limbo at best and probably purgatory. In either event, you'll think you've been in purgatory if you get stuck in the regular line during the hot, crowded part of the day.

FASTPASS, however, doesn't eliminate the need to arrive at the theme park early. Because each park offers at most ten FASTPASS attractions, you still need to get an early start if you want to see as much as possible in a single day. Plus, as we'll discuss later, there's only a limited supply of FASTPASSes available for each attraction on a given day. So, if you don't show up until the middle of the afternoon, you might discover that all the FASTPASSes have been distributed to other guests. FASTPASS does, happily, make it possible to see more with less waiting than ever before, and it's a great benefit to those who like to sleep late or who enjoy an afternoon or evening at the theme parks on their arrival day. It also enables you to postpone wet rides like the Grizzly River Run at Disney's California Adventure or Splash Mountain at Disneyland Park until the warmer part of the day.

Understanding the FASTPASS System

The basic purpose of the FASTPASS system is to reduce the waiting time for designated attractions by more equally distributing the arrival of guests at those attractions over the course of the day. This is accomplished by providing an incentive, a shorter wait in line, for guests who are willing to postpone experiencing the attraction until sometime later in the day. The system also, in effect, imposes a penalty—that is, being relegated to standby status—to those who opt not to use it (although as we shall see, spreading guest arrivals more equally decreases waiting time for standby guests as well).

When you insert your admission pass into a FASTPASS time clock, the machine spits out a small slip of paper about two-thirds the size of a credit card, small enough to fit in your wallet (but also small enough to lose easily). Printed on the paper will be the name of the attraction and a specific one-hour time window—for example, 1:15 to 2:15 p.m. You can return to enjoy the ride anytime from 1:15 until park closing.

Each person in your party must have his or her own FASTPASS.

When you report back to the attraction during your one-hour window, you'll enter a line marked "FASTPASS Return" that will route you more or less directly to the boarding area or preshow area. Each person in your party must have his or her own FASTPASS and be ready to show it to the Disney cast member at the entrance of the FASTPASS return line. Before you enter the boarding area (or theater) another cast member will collect your FASTPASS.

You may show up at any time after the period printed on your FASTPASS begins, and from our observation, no specific time is better or worse. This holds true because cast members are instructed to minimize waits for FASTPASS holders. Thus, if the FASTPASS return line is suddenly inundated (something that occurs more or less by chance), cast members rapidly intervene to reduce the FASTPASS line. This is done by admitting as many as 25 FASTPASS holders for each standby guest until the FASTPASS line is drawn down to an acceptable length. Though FASTPASS will lop off as much as 80% of the wait you'd experience in the regular line, you can still expect a short wait, but usually less than 20 minutes.

You can obtain a FASTPASS anytime after a park opens, though the FASTPASS return lines do not begin operating until about 35 to 50 minutes after opening. Thus, if the attractions at Disneyland Park open at 9 a.m., the FASTPASS time-clock machines will also be available at 9 a.m. and the FASTPASS line will begin operating at about 9:35 a.m.

Whatever time you obtain a FASTPASS, you can be assured of a period of time between when you receive your FASTPASS and the beginning of your return window. The interval can be as short as 30 minutes or as long as seven hours depending on park attendance, the popularity of the attraction, and the attraction's hourly capacity. As a general rule, the earlier in the day you secure a FASTPASS, the shorter the interval between time of issue and the beginning of your return window. If on a day that the park opens at 9 a.m., you pick up a FASTPASS for Splash Mountain at, say, 9:25 a.m., your recommended window for returning to ride would be something like 10 to 11 a.m., or perhaps 10:10 to 11:10 a.m. The exact time will be determined by how many other guests have obtained FAST-PASSes before you.

To more effectively distribute guests over the course of a day, the FASTPASS machines bump the one-hour return period back five minutes for a specific set number of passes issued (usually the number is equal to about 6% of the attraction's hourly capacity). When Splash Mountain opens at 9 a.m., for example, the first 125 people to obtain a FASTPASS will get a 10 to 11 a.m. recommended return window. The next 125 guests are issued FASTPASSes that can be used between 10:05 and 11:05 a.m., with the next 125 assigned a 10:10 to 11:10 a.m. time slot. And so it goes, with the time window dropping back five minutes for every 125 guests. The fewer guests who obtain FAST-PASSes for an attraction, the shorter the interval between the receipt of your pass and the return window. Conversely, the more guests issued FASTPASSes, the longer the interval. If an attraction is exceptionally popular, and/or its hourly capacity is relatively small, the return window might be pushed back all the way to park closing time. When this happens the FASTPASS machines stop pumping out passes. It would not be unusual, for example, for Maliboomer at Disney's California Adventure to distribute an entire day's allocation of FASTPASSes by 2 p.m. When this happens, the machines simply shut down and a sign is posted saying that FASTPASSes are all gone for the day.

Whereas rides routinely exhaust their daily FASTPASS supply, shows almost never do. FASTPASS machines at theaters try to balance attendance at each show so that the audience of any given performance is divided evenly between standby and FASTPASS guests. At shows, consequently, standby guests are not discriminated against to the degree experienced by standby guests at rides. In practice, FASTPASS diminishes the wait for standby guests. Generally, with very few exceptions, using the standby line at theater attractions requires a smaller investment of time than using FASTPASS.

FASTPASS GUIDELINES

- Don't mess with FASTPASS unless it can save you 30 minutes or more.
- If you arrive after a park opens, obtain a FASTPASS for your preferred FASTPASS attraction first thing.
- Do not obtain a FASTPASS for a theater attraction until you have experienced all of the FASTPASS rides on your itinerary (using FASTPASS at theater attractions usually requires a greater investment of time than using the standby line).
- Always check the FASTPASS return period before obtaining your FASTPASS.
- Obtain FASTPASSes for Space Mountain and Splash Mountain at Disneyland Park and for Soarin' over California and Mulholland Madness at DCA as early in the day as practicable.
- Try to obtain FASTPASSes for rides not mentioned above by 1 p.m.
- Don't depend on FASTPASSes being available for ride attractions after 2 p.m. during busier times of the year.
- Make sure everyone in your party has his or her own FASTPASS.
- Be mindful that you can obtain a second FASTPASS as soon as you enter the return period for your first FASTPASS or after two hours from issuance, whichever comes first.
- Be mindful of your FASTPASS return time, and plan intervening activities accordingly.

Disconnected FASTPASS Attractions

Some attractions' FASTPASS kiosks function independently and are not hooked up to the parkwide FASTPASS distribution system. Because a "disconnected" attraction has no way of knowing if you have a FASTPASS for another attraction, it will issue you a FAST-PASS at any time. In Disneyland Park, Roger Rabbit's Car Toon Spin is sometimes disconnected, as is Grizzly River Run at DCA. Disney can connect and disconnect FASTPASS attractions at will, so it's possible that the disconnected lineup will vary somewhat during your visit. Finally, the use of disconnected FASTPASS attractions is incorporated in our touring plans.

When to Use FASTPASS

Except as discussed below, there's no reason to use FASTPASS during the first 30 to 40 minutes a park is open. Lines for most attractions are quite manageable during this period. In addition, this is the only time of the day when the FASTPASS attractions exclusively serve those in the regular line. Regardless of time of day, however, if the wait in the regular line at a FASTPASS attraction is 25 to 30 minutes or less, we recommend joining the regular line.

Think about it. Using FASTPASS requires two trips to the same attraction: one to obtain the pass and one to use it. This means that you must invest time to secure the pass (by the way, sometimes there are lines at the FASTPASS machines!) and then later interrupt your touring and backtrack in order to use your FASTPASS. The additional time, effort, and touring modification required, therefore, are justified only if you can save more than 30 minutes. And don't forget: even in the FASTPASS line you must endure some waiting.

Tricks of the Trade

Although Disney stipulates that you can hold a FASTPASS to only one attraction at a time, it's possible to acquire a second FASTPASS before using the first. Let's say you obtain a FASTPASS to Buzz Lightyear at Disneyland Park with a return time slot of 10:15 to 11:15 a.m. Any time after your FASTPASS window begins, that is, anytime after 10:15 a.m., you will be able to obtain another FASTPASS, for Splash Mountain, for example. This is possible because the FASTPASS computer system monitors only the distribution of passes, ignoring whether or when a FASTPASS is used.

When obtaining FASTPASSes, it's faster and more considerate of other guests if one person obtains passes for your entire party. This means entrusting one individual with both your valuable park admission passes and your FASTPASSes, so choose wisely.

SAVING TIME IN LINE BY UNDERSTANDING THE RIDES

unofficial **TIP**
Use FASTPASS if the wait in the regular line is more than 30 minutes.

There are many different types of rides in Disneyland. Some rides, like It's a Small World, are engineered to carry several thousand people every hour. At the other extreme, rides such as Dumbo the Flying Elephant, can accommodate

FASTPASS ATTRACTIONS

DISNEYLAND PARK	DISNEY'S CALIFORNIA ADVENTURE
Autopia	California Screamin'
Big Thunder Mountain	Grizzly River Run
Buzz Lightyear Astro Blasters	Mulholland Madness*
Indiana Jones Adventure	Soarin' over California*
Roger Rabbit's Car Toon Spin*	*The Twilight Zone* Tower of Terror
Space Mountain*	
Splash Mountain*	

Denotes rides that routinely issue FASTPASSes for redemption three to seven hours later.

only around 500 people in an hour. Most rides fall somewhere in between. Lots of factors figure into how long you will have to wait to experience a particular ride: the popularity of the ride, how it loads and unloads, how many people can ride at one time, how many units (cars, rockets, boats, flying elephants, or whatever) of those available are in service at a given time, and how many staff personnel are available to operate the ride. Let's take them one by one:

1. HOW POPULAR IS THE RIDE? Newer rides like the *Finding Nemo* Submarine Voyage attract a lot of people, as do longtime favorites such as the Jungle Cruise. If you know a ride is popular, you need to learn a little more about how it operates to determine when might be the best time to ride. But a ride need not be especially popular to form long lines. The lines can be the result of less-than-desirable traffic engineering; that is, it takes so long to load and unload that a line builds up. This is the situation at the Mad Tea Party and Dumbo the Flying Elephant. Only a small percentage of the visitors to Disneyland Park (mostly children) ride Dumbo, for instance, but because it takes so long to load and unload, this ride can form long waiting lines.

2. HOW DOES THE RIDE LOAD AND UNLOAD? Some rides never stop. They are like a circular conveyor belt that goes around and around. We call these "continuous loaders." The Haunted Mansion is a continuous loader. The more cars or ships or whatever on the conveyor, the more people can be moved through in an hour. The Haunted Mansion has lots of cars on the conveyor belt and consequently can move more than 2,400 people an hour.

Other rides are "interval loaders." This means that cars are unloaded, loaded, and dispatched at certain set intervals (sometimes controlled manually and sometimes by a computer). Matterhorn Bobsleds is an interval loader. It has two separate tracks (in other words, the ride has been duplicated in the same facility). Each track can run up to ten sleds, released at 23-second or greater intervals (the bigger the crowd, the shorter the interval). In another kind of interval loader, like the Jungle Cruise, empty boats return to the starting point, where they line up waiting to be reloaded. In a third type of interval loader, one group of riders enters the vehicle while the last group of riders departs. We call these "in-and-out" interval loaders. Indiana Jones is a good example of an "in-and-out" interval loader. As a troop transport pulls up to the loading station, those who have just completed their ride exit to the left. At almost the same time, those waiting to ride enter the troop transport from the right. The troop transport is released to the dispatch point a few yards down the line where it is launched according to whatever second interval is being used. Interval loaders of both types can be very efficient at moving people if (1) the release (launch) interval is relatively short, and (2) the ride can accommodate a large number of vehicles in the system at one time. Since many boats can be floating through Pirates of the Caribbean at a given time and the release interval is short, almost 2,300 people an hour can see this attraction.

A third group of rides are "cycle rides." Another name for these same rides is "stop-and-go" rides; those waiting to ride exchange places with those who have just ridden. The main difference between "in-and-out" interval rides and cycle rides is that with a cycle ride the whole system shuts down when loading and unloading is in progress. While one boat is loading and unloading in It's a Small World, many other boats are proceeding through the ride. But when Dumbo the Flying Elephant touches down, the whole ride is at a standstill until the next flight is launched. Likewise, with the Orange Stinger, all riders dismount and the swings stand stationary until the next group is loaded and ready to ride.

In discussing a cycle ride, the amount of time the ride is in motion is called "ride time." The amount of time that the ride is idle while loading and unloading is called "load time." Load time plus ride time equals "cycle time," or the time expended from the start of one run of the ride until the start of the succeeding run. Cycle rides are the least efficient of all the Disneyland rides in terms of traffic engineering. Disneyland Park has seven cycle rides, while Disney's California Adventure has nine, an astonishing number for a modern park.

3. HOW MANY PEOPLE CAN RIDE AT ONE TIME? This figure is defined in terms of "per-ride capacity" or "system capacity." Either way, the figures refer to the number of people who can ride at the same time. Our discussion above illustrates that the greater a ride's carrying capacity (all other things being equal), the more visitors it can accommodate in an hour.

4. HOW MANY "UNITS" ARE IN SERVICE AT A GIVEN TIME? A "unit" is simply a term for the vehicle you sit in during your ride. At the Mad Tea Party the unit is a teacup, and at Alice in Wonderland it's a caterpillar. On some rides (mostly cycle rides), the number of units in operation at a given time is fixed. Thus, there are always 16 flying-elephant units

Cycle Rides

DISNEYLAND PARK

Fantasyland	Mickey's Toontown	Tomorrowland
Casey Jr. Circus Train	**Gadget's Go Coaster**	**Astro Orbiter**
Dumbo the Flying Elephant	**Goofy's Playhouse**	
King Arthur Carrousel		
Mad Tea Party		

DISNEY'S CALIFORNIA ADVENTURE

a bug's land	Paradise Pier
Flik's Flyers	**Golden Zephyr**
Francis Ladybug Boogie	**Jumpin' Jellyfish**
Tuck and Roll's Drive 'Em Buggies	**Maliboomer**
Sun Wheel	**Orange Stinger**
King Triton's Carousel	

operating on the Dumbo ride, 72 horses on King Arthur Carrousel, and so on. What this fixed number of units means to you is that there is no way to increase the carrying capacity of the ride by adding more units. On a busy day, therefore, the only way to carry more people each hour on a fixed-unit cycle ride is to shorten the loading time (which, as we will see in number 5 below, is sometimes impossible) or by decreasing the riding time, the actual time the ride is in motion. The bottom line on a busy day for a cycle ride is that you will wait longer and be rewarded for your wait with a shorter ride. This is why we try to steer you clear of the cycle rides unless you are willing to ride them early in the morning or late at night.

Other rides at Disneyland can increase their carrying capacity by adding units to the system as the crowds build. The Big Thunder Mountain Railroad is a good example. If attendance is very light, Big Thunder can start the day by running one of five available mine trains. When lines start to build, more mine trains can be placed into operation. At full capacity, a total of five trains can carry about 2,400 people an hour. Likewise, *Finding Nemo* can increase its capacity by adding more submarines, and Orange Stinger can do the same by adding more swings. Sometimes a long line will disappear almost instantly when new units are brought online. When an interval-loading ride places more units into operation, it usually shortens the dispatch interval, so more units are being dispatched more often.

5. HOW MANY CAST MEMBERS ARE AVAILABLE TO OPERATE THE RIDE?
Allocation of additional staff to a given ride can allow extra units to

be placed in operation, or additional loading areas or holding areas to be opened. Pirates of the Caribbean and It's a Small World can run two separate waiting lines and loading zones. The Haunted Mansion has a short "preshow," which is staged in a "stretch room." On busy days, a second stretch room can be activated, thus permitting a more continuous flow of visitors to the actual loading area. Additional staff make a world of difference on some cycle rides. Often, if not usually, one attendant will operate the Golden Zephyr. This single person must clear the visitors from the ride just completed, admit and seat visitors for the upcoming ride, check that all zephyrs are properly secured (which entails an inspection of each zephyr), return to the control panel, issue instructions to the riders, and finally, activate the ride (whew!). A second attendant allows for the division of these responsibilities and has the effect of cutting loading time by 25 to 50%.

BEWARE OF THE DARK, WET, ROUGH, AND SCARY

OOPS, ALMOST FORGOT: there's a member of our team you need to meet. Called a Wuffo, she's our very own character. She'll warn you when rides are too scary, too dark, or too wet. You'll bump into her throughout the book doing, well, what characters do. Pay attention to her—she knows what she's talking about.

SAVING TIME IN LINE BY UNDERSTANDING THE SHOWS

MANY OF THE FEATURED ATTRACTIONS at Disneyland are theater presentations. While they're not as complex as rides from a traffic-engineering viewpoint, a little enlightenment concerning their operation may save some touring time.

Most of Disneyland theater attractions operate in three distinct phases:

1. First, there are the visitors who are in the theater viewing the presentation.
2. Next, there are the visitors who have passed through the turnstile into a holding area or waiting lobby. These people will be admitted to the theater as soon as the current presentation is concluded. Several attractions offer a preshow in their waiting lobby to entertain the crowd until they are admitted to the main show.
3. Finally, there is the outside line. Visitors waiting here will enter the waiting lobby when there is room and then move into the theater when the audience turns over (is exchanged) between shows.

The theater capacity and popularity of the presentation, along with the level of attendance in the park, determine how long the lines will be at a given theater attraction. Except for holidays and other

Caution: *How Theater Attractions Work*

days of especially heavy attendance, the longest wait for a show usually does not exceed the length of one complete performance.

Since almost all Disneyland theater attractions run continuously, only stopping long enough for the previous audience to leave and the waiting audience to enter, a performance will be in progress when you arrive. If the *Enchanted Tiki Room* show lasts 15 minutes, the wait under normal circumstances should be 15 minutes if you were to arrive just after the show began.

All Disneyland theaters (except the Main Street Cinema and some amphitheater productions) are very strict when it comes to controlling access. Unlike at a regular movie theater, you can't just walk in during the middle of a performance; you will always have at least a short wait.

GUIDED TOURS AT DISNEYLAND PARK AND DCA

FOUR GUIDED TOURS ARE OFFERED. All require a valid park admission in addition to the price of the tour. All four tours can be booked up to 30 days in advance by calling ☎ 714-781-4400.

DISCOVER THE MAGIC Kids interact with Disney characters in a sort of treasure hunt to find clues to the treasure and avoid villainous characters. Designed for ages 5 to 9 years, the frenetic, fast-paced family program lasts approximately three hours and includes lunch. Prices are $59 for the first two tickets, $49 for the third and subsequent tickets.

WELCOME TO DISNEYLAND TOUR This two-and-a-half-hour tour provides a warp-speed look at pretty much the entire Disneyland Resort. Guides provide background and history of the parks, attractions, and sights as you tour both theme parks, Downtown Disney, and the Disney-owned hotels. Suffice it to say you'll do a lot of walking. The tour includes special reserved seats for a performance at a stage show or parade (selected locations), two FASTPASSes per person for use after the tour, and Priority Seating at a dining location (selected locations) for each ticketed guest. The tour is reasonably priced at $25.

A WALK IN WALT'S FOOTSTEPS This tour offers a historic perspective on both Disneyland Park and the man who created it. At three and a half hours, A Walk In Walt's Footsteps provides a lot of detail as it covers Disney's vision and the challenges in bringing the groundbreaking theme park to life. The tour includes a private lunch on the patio of the Disney Gallery. Highlights of the tour are an inside look at the Disneyland Railroad, a visit to the park's first animatronic attraction, and a glimpse of the lobby of Club 33, where Disney entertained his friends and dignitaries. Cost is $59 for all ages. (The tour is considered inappropriate for younger children.)

CRUZIN' DCA SEGWAY TOUR Launched in the summer of 2007, this tour begins with a Continental breakfast followed by learning how to operate a Segway Personal Transportation Vehicle. After successfully proving your driving skills by running a Segway obstacle course, you roll through Disney's California Adventure on a one-hour guided tour. The three-hour experience is $99 per person and includes all-day parking at Downtown Disney, the breakfast, a commemorative pin, and a group photo. Disneyland Resort Annual Passport holders receive a $20 discount. The tour is limited to ten participants and begins at 7 a.m. Participants must be at least 18 years old or at least 16 years old and accompanied by an adult guardian, weigh between 100 and 250 pounds, and sign a liability waiver before riding the Segway. Park admission is not included. Because the tour begins before the ticket booths open, it's necessary to purchase your theme park admission in advance.

PART TWO

ESSENTIALS

THE BARE NECESSITIES

CREDIT CARDS

AMERICAN EXPRESS, MASTERCARD, VISA, Discover, Japan Credit Bureau (JCB), and of course the Disneyland credit card are accepted for theme-park admission. Disneyland shops, fast-food and counter-service restaurants, sit-down restaurants, and the Disneyland Resort hotels also accept all the cards listed above. However, no credit cards are accepted in the theme park at vending carts.

RAIN

IF IT RAINS, GO ANYWAY; the bad weather will diminish the crowds. Additionally, most of the rides and attractions at the parks are under cover. Likewise, all but a few of the waiting areas are protected from inclement weather. If you get caught in an unexpected downpour, rain gear of varying sorts can be purchased at a number of shops.

VISITORS WITH SPECIAL NEEDS

DISABLED VISITORS Rental wheelchairs are available if needed. Most rides, shows, attractions, restrooms, and restaurants are engineered to accommodate the disabled. For specific inquiries call ☎ 714-781-7290. If you are in Disneyland Park and need some special assistance, go to City Hall on Main Street. At Disney's California Adventure Park (DCA), go to Guest Relations in the entrance plaza. Close-in parking is available for the disabled; inquire when you pay your parking fee.

VISITORS WITH DIETARY RESTRICTIONS Guests on special or restricted diets, including those requiring kosher meals, can arrange for assistance at City Hall on Main Street at Disneyland Park or at Guest Relations at DCA. For special service at Disneyland Resort restaurants, call the restaurant one day in advance for assistance.

FOREIGN-LANGUAGE ASSISTANCE Translation services are available to guests who do not speak English. Inquire by calling ☎ 714-781-7290 or by stopping in at City Hall at Disneyland Park or at Guest Relations at DCA.

LOST ADULTS Arrange a plan for regrouping with those in your party should you become separated. Failing this, you can leave a message at City Hall or Guest Relations for your missing person. For information concerning lost children, see page 156.

MESSAGES Messages for your fellow group members can be left at City Hall in Disneyland Park or at DCA Guest Relations.

CAR TROUBLE If you elected to decrease the chance of losing your keys by locking them in your car, or decided that your car might be easier to find if you left your lights on, you may have a little problem to deal with when you return to the parking lot. Fortunately, the security patrols that continually cruise the parking lots are equipped to handle these types of situations and can quickly put you back in business.

LOST AND FOUND If you lose (or find) something at Disneyland Park, the lost-and-found office is located in the same place where lockers are available (walk down Main Street toward the castle, and go to the end of the first cul-de-sac on the right). At DCA, inquire at Guest Relations. If you do not discover your loss until you have left the parks, call ☎ 714-781-4765.

EXCUSE ME, BUT WHERE CAN I FIND . . .

SOMEPLACE TO PUT ALL THESE PACKAGES? Lockers are available at both parks. A more convenient solution, if you plan to spend a minimum of two or more hours in the park, is to have the salesperson forward your purchases to Package Pick-Up. When you leave the park, they will be there waiting for you. If you are staying at a Disneyland Resort hotel, you can have your purchases delivered directly to your room.

A MIXED DRINK OR BEER? If you are in Disneyland Park, you are out of luck. You will have to exit the park and try one of the hotels. At DCA, alcoholic beverages are readily available.

SOME RAIN GEAR? At Disneyland, rain gear is available at most shops but is not always displayed. As the Disney people say, it is sold "under the counter." In other words, you have to ask for it. If you are caught without protection on a rainy day, don't slog around dripping. Rain gear is one of the few shopping bargains at Disneyland. Ponchos are $7 for adults and $5 for kids, and umbrellas are $10 and up.

A CURE FOR THIS HEADACHE? Aspirin and various other sundries can be purchased on Main Street at the Emporium in Disneyland Park and at Greetings from California at the DCA entrance plaza (they keep them behind the counter, so you have to ask).

A PRESCRIPTION FILLED? Unfortunately, there is no place in Disney-land Resort to have a prescription filled.

SUNTAN LOTION? Suntan lotion and various other sundries can be purchased in Disneyland Park on Main Street at the Emporium and at Greetings from California at the DCA entrance plaza (they keep them behind the counter, so you have to ask).

A SMOKE? You won't find cigarettes for sale at Disneyland parks, and you'll have a hard time finding a place to smoke any you bring with you. Smoking is strongly discouraged throughout the parks and resorts, though there are a few designated smoking areas.

FEMININE-HYGIENE PRODUCTS? These are available in most women's restrooms at Disneyland Resort.

CASH? At Disneyland Park, the Bank of Main Street offers the following services:

- Personal checks cashed for $100 or less if drawn on U.S. banks; presentation of a valid driver's license and a major credit card is required
- Cash for travelers' checks
- Exchange of foreign currency for dollars

In addition, cash advances on MasterCard and VISA credit cards are available for a fee at Starcade in Tomorrowland. If the cashier is closed, there are Automatic Teller Machines (ATMs) at these locations:

AT DISNEYLAND PARK

- Outside the main entrance
- On Main Street, next to The Walt Disney Story at the Town Square end
- At the entrance to Frontierland on the left
- Near the Fantasyland Theatre
- In Tomorrowland, near Starcade

AT DOWNTOWN DISNEY

- Next to Häagen-Dazs
- LEGO Imagination Center

AT DISNEY'S CALIFORNIA ADVENTURE

- Outside the main entrance
- At the phone and locker complex just inside the main entrance and to the right
- Near the restrooms to the left of the Redwood Creek Challenge Trail
- Near the restrooms at Hollywood Pictures Backlot
- Near the restrooms on Pacific Wharf
- To the left of Mulholland Madness at Paradise Pier
- Near the Sun Wheel at Paradise Pier

A PLACE TO LEAVE MY PET? Pets are not allowed in the parks (except for assistance dogs), but cooping up an animal in a hot car while you tour can yield disastrous results. Kennels and holding facilities are provided for the temporary care of your pets and are located at the parking garage. If you are adamant, the folks at the kennels will accept custody of just about any type of animal. Owners of pets, exotic or otherwise, must themselves place their charge in the assigned cage. Small pets (mice, hamsters, birds, snakes, turtles, alligators, and the like) must arrive in their own escape-proof quarters. Kennels cost $15 a day.

In addition to the above, there are several other details you may need to know:

- Advance reservations for animals are not accepted.
- No horses, llamas, or cattle are accepted.
- Kennels' hours are the same as theme-park operating hours.
- Pets may not be boarded overnight.
- Guests leaving exotic pets should supply food for their pet.
- On busy days, there is a one- to two-hour bottleneck at the kennel, beginning half an hour before the park opens. If you need to use the kennels on such a day, arrive at least an hour before the park's stated opening time.
- Pets are fed on request only (yours, not your pet's), and there is no additional charge for food.

CAMERAS AND FILM? If you do not have a camera, you can buy a disposable one, with or without a flash, in both parks. You can buy film throughout the parks. Finally, photo tips, including recommendations for settings and exposures, are provided in the Disneyland Park and DCA maps, both available for free when you enter.

PART THREE

DISNEYLAND *with* KIDS

The **BRUTAL TRUTH** *about* **FAMILY VACATIONS**

IT'S BEEN SUGGESTED that the phrase *family vacation* is a bit of an oxymoron. This is because you can never take a vacation from the responsibilities of parenting if your children are traveling with you. Though you leave work and normal routine far behind, your

children require as much attention, if not more, when traveling as they do at home.

Parenting on the road is an art. It requires imagination and organization. Think about it: you have to do all the usual stuff (feed, dress, bathe, supervise, teach, comfort, discipline, put to bed, and so on) in an atmosphere where your children are hyperstimulated, without the familiarity of place and the resources you take for granted at home. Although it's not impossible—and can even be fun—parenting on the road is not something you want to learn on the fly, particularly at Disneyland.

The point we want to drive home is that preparation, or the lack thereof, can make or break your Disneyland vacation. Believe us, you don't want to leave the success of your expensive Disney vacation to chance. But don't confuse chance with good luck. Chance is what happens when you fail to prepare; good luck is when preparation meets opportunity.

Your preparation can be organized into several categories, all of which we'll help you undertake. Broadly speaking, you need to prepare yourself and your children mentally, emotionally, physically, organizationally, and logistically. You also need a basic understanding of the two theme parks and a well-considered plan for how to go about seeing them.

MENTAL *and* EMOTIONAL PREPARATION

MENTAL PREPARATION BEGINS with realistic expectations about your Disney vacation and consideration of what each adult and child in your party most wants and needs from his or her Disneyland experience. Getting in touch with this aspect of planning requires a lot of introspection and good, open family communication.

DIVISION OF LABOR

TALK ABOUT WHAT YOU AND YOUR PARTNER need and what you expect to happen on the vacation. This discussion alone can preempt some unpleasant surprises mid-trip. If you are a two-parent (or two-adult) family, do you have a clear understanding of how the parenting workload is to be distributed? We've seen some distinctly disruptive misunderstandings in two-parent households in which one parent is (pardon the legalese) the primary caregiver. Often, the other parent expects the primary caregiver to function on vacation as she (or he) does at home. The primary caregiver, on the other hand, is ready for a break. She expects her partner to either shoulder the load equally or perhaps even assume the lion's share so she can have a real vacation. However you divide the responsibility, of course, is up to you. Just make sure you negotiate a clear understanding before you leave home.

TOGETHERNESS

ANOTHER DIMENSION TO CONSIDER is how much togetherness seems appropriate to you. For some parents, a vacation represents a rare opportunity to really connect with their children, to talk, exchange ideas, and get reacquainted. For others, a vacation affords the time to get a little distance, to enjoy a round of golf while the kids are enjoying the theme park. The point here is to think about your and your children's preferences and needs concerning your time together. A typical day at a Disney theme park provides the structure of experiencing attractions together, punctuated by periods of waiting in line, eating, and so on, which facilitate conversation and sharing. Most attractions can be enjoyed together by the whole family, regardless of age ranges. This allows for more consensus and less dissent when it comes to deciding what to see and do. For many parents and children, however, the rhythms of a Disneyland day seem to consist of passive entertainment experiences alternated with endless discussions of where to go and what to do next. As a mother from Winston-Salem, North Carolina, reported, "Our family mostly talked about what to do next with very little sharing or discussion about what we had seen. [The conversation] was pretty task-oriented."

Two observations: First, fighting the crowds and keeping the family moving along can easily escalate into a pressure-driven outing. Having an advance plan or itinerary eliminates moment-to-moment guesswork and decision making, thus creating more time for savoring and connecting. Second, external variables such as crowd size, noise, and weather, among others, can be so distracting as to preclude any meaningful togetherness. These negative impacts can be moderated, as previously discussed in Part One, by your being selective concerning the time of year, day of the week, and time of day you visit the theme parks. The bottom line is that you can achieve the degree of connection and togetherness you desire with a little advance planning and a realistic awareness of the distractions you will encounter.

LIGHTEN UP

PREPARE YOURSELF MENTALLY to be a little less compulsive on vacation about correcting small behavioral deviations and pounding home the lessons of life. Certainly, little Mildred will have to learn eventually that it's very un–Disney-like to take off her top at the pool. But there's plenty of time for that later. So what if Matt eats hamburgers for breakfast, lunch, and dinner every day? You can make him eat peas and broccoli when you get home. Roll with the little stuff, and remember when your children act out that they are wired to the max. At least some of that adrenaline is bound to spill out in undesirable ways. Coming down hard will send an already frayed little nervous system into orbit.

unofficial **TIP**
Try to schedule some time alone with each of your children—if not each day, then at least a couple of times during the trip.

SOMETHING FOR EVERYONE

IF YOU TRAVEL WITH AN INFANT, toddler, or any child who requires a lot of special attention, make sure that you have some energy and time remaining for the rest of your brood. In the course of your planning, invite each child to name something special to do or see at Disneyland with Mom or Dad alone. Work these special activities into your trip itinerary. Whatever else, if you commit, write it down so that you don't forget. Remember: a casually expressed willingness to do this or that may be perceived as a promise.

WHOSE IDEA WAS THIS, ANYWAY?

THE DISCORD THAT MANY VACATIONING families experience arises from the kids being on a completely different wavelength from Mom and Dad. Parents and grandparents are often worse than children when it comes to conjuring fantasy scenarios of what a Disneyland vacation will be like. It can be many things, but believe us when we tell you that there's a lot more to it than just riding Dumbo and seeing Mickey.

In our experience, most parents and nearly all grandparents expect children to enter a state of rapture at Disneyland, bouncing from attraction to attraction in wide-eyed wonder, appreciative beyond words to their adult benefactors. What they get, more often than not, is not even in the same ballpark. Preschoolers will, without a doubt, be wide-eyed, often with delight but also with a general sense of being overwhelmed by noise, crowds, and Disney characters as big as toolsheds. We've substantiated through thousands of interviews and surveys that the best part of a Disney vacation for a preschooler is the hotel swimming pool. With some grade-schoolers and pre-driving-age teens, you get near-manic hyperactivity coupled with periods of studied nonchalance. This last phenomenon, which relates to the importance of being "cool at all costs," translates into a maddening display of boredom and a "been there, done that" attitude. Older teens are frequently the exponential version of the younger teens and grade-schoolers, except without the manic behavior.

As a function of probability, you may escape many—but most likely not all—of the above behaviors. Even in the event that they are all visited on you, however, take heart; there are antidotes.

For preschoolers, you can keep things light and happy by limiting the time you spend in the theme parks. The most critical point is that the overstimulation of the parks must be balanced by adequate rest and more-mellow activities. For grade-schoolers and early teens, you can moderate the hyperactivity and false ennui by enlisting their help in planning the vacation, especially by allowing them to take a leading role in determining the itinerary for days at the theme parks. Being in charge of specific responsibilities that focus on the happiness of other family members also works well. One reader, for example,

*uno**fficial* **TIP**
The more information your kids have before arriving at Disneyland, the less likely they'll be to act out.

turned a 12-year-old liability into an asset by asking him to help guard against attractions that might frighten his 5-year-old sister. Knowledge enhances anticipation and at the same time affords a level of comfort and control that helps kids understand the big picture. The more they feel in control, the less they will act out of control.

BASIC CONSIDERATIONS:
Is Disneyland for You?

ALMOST ALL VISITORS ENJOY Disneyland on some level and find things to see and do that they like. In fact, for many, the theme park attractions are just the tip of the iceberg. The more salient question, then (since this is a family vacation), is whether the members of your family basically like the same things. If you do, fine. If not, how will you handle the differing agendas?

A mother from Toronto wrote a couple of years ago describing her husband's aversion to Disney's (in his terms) "phony, plastic, and idealized version of life." Touring the theme parks, he was a real cynic and managed to diminish the experience for the rest of the family. As it happened, however, Dad's pejorative point of view didn't extend to the area golf courses. So Mom packed him up and sent him golfing while the family enjoyed the theme parks.

If you have someone in your family who doesn't like theme parks or, for whatever reason, doesn't care for Disney's brand of entertainment, it helps to get the attitude out in the open. We recommend dealing with the person up front. Glossing over or ignoring the contrary opinion and hoping that "Tom will like it once he gets there" is naive and unrealistic. Either leave Tom at home or help him discover and plan activities that he will enjoy, resigning yourself in the process to the fact that the family won't be together at all times.

DIFFERENT FOLKS, DIFFERENT STROKES

IT'S NO SECRET THAT WE at the *Unofficial Guides* believe thorough planning is an essential key to a successful Disneyland vacation. It's also no secret that our emphasis on planning rubs some folks the wrong way. Bob's sister and her husband, for example, are spontaneous people and do not appreciate the concept of detailed planning or, more particularly, following one of our touring plans when they visit the theme parks. To them the most important thing is to relax, take things as they come, and enjoy the moment. Sometimes they arrive at 10:30 in the morning (impossibly late for us *Unofficial Guide* types), walk around enjoying the landscaping and architecture, and then sit with a cup of espresso; watching other guests race around the park like maniacs. They would be the first to admit that they don't see many attractions, but experiencing attractions is not what lights their sparklers.

Not coincidentally, most of our readers are big on planning. When they go to the theme park they want to experience the attractions, and the shorter the lines, the better. In a word, they are willing to sacrifice some spontaneity for touring efficiency.

We want you to have the best possible time, whatever that means to you, so plan (or not) according to your preference. The point here is that most families (unlike my sister and her husband) are not entirely in agreement on this planning versus spontaneity issue. If you are a serious planner and your oldest daughter and husband are free spirits, you've got the makings of a problem. In practice, the way this and similar scenarios shake out is that the planner (usually the more assertive or type A person) just takes over. Sometimes daughter and husband go along and everything works out, but just as often they feel resentful. There are as many ways of developing a win/win compromise as there are well-intentioned people on different sides of this situation. How you settle it is up to you. We're simply suggesting that you examine the problem and work out the solution before you go on vacation.

THE NATURE OF THE BEAST

THOUGH MANY PARENTS DON'T REALIZE IT, there is no law that says you must take your kids to Disneyland or Walt Disney World. Likewise, there's no law that says you will enjoy Disneyland. And although we will help you make the most of any visit, we can't change the basic nature of the beast—er, mouse. A Disneyland vacation is an active and physically demanding undertaking. Regimentation, getting up early, lots of walking, waiting in lines, fighting crowds, and (often) enduring the hot California sun are as intrinsic to a Disneyland vacation as stripes are to a zebra. Especially if you're traveling with children, you'll need a sense of humor, more than a modicum of patience, and the ability to roll with the punches.

KNOW THYSELF AND NOTHING TO EXCESS

THIS GOOD ADVICE WAS MADE AVAILABLE to ancient Greeks courtesy of the oracle of Apollo at Delphi, who gave us permission to pass it along to you. First, concerning the "know thyself" part, we want you to do some serious thinking concerning what you want in a vacation. We also want you to entertain the notion that having fun and deriving pleasure from your vacation may be very different indeed from doing and seeing as much as possible.

unofficial **TIP** You can have a perfectly wonderful time at Disneyland if you're realistic, organized, and prepared.

Because Disneyland Resort is expensive, many families confuse "seeing everything" in order to "get our money's worth" with having a great time. Sometimes the two are compatible, but more often they're not. So if sleeping in, relaxing with the paper over coffee, sunbathing by the pool, or taking a nap rank high on your vacation hit parade, you need to accord them due emphasis on your Disney visit (are you listening?), even if it means you see less of the theme parks.

Which brings us to the "nothing to excess" part. At the Disneyland parks, especially if you're touring with children, less is definitely more. Trust us, it's tough go full-tilt dawn to dusk in the theme parks. First you'll get tired, then you'll get cranky, and then you'll adopt a production mentality ("we've got three more rides and then we can go back to the hotel"). Finally, you'll hit the wall because you just can't maintain the pace.

Plan on seeing the Disneyland parks in bite-size chunks with plenty of sleeping, swimming, napping, and relaxing in between. Most Disneyland vacations are short. Even if you have to stay an extra day to build in some relaxation, you'll be happier while you're there and more rested when you get home. Ask yourself over and over in both the planning stage and while you are at Disneyland: what will contribute the greatest contentedness, satisfaction, and harmony? Trust your instincts. If stopping for ice cream or returning to the hotel for a dip feels like more fun than seeing another attraction, do it—even if it means wasting the remaining hours of an expensive admissions pass.

The **AGE THING**

THERE'S A LOT OF SERIOUS COGITATION among parents and grandparents in regard to how old a child should be before embarking on a trip to Disneyland. The answer, not always obvious, stems from the personalities and maturity of the children, and the personalities and parenting style of the adults.

Disneyland for Infants and Toddlers

We believe that traveling with infants and toddlers is a great idea. Developmentally, travel is a stimulating learning experience for even the youngest of children. Infants, of course, won't know Mickey Mouse from a draft horse but will respond to sun and shade, music, bright colors, and the extra attention they receive from you. From first steps to full mobility, toddlers respond to the excitement and spectacle of the Disneyland parks, though of course in a much different way than you do. Your toddler will prefer splashing in fountains and clambering over curbs and benches to experiencing most attractions, but no matter: he or she will still have a great time.

Somewhere between 4 and 6 years of age, your child will experience the first vacation that he or she will remember as an adult. Though more likely to remember the coziness of the hotel room than the theme parks, the child will be able to experience and comprehend many attractions and will be a much fuller participant in your vacation. Even so, his or her favorite activity is likely to be swimming in the hotel pool.

As concerns infants and toddlers, there are good reasons and bad reasons for vacationing at Disneyland. A good reason for taking your little one to Disneyland Resort is that you want to go and there's no one available to care for your child during your absence. Philosophically, we are very much against putting your life (including your vacation) on hold until your children are older.

unofficial **TIP**
Traveling with infants and toddlers sharpens parenting skills and makes the entire family more mobile and flexible, resulting in a richer, fuller life for all.

Especially if you have children of varying ages (or plan to, for that matter), it's better to take the show on the road than to wait until the youngest reaches the perceived ideal age. If your family includes a toddler or infant, you will find everything from private facilities for breastfeeding to changing tables in both men's and women's restrooms to facilitate baby's care. Your whole family will be able to tour together with fewer hassles than on a day's picnic outing at home.

A bad reason, however, for taking an infant or toddler to Disneyland Resort is that you think Disneyland is the perfect vacation destination for babies. It's not, so think again if you are contemplating Disneyland Resort primarily for your child's enjoyment. For starters, attractions are geared more toward older children and adults. Even designer play areas like the Pirate's Lair on Tom Sawyer Island in Disneyland Park are developed with older children in mind.

By way of example, Bob has a friend who bought a video camcorder when his first child was born. He delighted in documenting his son's reaction to various new experiences on video. One memorable night when the baby was about 18 months old, he taped the baby eating a variety of foods (from whipped cream to dill pickles) that he had never tried before. While some of the taste sensations elicited wild expressions and animated responses from the baby, the exercise was clearly intended for the amusement of Dad, not junior.

That said, let us stress that for the well prepared, taking a toddler to Disneyland Resort can be a totally glorious experience. There's truly nothing like watching your child respond to the color, the sound, the festivity, and, most of all, the characters. You'll return home with scrapbooks of photos that you will treasure forever. Your little one won't remember much, but never mind. Your memories will be unforgettable.

Along similar lines, remember when you were little and you got that nifty electric train for Christmas, the one Dad wouldn't let you play with? Did you ever wonder who that train was really for? Ask yourself the same question about your vacation to Disneyland Resort. Whose dream are you trying to make come true: yours or your child's?

If you elect to take your infant or toddler to Disneyland Resort, rest assured that their needs have been anticipated. The theme parks have centralized facilities for infant and toddler care. Everything necessary for changing diapers, preparing formula, and warming bottles and food is available. At the Disneyland Park, the Baby Center is next to the Plaza Inn at the end of Main Street and to the right. At DCA, the Baby Center is tucked out of the way next to the Mission Tortilla Factory in the Pacific Wharf area of the park. Dads in charge of little ones are welcome at the centers and can use most services offered. In addition, men's rooms in the theme parks have changing tables.

Infants and toddlers are allowed to experience any attraction that doesn't have minimum height or age restrictions. But as a Minneapolis mother reports, some attractions are better for babies than others:

Theater and boat rides are easier for babies (ours was almost 1 year old, not yet walking). Rides where there's a bar that comes down are doable, but harder. Peter Pan was our first encounter with this type, and we had barely gotten situated when I realized he might fall out of my grasp. The [3-D] films are too intense; the noise level is deafening, and the images inescapable. You don't have a rating system for babies, and I don't expect to see one, but I thought you might want to know what a baby thought (based on his reactions).

At the Park: Jungle Cruise—didn't get into it. Pirates—slept through it. Riverboat—the horn made him cry. Small World—wide-eyed, took it all in. Peter Pan—couldn't really sit on the seat. A bit dangerous. He didn't get into it. Railroad—liked the motion and scenery. Tiki Room—loved it. Danced, clapped, sang along. Honey, I Shrunk the Audience—we skipped due to recommendation of Disney worker that it got too loud and adults screamed throughout.

The same mom also advises:

We used a baby sling on our trip and thought it was great when standing in the lines—much better than a stroller, which you have to park before getting in line (and navigate through crowds). My baby was still nursing when we went. It is impractical to go to the baby station every time, so a nursing mom had better be comfortable about nursing in very public situations.

Two points in our reader's comment warrant elaboration. First,

the rental strollers at the theme parks are designed for toddlers and children up to 3 and 4 years old, but they're definitely not for infants. Still, if you bring pillows and padding, these strollers can be made to work. You can alternatively bring your own stroller, but unless it's collapsible, you will not be able to take it on Disney [parking lot] trams.

Even if you opt for a stroller (your own or a rental), we nevertheless recommend that you also bring a baby sling or baby/child backpack. Simply put, there will be many times in the theme parks when you will have to park the stroller and carry your child. As an aside, if you haven't checked out baby slings and packs lately, you'll be amazed by some of the technological advances made in these products.

The second point that needs addressing is our reader's perception that there are not many good places in the theme parks for breast-feeding unless you are accustomed to nursing in public. Many nursing moms recommend breast-feeding during a dark Disney theater presentation. This only works, however, if the presentation is long enough for the baby to finish nursing. Shows at the Hyperion Theater at DCA are long enough at about 45 minutes, but the theater is not as dark as those that show films. *Honey! I Shrunk the Audience* at Disneyland Park is way too loud, as is *Muppet Vision 3-D* at DCA. The best bet in either park is *Golden Dreams* at DCA, but the presentation lasts only 17 minutes.

Many Disney shows run back to back with only a minute or two in between to change the audience. If you want to breast-feed and require more time than the length of the show, tell the cast member on entering that you want to breast-feed and ask if you can remain in the theater and watch a second showing while your baby finishes.

If you can adjust to nursing in more public places with your breast and the baby's head covered with a shawl or some such, nursing will not be a problem at all. Even on the most crowded days, you can always find a back corner of a restaurant or a comparatively secluded park bench or garden spot to nurse.

unofficial **TIP**
Infants are easy travelers. As long as they are fed and comfortable, there is really no limit to what you can do when on the road with little ones. Food plus adequate rest is the perfect formula for happy babies.

Disneyland for 4-, 5-, and 6-year-olds

Kids in this age group vary immensely in their capacity to comprehend and enjoy Disneyland Resort. With this age group, the go–no-go decision is a judgment call. If your child is sturdy, easygoing, fairly adventuresome, and demonstrates a high degree of independence, the trip will probably work. On the other hand, if your child tires easily, is temperamental, or is a bit timid or reticent in embracing new experiences, you're much better off waiting a few years. Whereas the travel and sensory-overload problems of infants and toddlers can be addressed and (usually) remedied on the go, discontented 4- to 6-year-olds have the ability to stop a family dead in its tracks, as this mother of three from Cape May, New Jersey, attests:

My 5-year-old was scared pretty bad on Snow White our first day. From then on for the rest of the trip we had to coax and reassure her before each and every ride before she would go. It was like pulling teeth.

If you have a retiring, clinging, and/or difficult 4- to 6-year-old who, for whatever circumstances, will be part of your group, you can sidestep or diminish potential problems with a bit of pre-trip preparation. Even if your preschooler is plucky and game, the same prep measures (described later in this section) will enhance his or her experience and make life easier for the rest of the family.

Parents who understand that a visit with 3- to 6-year-old children is going to be more about the cumulative experience than about seeing it all will have a blast and wonderful memories of their children's amazement.

The Ideal Age

Although our readers report both successful trips as well as disasters with children of all ages, the consensus ideal children's ages for family compatibility and togetherness at Disneyland are 8 to 12 years. This age group is old enough, tall enough, and sufficiently stalwart to experience, understand, and appreciate practically all Disney attractions. Moreover, they are developed to the extent that they can get around the parks on their own steam without being carried or collapsing. Best of all, they are still young enough to enjoy being with Mom and Dad. From our experience, ages 10 to 12 are better than 8 and 9, though what you gain in maturity is at the cost of that irrepressible, wide-eyed wonder so prevalent in the 8- and 9-year-olds.

Disneyland for Teens

Teens love Disneyland, and for parents of teens Disneyland Resort is a nearly perfect, albeit expensive, vacation choice. Although your teens might not be as wide-eyed and impressionable as their younger sibs, they are at an age where they can sample, understand, and enjoy practically everything Disneyland Resort has to offer.

For parents, Disneyland Resort is a vacation destination where you can permit your teens an extraordinary amount of freedom. The entertainment is wholesome, the venues are safe, and the entire complex of hotels, theme parks, restaurants, and shopping is easily accessible on foot. Because most adolescents relish freedom, you may have difficulty keeping your teens with the rest of the family. Thus, if one of your objectives is to spend time with your teenage children during your Disneyland vacation, you will need to establish some clear-cut guidelines regarding togetherness and separateness before you leave home. Make your teens part of the discussion and try to meet them halfway in crafting a decision everyone can live with. For your teens, touring on their own at Disneyland is tantamount to being independent in an exotic city. It's intoxicating, to say the least, and can be an excellent learning experience, if not a rite of passage. In any event, we're not suggesting that you just turn them loose. Rather, we are just attempting to sensitize you to the fact that for your teens, there are some transcendent issues involved.

Most teens crave the company of other teens. If you have a solitary teen in your family, do not be surprised if he or she wants to invite a friend on your vacation. If you are invested in sharing intimate, quality time with your solitary teen, the presence of a friend will make this more difficult, if not impossible. However, if you turn down the request to bring a friend, be prepared to go the extra mile to be a companion to your teen at Disneyland. If you're a teen, it's not much fun to ride Space Mountain by yourself.

One specific issue that absolutely should be addressed before you leave home is what assistance (if any) you expect from your teen in regard to helping with younger children in the family. Once again, try to carve out a win–win compromise. Consider the case of the mother from Indiana who had a teenage daughter from an earlier marriage and two children under age 10 from a second marriage. After a couple of vacations where she thrust the unwilling teen into the position of being a surrogate parent to her stepsisters, the teen declined henceforth to participate in family vacations.

Some parents have written the *Unofficial Guide* asking if there are unsafe places at Disneyland Resort or places where teens simply should not be allowed to go. Although the answer depends more on your family values and the relative maturity of your teens than on Disneyland Resort, the basic answer is no. Though it's true that teens (or adults, for that matter) who are looking for trouble can find it anywhere, there is absolutely nothing at Disneyland Resort that could be construed as a precipitant or a catalyst. Be advised, however, that adults consume alcohol at most Disneyland Resort restaurants. Also, be aware that some of the movies available at the cinemas at Downtown Disney demand the same discretion you exercise when allowing your kids to see movies at home.

About **INVITING** *Your* **CHILDREN'S FRIENDS**

IF YOUR CHILDREN WANT TO INVITE FRIENDS on your Disneyland vacation, give your decision careful thought. There's more involved here than might be apparent. First, consider the logistics of numbers. Is there room in the car? Will you have to leave something at home that you had planned on taking to make room in the trunk for the friend's luggage? Will additional hotel rooms or a larger suite be required? Will the increased number of people in your group make it hard to get a table at a restaurant?

If you determine that you can logistically accommodate one or more friends, the next step is to consider how the inclusion of the friend will affect your group's dynamics. Generally speaking, the presence of a friend will make it harder to really connect with your own children. So if one of your vacation goals is an intimate bonding experience with your children, the addition of friends will possibly frustrate your attempts to realize that objective.

If family relationship building is not necessarily a primary objective of your vacation, it's quite possible that the inclusion of a friend will make life easier for you. This is especially true in the case of only children, who may otherwise depend exclusively on you to keep them happy and occupied. Having a friend along can take the pressure off and give you some much-needed breathing room.

If you decide to allow a friend to accompany you, limit the selection to children you know really well and whose parents you also know. Your Disneyland vacation is not the time to include "my friend Eddie from school" whom you've never met. Your children's friends who have spent time in your home will have a sense of your parenting style, and you will have a sense of their personality, behavior, and compatibility with your family. Assess the prospective child's potential to fit in well on a long trip. Is he or she polite, personable, fun to be with, and reasonably mature? Does he or she relate well to you and to the other members of your family?

Because a Disneyland vacation is not, for most of us, a spur-of-the-moment thing, you should have adequate time to evaluate potential candidate friends. A trip to the mall including a meal in a sit-down restaurant will tell you volumes about the friend. Likewise, inviting the friend to share dinner with the family and then spend the night will provide a lot of relevant information. Ideally this type of evaluation should take place early on in the normal course of family events, before you discuss the possibility of a friend joining you on your vacation. This will allow you to size things up without your child (or the friend) realizing that an evaluation is taking place.

By seizing the initiative, you can guide the outcome. Ann, a Springfield, Ohio, mom, for example, anticipated that her 12-year-old son would ask to take a friend on their vacation. As she pondered the various friends her son might propose, she came up with four names. One, an otherwise sweet child, had a medical condition that Ann felt unqualified to monitor or treat. A second friend was overly aggressive with younger children and was often socially inappropriate for his age. Two other friends, Chuck and Marty, with whom she had had a generally positive experience, were good candidates for the trip. After orchestrating some opportunities to spend time with each of the boys, she made her decision and asked her son, "Would you like to take Marty with us to Disney World?" Her son was delighted, and Ann had diplomatically preempted having to turn down friends her son might have proposed.

We recommend that you do the inviting, instead of your child, and that the invitation be extended parent to parent (to avoid disappointment, you might want to sound out the friend's parent before broaching the issue with your child). Observing this recommendation will allow you to query the friend's parents concerning food preferences, any medical conditions, how discipline is administered in the friend's family, how the friend's parents feel about the way you administer discipline, and the parents' expectation regarding religious observations while their child is in your care.

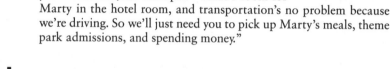

unofficial **TIP**
We suggest that you arrange for the friend's parents to reimburse you after the trip for things like restaurant meals and admissions. This is much easier than trying to balance the books after every expenditure.

Before you extend the invitation, give some serious thought to who pays for what. Make a specific proposal for financing the trip a part of your invitation, for example: "There's room for Marty in the hotel room, and transportation's no problem because we're driving. So we'll just need you to pick up Marty's meals, theme park admissions, and spending money."

A **FEW WORDS** *for* **SINGLE PARENTS**

BECAUSE SINGLE PARENTS GENERALLY are also working parents, planning a special getaway with your children can be the best way to spend some quality time together. But remember, the vacation is not just for your child—it's for you, too. You might invite a grandparent or a favorite aunt or uncle along; the other adult provides nice company for you, and your child will benefit from the time with family members. You might likewise consider inviting an adult friend.

Though bringing along an adult friend or family member is the best option, the reality is that many single parents don't have friends, grandparents, or favorite aunts or uncles who can make the trip. And while spending time with your child is wonderful, it is very difficult to match the energy level of your child if you are the sole focus of his or her world.

One alternative: try to meet other single parents at Disneyland. It may seem odd, but most of them are in the same boat as you; besides, all you have to do is ask. Another option, albeit expensive, is to take along a trustworthy babysitter (18 or up) to travel with you.

The easiest way to meet other single parents is to hang out at the hotel pool. Make your way there on the day you arrive, after traveling by car or plane and without enough time to blow a full admission ticket at a theme park. In any event, a couple of hours spent poolside is a relaxing way to start your vacation.

If you visit Disneyland Resort with another single parent, get adjoining rooms; take turns watching all the kids; and, on at least one night, get a sitter and enjoy an evening out.

Throughout this book we mention the importance of good planning and touring. For a single parent, this is an absolute must. In addition, make sure that every day you set aside some downtime back at the hotel.

Finally, don't try to spend every moment with your children on vacation. Instead, plan some activities for your children with other children. Then take advantage of your free time to do what you want to do: read a book, have a massage, take a long walk, or enjoy a catnap.

"He Who Hesitates Is Launched!"
TIPS *and* WARNINGS
for GRANDPARENTS

SENIORS OFTEN GET INTO PREDICAMENTS caused by touring with grandchildren. Run ragged and pressured to endure a blistering pace, many seniors just concentrate on surviving Disneyland rather than enjoying it. The theme parks have as much to offer older visitors as they do children, and seniors must either set the pace or dispatch the young folks to tour on their own.

An older reader from Alabaster, Alabama, writes:

> *The main thing I want to say is that being a senior is not for wussies. At Disney [parks] particularly, it requires courage and pluck. Things that used to be easy take a lot of effort, and sometimes your brain has to wait for your body to catch up. Half the time, your grandchildren treat you like a crumbling ruin, then turn around and trick you into getting on a roller coaster in the dark. What you need to tell seniors is that they have to be alert and not trust anyone. Not their children or even the Disney people, and especially not their grandchildren. When your grandchildren want you to go on a ride, don't follow along blindly like a lamb to the slaughter. Make sure you know what the ride is all about. Stand your ground and do not waffle. He who hesitates is launched!*

If you don't get to see much of your grandchildren, you might think that Disneyland is the perfect place for a little bonding and togetherness. Wrong! Disneyland can potentially send children into system overload and precipitates behaviors that pose a challenge even to adoring parents, never mind grandparents. You don't take your grandchildren straight to Disneyland for the same reason you don't buy your 16-year-old son a Ferrari: handling it safely and well requires some experience.

Begin by spending time with your grandchildren in an environment that you can control. Have them over one at a time for dinner and to spend the night. Check out how they respond to your oversight and discipline. Most of all, zero in on whether you are compatible, enjoy each other's company, and have fun together. Determine that you can set limits and that they will accept those limits. When you reach this stage, you can contemplate some outings to the zoo, the movies, the mall, or the state fair. Gauge how demanding your grandchildren are when you are out of the house. Eat a meal or two in a full-service restaurant to get a sense of their social skills and their ability to behave appropriately. Don't expect perfection, and be prepared to modify your behavior a little, too. As a senior friend of mine told her husband (none too decorously), "You can't see Disneyland sitting on a stick."

If you have a good relationship with your grandchildren and have had a positive one-on-one experience taking care of them, you might consider a trip to Disneyland. If you do, we have two recommendations. Visit Disneyland without them to get an idea of what you're getting into. A scouting trip will also provide you an opportunity to enjoy some of the attractions that won't be on the itinerary when you return with the grandkids.

Tips for Grandparents

1. It's best to take one grandchild at a time, two at the most. Cousins can be better than siblings because they don't fight as much. To preclude sibling jealousy, try connecting the trip to a child's milestone, such as finishing the sixth grade.

2. Let your grandchildren help plan the vacation, and keep the first one short. Be flexible, and don't overplan.

3. Discuss mealtimes and bedtime. Fortunately, many grandparents are on an early dinner schedule, which works nicely with younger children.

4. Gear plans to your grandchildren's age levels, because if they're not happy, you won't be happy.

5. Create an itinerary that offers some supervised activities for children in case you need a rest.

6. If you're traveling by car, this is the one time we highly recommend headphones. Kids' musical tastes are vastly different from most grandparents.' It's simply more enjoyable when everyone can listen to his or her own preferred style of music, at least for some portion of the trip.

7. Take along a night-light.

8. Carry a notarized statement from parents for permission for medical care in case of an emergency. Also be sure you have insurance information and copies of any prescriptions for medicines the kids may be on. Ditto for eyeglass prescriptions.

9. Tell your grandchildren about any medical problems you may have so they can be prepared if there's an emergency.

10. Many attractions and hotels offer discounts for seniors, so be sure you check ahead of time for bargains.

11. Plan your evening meal early to avoid long waits. And make Priority Seatings if you're dining in a popular spot, even if it's early. Take some crayons and paper to keep kids occupied.

If planning a family-friendly trip seems overwhelming, try **Grandtravel,** a tour operator–travel agent aimed at kids and their grandparents (call ☎ 800-247-7651 or visit **www.grandtrvl.com**).

HOW *to* CHILDPROOF
a HOTEL ROOM

TODDLERS AND SMALL CHILDREN up to 3 years of age (and sometimes older) can wreak mayhem if not outright disaster in a hotel room. They're mobile, curious, and amazingly fast, and they have a penchant for turning the most seemingly innocuous furnishing or decoration into a lethal weapon. Chances are you're pretty experienced when it comes to spotting potential dangers, but just in case you need a refresher course, here's what to look for.

Always begin by checking the room for hazards that you cannot neutralize, like balconies, chipping paint, cracked walls, sharp surfaces, shag carpeting, and windows that can't be secured shut. If you encounter anything that you don't like or is too much of a hassle to fix, ask for another room.

If you use a crib supplied by the hotel, make sure that the mattress is firm and covers the entire bottom of the crib. If there is a mattress cover, it should fit tightly. Slats should be 2⅜ inches (about the width of a soda can) or less apart. Test the drop sides to ensure that they work properly and that your child cannot release them accidentally. Examine the crib from all angles (including from underneath) to make sure it has been assembled correctly and that there are no sharp edges. Check for chipping paint and other potentially toxic substances that your child might ingest. Wipe down surfaces your child might touch or mouth to diminish the potential of infection transmitted from a previous occupant. Finally, position the crib away from drape cords, heaters, wall sockets, and air conditioners.

If your infant can turn over, we recommend changing him or her on a pad on the floor. Likewise, if you have a child seat of any sort, place it where it cannot be knocked over, and always strap your child in.

If your child can roll, crawl, or walk, you should bring about eight electrical outlet covers and some cord to tie cabinets shut and to bind drape cords and the like out of reach. Check for appliances, lamps, ashtrays, ice buckets, and anything else that your child might pull down on him- or herself. Have the hotel remove coffee tables with sharp edges, and both real and artificial plants that are within your child's reach. Round up items from table and counter tops such as matchbooks, courtesy toiletries, and drinking glasses and store them out of reach.

If the bathroom door can be accidentally locked, cover the locking mechanism with duct tape or a doorknob cover. Use the security chain or upper latch on the room's entrance door to ensure that your child doesn't open it without your knowledge.

Inspect the floor and remove pins, coins, and other foreign objects that your child might find. Don't forget to check under beds and furniture. One of the best tips we've heard came from a Fort Lauderdale,

Florida, mother who crawls around the room on her hands and knees in order to see possible hazards from her child's perspective.

If you rent a suite, you'll have more territory to childproof and will have to deal with the possible presence of cleaning supplies, a stove, a refrigerator, cooking utensils, and low cabinet doors, among other things. Sometimes the best option is to seal off the kitchen with a folding safety gate.

 # PHYSICAL PREPARATION

YOU'LL FIND THAT SOME PHYSICAL CONDITIONING, coupled with a realistic sense of the toll that Disneyland takes on your body, will preclude falling apart in the middle of your vacation. As one of our readers put it, "If you pay attention to eat, heat, feet, and sleep, you'll be OK."

As you contemplate the stamina of your family, it's important to understand that somebody is going to run out of steam first, and when they do, the whole family will be affected. Sometimes a cold drink or a snack will revive the flagging member. Sometimes, however, no amount of cajoling or treats will work. In this situation it's crucial that you recognize that the child, grandparent, or spouse is at the end of his or her rope. The correct decision is to get them back to the hotel. Pushing the exhausted beyond their capacity will spoil the day for them—and you. Accept that stamina and energy levels vary and be prepared to administer to members of your family who poop out. One more thing: no guilt trips. "We've driven 300 miles to take you to Disneyland and now you're going to ruin everything!" is not an appropriate response.

THE AGONY OF THE FEET

HERE'S A LITTLE FACTOID TO CHEW ON: If you spend a day at Disneyland Park, you will walk three to six miles! If you walk to the theme park from your hotel, you can add one to two miles and tack on another couple of miles if you park hop over to DCA. The walking, however, will be nothing like a five-mile hike in the woods. At Disneyland Park and DCA you will be in direct sunlight most of the time, will have to navigate through huge jostling crowds, will be walking on hot pavement, and will have to endure waits in line between bursts of walking. The bottom line, if you haven't figured it out, is that Disney theme parks (especially in the summer) are not for wimps!

Though most children are active, their normal play usually doesn't condition them for the exertion of touring a Disney theme park. We recommend starting a program of family walks six weeks or more before your trip. A Pennsylvania mom who did just that offers the following:

We had our 6-year-old begin walking with us a bit every day one month before leaving—when we arrived, her little legs could carry her and she had a lot of stamina.

The first thing you need to do, immediately after making your hotel reservation, is to get thee to a footery. Take the whole family to a shoe store and buy each member the best pair of walking, hiking, or running shoes you can afford. Wear exactly the kind of socks to try on the shoes that you will wear when using them to hike. Do not under any circumstances attempt to tour Disneyland shod in sandals, flip-flops, loafers, or any kind of high heel or platform shoe.

*uno*fficial **TIP**
If your children (or you, for that matter) think that wearing socks isn't cool, get over it! Bare feet, whether encased in Nikes, Weejuns, Docksiders, or Birkenstocks, will turn into lumps of throbbing red meat if you tackle a Disney park without socks.

Good socks are as important as good shoes. When you walk, your feet sweat like a mule in a peat bog, and moisture increases friction. To minimize friction, wear a pair of Smart Wool or CoolMax hiking socks, available at most outdoor retail (camping equipment) stores. To further combat moisture, dust your feet with some antifungal talcum powder.

All right, now you've got some good shoes and socks. The next thing to do is to break the shoes in. You can accomplish this painlessly by wearing the shoes in the course of normal activities for about three weeks.

Once the shoes are broken in, it's time to start walking. The whole family will need to toughen up their feet and build endurance. As you begin, remember that little people have little strides, and though your 6-year-old may create the appearance of running circles around you, consider that (1) he won't have the stamina to go at that pace very long, and (2) more to the point, he probably has to take two strides or so to every one of yours to keep up when you walk together.

Start by taking short walks around the neighborhood, walking on pavement, and increasing the distance about a quarter of a mile on each outing. Older children will shape up quickly. Younger children should build endurance more slowly and incrementally. Increase distance until

*uno*fficial **TIP**
Be sure to give your kids adequate recovery time between training walks (48 hours will usually be enough), however, or you'll make the problem worse.

you can manage a six- or seven-mile hike without requiring CPR. And remember, you're not training to be able to walk six or seven miles just once; at Disneyland you will be hiking five to seven miles or more almost every day of your visit. So unless you plan to crash after the first day, you've got to prepare your feet to walk long distances for three to five consecutive days.

Let's be honest and admit up front that not all feet are created equal. Some folks are blessed with really tough feet, whereas the feet of others sprout blisters if you look at them sideways. Assuming that there's nothing wrong with either shoes or socks, a few brisk walks will clue you in to what kind of feet the members of your family have. If you have a tenderfoot in your family, walks of incrementally increased distances will usually toughen up his or her feet to some extent. For those whose feet refuse to toughen, your only alternative is preventive care. After several walks, you will know where your tenderfoot tends to develop blisters. If you can anticipate where blisters will develop, you can cover sensitive spots in advance with moleskin, a friction-resistant adhesive dressing.

When you initiate your walking program, teach your children to tell you if they feel a "hot spot" on their feet. This is the warning that a blister is developing. If your kids are too young, too oblivious, too preoccupied, or don't understand the concept, your best bet is to make regular foot checks. Have your children remove their shoes and socks and present their feet for inspection. Look for red spots and blisters, and ask if they have any places on their feet that hurt.

unofficial **TIP**
If your child is age 8 or younger, we recommend regular foot inspections whether he or she under- stands the hot-spot idea or not. Even the brightest and most well-intentioned child will fail to sound off when distracted.

During your conditioning, and also at Disney- land, carry a foot emergency kit in your day pack or hip pack. The kit should contain gauze, Beta- dine antibiotic ointment, moleskin and an assort- ment of Band-Aid Blister Bandages, scissors, a sewing needle or some such to drain blisters, as well as matches to ster- ilize the needle. An extra pair of dry socks and talc are optional.

If you discover a hot spot, dry the foot and cover the spot immedi- ately with moleskin. Cut the covering large enough to cover the skin surrounding the hot spot. If you find that a blister has fully or par- tially developed, first air out and dry the foot. Next, using your sterile needle, drain the fluid but do not remove the top skin. Clean the area with your Betadine, and place a Band-Aid Blister Bandage over the blister. If you do not have moleskin or Band-Aid Blister Bandages, do not try to cover the hot spot or blister with regular Band-Aids. Regu- lar Band-Aids slip and wad up.

A stroller will provide the child the option of walking or riding, and, if he poops out, you won't have to carry him. Even if your child hardly uses the stroller at all, it serves as a convenient rolling depository for water bottles and other stuff you may not feel like carrying. Strollers at Disneyland are covered in detail on pages 138–142.

unofficial **TIP**
If you have a child who will physically fit in a stroller, rent one, no matter how well condi- tioned your family is.

SLEEP, REST, AND RELAXATION

OK, WE KNOW THAT THIS DISCUSSION is about physical prepara- tion before you go, but this concept is so absolutely critical that we need to tattoo it on your brain right now.

Physical conditioning is important but is not a substitute for rest. Even marathon runners need recovery time. If you push too hard and try to do too much, you'll either crash or, at a minimum, turn what should be fun into an ordeal. Rest means plenty of sleep at night, and if possible, naps during the afternoon, and planned breaks in your vacation itinerary. And don't forget that the brain needs rest and relaxation as well as the body. The stimulation inherent in touring a Disney theme park is enough to put many children and some adults into system overload. It is imperative that you remove your family from this unremitting assault on the senses and do something relaxing and quiet like swimming or reading.

The theme parks are pretty big, so don't try to see everything in one day. Even during the off-season, when the crowds are smaller and the temperatures more pleasant, the size of the theme parks will exhaust most children under age 8 by lunchtime. A Texas family underscores the importance of naps and rest:

Despite not following any of your "tours," we did follow the theme of visiting a specific park in the morning, leaving midafternoon for either a nap back at the room or a trip to the pool, and then returning to one of the parks in the evening. On the few occasions when we skipped your advice, I was muttering to myself by dinner. I can't tell you what I was muttering . . .

When it comes to naps, this mom does not mince words:

One last thing for parents of small kids—take the book's advice and get out of the park and take the nap, take the nap, TAKE THE NAP! Never in my life have I seen so many parents screaming at, ridiculing, or slapping their kids. (What a vacation!) Disney [parks are] overwhelming for kids and adults. Even though the rental strollers recline for sleeping, we noticed that most of the toddlers and preschoolers didn't give up and sleep until 5 p.m., several hours after the fun had worn off, and right about the time their parents wanted them to be awake and polite in a restaurant.

A mom from Rochester, New York, was equally adamant:

[You] absolutely must rest during the day. Kids went from 8 a.m. to 9 p.m. in the park. Kids did great that day, but we were all completely worthless the next day. Definitely must pace yourself. Don't ever try to do two full days of park sightseeing in a row.

If you plan to return to your hotel in midday and would like your room made up, let housekeeping know.

DEVELOPING *a* GOOD PLAN

ALLOW YOUR CHILDREN to participate in the planning of your time at Disneyland. Guide them diplomatically through the options, establishing advance decisions about what to do each day and how the day will be structured. Begin with your trip to Disneyland, deciding what time to depart, who sits by the window, whether to stop for meals or eat in the car, and so on. For the Disneyland part of your vacation, build consensus for wake-up call, bedtime, and building naps into the itinerary, and establish ground rules for eating, buying refreshments, and shopping. Determine the order for visiting the two theme parks and make a list of "must-see" attractions. To help you with filling in the blanks of your days, and especially to prevent you from spending most of your time standing in line, we offer a number of field-tested touring plans. The plans are designed to minimize your waiting time at each park by providing step-by-step itineraries that route you counter to the flow of traffic. The plans are explained in detail starting on page 79.

Generally, it's better to just sketch in the broad strokes on the master plan. The detail of what to do when you actually arrive at the park can be decided the night before you go, or with the help of one of our touring plans once you get there. Above all, be flexible. One important caveat, however: make sure you keep any promises or agreements that you make when planning. They may not seem important to you, but they will to your children, who will remember for a long, long time that you let them down.

*un*official **TIP**
To keep your thinking fresh and to adequately cover all bases, develop your plan in two or three family meetings no longer than 40 minutes each. You'll discover that all members of the family will devote a lot of thought to the plan both in and between meetings. Don't try to anticipate every conceivable contingency, or you'll end up with something as detailed and unworkable as the tax code.

The more you can agree to and nail down in advance, the less potential you'll have for disagreement and confrontation once you arrive. Because children are more comfortable with the tangible than the conceptual, and also because they sometimes have short memories, we recommend typing up all of your decisions and agreements and providing a copy to each child. Create a fun document, not a legalistic one. You'll find that your children will review it in anticipation of all the things they will see and do, will consult it often, and will even read it to their younger siblings.

By now you're probably wondering what one of these documents looks like, so here's a sample. Incidentally, this itinerary reflects the preferences of its creators, the Shelton family, and is not meant to be offered as an example of an ideal itinerary. It does, however, incorporate many of our most basic and strongly held recommendations, such as setting limits and guidelines in advance, getting enough rest, getting to the theme parks early, and saving time and money by having a cooler full of food for breakfast. As you will see, the Sheltons go pretty much full-tilt without much unstructured time and will probably be exhausted by the time they get home, but that's their choice. One more thing—the Sheltons visited Disneyland in late June, when all of the theme parks stay open late.

Notice that the Sheltons' itinerary on pages 127 and 128 provides minimum structure and maximum flexibility. It specifies which park the family will tour each day without attempting to nail down exactly what the family will do there. No matter how detailed your itinerary is, be prepared for surprises at Disneyland, both good and bad. If an unforeseen event renders part of the plan useless or impractical, just roll with it. And always remember that it's your itinerary; you created it, and you can change it. Just try to make any changes the result of family discussion and be especially careful not to scrap an element of the plan that your children perceive as something you promised them.

THE GREAT DISNEYLAND EXPEDITION

CO-CAPTAINS Mary and Jack Shelton

TEAM MEMBERS Lynn and Jimmy Shelton

EXPEDITION FUNDING The main Expedition Fund will cover everything except personal purchases. Each team member will receive $40 for souvenirs and personal purchases. Anything above $40 will be paid for by team members with their own money.

EXPEDITION GEAR Each team member will wear an official expedition T-shirt and carry a hip pack.

PRE-DEPARTURE Jack makes Priority Seating arrangements at Disneyland restaurants. Mary, Lynn, and Jimmy make up trail mix and other snacks for the hip packs.

Routines That Travel

If when at home you observe certain routines—for example, reading a book before bed or having a bath first thing in the morning—try to incorporate these familiar activities into your vacation schedule. They will provide your children with a sense of security and normalcy.

Maintaining a normal routine is especially important with toddlers, as a mother of two from Lawrenceville, Georgia, relates:

> *The first day, we tried an early start, so we woke the children (ages 2 and 4) and hurried them to get going. BAD IDEA with toddlers. This put them off schedule for naps and meals the rest of the day. It is best to let young ones stay on their regular schedule and see Disney at their own pace, and you'll have much more fun.*

 # LOGISTIC PREPARATION

WHEN WE RECENTLY LAUNCHED into our spiel about good logistic preparation for a Disneyland vacation, a friend from Phoenix said, "Wait, what's the big deal? You pack clothes, a few games for the car, then go!" So OK, we confess, that will work, but life can be sweeter and the vacation smoother (as well as less expensive) with the right gear.

SHELTON FAMILY ITINERARY

DAY 1: FRIDAY

6:30 p.m.	Dinner
After dinner	Pack car
10 p.m.	Lights out

DAY 2: SATURDAY

7 a.m.	Wake up!
7:15 a.m.	Breakfast
8 a.m.	Depart Portland for Hampton Inn, Oakland; Confirmation #DE56432; Lynn rides shotgun
About noon	Stop for lunch; Jimmy picks restaurant
7 p.m.	Dinner
9:30 p.m.	Lights out

DAY 3: SUNDAY

7 a.m.	Wake up!
7:30 a.m.	Breakfast
8:15 a.m.	Depart Oakland for Disneyland, Disneyland Hotel; Confirmation #L124532; Jimmy rides shotgun
About noon	Stop for lunch; Lynn picks restaurant
5 p.m.	Check in, buy park admissions, and unpack
6–7 p.m.	Mary and Jimmy shop for breakfast food for cooler
7:15 p.m.	Dinner at Rainforest Cafe at Downtown Disney
After dinner	Explore Downtown Disney
10 p.m.	Lights out

DAY 4: MONDAY

7 a.m.	Wake up! Cold breakfast from cooler in room
8 a.m.	Depart room for Disneyland Park
Noon	Lunch at park
1 p.m.	Return to hotel for swimming and a nap
5 p.m.	Return to park for touring, dinner, and *Fantasmic!*
9:30 p.m.	Return to hotel
10:30 p.m.	Lights out

DAY 5: TUESDAY

7 a.m.	Wake up! Cold breakfast from cooler in room
7:45 a.m.	Depart room for DCA

DAY 5: TUESDAY (CONTINUED)

Noon	Lunch at park
2:30 p.m.	Return to hotel for swimming and a nap
6 p.m.	Drive to dinner at Outback Steakhouse
7:30 p.m.	Return to DCA for touring
10 p.m.	Return to hotel
11 p.m.	Lights out

DAY 6: WEDNESDAY

ZZZZZZ!	Lazy morning—sleep in!
10:30 a.m.	Late-morning swim
Noon	Check out of Disneyland Hotel
1 p.m.	Fast food lunch
1:45 p.m.	Depart Anaheim for Hollywood; Sheraton Universal, Confirmation # 3542986X; Lynn rides shotgun
7:30 p.m.	Dinner at Universal CityWalk
9:15 p.m.	Return to hotel
10:30 p.m.	Lights out

DAY 7: THURSDAY

7 a.m.	Wake up! Cold breakfast from cooler in room
7:45 a.m.	Depart for Universal Studios
11:30 a.m.	Lunch at park
4:45 p.m.	Return to hotel for downtime
7:30 p.m.	Dinner at Zen Grill, 14543 Ventura Blvd., Sherman Oaks
10 p.m.	Return to hotel
11:45 p.m.	Lights out

DAY 8: FRIDAY

7:30 a.m.	Wake up!
8:30 a.m.	After fast-food breakfast, depart for Executive Inn, Sacramento; Confirmation #SD234; Jimmy rides shotgun
About noon	Stop for lunch; Lynn picks restaurant
7 p.m.	Dinner
10 p.m.	Lights out

DAY 9: SATURDAY

7 a.m.	Wake up!
7:45 a.m.	Depart for home after fast-food breakfast; Lynn rides shotgun
About noon	Stop for lunch; Jimmy picks restaurant
5:30 p.m.	Home sweet home!

CLOTHING

LET'S START WITH CLOTHES. We recommend springing for vacation uniforms. Buy for each child several sets of jeans (or shorts) and T-shirts, all matching, and all the same. For a one-week trip, as an example, get each child three or so pairs of khaki shorts, three or so light-yellow T-shirts, three pairs of SmartWool or CoolMax hiking socks. What's the point? First, you don't have to play fashion designer, coordinating a week's worth of stylish combos. Each morning the kids put on their uniform. It's simple, it saves time, and there are no decisions to make or arguments about

unofficial **TIP**
Give your teens the job of coming up with the logo for your shirts. They will love being the family designer.

what to wear. Second, uniforms make your children easier to spot and keep together in the theme parks. Third, the uniforms give your family, as well as the vacation itself, some added identity. If you're like the Shelton family who created the sample itinerary in the section on organizational planning, you might go so far as to create a logo for the trip to be printed on the shirts.

When it comes to buying your uniforms, we have a few suggestions. Purchase well-made, durable shorts or jeans that will serve your children well beyond the vacation. Active children can never have too many pairs of shorts or jeans. As far as the T-shirts go, buy short-sleeve shirts in light colors for warm weather, or long-sleeve, darker-colored T-shirts for cooler weather. We suggest that you purchase your colored shirts from a local T-shirt printing company. Cleverly listed under "T-shirts" (sometimes under "Screen Printing") in the Yellow Pages, these firms will be happy to sell you either printed T-shirts or unprinted T-shirts (called "blanks") with long or short sleeves. You can select from a wide choice of colors not generally available in retail clothing stores and will not have to worry about finding the sizes you need. Plus, the shirts will cost a fraction of what a clothing retailer would charge. Most shirts come in the more durable 100% cotton or in the more wrinkle-resistant 50% cotton and 50% polyester (50–50s). The cotton shirts are a little cooler and more comfortable in hot, humid weather. The 50–50s dry a bit faster if they get wet.

LABELS A great idea, especially for younger children, is to attach labels with your family name, hometown, the name of your hotel, the dates of your stay, and your cell phone number inside the shirt—for example:

HODDER FAMILY OF DENVER, CO.; CAMELOT INN; MAY 5–12; 303-662-2108

Instruct your smaller children to show the label to an adult if they get separated from you. Elimination of the child's first name (which most children of talking age can articulate in any event) allows you to order labels that are all the same, that can be used by anyone in the family, and that can also be affixed to such easily lost items as caps, hats, jackets, hip packs, ponchos, and umbrellas. If fooling with labels sounds like too much of a hassle, check out "When Kids Get Lost" (page 157) for some alternatives.

DRESSING FOR COOLER WEATHER Southern California experiences temperatures all over the scale from November through March, so it could be a bit chilly if you visit during those months. Our suggestion is to layer: for example, a breathable, waterproof or water-resistant Windbreaker over a light, long-sleeved polypro shirt over a long-sleeved T-shirt. As with the baffles of a sleeping bag or down coat, it is the air trapped between the layers that keeps you warm. If all the layers are thin, you won't be left with something bulky to cart around if you want to pull one or more off. Later in this section, we'll advocate wearing a hip pack. Each layer should be sufficiently compactible to fit easily in that hip pack along with whatever else is in it.

ACCESSORIES

I (BOB) WANTED TO CALL THIS PART "Belts and Stuff," but our editor (who obviously spends a lot of time at Macy's) thought "Accessories" put a finer point on it. In any event, we recommend pants for your children with reinforced elastic waistbands that eliminate the need to wear a belt (one less thing to find when you're trying to leave). If your children like belts or want to carry an item suspended from their belts, buy them military-style 1½-inch-wide web belts at any army–navy surplus or camping-equipment store. The belts weigh less than half as much as leather, are cooler, and are washable.

SUNGLASSES Smog notwithstanding, the California sun is so bright and the glare so blinding that we recommend sunglasses for each family member. For children and adults of all ages, a good accessory item is a polypro eyeglass strap for spectacles or sunglasses. The best models have a little device for adjusting the amount of slack in the strap. This allows your child to comfortably hang sunglasses from his or her neck when indoors or, alternately, to secure them fast to his or her head while experiencing a fast ride outdoors.

HIP PACKS AND WALLETS Unless you are touring with an infant or toddler, the largest thing anyone in your family should carry is a hip pack, or fanny pack. Each adult and child should have one. They should be large enough to carry at least a half-day's worth of snacks as well as other items deemed necessary (lip balm, bandanna, anti-bacterial hand gel, and so on) and still have enough room left to stash a hat, poncho, or light Windbreaker. We recommend buying full-sized hip packs at outdoor retailers as opposed to small, child-sized hip packs. The packs are light; can be made to fit any child large enough to tote a hip pack; have slip-resistant, comfortable, wide belting; and will last for years.

Do not carry billfolds or wallets, car keys, Disney Resort IDs, or room keys in your hip packs. We usually give this advice because hip packs are vulnerable to thieves (who snip them off and run), but pick-pocketing and theft are not all that common at Disneyland. In this instance, the advice stems from a tendency of children to inadvertently drop their wallet in the process of rummaging around in their hip packs for snacks and other items.

You should weed through your billfold and remove to a safe place anything that you will not need on your vacation (family photos, local library card, department store credit cards, business cards, movie-rental ID cards, and so on). In addition to having a lighter wallet to lug around, you will decrease your exposure in the event that your wallet is lost or stolen. When we are working at Disneyland, we carry a small profile billfold with a driver's license, a credit card, our room key, and a small amount of cash. Think about it: you don't need anything else.

DAY PACKS We see a lot of folks at Disneyland carrying day packs (that is, small, frameless backpacks) and/or water bottle belts that strap around your waist. Day packs might be a good choice if you plan to carry a lot of camera equipment or if you need to carry baby supplies on your person. Otherwise, try to travel as light as possible. Packs are hot, cumbersome, not very secure, and must be removed every time you get on a ride or sit down for a show. Hip packs, by way of contrast, can simply be rotated around the waist from your back to your abdomen if you need to sit down. Additionally, our observation has been that the contents of one day pack can usually be redistributed to two or so hip packs (except in the case of camera equipment).

CAPS We do not recommend caps (or hats of any kind) for children unless they are especially sun sensitive. Simply put, kids pull caps on and off as they enter and exit attractions, restrooms, and restaurants, and—big surprise—they lose them. In fact, they lose them by the thousands. You could provide a ball cap for every Little Leaguer in California from the caps that are lost at Disneyland each summer.

unofficial **TIP**
Equip each child with a big bandanna. Although bandannas come in handy for wiping noses, scouring ice cream from chins and mouths, and dabbing sweat from the forehead, they can also be tied around the neck to protect from sunburn.

If your children are partial to caps, there is a device sold at ski and camping supply stores that might increase the likelihood of the cap returning home with the child. Essentially, it's a short, light cord with little alligator clips on both ends. Hook one clip to the shirt collar and the other to the hat. It's a great little invention. Bob uses one when he skis in case his ball cap blows off.

RAIN GEAR Rain is a fact of life, although persistent rain day after day is unusual. Our suggestion is to check out the Weather Channel or weather forecasts on the Internet for three or so days before you leave home to see if there are any major storm systems heading for Southern California. Weather forecasting has improved to the extent that predictions concerning systems and fronts four to seven days out are now pretty reliable. If it appears that you might see some rough weather during your visit, you're better off bringing rain gear from home. If, however, nothing big is on the horizon weatherwise, you can take your chances.

We at the *Unofficial Guide* usually do not bring rain gear. Rain gear is pretty cheap at Disneyland, especially the ponchos for about $7 adults, $6 child, available in seemingly every retail shop. Moreover, in the theme parks, a surprising number of attractions and queuing areas are under cover. Finally, we prefer to travel light.

If you do find yourself in a big storm, however, you'll want to have both a poncho and an umbrella. As one *Unofficial* reader puts it, "Umbrellas make the rain much more bearable. When rain isn't beating down on your ponchoed head, it's easier to ignore."

And consider this tip from a Memphis, Tennessee, mom:

Scotchgard your shoes. The difference is unbelievable.

MISCELLANEOUS ITEMS

MEDICATION Some parents of hyperactive children on medication discontinue or decrease the child's normal dosage at the end of the school year. If you have such a child, be aware that the Disneyland parks might overly stimulate him or her. Consult your physician before altering your child's medication regimen. Also, if your child has attention-deficit disorder, remember that especially loud sounds can drive him or her right up the wall. Unfortunately, some Disney theater attractions are almost unbearably loud.

unofficial **TIP**
Often little ones fall asleep in their strollers (hallelujah!). Bring a large lightweight cloth and drape it over the stroller to cover your child from the sun. A few clothespins will keep it in place.

SUNSCREEN Overheating and sunburn are among the most common problems of younger children at Disneyland. Carry and use sunscreen of SPF 15 or higher. Be sure to put some on kids in strollers, even if the stroller has a canopy. Some of the worst cases of sunburn we've seen were on the exposed foreheads and feet of toddlers and infants in strollers. Protect skin from overexposure. To avoid overheating, rest regularly in the shade or in an air-conditioned restaurant or show.

WATER BOTTLES Don't count on keeping young children hydrated with soft drinks and stops at water fountains. Long lines may hamper buying refreshments, and fountains may not be handy. Furthermore, excited children may not realize or tell you that they're thirsty or hot. We recommend renting a stroller for children ages 6 and younger and carrying plastic bottles of water. Plastic squeeze bottles with caps run about $3 in all major parks.

COOLERS AND MINI-FRIDGES If you drive to Disneyland, bring two coolers: a small one for drinks in the car, and a large one for the hotel room. If you fly and rent a car, stop and purchase a large Styrofoam cooler, which can be discarded at the end of the trip. If you will be without a car, book a hotel with mini-fridges in each room. If mini-fridges aren't provided, rent one from the hotel.

Coolers and mini-fridges allow you to have breakfast in your hotel room, store snacks and lunch supplies to take to the theme parks, and supplant expensive vending machines for snacks and beverages at the hotel. To keep the contents of your cooler cold, we suggest freezing a two-gallon milk jug full of water before you head out. In a good cooler, it will take the jug five or more days to thaw. If you buy a Styrofoam cooler, you can use bagged ice and ice from the ice machine at your hotel. Even if you have to rent a mini-fridge, you will save a bundle of cash as well as significant time by reducing dependence on restaurant meals and expensive snacks and drinks purchased from vendors.

FOOD-PREP KIT If you plan to make sandwiches, bring along your favorite condiments and seasonings from home. A typical travel kit will include mayonnaise, ketchup, mustard, salt and pepper, and packets of sugar or artificial sweetener. Also throw in some plastic knives and spoons, paper napkins, plastic cups, and a box of zip-top plastic bags. For breakfast you will need some plastic bowls for cereal. Of course, you can buy this stuff in Anaheim, but you probably won't consume it all, so why waste the money? If you drink bottled beer or wine, bring a bottle opener and corkscrew.

unofficial **TIP**
About two weeks before arriving, ship a box to your hotel containing food, plastic cutlery, and toiletries, plus pretty much any other consumables that might come in handy during your stay. If you fly, this helps avoid overweight fees and problems with liquid restrictions for carry-on luggage.

ENERGY BOOSTERS Kids get cranky when they're hungry, and when that happens your entire group has a problem. Like many parents you might, for nutritional reasons, keep a tight rein on snacks available to your children at home. At Disneyland, however, maintaining energy and equanimity trumps between-meal snack discipline. For maximum zip and contentedness, give your kids snacks containing complex carbohydrates (fruits, crackers, nonfat energy bars, and the like) before they get hungry or show signs of exhaustion. You should avoid snacks that are high in fats and proteins because these foods take a long time to digest and will tend to unsettle your stomach if it's a hot day.

ELECTRONICS Regardless of your children's ages, always bring a night-light. Flashlights are also handy for finding stuff in a dark hotel room after the kids are asleep. If you are big coffee drinkers and if you drive, bring along a coffeemaker.

Walkmans and portable CD players with headphones as well as some electronic games are often controversial gear for a family outing. We recommend compromise. Headphones allow kids to create their own space even when they're with others, and that can be a safety valve. That said, try to agree before the trip on some headphone parameters, so you don't begin to feel as if they're being used to keep other family members and the trip itself at a distance. If you're traveling by car, take turns choosing the radio station, CD, or audio tape for part of the trip.

DON'T FORGET THE TENT This is not a joke and has nothing to do with camping. When Bob's daughter was preschool age, he about went crazy trying to get her to sleep in a shared hotel room. She was accustomed to having her own room at home and was hyperstimulated whenever she traveled. Bob tried makeshift curtains and room dividers and even rearranged the furniture in a few hotel rooms to create the illusion of a more private, separate space for her. It was all for naught. It wasn't until she was around 4 years old and Bob took her camping that he seized on an idea that had some promise. She liked the cozy, secure, womblike feel of a backpacking tent, and quieted down much more readily than she ever had in hotel rooms. So the next time the family stayed in a hotel, he pitched his backpacking tent in the corner of the room. In she went, nested for a bit, and fell asleep.

Since the time of Bob's daughter's childhood, there has been an astounding evolution in tent design. Responding to the needs of climbers and paddlers who often have to pitch tents on rocks (where it's impossible to drive stakes), tent manufacturers developed a broad range of tents with self-supporting frames that can be erected virtually anywhere without ropes or stakes. Affordable and sturdy, many are as simple to put up as opening an umbrella. So, if your child is too young for a room of his or her own, or you can't afford a second hotel room, try pitching a small tent. Modern tents are self-contained, with floors and an entrance that can be zipped up (or not) for privacy but cannot be locked. Kids appreciate having their own space and enjoy the adventure of being in a tent, even one set up in the corner of a hotel room. Sizes range from children's "play tents" with a two- to three-foot base to models large enough to sleep two or three husky teens. Light and compact when stored, a two-adult-size tent in its own storage bag (called a "stuff sack") will take up about one-tenth or less of a standard overhead bin on a commercial airliner. Another option for infants and toddlers is to drape a sheet over a portable crib or playpen to make a tent.

THE BOX Bob here: On one memorable Disneyland excursion when my children were younger, we started each morning with an immensely annoying, involuntary scavenger hunt. Invariably, seconds before our scheduled departure to the theme park, we discovered that some combination of shoes, billfolds, sunglasses, hip packs, or other necessities were unaccountably missing. For the next 15 minutes we would root through the room like pigs hunting truffles in an attempt to locate the absent items. Now I don't know about your kids, but when my kids lost a shoe or something, they always searched where it was easiest to look, as opposed to where the lost article was most likely to be. I would be jammed under a bed feeling around while my children stood in the middle of the room intently inspecting the ceiling. As my friends will tell you, I'm as open to a novel theory as the next guy, but we never did find any shoes on the ceiling. Anyway, here's what I finally did: I swung by a local store and mooched a big empty box. From then on, every time we returned to the room, I had the kids deposit shoes, hip packs, and other potentially wayward items in the box. After that the box was off limits until the next morning, when I doled out the contents.

PLASTIC GARBAGE BAGS There are two attractions, the Grizzly River Run raft ride at DCA and Splash Mountain in Disneyland Park, where you are certain to get wet and possibly soaked. If it's really hot and you don't care, then fine. But if it's cool or you're just not up for a soaking, bring a large plastic trash bag to the park. By cutting holes in the top and on the sides you can fashion a sack poncho that will keep your clothes from getting wet. On the raft ride, you will also get your feet wet. If you're not up for walking around in squishing, soaked shoes, bring a second, smaller plastic bag to wear over your feet while riding.

SUPPLIES FOR INFANTS AND TODDLERS

BASED ON RECOMMENDATIONS from hundreds of *Unofficial Guide* readers, here's what we suggest you carry with you when touring with infants and toddlers:

- A disposable diaper for every hour you plan to be away from your hotel room
- A plastic (or vinyl) diaper wrap with Velcro closures
- A cloth diaper or kitchen towel to put over your shoulder for burping
- Two receiving blankets: one to wrap the baby, one to lay the baby on or to drape over you when you nurse
- Ointment for diaper rash
- Moistened towelettes such as Handi-Wipes
- Prepared formula in bottles if you are not breast-feeding
- A washable bib, baby spoon, and baby food if your infant is eating solids
- For toddlers, a small toy for comfort and to keep them occupied during attractions

Baby-care centers at the theme parks will sell you just about anything that you forget or run out of. Like all things Disney, prices will be higher than elsewhere, but at least you won't need to detour to a drug store in the middle of your touring day.

REMEMBERING *Your* TRIP

1. Purchase a notebook for each child and spend some time each evening recording the events of the day. If your children have trouble getting motivated or don't know what to write about, start a discussion; otherwise, let them write or draw whatever they want to remember from the day's events.

2. Collect mementos along the way and create a treasure box in a small tin or cigar box. Months or years later, it's fun to look at postcards, pins, seashells, or ticket stubs to jump-start a memory.

3. Add inexpensive postcards to your photographs to create an album, then write a few words on each page to accompany the images.

4. Give each child a disposable camera to record his or her version of the trip. One 5-year-old snapped an entire series of photos that never showed anyone above the waist—his view of Disneyland (and the photos were priceless).

5. Nowadays, many families travel with a camcorder, though we recommend using one sparingly—parents end up viewing the trip through the lens rather than being in the moment. If you must, take it along, but only record a few moments of major sights (too much is boring anyway). And let the kids tape and narrate. On the topic of narration, speak loudly so as to be heard over the not insignificant background noise of the parks. Make use of lockers at all of the parks when the camcorder becomes a burden or when you're going to experience an attraction that might damage it or get it wet.   Unless you've got a camcorder designed for underwater shots, leave it behind on Splash Mountain, the Grizzly River Run, and any other ride where water is involved.

6. Another inexpensive way to record memories is a palm-size tape recorder. Let all family members describe their experiences. Hearing a small child's voice years later is so endearing, and those recorded descriptions will trigger an album's worth of memories, far more focused than what many novices capture with a camcorder.

Finally, when it comes to taking photos and collecting mementos, don't let the tail wag the dog. You are not going to Disneyland to build the biggest scrapbook in history. Or as this Houston mom put it:

> *Tell your readers to get a grip on the photography thing. We were so busy shooting pictures that we kind of lost the thread. We had to get our pictures developed when we got home to see what all we did* [while on vacation].

TRIAL RUN

IF YOU GIVE THOUGHTFUL CONSIDERATION to all areas of mental, physical, organizational, and logistical preparation discussed in this chapter, what remains is to familiarize yourself with the Disneyland parks and, of course, to conduct your field test. Yep, that's right, we want you to take the whole platoon on the road for a day to see if you are combat ready. No joke, this is important. You'll learn who tuckers out first, who's prone to developing blisters, who has to pee every 11 seconds, who keeps losing her cap, and, given the proper forum, how compatible your family is in terms of what you like to see and do.

For the most informative trial run, choose a local venue that requires lots of walking, dealing with crowds, and making decisions on how to spend your time. Regional theme parks and state fairs are your best bets, followed by large zoos and museums. Devote the whole day. Kick off the morning with an early start, just like you will at Disneyland, paying attention to who's organized and ready to go and who's dragging his or her butt and holding up the group. If you have to drive an hour or two to get to your test venue, no big deal. You may have to do some commuting at Disneyland, too. Spend the whole day, eat a couple meals, stay late.

Don't bias the sample (that is, mess with the outcome) by telling everyone you are practicing for Disneyland. Everyone behaves differently when they know they are being tested or evaluated. Your objective is not to run a perfect drill but to find out as much as you can about how the individuals in your family, as well as the family as a group, respond to and deal with everything they experience during the day. Pay attention to who moves quickly and who is slow; to who is adventuresome and who is reticent; to who keeps going and who needs frequent rest breaks; to who sets the agenda and who is content to follow; to who is easily agitated and who stays cool; to who tends to dawdle or wander off; to who is curious and who is bored; to who is demanding and who is accepting. You get the idea.

Discuss the findings of the test run with your spouse the next day. Don't be discouraged if your test day wasn't perfect; few (if any) are. Distinguish between problems that are remediable and problems that are intrinsic to your family's emotional or physical makeup (no amount of hiking, for example, will toughen up some people's feet).

Establish a plan for addressing remediable problems (further conditioning, setting limits before you go, trying harder to achieve family consensus, whatever) and develop strategies for minimizing or working around problems that are a fact of life (waking sleepyheads 15 minutes early, placing moleskin on likely blister sites before setting out, packing familiar food for the toddler who balks at restaurant fare). If you are an attentive observer, a fair diagnostician, and a creative problem solver, you'll be able to work out a significant percentage of the problems you're likely to encounter at Disneyland before you ever leave home.

ABOUT THE *UNOFFICIAL GUIDE* TOURING PLANS Parents who embark on one of our touring plans are often frustrated by the various interruptions and delays occasioned by their small children. In case you haven't given the subject much thought, here is what to expect:

1. Many small children will stop dead in their tracks whenever they see a Disney character. Our advice: live with it. An attempt to haul your children away before they have satisfied their curiosity is likely to precipitate anything from whining to a full-scale revolt.

2. The touring plans call for visiting attractions in a specified sequence, often skipping certain attractions along the way. Children do not like skipping *anything*! If they see something that attracts them they want to experience it *now*. Some children can be persuaded to skip attractions if parents explain things in advance. Other kids severely flip out at the threat of skipping something, particularly something in Fantasyland. A mom from Charleston, South Carolina, had this to say:

   Following the touring plans turned out to be a train wreck. The main problem with the plan is that it starts in Fantasyland. When we were on Dumbo, my 5-year-old saw eight dozen other things in Fantasyland she wanted to see. The long and the short is that after Dumbo, there was no getting her out of there.

3. Children seem to have a genetic instinct when it comes to finding restrooms. We have seen perfectly functional adults equipped with all manner of maps search interminably for a restroom. Small children, on the other hand, including those who cannot read, will head for the nearest restroom with the certainty of a homing pigeon. While you may skip certain attractions, you can be sure that your children will ferret out (and want to use) every restroom in the theme park.

STROLLERS

STROLLERS ARE AVAILABLE for about $8 at Disneyland and DCA. The rental covers the entire day and is good at both parks. If you rent a stroller and later decide to go back to your hotel for lunch, a swim, or a nap, turn in your stroller but hang on to your rental receipt. When you return to either park later in the day, present your receipt. You will be issued another stroller without an additional charge. The rental procedure is fast and efficient. Likewise, returning the stroller is a breeze. Even in the evening, when several hundred strollers are turned in following the laser-and-fireworks show, there is no wait or hassle.

The strollers come with sun canopies and small cargo compartments under the seat. For infants and toddlers, strollers are a must, and we recommend taking a small pillow or blanket with you to help make them more comfortable for your child during what may be long periods in the seat. We have also observed many sharp parents renting strollers for somewhat older children. Strollers prevent parents from having to carry children when they run out of steam and provide an easy, convenient way to carry water, snacks, diaper bags, and the like.

unofficial **TIP**
Strollers are also great for older kids who tire easily.

When you enter a show or board a ride, you will have to park your stroller, usually in an open, unprotected area. If it rains before you return, you'll need a cloth, towel, or spare diaper to dry off the stroller.

Bringing Your Own Stroller

You are allowed to bring your own stroller to the theme parks. However, only collapsible strollers are allowed on the monorail and parking-lot trams. Your stroller is unlikely to be stolen, but mark it with your name. We strongly recommend bringing your own stroller. In addition to the parks there is the walk from and to your hotel, the parking lot tram, or the bus/hotel-shuttle boarding area, not to mention many other occasions at your hotel or during shopping when you will be happy to have a stroller handy.

If you do not want to bring your own stroller you may consider buying one of the umbrella style collapsible strollers. Wal-Mart sells a very basic Winnie the Pooh collapsible stroller for $13.88. You may even consider ordering online at places such as **www.walmart.com, www.toysrus.com,** or **www.sears.com** and shipping it right to your hotel. Make sure you leave enough time between your order and arrival dates. When you are ready to go home, keep it or chuck it.

Having her own stroller was indispensable to a Mechanicsville, Virginia, mother of two toddlers:

How I was going to manage to get the kids from the parking lot to the park was a big worry for me before I made the trip. I didn't read anywhere that it was possible to walk to the entrance of the parks instead of taking the tram, so I wasn't sure I could do it.

I found that for me personally, since I have two kids ages 1 and 2, it was easier to walk to the entrance of the park from the parking lot with the kids in [my own] stroller than to take the kids out of the stroller, fold the stroller (while trying to control the two kids and associated gear), load the stroller and the kids onto the tram, etc. . . . No matter where I was parked, I could always just walk to the entrance. . . . it sometimes took a while, but it was easier for me.

An Oklahoma mom, however, reports a bad experience with bringing her own stroller:

The first time we took our kids we had a large stroller (big mistake). It is so much easier to rent one in the park. The large [personally owned] strollers are nearly impossible to get on [airport shuttle] buses and are a hassle at the airport. I remember feeling dread when a bus pulled up that was even semi-full of people. People look at you like you have a cage full of live chickens when you drag heavy strollers onto the bus.

The 357th Stroller Squadron: The Mowin' Mamas

Stroller Wars

Sometimes strollers disappear while you are enjoying a ride or a show. Do not be alarmed. You won't have to buy the missing stroller, and you will be issued a new stroller for your continued use. At Disneyland Park, a replacement center is located at the Star Trader in Tomorrowland. At DCA, stroller replacement centers are located across from

Soarin' Over California. Lost strollers can also be replaced at the main rental facility near the respective park entrances.

While replacing a ripped-off stroller is no big deal, it is an inconvenience. One family complained that their stroller had been taken six times in one day. Even with free replacements, larceny on this scale represents a lot of wasted time. Through our own experiments and suggestions from readers, we have developed several techniques for hanging on to your rented stroller:

unofficial **TIP**
Beware of stroller stealers. With so many identical strollers, it's easy to grab the wrong one. Mark yours with a bandanna or some other easily identifiable flag.

1. Write your name in permanent marker on a 6- by 9-inch card, put the card in a transparent freezer bag, and secure the bag to the handle of the stroller with masking or duct tape.

2. Affix something personal (but expendable) to the handle of the stroller. Evidently most strollers are pirated by mistake (since they all look the same) or because it's easier to swipe someone else's stroller (when yours disappears) than to troop off to the replacement center. Since most stroller theft is a function of confusion, laziness, or revenge, the average pram-pincher will balk at hauling off a stroller bearing another person's property. After trying several items, we concluded that a bright, inexpensive scarf or bandanna tied to the handle works well, and a sock partially stuffed with rags or paper works even better (the weirder and more personal the object, the greater the deterrent). Best of all is a dead mackerel dangling from the handle, though in truth, the kids who ride in the stroller prefer the other methods.

Bound and determined not to have her stroller ripped off, an Ann Arbor, Michigan, mother describes her stroller security plan as follows:

We used a variation on your stroller identification theme. We tied a clear plastic bag with a diaper in it onto the stroller. Jon even poured a little root beer on the diaper for effect. Needless to say, no one took our stroller, and it was easy to identify.

We receive quite a few letters from readers debating the pros and cons of bringing your own stroller versus renting one of Disney's. A mother from Falls Church, Virginia, with two small children opted for her own pram, commenting:

I was glad I took my own stroller, because the rented strollers aren't appropriate for infants (we had a 5-year-old and a 5-month-old in tow). No one said anything about me using a bike lock to secure our brand-new Aprica stroller. However, an attendant came over and told us not to lock it anywhere, because it's a fire hazard! (Outside?) When I politely asked the attendant if she wanted to be responsible for my $300 stroller, she told me to go ahead and lock it but not tell anyone! I observed the attendants constantly moving the strollers. This seems very confusing—no wonder people think their strollers are getting ripped off!

As the reader mentioned, Disney cast members often rearrange strollers parked outside an attraction. Sometimes this is done simply to "tidy up." At other times the strollers are moved to make additional room along a walkway. In any event, do not assume that your stroller is stolen because it is missing from the exact place you left it. Check around. Chances are it will be "neatly arranged" just a few feet away.

BABYSITTING

CHILD-CARE SERVICES ARE UNAVAILABLE in the Disney parks. There is a child-care facility, Pinocchio's Workshop, at the Grand Californian Hotel, but its services are available only to guests of the three Disneyland resort hotels. Children ages 5 to 12 can be left for up to four hours at a cost of $9 per hour, per child. Dinner is available for an additional fee. An independent organization called the Fullerton Childcare Agency, however, provides in-room sitting for infants and children. If you pay the tab, Fullerton Childcare sitters will even take your kids to Disneyland.

All sitters are experienced and licensed to drive, and the Fullerton Childcare Agency is fully insured. The basic rate for in-room sitting for one or two children is $48 for the first four hours, with a four-hour minimum, and $10 each hour thereafter. The charge for each additional child varies with the sitter. There is no transportation fee, but the client is expected to pay for parking when applicable. All fees and charges must be paid in cash at the end of the assignment. To reserve a sitter, one or two days' advance notice is requested. You can reach the Fullerton Childcare Agency by calling ☎ 714-528-1640.

DISNEY, KIDS, AND SCARY STUFF

DISNEYLAND PARK and Disney's California Adventure are family theme parks. Yet some of the Disney adventure rides can be intimidating to small children. On certain rides, such as Splash Mountain and the roller coasters (California Screamin', Space Mountain, Matterhorn Bobsleds, and Big Thunder Mountain Railroad), the ride itself may be frightening. On other rides, such as the Haunted Mansion and Snow White's Scary Adventures, it is the special effects. We recommend a little parent-child dialogue coupled with a "testing the water" approach. A child who is frightened by Pinocchio's Daring Journey should not have to sit through The Haunted Mansion. Likewise, if Big Thunder Mountain Railroad is too much, don't try Space Mountain or California Screamin'.

Disney rides and shows are adventures. They focus on the substance and themes of all adventure, and indeed of life itself: good and evil, beauty and the grotesque, fellowship and enmity, quest, and death. As you sample the variety of attractions at the Disney parks, you transcend the mundane spinning and bouncing of midway rides to a more thought-provoking and emotionally powerful entertainment experience. Though the endings are all happy, the impact of the

adventures, with Disney's gift for special effects, is often intimidating and occasionally frightening to small children.

There are rides with menacing witches, rides with burning towns, and rides with ghouls popping out of their graves, all done tongue-in-cheek and with a sense of humor, provided you are old enough to understand the joke. And there are bones, lots of bones—human bones, cattle bones, dinosaur bones, and whole skeletons are everywhere you look. There have to be more bones at Disneyland Park than at the Smithsonian and the UCLA Medical School combined. There is a stack of skulls at the headhunter's camp on the Jungle Cruise; a veritable platoon of skeletons sailing ghost ships in Pirates of the Caribbean; a macabre assemblage of skulls and skeletons in the Haunted Mansion; and more skulls, skeletons, and bones punctuating Snow White's Scary Adventures, Peter Pan's Flight, and Big Thunder Mountain Railroad, to name a few.

One reader wrote us after taking his preschool children on Star Tours:

We took a 4-year-old and a 5-year-old and they had the *#%^! scared out of them at Star Tours. We did this first thing in the morning and it took hours of Tom Sawyer Island and It's a Small World to get back to normal.

Our kids were the youngest by far in Star Tours. I assume that either other adults had more sense or were not such avid readers of your book. Preschoolers should start with Dumbo and work up to the Jungle Cruise in the late morning, after being revved up and before getting hungry, thirsty, or tired. Pirates of the Caribbean is out for preschoolers. You get the idea.

The reaction of young children to the inevitable system overload of Disney parks should be anticipated. Be sensitive, alert, and prepared for almost anything, even behavior that is out of character for

Small-child Fright-potential Chart

As a quick reference, we provide this chart to warn you which attractions to be wary of and why. Remember that the chart represents a generalization and that all kids are different. The chart relates specifically to kids 3 to 7 years of age. On average, as you would expect, children at the younger end of the age range are more likely to be frightened than children in their sixth or seventh year.

Disneyland Park

MAIN STREET, U.S.A.

Disneyland Railroad Tunnel with dinosaur display frightens some small children.
Disneyland: The First Magical 50 Years Not frightening in any respect.
Main Street Cinema Not frightening in any respect.
Main Street Vehicles Not frightening in any respect.

ADVENTURELAND

Enchanted Tiki Room A small thunderstorm momentarily surprises very
    young children.
Indiana Jones Adventure Visually intimidating, with intense effects and
    a jerky ride. Switching-off option provided (see page 152).
Jungle Cruise Moderately intense, with some macabre sights; a good
    test attraction for little ones.
Tarzan's Treehouse Not frightening in any respect.

NEW ORLEANS SQUARE

Haunted Mansion Name of attraction raises anxiety, as do sights and sounds
    of waiting area. An intense attraction with humorously presented macabre
    sights. The ride itself is gentle.
Pirates of the Caribbean Slightly intimidating queuing area; an intense boat
    ride with gruesome (though humorously presented) sights and two short,
    unexpected slides down flumes.

CRITTER COUNTRY

Davy Crockett's Explorer Canoes Not frightening in any respect.
The Many Adventures of Winnie the Pooh Not frightening in any respect.
Splash Mountain Visually intimidating from the outside. Moderately intense
    visual effects. The ride itself is somewhat hair-raising for all ages, culminating
    in a 52-foot plunge down a steep chute. Switching-off option provided (see
    page 152).

FRONTIERLAND

Big Thunder Mountain Railroad Visually intimidating from the outside with
    moderately intense visual effects. The roller coaster is wild enough to
    frighten many adults, particularly seniors. Switching-off option provided
    (see page 152).
Frontierland Shootin' Exposition Not frightening in any respect.
Golden Horseshoe Stage Not frightening in any respect.

Mark Twain **Riverboat** Not frightening in any respect.
Pirates Lair on Tom Sawyer Island Some very small children are intimidated by
    dark walk-through tunnels that can be easily avoided.
Sailing Ship *Columbia* Not frightening in any respect.

FANTASYLAND

Alice in Wonderland Pretty benign, but frightens a small percentage of
    preschoolers.
Casey Jr. Circus Train Not frightening in any respect.
Dumbo the Flying Elephant A tame midway ride; a great favorite of most
    small children.
It's a Small World Not frightening in any respect.
King Arthur Carrousel Not frightening in any respect.
Mad Tea Party Midway-type ride can induce motion sickness in all ages.
Matterhorn Bobsleds The ride itself is wilder than Big Thunder Mountain
    Railroad, but not as wild as Space Mountain. Switching off is an option
    (see page 152).
Mr. Toad's Wild Ride Name of ride intimidates some. Moderately
    intense spook-house genre attraction with jerky ride. Frightens only
    a small percentage of preschoolers.
Peter Pan's Flight Not frightening in any respect.
Pinocchio's Daring Journey Less frightening than Alice in Wonderland, but
    scares a few very young preschoolers.
Snow White's Scary Adventures Moderately intense spook-house-genre
    attraction with some grim characters. Absolutely terrifying to many preschoolers.
Storybook Land Canal Boats Not frightening in any respect.

MICKEY'S TOONTOWN

Chip 'n' Dale's Treehouse Not frightening in any respect.
Gadget's Go Coaster Tame as far as roller coasters go; frightens some
    small children.
Goofy's Playhouse Not frightening in any respect.
Mickey's House Not frightening in any respect.
Minnie's House Not frightening in any respect.
Miss Daisy, **Donald Duck's Boat** Not frightening in any respect.
Roger Rabbit's Car Toon Spin Intense special effects, coupled with a dark
    environment and wild ride; frightens many preschoolers.

TOMORROWLAND

Astro Orbiter Waiting area is visually intimidating to preschoolers. The ride is a
    lot higher, but just a bit wilder, than Dumbo.
Buzz Lightyear Astro Blasters Intense special effects plus a dark environment
    frighten some preschoolers.
Disneyland Monorail Not frightening in any respect.
Finding Nemo **Submarine Voyage** Being enclosed, as well as certain ride effects,
    may frighten preschoolers.

Small-child Fright-potential Chart (continued)

Disneyland Park (continued)

TOMORROWLAND (CONTINUED)

Honey, I Shrunk the Audience Extremely intense visual effects and the loud volume scare many preschoolers.

Space Mountain Very intense roller coaster in the dark; Disneyland's wildest ride and a scary roller coaster by anyone's standards. Switching-off option provided (see page 152).

Star Tours Extremely intense visually for all ages; the ride itself is one of the wildest in Disney's repertoire. Switching-off option provided (see page 152).

Tomorrowland Autopia The noise in the waiting area slightly intimidates preschoolers; otherwise, not frightening.

Disney's California Adventure Park

A BUG'S LAND

Bountiful Valley Farm Not frightening in any respect.

Flik's Fun Fair Rides and Playground Not frightening in any respect.

It's Tough to Be a Bug! Loud and extremely intense with special effects that will terrify children under 8 years or anyone with a fear of insects.

Ugly Bug Ball Not frightening in any respect.

GOLDEN STATE

Boudin Bakery Not frightening in any respect.

Golden Dreams Not frightening in any respect.

Golden Vine Winery Not frightening in any respect.

Mission Tortilla Factory Not frightening in any respect.

Redwood Creek Challenge Trail featuring *The Magic of Brother Bear* show. A bit overwhelming to preschoolers but not frightening.

your child at home. Most small children take Disney's variety of macabre trappings in stride, and others are quickly comforted by an arm around the shoulder or a little squeeze of the hand. For parents who have observed a tendency in their kids to become upset, we recommend taking it slowly and easily by sampling more benign adventures like the Jungle Cruise, gauging reactions, and discussing with children how they felt about the things they saw.

Sometimes, small children will rise above their anxiety in an effort to please their parents or siblings. This behavior, however, does not necessarily indicate a mastery of fear, much less enjoyment. If children come off a ride in ostensibly good shape, we recommend asking if they would like to go on the ride again (not necessarily right now, but sometime). The response to this question will usually give you a clue as to how much they actually enjoyed the experience. There is

Soarin' over California Frightens some children 7 years and under. Really a very sweet ride.

HOLLYWOOD PICTURES BACKLOT

Disney Animation Not frightening in any respect.
Hollywood Backlot Stage Not frightening in any respect.
Hyperion Theater Some productions are both very intense and loud.
Monsters, Inc.: **Mike and Sulley to the Rescue** May frighten children under 7 years of age.
Muppet Vision 3-D Intense and loud with a lot of special effects. Frightens some preschoolers.
Playhouse Disney—**Live on Stage** Not frightening in any respect.
The Twilight Zone **Tower of Terror** Frightening to guests of all ages.

PARADISE PIER

California Screamin' Frightening to guests of all ages.
Golden Zephyr Frightening to a small percentage of preschoolers.
Jumpin' Jellyfish The ride's appearance frightens some younger children. The ride itself is exceedingly tame.
King Triton's Carousel Not frightening in any respect.
Maliboomer Frightening to guests of all ages.
Mulholland Madness Frightening to the under-8 crowd.
Orange Stinger Height requirement keeps preschoolers from riding. Moderately intimidating to younger grade-schoolers.
S.S. *Rustworthy* Not frightening in any respect.
Sun Wheel The ride's appearance frightens some younger children. The ride itself is exceedingly tame.
Toy Story **Mania** Loud and intense but not frightening.

a lot of difference between having a good time and mustering the courage to get through something.

Evaluating a child's capacity to handle the visual and tactile effects of the Disney parks requires patience, understanding, and experimentation. Each of us, after all, has our own demons. If a child balks at or is frightened by a ride, respond constructively. Let your children know that lots of people, adults as well as children, are scared by what they see and feel. Help them understand that it is OK if they get frightened and that their fear does not lessen your love or respect. Take pains not to compound the discomfort by making a child feel inadequate; try not to undermine self-esteem, impugn courage, or subject a child to ridicule. Most of all, do not induce guilt, as if your child's trepidation is ruining the family's fun. When older siblings are present, it is sometimes necessary to restrain their taunting and teasing.

A visit to a Disney park is more than an outing or an adventure for a small child. It is a testing experience, a sort of controlled rite of passage. If you help your little one work through the challenges, the time can be immeasurably rewarding and a bonding experience for both of you.

The Fright Factor

While each youngster is different, there are essentially six attraction elements that alone or combined can push a child's buttons:

1 THE NAME OF THE ATTRACTION Small children will naturally be apprehensive about something called the "Haunted Mansion" or "Snow White's Scary Adventures" or "Orange Stinger."

2. THE VISUAL IMPACT OF THE ATTRACTION FROM OUTSIDE Splash Mountain, Maliboomer, the *Twilight Zone* Tower of Terror, and Big Thunder Mountain Railroad look scary enough to give even adults second thoughts. To many small kids, the rides are visually terrifying.

3. THE VISUAL IMPACT OF THE INDOOR QUEUING AREA Pirates of the Caribbean, with its dark bayou scene, and the Haunted Mansion, with its "stretch rooms," are capable of frightening small children before they even board the ride.

4. THE INTENSITY OF THE ATTRACTION Some attractions are so intense as to be overwhelming; they inundate the senses with sights, sounds, movement, and even smell. *Honey, I Shrunk the Audience, Muppet Vision 3-D,* and *It's Tough to Be a Bug!,* for instance, combine loud music, laser effects, lights, and 3-D cinematography to create a total sensory experience. For some preschoolers, this is two or three senses too many.

5. THE VISUAL IMPACT OF THE ATTRACTION ITSELF As previously discussed, the sights in various attractions range from falling boulders to lurking buzzards, from grazing dinosaurs to attacking hippos. What one child calmly absorbs may scare the owl poop out of another child the same age.

6. DARK Many Disneyland attractions are "dark" rides—that is, they operate indoors in a dark environment. For some children, this fact alone is sufficient to trigger significant apprehension. A child who is frightened on one dark ride, for example Snow White's Scary Adventures, may be unwilling to try other indoor rides.

7. THE RIDE ITSELF; THE TACTILE EXPERIENCE Some Disney rides are downright wild—wild enough to induce motion sickness, wrench backs, and generally discombobulate patrons of any age.

A Bit of Preparation

We receive many tips from parents relating how they prepared their small children for their Disneyland experience. A common strategy is to acquaint children with the characters and the stories behind the attractions by reading Disney books and watching Disney videos at home. A more direct approach is to rent Disneyland travel videos that actually show the various attractions. Concerning the latter, a father from Arlington, Virginia, reported:

> *My kids both loved The Haunted Mansion, with appropriate prepa-*
> *ration. We rented a tape before going so they could see it, and then I*
> *told them it was all "Mickey Mouse Magic" and that Mickey was*
> *just "joking you," to put it in their terms, and that there weren't any*
> *real ghosts, and that Mickey wouldn't let anyone actually get hurt.*

A mother from Gloucester, Massachusetts, handled her son's preparation a bit more extemporaneously:

> *The 3½-year-old liked It's a Small World [but] was afraid of The*
> *Haunted Mansion. We just pulled his hat over his face and quietly*
> *talked to him while we enjoyed [the ride].*

A Word about Height Requirements

A number of attractions require children to meet minimum height and age requirements, usually 40 inches tall to ride with an adult, or

40 inches and 7 years of age to ride alone. If you have children too short or too young to ride, you have several options, including switching off (described later in this chapter). Although the alternatives may resolve some practical and logistical issues, be forewarned that your smaller children might nonetheless be resentful of their older (or taller) siblings who qualify to ride. A mom from Virginia bumped into just such a situation, writing:

> You mention height requirements for rides but not the intense sibling jealousy this can generate. Frontierland was a real problem in that respect. Our very petite 5-year-old, to her outrage, was stuck hanging around while our 8-year-old went on Splash Mountain and [Big] Thunder Mountain with Grandma and Granddad, and the nearby alternatives weren't helpful [too long a line for rafts to Tom Sawyer Island, etc.]. If we had thought ahead, we would have left the younger kid back in Mickey's Toontown with one of the grown-ups for another roller coaster ride or two and then met up later at a designated point. The best areas had a playground or other quick attractions for short people near the rides with height requirements.

The reader makes a valid point, though splitting the group and then meeting later can be more complicated in practical terms than she might imagine. If you choose to split up, ask the Disney greeter at the entrance to the height-restricted attraction(s) how long the wait is. If you tack five minutes for riding onto the anticipated wait, and then add five or so minutes to exit and reach the meeting point, you'll have an approximate sense of how long the younger kids (and their supervising adult) will have to do other stuff. Our guess is that even with a long line for the rafts, the reader would have had more than sufficient time to take her daughter to Tom Sawyer Island while the sibs rode Splash Mountain and Big Thunder Mountain with the

POTENTIALLY PROBLEMATIC ATTRACTIONS FOR ADULTS		
Disneyland Park		
Adventureland	**Indiana Jones Adventure**	
Critter Country	**Splash Mountain**	
Fantasyland	**Mad Tea Party**	**Matterhorn Bobsleds**
Frontierland	**Big Thunder Mountain Railroad**	
Tomorrowland	**Space Mountain**	**Star Tours**
Disney's California Adventure Park		
Golden State	**Grizzly River Run**	
Hollywood Pictures Backlot	*Monsters, Inc.:* **Mike and Sulley to the Rescue** *The Twilight Zone* **Tower of Terror**	
Paradise Pier	**California Screamin'**	**Maliboomer**
	Mulholland Madness	

grandparents. For sure she had time to tour Tarzan's Treehouse in adjacent Adventureland.

Attractions that Eat Adults

You may spend so much energy worrying about Junior's welfare that you forget to take care of yourself. If the ride component of the attraction (that is, the actual motion and movement of the conveyance itself) is potentially disturbing, persons of any age may be adversely affected. At bottom left are several attractions likely to cause motion sickness or other problems for older children and adults. Fast, jerky rides are also noted with icons in the attraction profiles.

WAITING-LINE STRATEGIES *for* ADULTS *with* SMALL CHILDREN

CHILDREN HOLD UP BETTER through the day if you minimize the time they have to spend in lines. Arriving early and using the touring plans in this guide will reduce waiting time immensely. There are, however, additional measures you can employ to reduce stress on little ones.

1. LINE GAMES It is a smart parent who anticipates how restless children get waiting in line and how a little structured activity can relieve the stress and boredom. In the morning, kids handle the inactivity of waiting in line by discussing what they want to see and do during the course of the day. Later, however, as events wear on, they need a little help. Watching for, and counting, Disney characters is a good diversion. Simple guessing games like "20 Questions" also work well. Lines for rides move so continuously that games requiring pen and paper are cumbersome and impractical. Waiting in the holding area of a theater attraction, however, is a different story. Here, tic-tac-toe, hangman, drawing, and coloring can really make the time go by.

2. LAST-MINUTE ENTRY If a ride or show can accommodate an unusually large number of people at one time, it is often unnecessary to stand in line. The *Mark Twain* Riverboat in Frontierland is a good example. The boat holds about 450 people, usually more than are waiting in line to ride. Instead of standing uncomfortably in a crowd with dozens of other guests, grab a snack and sit in the shade until the boat arrives and loading is well under way. After the line has all but disappeared, go ahead and board.

In large-capacity theaters, like the one showing *Honey, I Shrunk the Audience* in Tomorrowland, ask the entrance greeter how long it will be until guests are admitted to the theater for the next show. If the answer is 15 minutes or more, use the time for a restroom break or to get a snack; you can return to the attraction just a few minutes before the show starts. You will not be permitted to carry any food or drink into the attraction, so make sure you have time to finish your snack before entering.

To help you determine which attractions to target for last-minute entry, we provide the following chart.

ATTRACTIONS YOU CAN USUALLY ENTER AT THE LAST MINUTE

Disneyland Park

Frontierland	*Mark Twain* Riverboat	Sailing Ship *Columbia*
Main Street, U.S.A.	*Disneyland: The First 50 Magical Years*	
Tomorrowland	*Honey, I Shrunk the Audience*	

Disney's California Adventure

Golden State	**Golden Dreams**

3. THE HAIL-MARY PASS Certain waiting lines are configured in such a way that you and your smaller children can pass under the rail to join your partner just before boarding or entry. This technique allows the kids and one adult to rest, snack, cool off, or tinkle, while another adult or older sibling does the waiting. Other guests are understanding when it comes to using this strategy to keep small children content. You are likely to meet hostile opposition, however, if you try to pass older children or more than one adult under the rail. Attractions where it is usually possible to complete a Hail-Mary pass are listed on the chart below.

ATTRACTIONS WHERE YOU CAN USUALLY COMPLETE A HAIL-MARY PASS

Disneyland Park

Adventureland	Jungle Cruise	Tarzan's Treehouse
Fantasyland	Casey Jr. Circus Train	Dumbo the Flying Elephant
	King Arthur Carrousel	Mad Tea Party
	Mr. Toad's Wild Ride	Peter Pan's Flight
	Snow White's Scary Adventures	Storybook Land Canal Boats
Tomorrowland	Tomorrowland Autopia	

Disney's California Adventure Park

Paradise Pier	Golden Zephyr	Jumpin' Jellyfish
	King Triton's Carousel	

4. SWITCHING OFF (AKA THE BABY SWAP) Several attractions have minimum height and/or age requirements, usually 40 inches tall to ride with an adult, or 7 years of age *and* 40 inches tall to ride alone. Some couples with children too small or too young forgo these attractions, while others split up and take turns riding separately. Missing out on some of Disney's best rides is an unnecessary sacrifice, and waiting in line twice for the same ride is a tremendous waste of time.

A better way to approach the problem is to take advantage of an option known as "switching off" or "The Baby Swap." Switching off requires at least two adults. Everybody waits in line together, both adults and children. When you reach a Disney attendant (known as a "greeter"), say you want to switch off. The greeter will allow everyone, including the small children, to enter the attraction. When you reach the loading area, one adult will ride while the other stays with the kids. The riding adult then disembarks and takes responsibility for the children while the other adult rides. A third adult in the party can ride twice, once with each of the switching-off adults, so they do not have to experience the attraction alone. The 13 attractions where switching off is routinely practiced are listed on the following chart.

ATTRACTIONS WHERE SWITCHING OFF IS COMMON		
Disneyland Park		
Adventureland	Indiana Jones Adventure	
Critter Country	Splash Mountain	
Fantasyland	Matterhorn Bobsleds	
Frontierland	Big Thunder Mountain Railroad	
Tomorrowland	Space Mountain	Star Tours
Disney's California Adventure Park		
Golden State	Grizzly River Run	Soarin' over California
Paradise Pier	California Screamin'	Maliboomer
	Mulholland Madness	Orange Stinger
Hollywood Pictures Backlot	*The Twilight Zone* Tower of Terror	

Disney has been experimenting with a new switching-off procedure for certain FASTPASS attractions. Here the cast member gives two FAST-PASSes to the parent who will be waiting with the child. That parent and the child then leave the queue and are free to do other things while the riding parent is waiting in line and experiencing the attraction. When the family regroups, the nonriding parent can use her FASTPASSes to ride, taking another member of the family with her if she desires.

An Ada, Michigan, mother who discovered that the procedure for switching off varies from attraction to attraction offered this suggestion:

> *Parents need to tell the very first attendant they come to that they would like to switch off. Each attraction has a different procedure for this. Tell every other attendant too, because they forget quickly.*

5. HOW TO RIDE TWICE IN A ROW WITHOUT WAITING Many small children like to ride a favorite attraction two or more times in succession. Riding the second time often gives the child a feeling of mastery and accomplishment. Unfortunately, repeat rides can be time-consuming, even in the early morning. If you ride Dumbo as soon as Disneyland Park opens, for instance, you will only have a one- or two-minute wait for your first ride. When you come back for your second ride, your wait will be about 12 minutes. If you want to ride a third time, count on a 20-minute or longer wait.

The "Baby Swap"

The best way for getting your child on the ride twice (or more) without blowing your whole morning is by using the "Chuck-Bubba Relay" (named in honor of a reader from Kentucky):

1. Mom and little Bubba enter the waiting line.
2. Dad lets a certain number of people go in front of him (32 in the case of Dumbo) and then gets in line.
3. As soon as the ride stops, Mom exits with little Bubba and passes him to Dad to ride the second time.
4. If everybody is really getting into this, Mom can hop in line again, no less than 32 people behind Dad.

The Chuck-Bubba Relay will not work on every ride because of differences in the way the waiting areas are configured (that is, it is impossible in some cases to exit the ride and make the pass). The rides where the Chuck-Bubba Relay does work appear on the chart below, along with the number of people to count off.

When practicing the Chuck-Bubba Relay, if you are the second adult in line, you will reach a point in the waiting area that is obviously the easiest place to make the hand-off. Sometimes this point is where those exiting the ride pass closest to those waiting to board. In any event, you will know it when you see it. Once there, if the first parent has not arrived with little Bubba, just let those behind you slip past until Bubba shows up.

ATTRACTIONS WHERE THE CHUCK-BUBBA RELAY USUALLY WORKS	
Disneyland Park	**Number of people between adults**
Alice in Wonderland **(tough, but possible)**	38 people
Casey Jr. Circus Train	34 people, if 2 trains are operating
Davy Crockett's Explorer Canoes	94 people, if 6 canoes are operating
Dumbo the Flying Elephant	32 people
King Arthur Carrousel	70 people
Mad Tea Party	53 people
Mr. Toad's Wild Ride	32 people
Peter Pan's Flight	25 people
Snow White's Scary Adventures	30 people
Disney's California Adventure Park	
Golden Zephyr	64 people
Jumpin' Jellyfish	16 people
King Triton's Carousel	64 people

6. LAST-MINUTE COLD FEET If your small child gets cold feet at the last minute after waiting for a ride (where there is no age or height requirement), you can usually arrange with the loading attendant for a switch-off. This situation arises frequently at Pirates of the Caribbean—small children lose their courage en route to the loading area.

There is no law that says you have to ride. If you get to the boarding area and someone is unhappy, just tell a Disney attendant you have changed your mind, and one will show you the way out.

7. THROW YOURSELF ON THE GRENADE, MILDRED! For by-the-book, do-the-right-thing parents determined to sacrifice themselves on behalf of their children, we provide a One-day Touring Plan for Disneyland Park called the Dumbo-or-Die-in-a-Day Touring Plan for Parents with Small Children. This touring plan, detailed starting on page 278, will ensure that you run yourself ragged. Designed to help you forfeit everything of personal interest for the sake of your children's pleasure, the plan is guaranteed to send you home battered and exhausted with extraordinary stories of devotion and heroic perseverance. By the way, the plan really works. Anyone under 8 years old will love it.

8. DISNEY'S CALIFORNIA ADVENTURE This is not a great park for little ones. With the exception of Flik's Fun Fair, three play areas, and a carousel, the remaining attractions will be either boring or too frightening for most preschoolers. Elementary school–age children will fare better but will probably be captivated by the low-capacity/long-line rides at the Paradise Pier district of the park. Although designed to be appealing to the eye, these attractions are simply gussied-up versions of midway rides your kids can enjoy less expensively and with a fraction of the wait at a local amusement park or state fair.

9. CATCH-22 AT THE TOMORROWLAND AUTOPIA Though the Autopia at Disneyland Park is a great treat for small children, they are required to be 52 inches tall in order to drive unassisted. Since very few children age 6 and under top this height, the ride is essentially withheld from the very age group that would most enjoy it. To resolve this catch-22, go on the ride with your small child. The attendants will assume that you will drive. After getting into the car, however, shift your child over behind the steering wheel. From your position you will still be able to control the foot pedals. To your child, it will feel like driving. Because the car travels on a self-guiding track, there is no way your child can make a mistake while steering.

LOST CHILDREN

LOST CHILDREN NORMALLY do not present much of a problem at Disneyland Resort. All Disney employees are schooled in handling such situations should they arise. If you lose a child while touring, report the situation to a Disney employee; then check in at City Hall (Disneyland Park) or Guest Relations (DCA) where lost-children logs are maintained. In an emergency, an alert can be issued throughout the park through internal communications. If a Disney cast member (employee) encounters a lost child, the cast member will escort the child immediately to the Baby Care Center located at the central-hub end of Main Street in Disneyland Park and at the entrance plaza in DCA.

unofficial **TIP**
We suggest that children younger than 8 years be color coded by dressing them in purple T-shirts or equally distinctive clothes.

It is amazingly easy to lose a child (or two) at a Disney park. It is a good idea to sew a label into each child's shirt that states his or her name, your name, and the name of your hotel. The same task can be accomplished less elegantly by writing the information on a strip of masking tape; hotel security professionals suggest that the information be printed in small letters, and that the tape be affixed to the outside of the child's shirt five inches or so below the armpit.

HOW KIDS GET LOST

CHILDREN GET SEPARATED from their parents every day at the Disney parks under circumstances that are remarkably similar (and predictable).

1. PREOCCUPIED SOLO PARENT In this scenario the only adult in the party is preoccupied with something like buying refreshments, loading the camera, or using the restroom. Junior is there one second and gone the next.

2. THE HIDDEN EXIT Sometimes parents wait on the sidelines while allowing two or more young children to experience a ride together. As it usually happens, the parents expect the kids to exit the attraction in one place, and, lo and behold, the young ones pop out somewhere else. The exits of some Disney attractions are considerably distant from the entrances. Make sure you know exactly where your children will emerge before letting them ride by themselves.

3. AFTER THE SHOW At the completion of many shows and rides, a Disney staffer will announce, "Check for personal belongings and take small children by the hand." When dozens, if not hundreds, of people leave an attraction at the same time, it is easy for parents to temporarily lose contact with their children unless they have them directly in tow.

4. RESTROOM PROBLEMS Mom tells 6-year-old Tommy, "I'll be sitting on this bench when you come out of the restroom." Three situations: One, Tommy exits through a different door and becomes disoriented (Mom may not know there is another door). Two, Mom decides belatedly that she will also use the restroom, and Tommy emerges to find her absent. Three, Mom pokes around in a shop while keeping an eye on the bench, but misses Tommy when he comes out.

If you can't be with your child in the restroom, make sure there is only one exit. Designate a meeting spot more distinctive than a bench, and be specific in your instructions: "I'll meet you by this flagpole. If you get out first, stay right here." Have your child repeat the directions back to you.

TIPS FOR KEEPING TRACK OF YOUR BROOD

- Same-colored T-shirts for the whole family will help you gather your troops in an easy and fun way. You can opt for just a uniform color or go the extra mile and have the T-shirts printed with a logo such as "The Brown Family's Assault on the Mouse." You might also include the date or the year of your visit. Your imagination is the limit. Light-colored T-shirts can even be autographed by the Disney characters.

- Clothing labels are great, of course. If you don't sew, buy labels that you can iron on the garment. If you own a cell phone, be sure to include the number on the label. If you do not own a cell phone, put in the phone number of the hotel where you'll be staying.

- In pet stores you can have name tags printed for a very reasonable price. These are great to add to necklaces and bracelets, or attach to your child's shoelaces or a belt loop.

- When you check into the hotel, take a business card of the hotel for each member in your party, especially those old enough to carry wallets and purses.

- Always agree on a meeting point before you see a parade, fireworks, and nighttime spectacles such as *Fantasmic!* Make sure the meeting place is in the park (as opposed to the car or someplace outside the front gate).

- If you have a digital camera you may elect to take a picture of your kids every morning. If they get lost the picture will show what they look like and what they are wearing.

- If all the members of your party have cell phones, it's easy to locate each other. Be aware, however, that the ambient noise in the parks is so loud that you probably won't hear your cell phone ring. Your best bet is to carry your phone in a front pants pocket and to program the phone to vibrate. If any of your younger kids carry cell phones, secure the phones with a strap.

- Save key tags and luggage tags for use on items you bring to the parks, including your stroller, diaper bag, and backpack or hip pack.

- Don't underestimate the power of the permanent marker, such as a Sharpie. They are great for labeling pretty much anything. Mini-Sharpies are sold as clip-ons and are great for collecting character autographs. The Sharpie will also serve well for writing down the location of your car in the parking lot.

5. PARADES There are many special parades and shows at the theme park during which the audience stands. Children, because they are small, tend to jockey around for a better view. By moving a little this way and a little that way, it is amazing how much distance kids can put between themselves and you before anyone notices.

6. MASS MOVEMENTS Another situation to guard against is when huge crowds disperse after shows, fireworks, parades, or at park closing.

With between 5,000 and 12,000 people suddenly moving at once, it is very easy to get separated from a small child or others in your party. Extra caution is recommended following the evening parades, fireworks, and *Fantasmic!* Families should develop specific plans for what to do and where to meet in the event they are separated.

7. CHARACTER GREETINGS A fair amount of activity and confusion is commonplace when the Disney characters are on the scene. See the next section on meeting the Disney characters.

The DISNEY CHARACTERS

FOR YEARS THE COSTUMED, walking versions of Mickey, Minnie, Donald, Goofy, and others have been a colorful supporting cast at Disneyland and Walt Disney World. Known unpretentiously as the "Disney characters," these large and friendly figures help provide a link between Disney animated films and the Disney theme parks.

Audiences, it has been observed, cry during the sad parts of Disney animated films and cheer when the villain is vanquished. To the emotionally invested, the characters in these features are as real as next-door neighbors; never mind that they are simply drawings on plastic. In recent years, the theme-park personifications of Disney characters have likewise become real to us. For thousands of visitors, it is not just some person in a mouse costume they see, it is really Mickey. Similarly, running into Goofy or Snow White in Fantasyland is a memory to be treasured, an encounter with a real celebrity.

About 250 of the Disney animated-film characters have been brought to life in costume. Of these, a relatively small number (about 50) are "greeters" (the Disney term for characters who mix with the patrons). The remaining characters are relegated exclusively to performing in shows or participating in parades. Some only appear once or twice a year, usually in Christmas parades or Disney anniversary celebrations.

CHARACTER ENCOUNTERS

CHARACTER WATCHING has developed into a pastime. Where families were once content to stumble across a character occasionally, they now relentlessly pursue them armed with autograph books and cameras. For those who pay attention, some characters are much more frequently encountered than others. Mickey, Minnie, and Goofy, for example, are seemingly everywhere, while Thumper comes out only on rare occasions. Other characters can be seen regularly, but limit themselves to a specific location.

The fact that some characters are seldom seen has turned character watching into character collecting. Mickey Mouse may be the best known and most loved character, but from a collector's perspective he is also the most common. To get an autograph from Mickey is no big deal, but Daisy Duck's signature is a real coup. Commercially tapping into the character-collecting movement, Disney sells autograph books throughout the parks.

PREPARING YOUR CHILDREN TO MEET THE CHARACTERS Because most small children are not expecting Minnie Mouse to be the size of a forklift, it's best to discuss the characters with your kids before you go. Almost all of the characters are quite large, and several, like Br'er Bear, are huge! All of them can be extremely intimidating to a preschooler.

unofficial **TIP**
Don't underestimate your child's excitement at meeting the Disney characters—but also be aware that very small kids may find the large, costumed characters a little frightening.

On first encounter, it is important not to thrust your child upon the character. Allow the little one to come to terms with this big thing from whatever distance the child feels safe. If two adults are present, one should stay close to the youngster while the other approaches the character and demonstrates that the character is safe and friendly. Some kids warm to the characters immediately, while some never do. Most take a little time, and often require several different encounters.

There are two kinds of characters: those whose costume includes a face-covering headpiece (animal characters plus some human characters like Captain Hook), and "face characters," or actors who resemble the cartoon characters to such an extent that no mask or headpiece is necessary. Face characters include Mary Poppins, Ariel, Jasmine, Aladdin, Cinderella, Mulan, Tarzan, Jane, Belle, Snow White, and Prince Charming, to name a few.

Only the face characters are allowed to speak. Headpiece characters, called "furs" in Disney-speak, do not talk or make noises of any kind.

unofficial **TIP**
Explain to your children that the headpiece characters do not talk. Keep in mind, too, that the characters are clumsy and have a limited field of vision.

Because the cast members could not possibly imitate the distinctive cinema voice of the character, the Disney folks have determined it is more effective to keep them silent. Lack of speech notwithstanding, the headpiece characters are extremely warm and responsive, and they communicate very effectively with gestures. As with the characters' size, children need to be forewarned that the characters do not talk.

Parents need to understand that some of the character costumes are very cumbersome and that cast members often suffer from very poor visibility. You have to look closely, but the eye holes are frequently in the mouth of the costume or even down on the neck. What this means in practical terms is that the characters are sort of clumsy and have a limited field of vision. Children who approach the character from the back or the side may not be noticed, even if the child is touching the character. It is perfectly possible in this situation for the character to accidentally step on the child or knock him or her down.

The best way for a child to approach a character is from the front, and occasionally not even this works. For example, the various duck characters (Donald, Daisy, Uncle Scrooge, and so on), have to peer around their bills. If it appears that the character is ignoring your child, pick your child up and hold her in front of the character until the character responds.

It is OK to touch, pat, or hug the character if your child is so inclined. Understanding the unpredictability of children, the characters will keep their feet very still, particularly refraining from moving backward or to the side. Most of the characters will sign autographs or pose for pictures. Once again, be sure to approach from the front so that the character will understand your intentions. If your child collects autographs, it is a good idea to carry a big, fat pen about the size of a Magic Marker. The costumes make it exceedingly difficult for the characters to wield a smaller pen, so the bigger the better.

THE BIG HURT Many children expect to bump into Mickey the minute they enter a park and are disappointed when he is not around. If your children are unable to settle down and enjoy things until they see Mickey, simply ask a Disney cast member where to find him. If the cast member does not know Mickey's whereabouts, he or she can find out for you in short order.

"THEN SOME CONFUSION HAPPENED" Be forewarned that character encounters give rise to a situation during which small children sometimes get lost. There is usually a lot of activity around a character, with both adults and children touching the character or posing for pictures. In the most common scenario, the parents stay in the crowd while their child marches up to get acquainted. With the excitement of the encounter, all the milling people, and the character moving around, a child may get turned around and head off in the wrong direction. In the words of a Salt Lake City mom: "Milo was shaking hands with Dopey one minute, then some confusion happened and he [Milo] was gone." Families with several small children, and parents who are busy fooling around with cameras, can lose track of a youngster in a heartbeat. Our recommendation for parents of preschoolers is to stay with the kids when they meet the characters, stepping back only long enough to take a picture, if necessary.

MEETING CHARACTERS You can *see* the Disney characters in live shows and in parades. For times, consult your *Times Guide*. If you have the time and money, you can share a meal with the characters (more about this later). But if you want to *meet* the characters, get autographs, and take photos, it's helpful to know where the characters hang out.

Responding to guest requests, Disneyland Resort has added a lot of information about characters to its handout park maps and entertainment *Times Guide*. A listing specifies where and when certain characters will be available and also provides information on character dining. On the maps of the parks themselves, yellow stars are used to denote locations where characters can be found.

At Disney's California Adventure Park, look for characters in Hollywood near the Animation Building, in parades, and in shows at the Hyperion Theater. Elsewhere around the park, characters will be less in evidence than at Disneyland Park, but they will make periodic appearances at Flik's Fun Fair and Sunshine Plaza (the central hub).

The last few years have seen a number of Disney initiatives aimed at satisfying guests' inexhaustible desire to meet the characters. At Disneyland Park, Disney relegated four (Mickey, Minnie, Pluto, and Donald) of the "fab five" to all-day tours of duty in Mickey's Toontown. The fifth "fab," Goofy, works a similar schedule most days in Frontierland. Likewise, Pooh and Tigger can usually be found in Critter Country, Beauty and the Beast in Fantasyland, and Aladdin and Jasmine in Adventureland. Characters less in demand roam the "lands" consistent with their image (Br'er Bear and Br'er Fox in Critter Country, for example).

While making the characters routinely available has taken the guesswork out of finding them, it has likewise robbed character encounters of much of their surprise and spontaneity. Instead of chancing on a character as you turn a corner, it is much more common now to wait in a queue in order to meet the character. Speaking of which, be aware that lines for face characters move *m-u-c-h* more slowly than do lines for nonspeaking characters, as you might surmise. Because face characters are allowed to talk, they do, often engaging children in lengthy conversations, much to the consternation of the families stuck in the queue.

If you believe that there are already quite enough lines in Disneyland Park, and, furthermore, if you prefer to bump into your characters on the run, here's a quick rundown of where the bears and chipmunks roam. There will almost always be a character in Town Square on Main Street and often at the central hub. Snow White,

Cinderella, and Princess Aurora hang out in the courtyard of the castle; the aforementioned Br'ers cruise Critter Country; and Pocahontas meets and greets in Frontierland. Any characters whom we haven't specifically mentioned generally continue to turn up randomly throughout the park.

Characters are also featured in the afternoon and evening parades, Frontierland waterfront shows, *Fantasmic!*, and shows on the Fantasyland Theatre stage. Characters also play a major role in shows at the Tomorrowland Terrace stage. Performance times for all of the shows and parades are listed in the Disneyland Park's daily *Times Guide* entertainment listings. After the shows, characters will sometimes stick around to greet the audience.

Mickey Mouse is available to meet guests and pose for photos all day long in his dressing room at Mickey's Movie Barn in Mickey's

Toontown. To reach the Movie Barn, proceed through the front door of Mickey's House and follow the crowd. If the line extends back to the entrance of Mickey's House, it will take you about 25 to 30 minutes to actually reach Mickey. When you finally get to his dressing room, one or two families at a time are admitted for a short personal audience with Mickey.

Many children are so excited about meeting Mickey that they cannot relax to enjoy the other attractions. If Mickey looms large in your child's day, board the Disneyland Railroad at the Main Street Station as soon as you arrive at the park, and proceed directly to Mickey's Toontown (half a circuit). If you visit Mickey before 10 a.m., your wait will be short.

Minnie receives guests at her house most of the day as well, and Donald and Pluto are frequently available for photos and autographs in the gazebo situated in front of the Toontown Town Hall. There is, of course, a separate line for each character. Also, be aware that the characters bug out for parades and certain other special performances. Check the daily *Entertainment Times Guide* for performance times and plan your Toontown visit accordingly.

CHARACTER DINING

FRATERNIZING WITH DISNEY CHARACTERS has become so popular that Disney offers character breakfasts, brunches, and dinners where families can dine in the presence of Mickey, Minnie, Goofy, and other costumed versions of animated celebrities. Besides grabbing customers from Denny's and McDonald's, character meals provide a familiar, controlled setting in which young children can warm gradually to the characters. All meals are attended by several characters. Adult prices apply to persons age 10 or older, children's prices to ages 3 to 9. Little ones under age 3 eat free.

unofficial **TIP**
Arrange Priority Seating as far in advance as possible. Your wait for a table will usually be less than 15 minutes.

Because character dining is very popular, we recommend that you arrange Priority Seating as far in advance as possible. Priority Seating is Disney's version of a reservation—you arrive at an appointed time and the restaurant will be expecting you, but no specific table will be set aside. Instead, you will be seated at the first available table. The "priority" part simply means that you will be seated ahead of walk-ins. In practice the system works reasonably well, and your wait for a table will usually be less than 15 minutes.

CHARACTER DINING: WHAT TO EXPECT Character meals are bustling affairs, held in hotels' or theme parks' largest table-service or "buffeteria" restaurants. Character breakfasts (there are five) offer a fixed menu served family-style or as a buffet. The typical family-style breakfast includes scrambled eggs; bacon, sausage, and ham; hash browns; waffles, pancakes, or French toast; biscuits, rolls, or pastries; and fruit. The meal is served in large skillets or platters at your table. If you run out of something, you can order seconds (or thirds) at no additional charge. Buffets offer much the same fare, but you have to fetch it yourself. The only character dinner at Disneyland Resort is a buffet serving standard American fare.

Whatever the meal, characters circulate around the room while you eat. During your meal, each of the three to five characters present will visit your table, arriving one at a time to cuddle the kids (and sometimes the adults), pose for photos, and sign autographs. Keep autograph books (with pens) and loaded cameras handy. For the best photos, adults should sit across the table from their children. Always seat the children where characters can reach them most easily. If a table is against a wall, for example, adults should sit with their backs to the wall and children should sit nearest the aisle.

You will not be rushed to leave after you've eaten. Feel free to ask for seconds on coffee or juice, and stay as long as you wish. Remember, however, that there might be lots of eager children and adults waiting not so patiently to be admitted.

You can dine with Disney characters at the Plaza Inn in Disneyland Park, at Goofy's Kitchen at the Disneyland Hotel, at Ariel's Grotto at DCA, at the Storytellers Cafe at the Grand Californian Hotel, and at the PCH Grill at the Paradise Pier Hotel. For information about character meals and to make Priority Seatings, call ☎ 714-781-DINE (3463).

PLAZA INN Located at the end of Main Street and to the right, the Plaza Inn character buffet is usually packed because it hosts character breakfasts that are included in vacation packages sold by the Walt Disney Travel Sales Center. Served from opening until 11 a.m., the buffet costs $24 for adults and $13 for children. Characters present usually include Mickey, Minnie, Goofy, Pluto, and Chip 'n' Dale. Priority Seating is recommended.

ARIEL'S DISNEY PRINCESS CELEBRATION Overlooking Paradise Bay, Avalon Cove restaurant hosts a lunch and dinner with Ariel and friends daily until one hour before park closing. The admission costs for both are $26 for adults and $17.33 for children. Priority Seating is recommended.

GOOFY'S KITCHEN Located at the Disneyland Hotel, Goofy's Kitchen serves a character breakfast buffet from 7 a.m. until 12 p.m. (2 p.m. weekends) and a character dinner buffet 5 to 9 p.m. Breakfast is $27.25 for adults and $15 for kids. Dinners run $36 (!) and $15, respectively. Goofy, of course, is the head character, but he's usually joined by Minnie, Pluto, and others. Priority Seating is recommended.

STORYTELLERS CAFE Storytellers Cafe, located at the Grand Californian Hotel, is the most attractive of the character-meal venues. A

"Casting!" This is George at the character breakfast. There's been a mistake. We were supposed to get the Assorted Character Packages with one Mickey, one Goofy, one Donald, one Pluto. . . ."

breakfast buffet is served from 6:30 until 11 a.m. Cost is $27.25 for adults and $15 for children. Chip 'n' Dale, the featured characters, are usually assisted by Pluto. Priority Seating is recommended.

PCH GRILL PCH Grill at the Paradise Pier Hotel serves a Lilo and Stitch Aloha breakfast buffet from 6:30 until 11 a.m. that features traditional Japanese breakfast items in addition to the usual American fare. Prices are $27.25 for adults and $15 for kids. Lilo and Stitch entertain you with a luau and Hawaiian music. Priority Seating is recommended.

PART FOUR

DINING *and* SHOPPING *in and around* DISNEYLAND

DINING *in* DISNEYLAND RESORT

IN THIS SECTION, we aim to help you find good food without going broke or tripping over one of Disneyland Resort's many culinary land mines. More than 50 restaurants operate in Disneyland Resort, including about 20 full-service restaurants, several of which are inside the theme parks. Collectively, Disney restaurants offer reasonable variety, serving everything from Louisiana Creole to Texas barbecue, but sadly, international cuisines other than Mexican and Italian are not represented. Most restaurants are expensive, and many serve less than distinguished fare, but the culinary scene gets better every year.

GETTING IT RIGHT

ALTHOUGH WE WORK HARD to be objective and accurate, many readers think we're too critical of the restaurants at both Disneyland and Walt Disney World in Florida. A reader from Couderport, Pennsylvania, is typical, writing:

> *You are tough on all Disney dining. . . . Everyone has to eat while there, so it benefits no one to be this critical. Lighten up a little bit and make your dining recommendations in the same spirit as the rest of the book.*

In a similar vein, a Charleston, West Virginia, woman came out swinging:

> *Get a life! It's crazy and unrealistic to be so snobbish about restaurants at a theme park. Considering the number of people Disney feeds each day, I think they do a darn good job. Also, you act so surprised that the food is expensive. Have you ever eaten at an airport? HELLO IN THERE? . . . Surprise, you're a captive! It's a theme park!*

And a mom from Erie, Pennsylvania, struck a practical note, writing:

> Most of the food is OK. Certainly in our experience, more of it is good than bad. If you pay attention to what other visitors say and what's in the guidebooks, you can avoid the yucky places. It's true that you pay more than you should, but it's more convenient [to eat Disney food] than to run around trying to find cheaper restaurants somewhere else. Who needs more running around?

As you might infer from the reader comments above, getting our dining coverage right is a bit of a challenge. While researching and reviewing restaurants may appear to be a straightforward endeavor, we can assure you that it is fraught with peril. We've read dining reviews by writers who turn up their noses at anything except four-star French restaurants (of which there are a whole lot fewer than people think). Likewise, we've seen reviewers who totally avoid Thai and Indian restaurants (among others) because they don't understand those cuisines, and we've read critiques absolutely devoid of criticism, written by "experts" unwilling to risk offending the sources of their free meals. Finally, we've seen reviews that are wholly based on surveys submitted by diners whose credentials for evaluating fine dining are mysterious at best and questionable at least.

unofficial **TIP**
It's necessary, we believe, to present both an expert and a popular opinion of each restaurant.

How, then, do we go about presenting the best possible dining coverage? What is the best way to get it right? We at the *Unofficial Guide* have elected to begin with highly qualified culinary experts and then balance their opinions with those of our readers.

The expert opinion is essential, because it's important to be able to differentiate what the restaurant really serves from what it purports to serve. Many years ago in Lexington, Kentucky, by way of example, there was only one Chinese restaurant. It was wildly successful even though it was Chinese in name only. Still, its specialty dishes—essentially American vegetable casseroles smothered in cornstarch—were happily consumed by patrons who had never been exposed to real Chinese cooking. The food wasn't bad, mind you, but it wasn't Chinese either. Visitors from out of town, inquiring about a good local Chinese restaurant, were often directed to this place. As you would expect, they were routinely horrified by the fare.

In this guide, we think you deserve to know whether or not you're getting the real thing. If we recommend, say, the shrimp rémoulade (shrimp served cold in a mayonnaise-based sauce with chopped onion, Creole mustard, and paprika) at Blue Bayou, it's pretty essential that our dining critics know what shrimp rémoulade is, how it should be prepared, how it should be served, and how it should taste. Likewise with the béarnaise sauce at Steakhouse 55 at the Disneyland Hotel, or the paella at Catal Restaurant in Downtown Disney. In our opinion, it's almost impossible to publish a creditable restaurant review without the help of a knowledgeable, professional dining critic.

The ultimate test of success for a restaurant, however, is not the authenticity of its dishes but the satisfaction of its patrons. If diners have a bad experience and don't come back, the restaurant will fail. Thus, we regard our experts' opinions and our readers' feedback as two halves of a whole: both are necessary to inform your dining decisions.

Our experts are knowledgeable, seasoned professionals who have studied culinary arts around the world and who have written cookbooks or columns. They are well versed in ethnic dishes and have studied many of the cuisines of the world in their native lands. As at home at a Tupelo, Mississippi, catfish shack as at an exclusive French restaurant on New York's Upper East Side, they have no prejudice about high or low cuisine. Equally important, our experts conduct their reviews anonymously and always pay full menu prices for their meals.

To be as fair and thorough as possible, we will, in subsequent editions, display our readers' collective opinion of each restaurant right alongside our dining critics' evaluations. Because this dining chapter is new to *The Unofficial Guide to Disneyland*, it will take a year to collect surveys from readers and add your opinions to our restaurant profiles. We encourage you, therefore, to fill out the dining survey in the back of this guide. If you want to share your dining experience in depth, write to us at the address listed on page 8, or e-mail us at **unofficialguides@menasharidge.com.**

DISNEY DINING 101

DISNEYLAND RESORT RESTAURANT RESERVATIONS: WHAT'S IN A NAME

DISNEY TINKERS CEASELESSLY with its restaurant-reservations policy. A few years back, reservations for full-service eateries were replaced with Priority Seating, a confusing system with a befuddling name that issues reservations which aren't exactly reservations. When you call Disney Dining at ☎ 714-781-3463, option 4, your name and essential information are taken, well, as if you were making a reservation. The Disney representative then tells you that you have Priority Seating for the restaurant on the date and time you requested, usually explaining that "Priority" means you will be seated ahead of walk-ins—that is, those guests without Priority Seating.

unofficial **TIP**
Priority Seating is available to all Disneyland visitors—not just guests of the resort hotels. In the theme parks, you can make Priority Seatings for later in the day at the door of the restaurant.

BEHIND THE SCENES AT
DISNEYLAND RESORT DINING

DISNEY RESTAURANTS OPERATE on what they call a "template system." Instead of scheduling Priority Seating for actual tables, reservationists fill time slots. The number of slots available is based on the average observed length of time that guests occupy a table at a particular restaurant, adjusted for seasonality.

Here's a rough example of how it works: Let's say the Blue Bayou Restaurant at Disneyland Park has 38 tables for four and 10 tables for six, and that the average length of time for a family to be seated, order, eat, pay, and depart is 40 minutes. Add 5 minutes to bus the table and set it up for the next guests, and the tables are turning every 45 minutes. The restaurant provides Disneyland Resort Dining (DRD) with a computer template of its capacity, along with the average time the table is occupied. Thus, when DRD makes Priority Seatings for four people at 6:15 p.m., the system removes one table for four from overall capacity for 45 minutes. The template on the reservationist's computer indicates that the table will not be available for reassignment until 7 p.m. (45 minutes later). And so it goes for all the tables in the restaurant, each being subtracted from overall capacity for 45 minutes, then listed as available again, then assigned to other guests and subtracted again, and so on, throughout the meal period. DRD tries to fill every time slot for every seat in the restaurant, or come as close to filling every slot as possible. No seats—repeat, none—are *reserved* for walk-ins, though all restaurants accommodate such customers on a space-available basis.

Templates are filled differently depending on the season. During slower times of year, when Priority Seatings are easier to get, DRD will overbook a restaurant for each time slot, assuming that there will be a lot of no-shows. During busy times of year, when Priority Seatings are harder to come by, there are very few no-shows, so the restaurant is booked according to its actual capacity.

With Priority Seating, your wait will almost always be less than 20 minutes during peak hours, and often less than 10 minutes. If you just walk in, especially during busier seasons, expect to wait 40 to 75 minutes.

GETTING YOUR ACT TOGETHER

IF YOU WANT TO PATRONIZE any of the Disneyland Resort full-service restaurants, especially buffets or character-dining eateries, you should consider Priority Seating (call ☎ 714-781-3463, option 4, up to 60 days in advance). DRD handles Priority Seatings for both Disney-owned and independent restaurants at the theme parks, Disney hotels, and Downtown Disney. The sole exception is the **Rainforest Cafe** at Downtown Disney, which makes its own reservations at ☎ 714-772-0413.

If you fail to make Priority Seatings before you leave home, or if you want to make your dining decisions spontaneously, your chances of getting a table at the restaurant of your choice are good. Blue Bayou at Disneyland Park, Napa Rose at the Grand Californian Hotel, and the various character-meal venues are the most likely to sell out. If, however, you visit Disneyland during a very busy time of year, it's to your advantage to make Priority Seatings.

If you poop out at the theme park and you don't feel like using your Priority Seating, there's no penalty. Also be aware that if you're a no-show for a particular Priority Seating, it won't affect any other such seatings you may have made. If you're running late, however, the restaurant will void your Priority Seating 15 minutes after the scheduled time. If you've lined up many seatings, it's a good idea to phone DRD a few days before you arrive to make sure everything's in order. If you stay at a Disney resort, Guest Services can print out a summary of all your Priority Seatings. If you have a seating for a theme-park restaurant at a time before opening, as is sometimes the case for a character breakfast, simply proceed to the turnstiles and inform a cast member, who will admit you to the park.

unofficial **TIP**
Disney Kids' Meals are now for ages 3–9; the cutoff used to be age 11.

DRESS

DRESS IS INFORMAL at all theme-park restaurants, but "dressy casual" is appropriate for resort restaurants such as Steakhouse 55 and Napa Rose. That means dress slacks (or dress shorts) with a collared shirt for men and slacks, skirts, or dress shorts with a blouse or sweater (or a dress) for women.

FOOD ALLERGIES AND SPECIAL REQUESTS

IF YOU HAVE FOOD ALLERGIES or follow a specific type of diet (such as kosher), make your needs known when you arrange your Priority Seating. Does it work? Well, a Phillipsburg, New Jersey, mom reports her family's experience:

> My 6-year-old has many food allergies, and we often have to bring food with us to restaurants when we go out to eat. I was able to make reservations at the Disney restaurants in advance and indicate these allergies to the reservation clerk. When we arrived at the restaurants, the staff was already aware of my child's allergies and assigned our table a chef who double-checked the list of allergies with us. Each member of the waitstaff was also informed of the allergies. The chefs were very nice and made my son feel very special (to the point where my other family members felt a little jealous).

A FEW CAVEATS

Before you begin eating your way through Disneyland, take our advice:

1. However creative and enticing the menu descriptions, avoid fancy food at full-service restaurants in the theme parks. Order dishes that the

kitchen is unlikely to botch. An exception to this caveat is the Vineyard Room at DCA.

2. Don't order baked, broiled, poached, or grilled seafood unless the restaurant specializes in seafood or rates at least ★★★½ in our dining profiles.

3. Theme-park restaurants rush their customers in order to make room for the next group of diners. Eating at high speed may appeal to a family with young, restless children, but for people wanting to relax, it's more like dining in a pressure chamber.

   If you want to linger over your expensive meal, don't order your entire dinner at once. Order drinks, study the menu while you sip, then order appetizers. Tell the waiter you need more time to decide among entrees. Order your main course only after appetizers have been served. Dawdle over coffee and dessert.

4. If you're dining in a theme park and cost is an issue, make lunch your main meal. Entrees are similar to those on the dinner menu, but prices are significantly lower.

DISNEYLAND RESORT RESTAURANT CATEGORIES

IN GENERAL, FOOD AND BEVERAGE OFFERINGS at Disneyland Resort are defined by service, price, and convenience:

FULL-SERVICE RESTAURANTS Full-service restaurants are in all Disneyland Resort hotels, both theme parks, and Downtown Disney. Disney operates most of the restaurants in the theme parks and its hotels; contractors or franchisees operate those at Downtown Disney. The restaurants accept VISA, MasterCard, American Express, Discover, Diners Club, and the Disney Credit Card.

BUFFETS AND FIXED-PRICE MEALS With set-price character meals such as Ariel's Grotto at DCA, you can choose one item each from a limited selection of appetizers, salads, main courses, and desserts. Character buffets such as the one at Goofy's Kitchen in the Disneyland Hotel have a separate children's menu featuring grub like hot dogs, burgers, chicken nuggets, pizza, macaroni and cheese, and spaghetti and meatballs. Priority Seating is highly recommended for all character meals.

COUNTER SERVICE Counter-service fast food is available at both theme parks and Downtown Disney. The food compares in quality with McDonald's, Captain D's, Pizza Hut, or Taco Bell but is more expensive, though it's often served in larger portions.

HARD CHOICES

DINING DECISIONS WILL DEFINITELY AFFECT your Disneyland Resort experience. If you're short on time and you want to see the theme parks, avoid full service. Ditto if you're short on funds. If you want to try a Disney full-service restaurant, arrange Priority Seating— this won't reserve you a table, but it will minimize your wait.

Integrating Meals into the *Unofficial Guide* Touring Plans

Arrive before the park of your choice opens. Tour expeditiously, using your chosen plan (taking as few breaks as possible), until about 11 to 11:30 a.m. Once the park becomes crowded around midday, meals and other breaks won't affect the plan's efficiency. If you intend to stay in the park for evening parades, fireworks, or other events, eat dinner early enough to be finished in time for the festivities.

Character Dining

A number of restaurants, primarily those that serve all-you-can-eat buffets and family-style meals, offer character dining. At character meals, you pay a fixed price and dine in the presence of one to five Disney characters who circulate throughout the restaurant, hugging children (and sometimes adults), posing for photos, and signing autographs. Character breakfasts, lunches, and dinners are served at restaurants in and out of the theme parks. For an extensive discussion of character dining, see page 164 in Part Three, Disneyland with Kids.

FULL-SERVICE DINING FOR FAMILIES WITH YOUNG CHILDREN

NO MATTER HOW FORMAL a restaurant appears, the staff is accustomed to wiggling, impatient, and often boisterous children. In Disneyland Resort's finest dining rooms, it's not unusual to find at least two dozen young diners attired in basic black . . . mouse ears.

Almost all Disney restaurants offer children's menus, and all have booster seats and high chairs. Well aware of how tough it may be for children to sit still for an extended period of time, waiters will supply little ones with crackers and rolls and serve your dinner much faster than in comparable restaurants elsewhere. In fact, letters from readers suggest that being served too quickly is much more common than having a long wait.

QUIET, ROMANTIC PLACES TO EAT

RESTAURANTS WITH GOOD FOOD *and* a couple-friendly ambience are rare in the theme parks. Only two Disneyland dining spots satisfy both requirements: **Blue Bayou** at Disneyland Park and the **Vineyard Room** at DCA. Among the hotels, **Napa Rose** at the Grand Californian and **Steakhouse 55** at the Disneyland Hotel are the leading candidates for a romantic adult-dining experience. At Downtown Disney, try **Ralph Brennan's Jazz Cafe**—ask for a quiet table, though, if you're not interested in the jazz.

Eating later in the evening and choosing a restaurant we've mentioned will improve your chances for intimate dining; nevertheless, know that children, well behaved or otherwise, are everywhere at Disneyland, and you can't escape them.

unofficial **TIP** Bottom line: young children are the rule, not the exception, at Disney restaurants.

FAST FOOD IN THE THEME PARKS

BECAUSE MOST MEALS DURING a Disneyland vacation are consumed on the run while touring, we'll tackle counter-service and vendor foods first. Plentiful at all theme parks are hot dogs, hamburgers, chicken sandwiches, salads, and pizza. They're augmented by special items that relate to the park's theme or the part of the park you're touring. In the Alpine village setting of Fantasyland, for example, counter-service bratwurst and knockwurst are sold; in New Orleans Square, Cajun and Creole dishes are available. Counter-service prices are fairly consistent from park to park. Expect to pay the same amount for your coffee or hot dog at DCA that you would at Disneyland Park.

Getting your act together in regard to counter service is more a matter of courtesy than necessity. Rude guests rank fifth among reader complaints. A mother from Fort Wayne, Indiana, points out that indecision can be as maddening as outright discourtesy, especially when you're hungry:

> Every fast-food restaurant has menu signs the size of billboards, but do you think anybody reads them? People waiting in line spend enough time in front of these signs to memorize them and still don't have a clue what they want when they finally get to the order taker. If by some miracle they've managed to choose between the hot dog and the hamburger, they then fiddle around another ten minutes deciding what size Coke to order. Tell your readers PULEEEZ get their orders together ahead of time!

A North Carolina reader offers a tip about counter-service food lines:

> [Many] counter-service registers serve two queues each, one to the left and one to the right of each register. People are not used to this and will instinctively line up in one queue per register, typically on the right side, leaving the left vacant. We had register operators wave us up to the front several times to start a left queue instead of waiting behind others on the right.

Healthful Food at Disneyland Resort

One of the most commendable developments in food service at Disneyland has been the introduction of healthier foods and snacks. Diabetics, vegetarians, weight watchers, those requiring kosher meals, and guests on restricted diets should have no trouble finding something to eat. The same goes for anyone seeking wholesome, nutritious food. Health-conscious choices are available at most fast-food counters and even from vendors.

Cutting Your Dining Time at the Theme Parks

Even if you confine your meals to vendor and counter-service fast food, you lose a lot of time getting sustenance in the theme parks. At Disneyland Park and DCA, everything begins with a line and ends with a cash register. When it comes to fast food, "fast" may apply to the time you spend eating it, not the time invested in obtaining it.

Here are suggestions for minimizing the time you spend hunting and gathering food:

1. Don't waste touring time on breakfast at the parks. Restaurants outside Disneyland offer some outstanding breakfast specials. Many hotels furnish small refrigerators in their guest rooms, or you can rent one. If you can get by on cold cereal, rolls, fruit, and juice, having a fridge in your room will save a ton of time. If you can't get a fridge, bring a cooler.

2. After a good breakfast, buy snacks from vendors in the parks as you tour, or stuff some snacks in a fanny pack. This is very important if you're on a tight schedule and can't spend a lot of time waiting in line for food.

3. All theme-park restaurants are busiest between 11:30 a.m. and 2:15 p.m. for lunch and 6 and 9 p.m. for dinner. For shorter lines and faster service, don't eat during these hours, especially 12:30 to 1:30 p.m.

4. Many counter-service restaurants sell cold sandwiches. Buy a cold lunch (except for drinks) before 11:30 a.m., and carry it until you're ready to eat. Ditto for dinner. Bring small plastic bags in which to pack the food; purchase drinks at the appropriate time from any convenient vendor.

5. Most fast-food eateries have more than one service window. Regardless of the time of day, check the lines at all windows before queuing. Sometimes a window that's staffed but out of the way will have a much shorter line or none at all. Note, however, that some windows may offer only certain items.

6. If you're short on time and the park closes early, stay until closing and eat dinner outside Disneyland before returning to your hotel. If the park stays open late, eat dinner about 4 or 4:30 p.m. at the restaurant of your choice. You should miss the last wave of lunchers and sneak in just ahead of the dinner crowd.

Beyond Counter Service: Tips for Saving Money on Food

Though buying food from counter-service restaurants and vendors will save you time and money compared with full-service dining, additional strategies can bolster your budget and maintain your waistline. Here are some suggestions our readers have offered over the years:

1. Go to Disneyland during a period of fasting and abstinence. You can save a fortune *and* save your soul!

2. Wear clothes that are slightly too small and make you feel like dieting. (No spandex allowed!)

3. Whenever you're feeling hungry, ride the Mad Tea Party, California Screamin', or other attractions that can induce motion sickness.

4. Leave your cash and credit cards at your hotel. Buy food only with money your children fish out of fountains and wishing wells.

Cost-conscious readers also have volunteered ideas for stretching food dollars. A Missouri mom writes:

> I have shared our very successful meal plan with many families. We shopped and arrived with our steel Coleman cooler well stocked with milk and sandwich fixings. I froze a block of ice in a milk bottle, and we replenished it daily from the resort ice machine. I also froze small packages of deli-type meats for later in the week. We ate cereal, milk, and fruit each morning, with boxed juices. I also had a hot pot to boil water for instant coffee, oatmeal, and soup.
>
> Each child had a belt bag of his own, which he filled from a special box of "goodies" each day. I made a great mystery of filling that box in the weeks before the trip. Some things were actual food, like packages of crackers and cheese, packets of peanuts and raisins. Some were worthless junk, like candy and gum. They grazed from their belt bags at will throughout the day, with no interference from Mom and Dad. Each also had a small, rectangular plastic water bottle that could hang on the belt. We filled these at water fountains before getting into lines and were the envy of many.
>
> We left the park before noon, ate sandwiches, chips, and soda in the room, and napped. We purchased our evening meal in the park, at a counter-service eatery. We budgeted for both morning and evening snacks from a vendor but often did not need them. It made the occasional treat all the more special. Our cooler had been pretty much emptied by the end of the week, but the block of ice was still there.

A mom from Whiteland, Indiana, who purchases drinks in the parks, offers this suggestion:

> One "must-take" item if you're traveling with younger kids is a supply of small paper or plastic cups to split drinks, which are both huge and expensive.

We interviewed one woman who brought a huge picnic for her family of five packed in a large diaper–baby paraphernalia bag. She stowed the bag in a locker on Main Street and retrieved it when the family was hungry.

Note: Disney has a rule against bringing your own food and drink into the parks. Although since 9/11 all packs, purses, diaper bags, and such have been searched, security usually does not enforce the ban.

THEME-PARK COUNTER-SERVICE RESTAURANT *Mini-profiles*

TO HELP YOU FIND PALATABLE fast-service foods that suit your taste, we've developed mini-profiles of Disneyland Park and DCA counter-service restaurants. The restaurants are listed alphabetically by park. Detailed profiles of all Disneyland full-service restaurants follow this section.

The restaurants profiled below are rated for quality and portion size as well as value. The value rating ranges from A to F as follows:

unofficial **TIP**
Restaurants with a "Disney's Munch Inc." logo on their menu boards (showing three red cogwheels in the shape of Mickey's head) offer special meals for kids ages 3–9. Menu items frequently available include mini-pizzas, mac and cheese, chicken tenders, and PB&J.

A = Exceptional value; a real bargain

B = Good value

C = Fair value; you get exactly what you pay for

D = Somewhat overpriced

F = Extremely overpriced

DISNEYLAND PARK

Bengal Barbecue

QUALITY Good–excellent	VALUE C	PORTION Small–medium	LOCATION Adventureland

Selections Beef, chicken, and vegetable skewers; fruit cups.
Comments Skewers are small, but nothing costs more that $4. Try the hot-and-spicy Banyan Beef Skewer.

Daisy's Diner

QUALITY Good	VALUE C	PORTION Medium	LOCATION Mickey's Toontown

Selections Pepperoni and cheese pizzas.
Comments Fine for eating on the run—there's no place convenient to sit.

Enchanted Cottage

QUALITY Excellent	VALUE C	PORTION Medium	LOCATION Fantasyland

Selections Bratwurst and knockwurst with peppers and onions or sauerkraut; Bavarian pretzels.
Comments Built as a concession stand for the adjoining Fantasyland Theatre (next to the Fantasyland railroad station), the Enchanted Cottage is often overlooked by lunch and dinner crowds.

French Market Restaurant

QUALITY Fair	VALUE C	PORTION Medium	LOCATION New Orleans Square

Selections Jambalaya, beef stew, fried chicken, chicken sandwiches, salads.
Comments Hearty but not overly tasty fare.

Golden Horseshoe

QUALITY Good	VALUE C	PORTION Medium–large	LOCATION Frontierland

Selections Chicken tenders, fish and chips, mozzarella strips, chili, cheese fries, and ice-cream sundaes.
Comments The Golden Horseshoe hosts the best live entertainment in the park. Try to combine lunch with a show.

Hungry Bear Restaurant

QUALITY Good   VALUE C   PORTION Medium–large   LOCATION Critter Country

Selections Burgers, chicken sandwiches, corn dogs, chicken tenders, salads, and turkey club sandwiches. All are served with fries or chips except the salads.

Comments An out-of-the-way, reasonably tranquil venue. Sit on the deck overlooking the Rivers of America.

Pluto's Dog House

QUALITY Good   VALUE C   PORTION Medium   LOCATION Mickey's Toontown

Selections Mini–hot dogs, knockwurst, bratwurst, mac and cheese.

Comments Food's not bad, but there's really no place to sit and eat it.

Rancho del Zocalo Restaurante

QUALITY Good   VALUE B   PORTION Medium–large   LOCATION Frontierland

Selections Mexican grilled chicken, enchilada platters, taco platters, *carne asada*.

Comments See page 194 for a full profile.

Redd Rockett's Pizza Port

QUALITY Good   VALUE C   PORTION Medium   LOCATION Tomorrowland

Selections Pasta, pizza, salads.

Comments Redd Rockett's is set up cafeteria-style—which usually means less waiting. The venue has an A/C system on steroids, making it a really cool place on a really hot day.

Refreshment Corner

QUALITY Good   VALUE C   PORTION Medium   LOCATION Main Street, U.S.A.

Selections Hot dogs, chili-cheese dogs, chili in a bread bowl.

Comments Not much of a selection, but the dogs are good. Limited seating.

River Belle Terrace

QUALITY Excellent   VALUE B   PORTION Large   LOCATION Frontierland

Selections Barbecued chicken and pork, salmon, grilled-chicken salad, turkey sandwiches, vegetable stew, clam chowder, PB&J, mac and cheese.

Comments See page 195 for a full profile.

Royal Street Veranda

QUALITY Fair   VALUE D   PORTION Large   LOCATION New Orleans Square

Selections Steak gumbo, vegetarian gumbo, clam chowder, all served in a sourdough bread bowl.

Comments So-so gumbo. Most of the meal is the bread bowl.

Stage Door Cafe

QUALITY Good   VALUE C   PORTION Medium–large   LOCATION Frontierland

Selections Chicken tenders, fish and chips, mozzarella strips, funnel cakes, PB&J.

Comments You can find better fare next door at the Golden Horseshoe.

Tomorrowland Terrace

| QUALITY Good | VALUE B | PORTION Medium–large | LOCATION Tomorrowland |

Selections Turkey club, veggie, grilled chicken, and roast beef–Cheddar sandwiches; burgers; salads.

Comments One of the park's largest restaurants, featuring a broad array of selections. Seating is available outdoors overlooking the Tomorrowland Terrace stage, which hosts live music and the popular Jedi Training Academy.

Vendor Treats

| LOCATION Throughout the park |

Selections Popcorn, French fries, smoked turkey legs, ice cream, churros, chimichangas.

Comments We love the smoked turkey legs—big enough for a whole meal, and only $6. Plus, there's something delightfully Neanderthal and exhibitionist about tucking into a huge, meaty bone as you stroll the park.

Village Haus

| QUALITY Fair–Good | VALUE C | PORTION Medium | LOCATION Fantasyland |

Selections Chicken tenders, mini–hot dog combo, mac-and-cheese meals for adults and toddlers, burgers, pizza, turkey club sandwiches, salads.

Comments Crowds and poor lighting limit the appeal of this Alpine-themed restaurant.

DISNEY'S CALIFORNIA ADVENTURE

Award Wieners

| QUALITY Good | VALUE B | PORTION Medium–large | LOCATION Hollywood Pictures Backlot |

Selections Chili-cheese dogs, hot dogs, smoked-sausage sandwiches, chili fries.

Comments This is a streetside counter with no seating.

Bountiful Valley Farmers Market

| QUALITY Good | VALUE C | PORTION Medium | LOCATION a bug's land |

Selections Chicken, fried fish, mozzarella strips.

Comments The selection is a little anemic, but the restaurant is situated in the quietest, least frenetic part of the park.

Burger Invasion

| QUALITY Good | VALUE C | PORTION Medium–large | LOCATION Paradise Pier |

Selections Burger Invasion is a McDonald's with most of the same menu items as your neighborhood Mickey D's.

Comments Most selections are available only as combos with fries.

Cocina Cucamonga Mexican Grill

QUALITY Good	VALUE C	PORTION Medium	LOCATION Pacific Wharf

Selections Tacos and nachos, desserts.

Comments The grill uses fresh tortillas from the nearby Mission Tortilla Factory.

Pacific Wharf Cafe

QUALITY Good	VALUE C	PORTION Medium–large	LOCATION Pacific Wharf

Selections Fresh soups and salads served in large, hollowed-out sourdough loaves; burgers, hot dogs, and mac and cheese for the kids.

Comments One of the best counter-service eateries in the park. We provide a full profile of the restaurant on page 191.

Pizza Oom Mow Mow

QUALITY Good	VALUE D	PORTION Medium–large	LOCATION Paradise Pier

Selections Sausage, cheese, Hawaiian, and barbecue-chicken pizza; pasta; salads.

Comments Slices are $6, whole pizzas about $32.

Taste Pilots' Grill

QUALITY Good	VALUE C	PORTION Medium–large	LOCATION Condor Flats

Selections Burgers, ribs, chicken sandwiches.

Comments Taste Pilots' Grill boasts the largest seating capacity, both indoors and out, of any DCA eatery. Because of crowds at the popular Soarin' over California attraction nearby, this is also the park's busiest restaurant.

DISNEYLAND RESORT RESTAURANTS:
Rated and Ranked

TO HELP YOU MAKE YOUR DINING CHOICES, we've developed profiles of full-service restaurants at Disneyland Resort. Each profile lets you quickly check the restaurant's cuisine, location, star rating, cost range, quality rating, and value rating. Profiles are listed alphabetically by restaurant. In addition to all full-service restaurants, we also list and profile a couple of delis and several self-serve restaurants in the theme parks that transcend basic burgers, hot dogs, and pizza.

STAR RATING The star rating represents the entire dining experience: style, service, and ambience, in addition to taste, presentation, and quality of food. Five stars, the highest rating, indicates that the restaurant offers the best of everything. Four-star restaurants are above average, and three-star restaurants offer good, though not necessarily memorable, meals. Two-star restaurants serve mediocre fare, and one-star restaurants are below average. (Our star ratings don't correspond to ratings awarded by AAA, Mobil, Zagat, or other restaurant reviewers.)

COST RANGE The next rating tells how much a complete meal will cost: a main dish with vegetable or side dish and a choice of soup or salad. Appetizers, desserts, drinks, and tips aren't included. We've rated the cost as inexpensive, moderate, or expensive.

Inexpensive	$12 or less per person
Moderate	$13–$23 per person
Expensive	More than $23 per person

QUALITY RATING The food quality is rated on a scale of one to five stars, five being the best. The quality rating is based on the taste, freshness of ingredients, preparation, presentation, and creativity of food served. There is no consideration of price. If you want the best food available and cost is no issue, you need look no further than the quality ratings.

VALUE RATING If, on the other hand, you are looking for both quality and value, check the value rating, also expressed as stars.

★★★★★	Exceptional value; a real bargain
★★★★	Good value
★★★	Fair value; you get exactly what you pay for
★★	Somewhat overpriced
★	Significantly overpriced

PAYMENT All Disney restaurants accept American Express, Master-Card, VISA, Diners Club, Discover, the Disney Credit Card, and JCB (Japanese Credit Bureau).

BEER, WINE, AND MIXED DRINKS Available at all restaurants except those at Disneyland Park.

Ariel's Grotto ★★★

CHARACTER DINING   MODERATE   QUALITY ★★★   VALUE ★★★½

Disney's California Adventure; ☎ 714-781-DINE

Priority Seating Recommended. **When to go** Lunch and dinner. **Entree range** Fixed-price meals, $13.99–$20.99. **Service** ★★★★. **Friendliness** ★★★★½. **Liquor service** Adult beverages available at The Cove bar upstairs. **Dress** Casual. **Disabled access** Yes. **Customers** Theme-park and hotel guests. **Lunch and dinner** Daily, 10 a.m.–6 p.m.

SETTING AND ATMOSPHERE You're "under the sea" with bright 3-D ocean-themed murals, jellyfish lanterns, and seashell tables, all with views of the wharf, Paradise Lagoon, and Paradise Pier. The overstuffed semicircular booths along the back wall are the best seats in the house and well worth waiting for.

Disneyland Resort Restaurants by Cuisine

CUISINE	LOCATION	OVERALL RATING	COST	QUALITY RATING	VALUE RATING
AMERICAN					
Steakhouse 55*	Disneyland Hotel	★★★★	V. Exp	★★★★	★★★★
Hook's Pointe	Disneyland Hotel	★★★½	Exp	★★★½	★★★
Carnation Cafe*	Disneyland Park	★★½	Mod	★★½	★★½
Rainforest Cafe*	Downtown Disney	★★½	Mod	★★	★½
Plaza Inn*	Disneyland Park	★½	Mod	★½	★½
BARBECUE					
River Belle Terrace	Disneyland Park	★★	Mod	★★	★★
CALIFORNIA/FUSION					
Napa Rose	Grand Californian	★★★★½	V. Exp	★★★★½	★★★★
Vineyard Room	DCA	★★★★	Exp	★★★★½	★★★½
Storytellers Cafe*	Grand Californian	★★★★	Exp	★★★★	★★★
Wine Country Trattoria	DCA	★★★★	Mod	★★★★	★★★½
CAJUN/CREOLE					
Ralph Brennan's Jazz Cafe*.	Downtown Disney	★★★★	Mod	★★★★	★★★★
Café Orléans*	Disneyland Park	★★★½	Mod	★★★½	★★★★
Blue Bayou	Disneyland Park	★★★½	Exp	★★★½	★★½
House of Blues	Downtown Disney	★★	Mod	★★	★★
CHARACTER DINING					
Storytellers Cafe*	Grand Californian	★★★★	Exp	★★★★	★★★
PCH Grill*	Paradise Pier Hotel	★★★★	Mod	★★★½	★★★½
Ariel's Grotto	DCA	★★★	Mod	★★★	★★★½
Goofy's Kitchen*	Disneyland Hotel	★★½	Exp	★★	★★
Plaza Inn*	Disneyland Park	★½	Mod	★½	★½

CUISINE	LOCATION	OVERALL RATING	COST	QUALITY RATING	VALUE RATING
DELI/BAKERY					
La Brea Bakery & Cafe*	**Downtown Disney**	★★★	Inexp	★★½	★★★
Napolini Delicatessen*	**Downtown Disney**	★★½	Inexp	★★½	★½
HEALTHY/VEGETARIAN					
Pacific Wharf Cafe	**DCA**	★★★	Inexp	★★★	★★★★
ITALIAN					
Naples Restaurant & Pizzeria	**Downtown Disney**	★★½	Mod	★★½	★★½
Napolini Delicatessen	**Downtown Disney**	★★½	Inexp	★★½	★½
JAPANESE/SUSHI					
Yamabuki	**Paradise Pier Hotel**	★★	V. Exp	★★	★★
MEDITERRANEAN					
Catal Restaurant & Uva Bar*	**Downtown Disney**	★★★	Mod	★★★	★★★
MEXICAN					
Tortilla Jo's	**Downtown Disney**	★★★	Inexp	★★★	★★★½
Rancho del Zocalo Restaurante	**Disneyland Park**	★★	Inexp	★★	★★
PACIFIC RIM					
PCH Grill*	**Paradise Pier Hotel**	★★★★	Mod	★★★½	★★★½
STEAK					
Steakhouse 55*	**Disneyland Hotel**	★★★★	V. Exp	★★★★	★★★★

*Serves breakfast.

HOUSE SPECIALTIES American comfort foods include a generous portion of meat loaf and Cheddar mashed potatoes, along with a very tasty Avalon Caesar salad for adults. Kid favorites include a hot dog–mac-and-cheese combo, fish and chips, and "swell sketti" (spaghetti under a bland marinara sauce).

OTHER RECOMMENDATIONS Adults won't feel cheated by a decent selection of sandwiches, entrees, and salads (most notably a shrimp Cobb) when the kids insist on dining here.

SUMMARY AND COMMENTS In a word, Ariel's Grotto is *fun,* even for adults. Kids will love the fact that Ariel and two to four other Disney princesses—Snow White, Cinderella, Sleeping Beauty, or Belle from *Beauty and the Beast*—are on hand for pictures and autographs. One set price buys adults a starter soup or salad, main course, and dessert, or a kids' appetizer of celery and carrot sticks with ranch dressing, a main course, and dessert (slices of Granny Smith apples and caramel dipping sauce or fruit parfait). Even toddlers will enjoy the bright surroundings and nonthreatening character visits. Adults, if they feel the need, can escape upstairs to The Cove, the only full bar in the park, for a cocktail, glass of wine, or bottle of beer. Demand is high here for obvious reasons, so book your Priority Seating early and avoid the long waits in peak season.

Blue Bayou ★★★½

AMERICAN/CONTINENTAL   EXPENSIVE   QUALITY ★★★½   VALUE ★★½

Disneyland Park; ☎ 714-781-DINE

Priority Seating Required. **When to go** Early or late lunch, early evening. **Entree range** $19–$35. **Service** ★★★. **Friendliness** ★★★. **Dress** Casual. **Disabled access** Yes. **Lunch** Daily, 11 a.m.–4 p.m. **Dinner** Nightly, 5:30–10 p.m.

SETTING AND ATMOSPHERE The Blue Bayou overlooks Pirates of the Caribbean and maintains an appropriately dark, moist ambience. The best tables ring the perimeter and afford a view of the faux bayou, replete with fireflies flickering among the weeping willows and mangroves; dilapidated houseboats; and soft lantern lights. If you're not lucky enough to get a table bayou-side, there's still enough wrought iron, uneven lighting, and twilight allure to soften the most hardened soul.

HOUSE SPECIALTIES Five-pepper roasted prime rib of beef, Gulf-Stream jumboshrimp rémoulade, and Le Special de Monte Cristo sandwich.

OTHER RECOMMENDATIONS Buccaneer's short ribs, Tesoro Island chicken.

SUMMARY AND COMMENTS Easily the best restaurant in Disneyland Park, Blue Bayou is as close to fine dining as you'll get here. The restaurant fills quickly and stays busy, so make Priority Seatings before you leave home (up to 60 days in advance) or obtain a same-day Priority Seating at the restaurant door as soon as you get to the park. Although there's a children's menu, this isn't the place to bring wound-up or tired kids for a leisurely meal; they'll be bored, and eventually even the best-behaved youngsters will find something to do with the swords they just scored in the New Orleans Square gift shops. Tables are tightly packed, and nothing disrupts the busy servers more than wild kids up and out of their seats.

Blue Bayou is more of a place where adults can escape the noise and happy chaos in the rest of the park without having to exit the gates. We love the Monte Cristo sandwich, a deep-fried turkey, ham, and cheese creation you don't find on many menus these days. Side dishes, including the Blue Bayou potatoes, a house gratin, and fresh vegetables, are quite good as well. The Key lime pie is also a crowd-pleaser. Servers are Disney-pleasant, if a tad rushed by the constant bustle, but they're more than happy to accommodate the random request. And our hat is off to whoever bakes their dinner rolls—they're great! All things considered, this is a solid restaurant with the best, most satisfying adult menu in the park.

Café Orléans ★★★½

CAJUN/CREOLE	MODERATE	QUALITY ★★★½	VALUE ★★★★

Disneyland Park; ☎ **714-781-**DINE

Priority Seating Recommended. **When to go** Early or late lunch, early evening. **Entree range** $14–$16. **Service** ★★★½. **Friendliness** ★★★★. **Dress** Casual. **Disabled access** Yes. **Breakfast–dinner** Daily, 8 a.m.–midnight.

SETTING AND ATMOSPHERE Across the alley from Blue Bayou, Café Orléans overlooks the Rivers of America. There's a small patio and limited inside seating, but the tableside service offers a nice break from the serve-your-self and buffet options in the same price range. After a day of traipsing around the park, it's nice to kick back amid the wrought-iron and scrolled-wood accents.

HOUSE SPECIALTIES The chef's *pommes frites* have to be among the best sides in the park: traditional thick-cut French fries tossed with Parmesan cheese, garlic, and parsley and served with a mildly spicy Cajun rémoulade sauce. Breakfast beignets are also a treat.

OTHER RECOMMENDATIONS A decent French onion soup with a cap of melted Gruyère cheese; an artery-clogging Monte Cristo sandwich in two versions, traditional and three-cheese.

SUMMARY AND COMMENTS The *pommes frites* are worth the price of admission. If you don't eat anything else in the park your entire visit, try these. We like to hit Café Orléans for a midafternoon break, kick our feet up for a soda or iced tea, and pick through a plate of the fries while we people-watch. The small menu makes ordering easy, provided you bring a big appetite and aren't afraid of a little cholesterol and trans fat. The Monte Cristo sandwiches are as good as Blue Bayou's, and a few bucks cheaper. Kids will love the three-cheese version: Swiss, mozzarella, and double-cream Brie between thick slices of deep-fried egg-battered bread. The gumbo is passable, if a little bland, while the salads, including a black-ened-chicken Caesar and the Crescent City salad (a mix of baby spinach, field greens, caramelized pecans, roasted corn, grapes, orange slices, and pan-seared salmon in an orange-cilantro vinaigrette), are very good. For something a little different, try the crepes—paper-thin pancakes stuffed with a variety of fillings, including chicken gumbo and seafood. Servers can get a bit testy if the crowd is impatient, but only the truly sensitive will notice.

Carnation Cafe ★★½

| AMERICAN/SANDWICHES | MODERATE | QUALITY ★★½ | VALUE ★★½ |

Disneyland Park; ☎ 714-781-DINE

Priority Seating Recommended. **When to go** Breakfast or late lunch. **Entree range** $10–$20. **Service** ★★★½. **Friendliness** ★★★★. **Dress** Casual. **Disabled access** Yes. **Breakfast and lunch** Daily, 8 a.m.–2 p.m.

SETTING AND ATMOSPHERE A Main Street staple since the park opened in 1955, the Carnation Cafe serves up an American menu heavy (pun intended) with traditional favorites—chicken potpie and pot roast, pancakes and waffles, and "butcher block" sandwiches—in a parlor circa 1890. There's lots of brass, marble, and bright white accents, plus a terrific patio for people-watching.

HOUSE SPECIALTIES Chicken potpie, on the menu since forever, is a perennial favorite, with chunks of white-meat chicken, chopped veggies, and potato swimming in a sea of thick, creamy gravy and baked into a buttery, flaky piecrust.

OTHER RECOMMENDATIONS A nice selection of deli-style sandwiches, featuring ham, roast beef, or turkey piled on slabs of thick-cut shepherd's bread; dressed with mayo, lettuce, and tomato; and served with a dill-pickle slice and a choice of sides.

SUMMARY AND COMMENTS The Carnation Cafe is another compromise spot—a place where the adults can find a decent plate, the kids can choose from a spate of their favorites, and no one's going to go broke picking up the tab. Because of its central location along Main Street, close to bathrooms and right across from the locker facility, it gets wicked busy, so much so that it's not unusual to see waiting lines stretching down the street. Service is friendly and unusually patient; someone's briefed these young cast members on how an hour's wait and low blood sugar can erode a diner's mood. Once you're seated, the order comes quickly and with a smile. This place also serves one of the best cups of coffee in the Kingdom.

Catal Restaurant & Uva Bar ★★★

| MEDITERRANEAN | MODERATE | QUALITY ★★★ | VALUE ★★★ |

Downtown Disney; ☎ 714-774-4442; www.patinagroup.com/catal

Priority Seating Recommended. **When to go** Dinner. **Entree range** $19–$37. **Service** ★★★. **Friendliness** ★★½. **Liquor service** Full bar and extensive wine list. **Dress** Dressy casual. **Disabled access** Yes. **Hours** *Catal:* dinner, Sunday–Thursday, 5–10 p.m., Friday and Saturday until 11 p.m.; *Uva Bar:* breakfast, lunch, and dinner, Sunday–Thursday, 8 a.m.–10 p.m., Friday and Saturday until 11 p.m.

SETTING AND ATMOSPHERE Uva Bar, a circular open-air lounge, sits immediately outside the restaurant and is a good place for a quick bite (sans line) or a leisurely cocktail while you watch the crowds go by. Inside is an elegant Art Deco–inspired restaurant with hardwood floors, spacious dining areas, and fine accoutrements. There are two fireplaces and a large central bar; a narrow balcony with tables wraps around the entire top floor.

HOUSE SPECIALTIES Tapas, marinated Mediterranean-olive plate, and various small plates outside at the bar; rotisserie chicken in a sweet garlic au jus reduction and bone-in New York steak with béarnaise sauce inside.

OTHER RECOMMENDATIONS A huge and very tasty plate of paella with bay scallops, clams, mussels, shrimp, chicken, chorizo sausage, saffron rice, and garlic aioli; a Moroccan-inspired lamb shank with olive potatoes and lemon confit.

SUMMARY AND COMMENTS Catal and Uva Bar are a Patina Group pairing, one in a chain of eateries operated by celebrity chef Joachim Splichal. Despite their overblown descriptions and gourmandese, the menu is pretty straightforward. The small plates—mainly appetizers, salads, and a few pasta dishes—are better than the rest of the menu and a real value for the money. When the weather cooperates, Uva is the better of the two venues. Be cautious when ordering some of the more complex or unusual offerings, including the duck and rabbit: they can be very inconsistent and terribly fatty. Side dishes shine, though. Price notwithstanding, this is a very adult experience.

Goofy's Kitchen ★★½

CHARACTER DINING/BUFFET	EXPENSIVE	QUALITY ★★	VALUE ★★

Disneyland Hotel; ☎ 714-781-DINE

Priority Seating Recommended. **When to go** Anytime with the kids. **Entree range** $20–$30. **Service** ★★★★. **Friendliness** ★★★½. **Dress** Casual. **Disabled access** Yes. **Breakfast** Daily, 8–11:30 a.m. **Lunch** Daily, 12–4 p.m. **Dinner** Nightly, 5–10 p.m.

SETTING AND ATMOSPHERE "Goofy's" says it all. A bright, modern, and easy-to-navigate buffet makes it simple for Goofy and up to four other characters to "help" patrons fill their plates. Adults take one for the kids here: the energy is high, the food is just OK, and the bill is, well, too much. But children will love the bright neon lights, the slide-around booths, and the opportunity to choose everything that goes on their plates.

HOUSE SPECIALTIES Breakfast is your best bet. Selections such as character-shaped pancakes, waffles, and scrambled eggs hold up well under the heat lamps, and you can customize your own omelet. The kids will also flip for the peanut-butter-and-jelly pizza.

OTHER RECOMMENDATIONS Kids of all ages will like the yogurt bar, where you can mix and match flavors and toppings.

SUMMARY AND COMMENTS This is definitely a youth-oriented excursion—the noise can be deafening, and the food is an afterthought. Add a few costumed Disney characters, and any notion of control and calm fly right out the window (think Chuck E. Cheese times ten and a C-note expense for a family of four). Little ones will love a special birthday event here; call ahead for arrangements.

Hook's Pointe ★★★½

AMERICAN	EXPENSIVE	QUALITY ★★★½	VALUE ★★★

Disneyland Hotel; ☎ 714-781-DINE

Priority Seating Recommended. **When to go** Dinner with the kids. **Entree range** $20–$30. **Service** ★★★★. **Friendliness** ★★★½. **Liquor service** Wine list and full bar. **Dress** Casual. **Disabled access** Yes. **Dinner** Nightly, 5–10 p.m.

SETTING AND ATMOSPHERE Squint your eyes and imagine, just for a moment, that you're dining with the infamous Captain Hook in his quarters aboard his notorious pirate ship, the *Jolly Roger*. It's not that far a reach at Hook's Pointe—though it probably smells better than the imaginary quarters thanks to the pungent aroma of the mesquite grill. Surrounded by the lush grounds of the Never Land Pool, this little bistro offers a comfortable respite with a little something for everyone.

HOUSE SPECIALTIES Management hesitates to call Hook's Pointe a fish house, but there's a large selection of seafood on the menu, most of it good. The ahi tuna has an Asian-influenced ginger glaze, the grilled shrimp comes with a tangy citrus sauce, and the grilled salmon is finished with a tomato-based vinaigrette.

OTHER RECOMMENDATIONS An excellent selection of appetizers, including a really good calamari dish and a crab-and-spinach spread on pita bread. If you want to hold out for something other than fish for the main course, the Kansas City pork chop is a real treat, thick and juicy (when it's not overdone), and the Thunder Cove penne (pasta with portobello mushrooms, fresh vegetables, and feta cheese tossed in olive oil, shallots, and garlic) is terrific.

SUMMARY AND COMMENTS Another great compromise restaurant, sure to please everyone on the dinner guest list. Kids will love the setting and ambience, and if they haven't yet had their fill of mac and cheese, burgers, and chicken strips, they don't have to ponder the menu for long. Adults, too, will appreciate the subtlety of the decor, both for its comfort and appeal to the younger generation and for the original recipes exiting the kitchen. The mesquite-grilled specialties are sure bets, simple and full of zest.

House of Blues ★★

CAJUN/CREOLE	MODERATE	QUALITY ★★	VALUE ★★

Downtown Disney; ☎ 714-778-BLUE;
www.hob.com/venues/clubvenues/anaheim

Priority Seating Recommended. **When to go** Dinner. **Entree range** $11–$28. **Service** ★★★. **Friendliness** ★★½. **Liquor service** Wine list and full bar. **Dress** Casual. **Disabled access** Yes. **Dinner** Nightly, 7–11 p.m.

SETTING AND ATMOSPHERE Think rustic-but-trendy blues club somewhere along the Mississippi River, maybe St. Louis. It's dark except for outside patios and a second-story terrace, with hardwood floors, small, intimate tables, and indirect lighting.

HOUSE SPECIALTIES The finger food is always safe, and the sandwiches, especially the Blues burger and the shrimp po'boy, are worth a taste.

OTHER RECOMMENDATIONS The Elwood blackened-chicken sandwich, jambalaya, red beans and rice with sausage.

SUMMARY AND COMMENTS The House of Blues is first and foremost a major concert site, with marquee names, up-and-comers, and strong local talent taking the stage every night. Food is a secondary thought. Tables are small and scrunched close together for maximum capacity. It's best to stick with the basics: finger foods, sandwiches, and salads. Some of the decidedly Southern fare, such as the jambalaya and fried chicken with country gravy, is pretty good, but you won't leave raving about the food. And unless stated otherwise, this is strictly an adult venue (18 and older).

La Brea Bakery & Cafe ★★★

BAKERY/DELI	INEXPENSIVE	QUALITY ★★½	VALUE ★★★

Downtown Disney; ☎ 714-490-4233; www.labreabakery.com/cafes

Priority Seating Available. **When to go** Breakfast. **Entree range** $7–$26. **Service** ★★. **Friendliness** ★★. **Dress** Casual. **Disabled access** Yes. **Breakfast–dinner** Sunday–Friday, 8 a.m.–9 p.m., Saturday until 11 p.m.; express dining, Sunday–Friday until 10 p.m., Saturday until 11 p.m.

SETTING AND ATMOSPHERE This indoor-outdoor space is rich with the yeasty aromas of breads and cakes, plus whiffs of herbs and spices. Hardwood floors and large glass display counters distinguish the dining room. A pleasant patio with colorful umbrellas fronting the cafe is the perfect perch for a quick cappuccino and pastry while you watch the hordes head to work or play in the parks.

HOUSE SPECIALTIES For breakfast, nothing beats a crumbly maple-walnut scone or a big, yeasty fruit muffin and your coffee drink of choice. The panini sandwiches at lunch and dinner are better than the ones across the way at Napolini.

OTHER RECOMMENDATIONS Take home one or more loaves of the artisanal breads to snack on later. Or try this sandwich on for size: thick sourdough layered with warm shaved Parmesan and Gruyère cheeses and grilled, marinated white asparagus.

SUMMARY AND COMMENTS It's all about the bread . . . and the muffins, pastries, scones, desserts, and anything else containing baked flour and yeast. Breakfast is the obvious time to enjoy La Brea Bakery (they also serve a mean cup of joe), and if you must supplement your daily carbohydrate fix, you can add an egg dish (the omelets are good) and a side of bacon or sausage. At lunch and dinner, the salads and sandwiches take over. Servers seem a little more impatient than most; you'll notice a big difference from the smiling Disneyites inside the parks. It's a great place to gather the troops before a long day inside the parks or as a midday escape. Get there early—it's the first eatery at the east end of the resort entrance, and a popular starting (and ending) place for tourists and locals alike.

Napa Rose ★★★★½

CALIFORNIA/FUSION	VERY EXPENSIVE	QUALITY ★★★★½	VALUE ★★★★

Grand Californian Hotel; ☎ 714-781-DINE

Priority Seating Recommended. **When to go** Dinner. **Entree range** $29–$75. **Service** ★★★★★. **Friendliness** ★★★★. **Liquor service** Impressive wine list. **Dress** Dressy casual. **Disabled access** Yes. **Dinner** Nightly, 5–10 p.m.

SETTING AND ATMOSPHERE The Napa Rose is Disneyland Resort's flagship fine-dining experience. The Grand Californian's Craftsman theme is carried into this premier room with sweeping views of Disney's California Adventure from virtually every table. A large, open demonstration kitchen lets you watch the magic happen, and wine, in all of its glory, is displayed at every turn. Fine linens, china, and flatware are the norm. This is an absolutely gorgeous room with food and service to match.

HOUSE SPECIALTIES The menu, rotated seasonally, focuses on the cuisine of California's wine region, ranch lands, farm belts, and coastline. Wine finds its way onto most of the menu in sauces, reductions, infusions, and dressings. The grilled Angus New York strip steak features an understated Cabernet reduction; ocean trout (a hearty, full-bodied cousin of the freshwater trout) is crusted with cashews and served with baked apples and sautéed coastal mushrooms.

OTHER RECOMMENDATIONS Game meat, ranch and free-range beef and poultry, and the chef's prix fixe Vintner's Table are constantly changing and always exciting.

SUMMARY AND COMMENTS Napa Rose may be the best restaurant in Anaheim and has been at the top of most critics' lists since its debut. Top talent in the kitchen and in the dining room—a beautiful space with panoramic views and a wine cellar second to none—make this an incomparable gustatory experience. Every server has earned sommelier status, a designation that takes years of study and practical experience with wine and winemaking. Look for unusual ingredients (Tahitian vanilla, smoked sturgeon, truffled quail eggs, lemongrass, almond oil) married to top-notch staples (Colorado lamb, Berkshire pork, pheasant breast, white asparagus), all deftly handled by a world-class kitchen crew. And although staff are very accommodating in the usual Disney manner, this is definitely not an adventure for the kids.

Naples Restaurant & Pizzeria ★★½

ITALIAN	MODERATE	QUALITY ★★½	VALUE ★★½

Downtown Disney; ☎ 714-766-6200; www.patinagroup.com/naples

Priority Seating Recommended. **When to go** Late lunch or early dinner. **Entree range** $14–$32. **Service** ★★. **Friendliness** ★★½. **Liquor service** Extensive wine list and full bar. **Dress** Casual. **Disabled access** Yes. **Lunch and dinner** Sunday–Thursday, 11 a.m.–10 p.m.; Friday and Saturday until 11 p.m.

SETTING AND ATMOSPHERE Food aside, this is a really fun restaurant: modern, colorful, and spacious, with tile floors, an open demonstration kitchen, and whimsical design touches that mirror nearby Disneyland. It's also noisy and crowded, typically filled with families. During peak hours, it's difficult to hear yourself think, let alone carry on a meaningful conversation. Nonetheless, it's a great gathering place, and there's something to appeal to everyone from small children to adults.

HOUSE SPECIALTIES Wood-fired Neapolitan-style pizzas: thin, crispy crusts with a hearty, almost spicy red sauce; handmade mozzarella cheese; and fresh toppings of choice.

OTHER RECOMMENDATIONS The family-style dinners give you a choice of salads, soups, and pasta (think tubs of spaghetti and four-cheese ravioli) served en masse and, if everyone can agree, make a great bargain.

SUMMARY AND COMMENTS Another Patina–Joachim Splichal venture where most of the effort went into the design. While the menu seems sophisticated, the recipes are rather bland and uninspired with a few exceptions. Some of the nonpasta entrees—pan-roasted white fish with fennel-and-tomato vinaigrette and a citrus-and-herb-rubbed chicken, for example—are the real highlights. The kids will enjoy the colorful decor and activities (the occasional balloon-animal artist makes tableside visits); adults can get a good glass of wine or a cocktail and feed the entire crew for less than $100.

Napolini Delicatessen ★★½

ITALIAN/DELI	INEXPENSIVE	QUALITY ★★½	VALUE ★½

Downtown Disney; ☎ 714-766-6200

Priority Seating None—first come, first served. When to go Lunch or a quick dinner. Entree range $7–$12. Service ★★. Friendliness ★★½. Liquor service Wine and beer only. Dress Casual. Disabled access Yes. Breakfast–dinner Sunday–Thursday, 8 a.m.–10 p.m.; Friday and Saturday until midnight.

SETTING AND ATMOSPHERE This is next-door Naples's cousin—a quick-in, quick-out deli with most of what you'd expect, from swinging salamis to large jars of peppers. Counter and table service are sketchy and poorly supervised.

HOUSE SPECIALTIES Wood-fired Neapolitan-style pizzas, paninis, and salads.

OTHER RECOMMENDATIONS The pastas are hit or miss—the angel hair with pesto was terrific, while the rigatoni in marinara was a gooey, uninspired mess.

SUMMARY AND COMMENTS Don't set your expectations too high and you won't be disappointed here. Best bet is the paninis—grilled sandwiches on thick Italian bread, loaded to order with salami, veggies, peppers, onions, and such. Servers get flustered easily, and order mistakes are common (our guess is that Napolini serves as a training ground for Naples). Noise spills over from Naples on busy nights, as do impatient diners who don't want to wait for a table next door, making for a volatile mix that can have you feeling very uncomfortable in a hurry. But maybe that's the plan: to get you in with the sweet, spicy aromas of Italian cooking and then out quickly.

Pacific Wharf Cafe ★★★

HEALTHY/VEGETARIAN	INEXPENSIVE	QUALITY ★★★	VALUE ★★★★

Disney's California Adventure; ☎ 714-781-DINE

Priority Seating Not available. When to go Lunch and dinner. Entree range $4.99–$19. Service ★★. Friendliness ★★★. Dress Casual. Liquor service Beers on tap, substantial wine list. Disabled access Yes. Lunch and dinner Daily, 10 a.m.–6 p.m.

SETTING AND ATMOSPHERE A little slice of pier life, Cape Cod–style, with wooden floors, large wooden-framed windows amid blue-and-white trim, and hurricane lamps.

HOUSE SPECIALTIES Fresh soups and salads served in large, hollowed-out sourdough loaves for grown-ups, and comfort foods such as burgers, hot dogs, and mac and cheese for the kids. The crab Louis and the Mexican Caesar are very popular, as is the signature creamy mushroom soup.

OTHER RECOMMENDATIONS If you're really hungry, go for a rack of the barbecued baby back ribs: double-cut pork, slow-roasted with a lip-smackingly sweet-and-sour sauce and served with "Cali" slaw (the usual cabbage mix with a tangy white balsamic–honey dressing). Or try the half-pound Big Kahuna burger with avocado and bacon. For dessert, there's a killer sundae that starts with ten scoops of ice cream and concludes with the kitchen sink (it's easier to tell them what you *don't* want on it).

SUMMARY AND COMMENTS This is another great compromise restaurant, with food and ambience that adults will appreciate as well as a very kid-friendly menu (burgers, chicken strips, pizza). The real lure for kids? Ice cream! The Pacific Wharf serves up a host of specialty sundaes, including the aforementioned, a hefty banana split, and a pastry–ice cream hybrid called the Kilauea Molten Apple Pie. A full view of Paradise Cove and friendly Disney service make this an easy place to gather for a snack, a full-blown meal, or a dessert that won't bankrupt you.

PCH Grill ★★★★

PACIFIC RIM	MODERATE	QUALITY ★★★½	VALUE ★★★½

**Disneyland Paradise Pier Hotel, 1717 South Disneyland Drive;
☎ 714-781-DINE**

Priority Seating Available. **When to go** Breakfast and dinner. **Entree range** $20–$30. **Service ★★★★. Friendliness ★★★½. Liquor service** Wine and beer. **Dress** Casual. **Disabled access** Yes. **Breakfast and dinner** Daily, 6:30–10:30 a.m., 5–11 p.m.

SETTING AND ATMOSPHERE A taste of Southern California beach life: bright primary colors, potted palms, and decorative elements such as surfboards and beach chairs.

HOUSE SPECIALTIES Wood-fired pizzas, sake-marinated black sea bass.

OTHER RECOMMENDATIONS Panko shrimp in mango sauce.

SUMMARY AND COMMENTS If you can take one more character breakfast, this time with Lilo and Stitch, get the kids up early and hit the "beach." The food improves at dinner, when the chef breaks out his Pacific Rim and Asian-fusion menus. While parents can get their fill of sushi appetizers and exotic fish dishes, kids can stick with burgers and design-your-own pizzas.

Plaza Inn ★½

CHARACTER DINING	MODERATE	QUALITY ★½	VALUE ★½

Disneyland Park; ☎ 714-781-DINE

Priority Seating Recommended. **When to go** When you're desperate, the kids insist, or you arrive right at the meal switch. **Entree range** $10–$20. **Service** ★★½. **Friendliness** ★★. **Dress** Casual. **Disabled access** Yes. **Breakfast–dinner** Daily, 8 a.m.–midnight.

SETTING AND ATMOSPHERE   Probably the high point of your meal at the Plaza Inn is the gorgeous Victorian-B&B ambience—comfortable, widely spaced tables in a spacious dining room with lots of brocade and brass. A pleasant patio with huge umbrellas rings the east end of the circle at the top of Main Street.

HOUSE SPECIALTIES   The steam tables are hit or-miss; see if you can catch something being freshly delivered. Best bets are the pot roast and the broasted chicken.

OTHER RECOMMENDATIONS   The little ones will love the character breakfast hosted by Minnie Mouse and two to four other characters. Adults will suffer through rubbery pancakes and soggy bacon.

SUMMARY AND COMMENTS   Don't expect fine dining when you book a table at the Plaza Inn. Unless you hit this place right when everything comes fresh, during the transitions from breakfast to lunch and from lunch to dinner, it's your basic been-in-the-steam-table-too-long scenario. A lot of effort goes into making the food look enticing, but huge sacrifices are made in the taste and texture departments.

Rainforest Cafe   ★★½

AMERICAN	MODERATE	QUALITY ★★	VALUE ★½

Downtown Disney; ☎ 714-772-0413; www.rainforestcafe.com

Priority Seating Not available. **When to go** Lunch or dinner. **Entree range** $7–$28. **Service** ★★. **Friendliness** ★★★. **Dress** Casual. **Liquor service** Full bar. **Disabled access** Yes. **Breakfast–dinner** Sunday–Thursday, 8 a.m.–10:30 p.m.; Friday and Saturday until midnight.

SETTING AND ATMOSPHERE   Couldn't get enough of the Jungle Cruise next door *and* you're starving? Exit the park and head to the Rainforest Cafe, a lush tropical experience that attracts a few thousand of your fellow diners on a daily basis. Take a safari through the winding sections of greenery, faux wildlife, and piped-in jungle sounds, and wade through a menu as large as the Orinoco Basin.

HOUSE SPECIALTIES   Stick to the basics: burgers, simple sandwiches, and salads. The Jungle Chopped Salad—a huge mix of romaine and iceberg greens, olives, cucumbers, cranberries, candied pecans, red cabbage, carrots, crumbled blue cheese, and grilled chicken in a raspberry vinaigrette—is arguably the best one on the menu.

OTHER RECOMMENDATIONS   The Mojo Bones (barbecued baby back ribs) are tasty; the Volcano chocolate dessert (complete with sparkler top) is gargantuan but irresistible. The sandwich wraps are also recommended.

SUMMARY AND COMMENTS   If the Adventureland experience just doesn't satisfy your lust for all things green, moist, and lush, this is the place for you. The menu is massive (maybe a little too large) and mostly palatable, but none of it is truly great. They do make up in quantity for any lack of quality; plates are enough for two in most circumstances. Children love the rain-forest theme, and you can count on any number of the chain's signature animal characters to show up during the meal for photo ops and a little interaction with the kiddies. All in all, a bit distracting—but maybe that's the point.

Ralph Brennan's Jazz Cafe ★★★★

| CAJUN/CREOLE | MODERATE | QUALITY ★★★★ | VALUE ★★★★ |

Downtown Disney; ☎ 714-775-5200; www.rbjazzkitchen.com

Priority Seating Available. **When to go** Lunch or dinner. **Entree range** $13–$25. **Service** ★★. **Friendliness** ★★★. **Liquor service** Full bar. **Dress** Casual. **Disabled access** Yes. **Hours** *Express breakfast:* daily, 8–10 a.m.; *lunch:* daily, 11 a.m.–4, p.m.; *dinner:* Sunday–Thursday, 4:30–10 p.m., Friday and Saturday until 11 p.m.; *Sunday zydeco jazz brunch:* 11 a.m.–4 p.m.

SETTING AND ATMOSPHERE Take a step back in time and space to the 19th-century French Quarter of New Orleans. Almost half the seating area is an open-air courtyard surrounded by wrought iron, hanging ferns, and milled hardwood. Above a small stage where live jazz plays daily, there's a pounded-copper ceiling; to stage left is a beautiful enamel-finished grand piano. You can people-watch from a balcony dining area, but no matter where you sit, you're going to enjoy the ambience.

HOUSE SPECIALTIES We loved the blackened-chicken ravioli: white-meat chicken blackened on the grill and served over deep-fried pillows of cheese-stuffed pasta in a pumpkin-pesto sauce. The pecan-crusted catfish—a fillet crusted with pecan flour and panfried—is served with sweet-potato dirty rice and spaghetti squash.

OTHER RECOMMENDATIONS Shrimp Creole, filet mignon with Creole spice rub, and pasta jambalaya are all good.

SUMMARY AND COMMENTS This is one of our favorite restaurants in or immediately around the resort. As the Brennan family is intimately involved with every aspect of the menu, both its authenticity and execution are exceptional. Servers, including actual Southerners and even a smattering of Louisiana natives, exude laid-back, gracious attitude without missing a lick. Add live jazz to the mix (the zydeco brunch is really fun), and you have one of Disneyland's ultimate dining experiences. Small children (and probably even preteens and teens) aren't going to appreciate the finer qualities here—this is a dining experience best suited to adults.

Rancho del Zocalo Restaurante ★★

| MEXICAN | INEXPENSIVE | QUALITY ★★ | VALUE ★★ |

Disneyland Park; ☎ 714-781-DINE

Priority Seating Not available. **When to go** Early lunch or early dinner. **Entree range** $10–$20. **Service** ★★½. **Friendliness** ★★★. **Dress** Casual. **Disabled access** Yes. **Lunch and dinner** Daily, 11 a.m.–10 p.m.

SETTING AND ATMOSPHERE Welcome to the hacienda! Faux adobe, open wooden beams, and Mexican tilework ring a dark interior and covered outdoor patio. Tucked away from the throngs and major thoroughfares in the northeast area of Frontierland, this can be a nice, quiet place for a meal.

HOUSE SPECIALTIES The enchiladas are quite good, probably because they lend themselves to the buffet-style dining here.

OTHER RECOMMENDATIONS Hit or miss: if you can catch a tray of tacos, burritos, or grilled chicken fresh from the commissary, you score.

SUMMARY AND COMMENTS Three words sum up the Zocalo: "Mexican, cafeteria-style." On the bright side, most of the cuisine holds up well under the heat lamps and over the steam tables, the enchiladas and grilled chicken in particular. The rest of the menu—the typical tacos, burritos, Mexican rice, and refried beans—is resolutely average, except at opening or right before the dinner rush, when the food is fresh and uncorrupted. The tortillas, both corn and flour, are pretty tasty. Zocalo is also a great choice when you've brought the kids along and you can't possibly choke down another hot dog, burger, or pizza slice.

River Belle Terrace ★★

WESTERN/BARBECUE	MODERATE	QUALITY ★★	VALUE ★★

Disneyland Park; ☎ 714-781-DINE

Priority Seating Not available **When to go** Breakfast and snacks. **Entree range** $10–$20. **Service** ★★½. **Friendliness** ★★★. **Dress** Casual. **Disabled access** Yes. **Breakfast–dinner** Daily, 9 a.m.–10 p.m.

SETTING AND ATMOSPHERE The decor befits the River Belle Terrace's location in the heart of Frontierland. Abundant wrought iron and wood siding suggest an elegant Western façade. Inside, large shuttered windows belie a small dining area; most of the seating is outdoors on a large patio covered with colorful umbrellas.

HOUSE SPECIALTIES The pancakes, country potatoes, and bacon are diner favorites. Little kids love the Mickey-shaped peanut-butter-and-jelly sandwiches.

OTHER RECOMMENDATIONS Barbecued items, including chicken and ribs, are messy-but-perfect "tweener" food ('tween lunch and dinner).

SUMMARY AND COMMENTS This original eatery survives by keeping the menu fresh and flexible. Disney lore places Walt himself here every morning for a breakfast of Mickey pancakes, scrambled eggs, bacon and sausage, and large, scrumptious cinnamon rolls dripping with buttercream frosting. We like this place for light lunches or dinners, when you don't want to take a lot of time for a formal sit-down meal. Grab a rack of ribs, a PB&J or a couple of mini–corn dogs for the kids, and a tall lemonade, and people-watch from the patio.

Steakhouse 55 ★★★★

AMERICAN	VERY EXPENSIVE	QUALITY ★★★★	VALUE ★★★★

Disneyland Hotel; ☎ 714-781-DINE

Priority Seating Recommended. **When to go** Breakfast or dinner. **Entree range** $22–$49. **Service** ★★★★★. **Friendliness** ★★★★. **Liquor service** Award-winning wine list and full bar. **Dress** Dressy casual. **Disabled access** Yes. **Breakfast** Daily, 8–11:30 a.m. **Lunch** Daily, 11:30 a.m.–2:30 p.m. **Dinner** Nightly, 5–10 p.m.

SETTING AND ATMOSPHERE Steakhouse 55 is a classic American steak house with large, overstuffed booths; white-linen napkins and tablecloths; and rich wood accents. The aroma of sizzling meat permeates the air, and servers are more than happy to show you the steak the chef is about to grill for you.

HOUSE SPECIALTIES Beef: it's what's for dinner! Classic Certified Angus cuts such as New York, filet mignon, and bone-in rib eye (with a signature spice rub) are sure bets. Breakfast is surprisingly good; the huevos rancheros (eggs, black beans, pico de gallo, guacamole, and sour cream) are a satisfying gut buster.

OTHER RECOMMENDATIONS If you're not in the mood for red meat, the fish is fresh and always good. The baby-spinach salad, served with a warm applewood-smoked-bacon vinaigrette, is deliciously simple and an excellent starter.

SUMMARY AND COMMENTS The old Granville's changed its name but not its menu when it became Steakhouse 55. It's still the best-kept secret in Anaheim, and the second best steak restaurant. The menu and decor are straightforward and pleasingly simple, just as they should be at a steak house. Any of the beef cuts are sure to please depending on your taste—the filet: no flavor but butter tender; the bone-in rib eye: massive; the New York strip: hearty and full-blooded. The service is Disney-efficient and always accompanied by a smile. And although there's a kids' menu, it's best to feed the little ones early and leave them at your hotel room—you'll want to linger a while here, maybe over a glass of Cognac.

Storytellers Cafe ★★★★

CALIFORNIA CUISINE/CHARACTER DINING EXPENSIVE QUALITY ★★★★ VALUE ★★★

Grand Californian Hotel; ☎ 714-781-DINE

Priority Seating Recommended. **When to go** Breakfast or dinner. **Entree range** $20–$30. **Service** ★★★★★. **Friendliness** ★★★★. **Liquor service** Extensive wine list and full bar. **Dress** Casual. **Disabled access** Yes. **Breakfast–dinner** Daily, 8 a.m.–10 p.m.

SETTING AND ATMOSPHERE The Storytellers Cafe carries the Grand Californian's Arts and Crafts theme throughout, with large, open beams; natural wood and wood carvings; milled stone; and stained glass. The walls are adorned with impressive murals depicting the state's rich literary history, from Mark Twain's "The Celebrated Jumping Frog of Calaveras County" to Scott O'Dell's *Island of the Blue Dolphins.*

HOUSE SPECIALTIES Children under age 10 will love the character breakfast. Chip 'n' Dale, Goofy, and other Disney celebrities visit the tables, sign autographs, and pose for photos between bites of omelets, waffles, and hotcakes. Wood-fired pizzas at lunch and for dinner are also exceptionally tasty.

OTHER RECOMMENDATIONS Health-conscious diners will love the cafe's salads, such as the Storyteller's Salad (baby greens, white asparagus, and orange slices topped with a white-balsamic vinaigrette). The chicken melt is one of the best sandwiches on the planet, and if you like barbecue, don't miss the rack of Santa Maria–style baby back ribs.

SUMMARY AND COMMENTS You may experience a little sticker shock at first, but there's real value here. It's not quite on par with Napa Rose across the way, but the same dedication to quality and originality are in evidence in everything from the menu to the service. Kids will find lots to like about the menu, along with enough distractions between the colorful menus, murals, and character visits to let the adults enjoy a wide range of menu options (from pastas to steaks to fresh fish) and a leisurely cocktail or glass of wine. You'll want to save some room for dessert, too—who could pass up warm seasonal-fruit cobbler heaped with vanilla ice cream or a chocolate fondue for two (or more) with pound cake, biscotti, assorted chopped fruit, and banana fritters?

Tortilla Jo's ★★★

MEXICAN	INEXPENSIVE	QUALITY ★★★	VALUE ★★★½

Downtown Disney; ☎ 714-535-5000; www.patinagroup.com/tortillajos

Priority Seating Available. When to go Lunch or dinner. Entree range $7–$20. Service ★★½. Friendliness ★★★. Liquor service Full bar. Dress Casual. Disabled access Yes. Lunch and dinner Sunday–Thursday, 11 a.m.–10 p.m., Friday and Saturday until 11 p.m.; *taqueria:* Sunday–Thursday, 11 a.m.–11:30 p.m., Friday and Saturday until 1 a.m.

SETTING AND ATMOSPHERE Old-world Mexico meets California modern. Mexican touchstones like glazed tiles; thick, crude glass; and wrought iron accent a sweeping, open dining room with modern, eclectic touches. There's a taqueria where you can grab a quick bite on the run and an outdoor cantina where the bartender pours from a huge selection of more than 100 premium and super-premium tequilas. The place goes crazy on the weekends, so gird yourself for a raucous, booze-shooting, beer-chasing good time.

HOUSE SPECIALTIES Start with the *queso fundido,* a pot of melted cheese plumped up with diced tomatoes and poblano chiles, and/or a bowl of the guacamole. The Yucatan chicken, a rotisserie half-bird with a red-chile glaze and caramelized pineapple, is delicious, as are the fiery habanero-tequila pork ribs.

OTHER RECOMMENDATIONS Try the *tortas,* Mexican-style sandwiches served on traditional *telera* bread. The chicken torta is made with sliced chicken breast, homemade mango-banana salsa, and chipotle mayonnaise; the steak version comes with grilled *carne asada,* fresh Mexican soft cheese, red onion, tomato, avocado, and lettuce.

SUMMARY AND COMMENTS Another Patina Group eatery from über-chef Joachim Splichal, Tortilla Jo's is upscale Mexican with a culinary twist. The menu is grounded in the dishes we know and love, including soft tacos, burritos, carnitas, and fajitas, but Splichal and his minions put their twist on just about everything. Of all the Patina Group restaurants in Downtown Disney, this one is the best and the most fun. The menu (and the loosey-goosey crowd) may be too much for the kids, but adults will appreciate a shot of Sauza Comemorativo tequila and a long, tall glass of ice-cold Corona beer.

Vineyard Room ★★★★

CALIFORNIA NOUVELLE   EXPENSIVE   QUALITY ★★★★½   VALUE ★★★½

Disney's California Adventure; ☎ 714-781-DINE

Priority Seating Recommended. **When to go** Dinner. **Entree range** $15–$34. **Service** ★★★★. **Friendliness** ★★★½. **Liquor service** Varied wine list, beer, and full bar. **Dress** Casual. **Disabled access** Yes. **Dinner** Friday–Sunday, 5–10 p.m.

SETTING AND ATMOSPHERE All the tables here are on the "patio," a partially enclosed room with space heaters and air-conditioning for weather extremes. Tile, adobe, and wrought iron adorn this hacienda-style eatery; simple sconces and chandeliers call to mind Champagne flutes. It's either a little short on ambience or elegantly simple, depending on your take and taste, especially as DCA's flagship restaurant. But all the requisite fine-dining touches are here, including white-linen table-cloths, elegant flatware, and expensive china.

HOUSE SPECIALTIES Executive chef Gloria Tae and *chef de cuisine* Janine Ruozi design and execute a nightly three-course menu complemented by matching wines, mostly from California's Central Coast. Chilled watermelon soup, pan-roasted filet, and peach-berry parfait exemplify an evening's fare.

OTHER RECOMMENDATIONS The rib-eye steak with sweet-corn gratin, balsamic fried onions, haricots verts, and Cabernet demi-glacé.

SUMMARY AND COMMENTS Easily the best restaurant in either park, the Vineyard Room is foodie heaven. The menu is well thought out and expertly executed, with such delights as five-spice double-cut pork chops, braised lamb shank, and a tantalizing fennel-and-coriander-crusted ahi steak. Among the starter selections are fresh salads, a really tasty pan-roasted whole artichoke, and various soups. Small plates include sliced-to-order prosciutto with grilled marinated figs and shaved pecorino cheese, and an Asian-influenced crispy quail with orange glaze and garlic coleslaw. Sitting above the fray on the second story of Disney's California Adventure's Wine Country, the Vineyard Room is a quiet oasis where you can enjoy a glass (or bottle) of fine wine or a cocktail and savor a leisurely meal. There's a limited kids' menu, but make no mistake: as with other higher-end eateries in the parks, this is a very grown-up experience.

Wine Country Trattoria ★★★★

CALIFORNIA NOUVELLE   MODERATE   QUALITY ★★★★   VALUE ★★★½

Disney's California Adventure; ☎ 714-781-DINE

Priority Seating Recommended. **When to go** Lunch or dinner. **Entree range** $5–$13. **Service** ★★. **Friendliness** ★★. **Liquor service** Wine and beer. **Dress** Casual. **Disabled access** Yes. **Lunch and dinner** Daily, 11 a.m.–9:30 p.m.

SETTING AND ATMOSPHERE Whether you choose the patio outside or the "patio" inside, this spacious bistro captures the California-casual mood, complete with an open kitchen. Plenty of tile, wood, and trellised greenery whisk you away from downtown Anaheim and posit you in the middle of California wine country. This is yet another easy place for adults to park for a while and get away from the frantic pace of the amusement park.

HOUSE SPECIALTIES Any of the entree salads, the panini-style chicken sandwich, and three kinds of lasagna.

OTHER RECOMMENDATIONS Meatball sandwich.

SUMMARY AND COMMENTS The Trattoria is a popular spot for a light meal and a glass of wine, and sometimes the waitstaff shows the stress of the constant pressure of so much volume. The pizzetta salad—a large plate of fresh romaine lettuce, Roma tomatoes, Kalamata olives, crumbled blue cheese, and a light, creamy Italian dressing over warm pizza-dough crust—is terrific and big enough for the heartiest appetite. The lasagnas are disappointing, with gooey, overcooked pasta; skimpy layers of meat, vegetables, and cheese; and limp, unremarkable sauces. The premeal basket of breads is fresh and unique: a sampler of thick-crusted herbed sourdough, spiced breadsticks, and olive bread served with a tasty olive tapenade. There's a decent selection of wines by the glass and beer, with an affinity toward California varietals and popular brews. In our opinion the second-best restaurant at the theme parks, Wine Country Trattoria appeals more to adults without children. Compared with other options, it's likely to bore kids quickly.

Yamabuki ★★

JAPANESE/SUSHI	VERY EXPENSIVE	QUALITY ★★	VALUE ★★

Disneyland Paradise Pier Hotel, 1717 South Disneyland Drive;
☎ **714-781-**DINE

Priority Seating Recommended. **When to go** Lunch or dinner. **Entree range** $12–$49. **Service** ★★½. **Friendliness** ★★★. **Liquor service** Good wine selection and full bar. **Dress** Casual. **Disabled access** Yes. **Lunch** Daily, 11:30 a.m.–2 p.m. **Dinner** Nightly, 5:30–8:30 p.m.

SETTING AND ATMOSPHERE A traditional Japanese dinner house with low-slung tables, paper lanterns, and geisha-attired servers. Beautiful at night.

HOUSE SPECIALTIES Sushi bar with most of what you'd expect, from California rolls to more-exotic fare such as eel and octopus; teriyaki beef and chicken.

OTHER RECOMMENDATIONS The sukiyaki is passable and a communal dish that many will like, especially if you like to play with your food.

SUMMARY AND COMMENTS Very inconsistent—good one day and absolutely terrible the next. The pricey sushi bar is good for a few standards, not so much for other dishes (one evening's vinegared rice was like little bricks of pure rice vinegar; the next evening's was pasty with nary a hint of vinegar). Service is also spotty, gracious enough but often slow and unresponsive. Stick to the basics such as teriyaki and tempura, and you take less of a risk. On a high note, the kids' *bento* (box) menus are a real hit with the younger generation and a much healthier alternative to most kiddie fare.

DINING *outside*
DISNEYLAND RESORT

UNOFFICIAL GUIDE RESEARCHERS LOVE good food and invest a fair amount of time scouting new places to eat. And because food at Disneyland Resort (all of the Disney complex including the theme parks, hotels, and Downtown Disney) is so expensive, we (like you) have an economic incentive for finding palatable meals off campus. Unfortunately, the area surrounding Disneyland is not exactly a culinary nirvana. If you thrive on fast food and the fare at chain restaurants, you'll be as happy as a honeybee on an orange blossom. If, however, you want a superlative dining experience, the pickings are slim. That said, the average Disneyland visitor only stays for two to four nights, and there are more than enough fine-dining venues outside Disneyland Resort to keep you happy for that amount of time. Good ethnic dining, however, is woefully underrepresented. Especially hard to find are high-quality Thai, Chinese, Mexican, Japanese, Korean, and Greek restaurants. We've confined our coverage to restaurants you can reach by car or cab in 15 minutes or less. If you're willing to range farther afield, your choices increase exponentially.

Among specialty restaurants in and out of Disneyland Resort, location and price will determine your choice. There is, for example, a decent Italian restaurant in Downtown Disney and several independent Italian eateries within five miles of the Disney complex. Which one you select depends on how much you want to spend and how convenient the place is.

Better restaurants outside Disneyland Resort cater primarily to adults and aren't as well equipped to deal with children. This is a plus, however, if you're looking to escape children and eat in peace and quiet.

BUFFETS AND MEAL DEALS OUTSIDE DISNEYLAND RESORT

BUFFETS, RESTAURANT SPECIALS, AND DISCOUNT DINING abound in the area surrounding Disneyland Resort, especially on Harbor Boulevard and Katella Avenue. The local visitor magazines, distributed free at non-Disney hotels, among other places, are packed with advertisements and discount coupons for seafood feasts, buffets (Chinese, Indian, and the like), and a host of combination specials for everything from lobster to barbecue. For a family trying to economize on meals, some of the come-ons are mighty attractive. But are these places any good? Is the food fresh, tasty, and appealing? Are the restaurants clean and inviting? Armed with little more than a roll of Tums, the *Unofficial* research team tried all the eateries that advertise heavily in the tourist publications. Here's what we discovered.

CHINESE SUPER BUFFETS Whoa! Talk about an oxymoron. If you've ever tried preparing Chinese food, especially a stir-fry, you know that split-second timing is required to avoid overcooking. So it should come as no big surprise that Chinese dishes languishing on a buffet lose their freshness, texture, and flavor in a hurry. On the bright side, however, the super buffets are so cheap you really can't go wrong. So what if it's not the best Chinese food you've ever had if you can scarf down all you want for ten bucks? All the Chinese buffets serve chicken prepared a dozen different ways but also offer such goodies as peel-and-eat shrimp, various fish and shellfish, the occasional carved meat, salads, soups, and sometimes sushi. Desserts are usually lackluster, but most folks are too stuffed to eat them anyway. Chinese buffets, super and otherwise, within a 15-minute drive of Disneyland Resort include:

INTERNATIONAL BUFFET & GRILL 12761 Harbor Boulevard, Garden Grove; ☎ 714-530-2288. Dinner: $11.98 weekdays and $13.98 on weekends for adults, $6.98 for children ages 6 to 10 and $4.98 for ages 3 to 5. Discount coupons available. Features grilled meat, shellfish, and Mongolian barbecue in addition to Chinese dishes.

JOY'S CAFE 512 East Katella Avenue, Anaheim; ☎ 714-639-2588. Dinner: $9.99 adults, $6.99 kids 3 to 10. Discount coupons available. Features sushi and shellfish in addition to Chinese.

WORLD BUFFET 12125 Brookhurst Street, Garden Grove; ☎ 714-534-1588. Dinner: $10.99 weekdays and $11.99 on weekends for adults, $6.49 for children ages 6 to 9 and $4.29 for ages 3 to 5. Discount coupons available. Serves pizza and sushi in addition to Chinese offerings.

INDIAN BUFFETS Indian food works much better on a buffet than Chinese food. The mainstay of Indian buffets is curries. *Curry,* you may be surprised to know, is essentially the Indian word for "stew." Curry powder, as sold in the United States, is nothing more than a blend of spices prepackaged to flavor a stew. In India, each curry is prepared with a different combination of spices, and no self-respecting cook would dream of using an off-the-shelf mix. The salient point about Indian buffets is that curries, unlike stir-fries, actually improve with a little aging. If you've ever reheated a leftover stew at home and noticed that it tasted better the second time around, it's because the flavors and ingredients continued to marry during the storage period, making the stew richer and tastier.

In the Disneyland Resort area, most Indian restaurants offer buffets at lunch only—not too convenient if you plan on spending your day at the theme parks. If you're out shopping or taking a day off, here are some Indian buffets worth trying:

GANDHI PALACE Ramada Plaza Hotel, 515 West Katella Avenue; ☎ 714-808-6777. Lunch buffet: Monday through Saturday, $7.95; Sunday brunch: $10.99. Discount coupons available.

TANDOOR 1132 East Katella Avenue, Orange; ☎ 714-538-2234. Lunch buffet: Monday through Saturday, $7.95; Sunday brunch: $10.99. Discount coupons available.

SALAD BUFFETS The most popular of these in the Disneyland Resort area is **Souplantation** (5939 West Chapman Avenue, Garden Grove; ☎ 714-895-1314). The buffet features prepared salads and an extensive array of ingredients to build your own. In addition to the rabbit food, Souplantation offers a variety of soups, a modest pasta bar, a baked-potato bar, an assortment of fresh fruit, and ice-cream sundaes. Dinner runs $8.99 for adults, $4.49 for children ages 6 to 12, and $1.99 for children ages 3 to 5. Lunch is $7.29 for adults; kids eat for the same price as at dinner.

FAMILY RESTAURANTS Three **Denny's,** featuring dauntingly enormous breakfast specials for $5.99, are within a mile of Disneyland Resort. The 1610 South Harbor Boulevard location is across the street from Disneyland's main pedestrian and hotel-shuttle entrance; a second Denny's is a quarter mile south at 2080 South Harbor Boulevard; and closer to the Anaheim Convention Center is the 1168 West Katella location.

Though not as inexpensive as Denny's, **Mimi's Cafe,** at 1400 South Harbor Boulevard, is the best family restaurant in the area surrounding Disneyland. The breakfast, lunch, and dinner menus are all extensive. We always drop by at lunch for Mimi's excellent liver and onions.

BEST HAMBURGER In-N-Out Burger, 600 South Brookhurst Street, Anaheim; ☎ 800-786-1000. This small, family-owned chain is the gold standard for burgers. Hamburgers, cheeseburgers, fries, and shakes are all they do—and nobody does them better. Ask for the Double-Double (double meat, double cheese), "Animal Style" (heavy on all the condiments). Another thing: the burgers are exponentially better if eaten on the spot. Even hauling them back to the hotel takes a little luster off the patty.

ANAHEIM-AREA FULL-SERVICE RESTAURANTS

SOUTHERN CALIFORNIA is a mother lode of wonderful dining, and if we directed you to Newport Beach, La Jolla, or L.A., we could guarantee you a fantastic eating experience every night. In that you've chosen Disneyland as your destination, however, we've elected to profile only solid restaurants that you can reach by car or cab in 15 minutes or less. That said, here are our picks.

Anaheim White House ★★★★½

ITALIAN	EXPENSIVE	QUALITY ★★★★½	VALUE ★★★½

887 South Anaheim Boulevard; ☎ 714-772-1381;
www.anaheimwhitehouse.com

Reservations Recommended. **When to go** Dinner. **Entree range** $22–$40. **Service** ★★★★★. **Friendliness** ★★★½. **Liquor service** Full bar, plentiful wine list. **Dress** Business casual. **Disabled access** Yes. **Lunch** Monday–Friday, 11 a.m.– 2 p.m. **Dinner** Nightly, 5–10 p.m. **Sunday brunch** 11 a.m.–3 p.m.

SETTING AND ATMOSPHERE Another local institution, the Anaheim White House sits in a restored Victorian originally built in 1909. It has nine different dining rooms, all with thick gold-and-white drapes and bright-gold accents against a bright-white background. Tables are set with fine bone china and the best flatware. Service is extremely gracious, willing, and knowledgeable.

HOUSE SPECIALTIES Italian seafood recipes from northern Italy highlight an extensive menu, each dish sporting the name of a famous Italian or Italian American celebrity—for example, the Gwen Stefani Ravioli (little pasta pillows stuffed with lobster in a ginger-citrus sauce), named for the Anaheim-born pop star, and the Fendi Prawns (giant shrimp baked in their shells and served over pasta with fresh herbs and a sautéed-scallop garnish), a culinary tribute to the ultra-glam Milan fashion house.

OTHER RECOMMENDATIONS Chicken stuffed with ham and fontina cheese in a light mushroom sauce.

SUMMARY AND COMMENTS The White House only seems to get better. The menu of northern Italian recipes is kept fresh and timely, and service is spot-on. This is an elegant, expensive restaurant—leave the kids at home.

The Catch ★★½

SEAFOOD	MODERATE	QUALITY ★★½	VALUE ★★★

1929 South State College Boulevard; ☎ 714-935-0101;
www.catchanaheim.com

Reservations Recommended. **When to go** Dinner. **Entree range** $15–$38. **Service** ★★. **Friendliness** ★★★. **Liquor service** Wine list and full bar. **Dress** Casual. **Disabled access** Yes. **Lunch** Monday–Friday, 11 a.m.–4 p.m. **Dinner** Nightly, 5–9 p.m.

SETTING AND ATMOSPHERE Dining at The Catch is like stepping into a 19th-century Cape Cod lighthouse, with abundant wood, tile floors, stained glass, and Tiffany lighting. There's both an 11-seat oyster bar and a spacious lounge; the kitchen is open, and it's fun to watch the help prepare the fish, cook it, and dress it before it arrives at the table.

HOUSE SPECIALTIES Anything with fins and gills. The miso Chilean sea bass—a fresh fillet caramelized and sautéed—is a sure winner, as is the blackened ahi.

OTHER RECOMMENDATIONS The king-crab legs and Australian lobster tail are popular, straightforward, and hard to mess up.

Anaheim-area Restaurants by Cuisine

CUISINE/ LOCATION	OVERALL RATING	COST	QUALITY RATING	VALUE RATING
AMERICAN				
Mr. Stox E. Katella Ave.	★★★½	Exp	★★★½	★★★
GERMAN				
The Phoenix Club S. Sanderson Dr.	★★★	Mod	★★★½	★★★
ITALIAN				
Anaheim White House S. Anaheim Blvd.	★★★★½	Exp	★★★★½	★★★½
Luigi's D'Italia S. State College Blvd.	★★★½	Inexp	★★★½	★★★★
PRIME RIB				
Mr. Stox E. Katella Ave.	★★★½	Exp	★★★½	★★★
SEAFOOD				
The Catch S. State College Blvd.	★★½	Mod	★★½	★★★
STEAK				
JW's Steakhouse Marriott Anaheim	★★★★	Exp	★★★★	★★★★
Morton's S. Harbor Blvd.	★★★★	Exp	★★★½	★★★½
VIETNAMESE				
Pho Republic S. Anaheim Blvd.	★★★½	Inexp	★★★½	★★★½

SUMMARY AND COMMENTS This is the fish house that's always just shy of being great. Because of its proximity to the baseball stadium, the hockey arena, and local businesses, it's always busy and a popular watering hole for hometown athletes and sports writers. The food is uneven, so stick to the basics. When the kitchen wanders into more-complex recipes, things begin to break down. The ambience, though, is both visually pleasant and uproariously noisy. Service is spotty and sometimes seemingly uncaring, as if they're doing you a favor.

Ethnic Eats in and around Anaheim

BEST CHINESE

Grand China Restaurant 575 Chapman Avenue, Anaheim; ☎ 714-740-1888. Really outstanding service differentiates this spot from its nearby competitors. The menu's pretty standard, but what they do they do well, and with a big smile. The broccoli with beef and sweet-and-sour chicken are first-rate.

BEST INDIAN

Tandoor 1132 East Katella Avenue, Orange; ☎ 714-538-2234. The lunch buffet is good, but the fresh tandoor in the evening is exceptional. Offers regional dishes not found at a lot of Indian restaurants.

BEST JAPANESE

Koji's Sushi & Shabu Shabu Block of Orange, 20 City Boulevard, Orange; ☎ 714-769-0200. Lively sushi chefs, an ever-evolving sushi and sashimi menu (focusing on super fresh fish), and a make-your-own shabu shabu station earn this place high marks, especially if you're looking for a really good time with your meal. Very popular with local hipsters. Also in Orange, check out **Koisan Japanese Cuisine** (1132 East Katella; ☎ 714-639-2330). Cozy and intimate, it's perfect for theme-park decompression, and the menu is pretty extensive.

BEST MEDITERRANEAN

Zankou Chicken 2424 West Ball Road, Anaheim; ☎ 714-229-2060. Forget this place is a chain, disregard the cheesy ambience, and go for the spit-roasted chicken, hummus, and *shwarma* beef. Inexpensive and delicious.

BEST MEXICAN

Casa Gamino 1228 South Brookhurst, Anaheim; ☎ 714-956-1120. A great spot just a few blocks from Disneyland with awesome margaritas, killer burritos, and some of the best *albóndigas* (meatball soup) this side of the border.

BEST THAI

Thai & Thai 150 East Katella Avenue, Anaheim; ☎ 714-635-3060. Great Thai place with exceptional curry (red and hot, hot, hot), plus traditional favorites such as pad thai and satay. Unusually gracious service.

JW's Steakhouse ★★★★

STEAK	EXPENSIVE	QUALITY ★★★★	VALUE ★★★★

Marriott Anaheim, 700 West Convention Way; ☎ 714-703-3187

Reservations Recommended. **When to go** Dinner. **Entree range** $18–$55. **Service** ★★★★. **Friendliness** ★★★★. **Liquor service** Wine list and full bar. **Dress** Dressy casual. **Disabled access** Yes. **Dinner** Nightly, generally 5–10 p.m. (hours vary according to hotel occupancy; there's no set schedule).

SETTING AND ATMOSPHERE The restaurant was included in the general remodel of the hotel and grounds and is, in a word, gorgeous. Minimalist modern with an Asian touch.

HOUSE SPECIALTIES Steak . . . almost any of the featured cuts are outstanding. Try the Kobe flatiron, rubbed with spices and pepper, grilled to order, and served as a cutlet. It's an underrated cut that's as lean as most filets and more flavorful than a sirloin.

OTHER RECOMMENDATIONS Wedge salad: one quarter head of iceberg lettuce with Gorgonzola-cheese dressing and maple bacon.

SUMMARY AND COMMENTS Right around the corner and down the street from Morton's, JW's actually serves a better steak in a nicer room with better service. The room is absolutely stunning (ask for the cozy, private nook behind the fireplace), the meat nearly flawless, the service sharp and warm. The trick is to catch the restaurant open: the hotel closes it when occupancy falls, so operating hours can be erratic.

Luigi's D'Italia ★★★½

| ITALIAN | INEXPENSIVE | QUALITY ★★★½ | VALUE ★★★★ |

801 South State College Boulevard; ☎ 714-490-0990

Reservations Recommended. **When to go** Lunch or dinner. **Entree range** $7–$20. **Service** ★★½. **Friendliness** ★★★. **Liquor service** Wine and beer. **Dress** Casual. **Disabled access** Yes. **Lunch and dinner** Daily, 11 a.m.–10 p.m.

SETTING AND ATMOSPHERE Classic tacky Italian, reminiscent of just about every neighborhood mom-and-pop pizzeria in America (think faux grapevines, funky murals, and Chianti-bottle candle holders). But there is something homey and comforting in this, and the service is generally warm and friendly.

HOUSE SPECIALTIES Better-than-average hand-tossed pizzas with all the familiar toppings (pepperoni, mushroom, sausage, and such); a very tasty (and hearty) eggplant Sorrentino.

OTHER RECOMMENDATIONS The pastas, including a superb spaghetti Bolognese, are commendable.

SUMMARY AND COMMENTS When the pocketbook can't take another huge hit no matter how good the menu looks, head to Luigi's. Old-fashioned Italian fare, a welcoming (if kitschy) ambience, and friendly smiles await. The pizzas and pastas, Italian staples, are all familiar, hearty, and tasty, if not overly generous in their portions. The kids will love watching the pizzas get tossed, and your credit card will breathe a sigh of relief.

Mr. Stox ★★★½

| AMERICAN/CONTEMPORARY | EXPENSIVE | QUALITY ★★★½ | VALUE ★★★ |

1105 East Katella Avenue; ☎ 714-634-2994; www.mrstox.com

Reservations Recommended. **When to go** Dinner. **Entree range** $18–$48. **Service** ★★★★. **Friendliness** ★★★. **Liquor service** Extensive wine list and full bar. **Dress** Business casual. **Disabled access** Yes. **Lunch** Monday–Friday, 11:30 a.m.–2:30 p.m. **Dinner** Nightly, 5:30–10 p.m.

SETTING AND ATMOSPHERE One of the oldest restaurants under continuous ownership in Orange County, Mr. Stox is a beacon of tradition and continuity. Founded and owned by local foodies and wine aficionados Chick, Debbie, and Tom Marshall, the restaurant is a timeless experience in good taste, comfort, and warmth. The dining rooms and lounge exude a simple, contemporary air reflective of the California experience, with works by local artists adorning the walls.

HOUSE SPECIALTIES Chef Scott Razeck does a seasonal menu, heavy on local flavors with a contemporary twist. The duck, a mesquite-grilled breast and confit of leg, is outstanding, as are the Maryland blue-crab cakes with Dijon-mustard sauce and spicy peanut coleslaw.

OTHER RECOMMENDATIONS The prime rib is always good—reliably rich and tender.

SUMMARY AND COMMENTS The Marshalls are Orange County's first family of haute cuisine and their flagship, Mr. Stox, a virtual landmark among epicureans. They have one of the largest and deepest wine cellars in the county and regularly sponsor cooking and demonstration events. This is where you'll find the area's chefs dining on their night off.

Morton's ★★★★

STEAK HOUSE	EXPENSIVE	QUALITY ★★★½	VALUE ★★★½

1895 South Harbor Boulevard; ☎ 714-624-0101; www.mortons.com

Reservations Recommended. When to go Dinner. Entree range $18–$49. Service ★★★★. Friendliness ★★★½. Liquor service Extensive wine list and full bar. Dress Dressy casual. Disabled access Yes. Dinner Monday–Saturday, 5:30–11 p.m.; Sunday, 5–10 p.m.

SETTING AND ATMOSPHERE Classic steak house with overstuffed booths, soft lighting, and dark hardwoods.

HOUSE SPECIALTIES Go for the double-cut filet mignon with béarnaise sauce, a classic.

OTHER RECOMMENDATIONS The double-cut bone-in rib eye is a Chicago staple and a beef eater's dream: 22 ounces of prime steak, grilled to order.

SUMMARY AND COMMENTS Morton's is a carnivore's delight . . . beef, lamb, pork, and chicken dominate the menu. Of course, there's a smattering of fish options, including shrimp in several different iterations, but this place is really about the beef. Lots of classic recipes, such as steak Diane and veal Oscar.

Pho Republic ★★★½

VIETNAMESE	INEXPENSIVE	QUALITY ★★★½	VALUE ★★★½

30 South Anaheim Boulevard, Old Historic Anaheim District;
☎ 714-999-1200; www.pho-republic.com

Reservations Recommended. When to go Dinner. Entree range $5–$12. Service ★★★★. Friendliness ★★★½. Liquor service Limited wine list and beer. Dress Casual. Disabled access Yes. Lunch and dinner Sunday–Thursday, 11 a.m.–9 p.m.; Friday and Saturday until 10 p.m.

SETTING AND ATMOSPHERE Pho Republic is a typical Asian restaurant. Bamboo and flowering greenery, Asian landscapes on the walls, and Buddha highlight the decor.

HOUSE SPECIALTIES *Pho* (pronounced "pha"), the ubiquitous noodle soup of Vietnam, is served here in ten different recipes, ranging from *pho do bien* (shrimp, squid, and fish cakes in chicken broth) to *pho tai nam gau gan sach* (beef broth with round steak, crispy beef fat, soft tendon, and tripe). What sandwiches are to Americans, pho is to the Vietnamese.

OTHER RECOMMENDATIONS Shaken beef (diced beef wok seared in a signature sauce and served with rice), Mekong River roasted chicken (half a bird marinated in five spices and rice wine).

SUMMARY AND COMMENTS Little Saigon, the largest Vietnamese community in the United States, is just a few miles southwest of Disneyland, so it's no surprise that a small gem like Pho Republic is within easy reach of the parks. Expect a sea of ethnic faces (a testimony to the eatery's authenticity and popularity) and a menu long on selections and short on price. An entire family can eat heartily here for about half of what it would cost to dine elsewhere, if the kids can take something a little more exotic (a kids' menu eliminates the fiery spice found in some Vietnamese cuisine). Service is efficient and a tad language challenged, but very helpful when you're navigating the exotic menu.

The Phoenix Club ★★★

| GERMAN | MODERATE | QUALITY ★★★½ | VALUE ★★★ |

1340 South Sanderson Drive, behind Honda Arena; ☎ 714-563-4166; www.thephoenixclub.com

Reservations Recommended. **When to go** Lunch or dinner. **Entree range** $9–$28. **Service** ★★★. **Friendliness** ★★★★. **Liquor service** Wine list, extensive draft-beer offerings, and full bar. **Dress** Casual. **Disabled access** Yes. **Lunch** Tuesday–Friday, 11:30 a.m.–1:30 p.m. **Dinner** Sunday and Tuesday–Thursday, 5–9 p.m.; Friday and Saturday until 10 p.m.

SETTING AND ATMOSPHERE Once a private club reserved for family members of the original German settlers of Anaheim and more recent émigrés, this famous landmark is now open to the public (members are still welcome and enjoy a few extra privileges). Choose from the formal, elegantly appointed Loreley dining room or the boisterous Bierstube, with more than a half-dozen German beers on tap. The Bierstube's menu is more limited than the Loreley's, trending toward less-fancy preparations, but it's these basic dishes that keep folks coming back. Where the Loreley is quiet and peaceful, the Bierstube is conducive to raucous eating, drinking, and carousing. Live music seems omnipresent, from local and guest polka bands to renowned accordion artists.

HOUSE SPECIALTIES Wursts, kraut, pork roast, mixed platters, wiener schnitzel, and sauerbraten are the best in a 100-mile radius.

OTHER RECOMMENDATIONS Pork in creamy Champagne-mushroom sauce.

SUMMARY AND COMMENTS The bastion of Anaheim's founding families and subsequent waves of German immigrants, The Phoenix Club offers a little taste of the *vaterland* far from home. The food is good, occasionally great; the beer is always cold; and the help is always ready to show you a good time, German or not. During Oktoberfest, the place rocks. The kids will love the early reminders of a rough and rural Anaheim and the oompah bands; Mom and Dad will love the German beers; and everyone will love the sweet-and-sour flavors of German cuisine

SHOPPING *at* DISNEYLAND

SHOPS ADD REALISM AND ATMOSPHERE to the various theme settings and offer souvenirs, clothing, novelties, jewelry, decorator items, and more. Much of the merchandise displayed (with the exception of Disney trademark souvenir items), though, is available back home and elsewhere, so we recommend bypassing the shops on a one-day visit. If you have two or more days to spend at Disneyland Resort, browse in the early afternoon, when many attractions are crowded.

Our recommendations notwithstanding, we realize that for many guests Disney souvenirs and memorabilia are irresistible. One of our readers writes:

> *People have a compelling need to buy Disney stuff at Disneyland. When you get home, you wonder why you ever got a cashmere sweater with Mickey Mouse embroidered on the breast, or a tie with tiny Goofys all over it. Maybe they put something in the food?*

If you don't want to lug your packages around, you can leave them at the information stand just inside the front gate and pick them up as you exit the park. Note that retrieving your purchases might take a while if you depart after a parade or fireworks show or at closing, when guests exit en masse. If you're staying at a Disneyland Resort hotel, your loot will be delivered directly to your room on request. If you have a problem with your purchases or need to make a return, call Disneyland Exclusive Merchandise at ☎ 800-760-3566, Monday through Friday, from 8 a.m. to 5 p.m. PST, and Saturday from 8 a.m. to 4 p.m PST.

DOWNTOWN DISNEY

DOWNTOWN DISNEY, verdant and landscaped by day, pops alive with neon and glitter at night. The complex offers more than 300,000 square feet of specialty shopping, clubs, restaurants, and movie theaters. Many of the restaurants offer entertainment in addition to dining, including **House of Blues** and **Ralph Brennan's Jazz Kitchen.** The **ESPN Zone** is a sports bar and restaurant with dozens of giant TV screens. Other restaurant options include the **Naples Ristorante e Pizzeria, Tortilla Jo's** Mexican restaurant, and jungle-themed dining at the **Rainforest Cafe.**

If you're not hungry, there's always shopping and a 12-theater **AMC Movieplex** to keep you occupied. A 40,000-square-foot **World of Disney** store, the second largest on the planet, anchors the shopping scene. Other retailers include **Compass Books; Basin,** a bath store; **Starabilias**

downtown disney

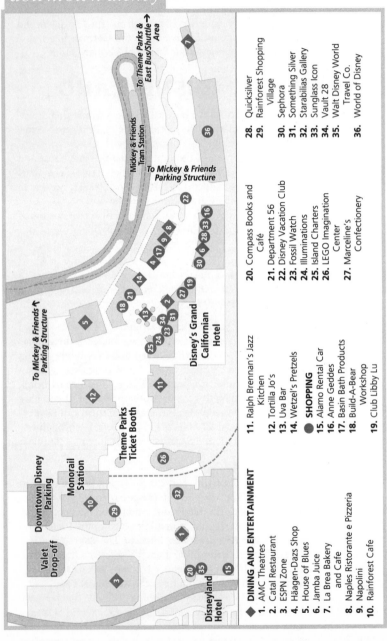

To Theme Parks &
East Bus/Shuttle → Area

Mickey & Friends
Tram Station

**To Mickey & Friends
Parking Structure**

To Mickey & Friends ↖
Parking Structure

**Theme Parks
Ticket Booth**

**Disney's Grand
Californian
Hotel**

**Downtown Disney
Parking**

**Monorail
Station**

**Valet
Drop-off**

**Disneyland
Hotel**

◆ **DINING AND ENTERTAINMENT**
1. AMC Theatres
2. Catal Restaurant
3. ESPN Zone
4. Häagen-Dazs Shop
5. House of Blues
6. Jamba Juice
7. La Brea Bakery
   and Cafe
8. Naples Ristorante e Pizzeria
9. Napolini
10. Rainforest Cafe

11. Ralph Brennan's Jazz
    Kitchen
12. Tortilla Jo's
13. Uva Bar
14. Wetzel's Pretzels

● **SHOPPING**
15. Alamo Rental Car
16. Anne Geddes
17. Basin Bath Products
18. Build-A-Bear
    Workshop
19. Club Libby Lu

20. Compass Books and
    Café
21. Department 56
22. Disney Vacation Club
23. Fossil Watch
24. Illuminations
25. Island Charters
26. LEGO Imagination
    Center
27. Marceline's
    Confectionery

28. Quicksilver
29. Rainforest Shopping
    Village
30. Sephora
31. Something Silver
32. Starabilias Gallery
33. Sunglass Icon
34. Vault 28
35. Walt Disney World
    Travel Co.
36. World of Disney

Gallery for antiques, memorabilia, and gifts; **Department 56** for hand-crafted collectibles; cosmetics at **Sephora; Something Silver** specializing in jewelry; and **Club Libby Lu** for little girl dress-up stuff. The **LEGO Imagination Center** features interactive play tables where children build whatever their imaginations conjure up with LEGO bricks.

Though most of the Downtown Disney shops are pretty interesting, the **Build-A-Bear Workshop** is a must-visit. Here, you choose from among a couple dozen unstuffed bearskins ranging in price from $12 to $25. Types vary from pandas to old-fashioned teddy bears and everything in between. Once you have a bear, you have the option of choosing a sound box to be implanted when the bear gets stuffed. Activated when you handle the bear, the sound box (depending on which one you choose) can say hello, sing a song, recite a poem, giggle, or growl (nicely, of course). Next, you proceed to the stuffing machine. This contraption is a big transparent box with stuffing whirling around inside on air currents. When the stuffer depresses a foot pedal, the stuffing is sucked out of the machine into a hose with a sharpish stainless-steel nozzle on the end. This last is inserted into the flaccid bearskin until the skin is appropriately plumped. Stuffing the bear requires much reaming of the aforementioned nozzle throughout the bear's head and innards. Because all this is somewhat disquieting to witness, you must think sweet thoughts about how your finished bear will look as opposed to what he's going through at the moment. Before sewing the bear up, you insert a little red heart and make a wish (probably that you don't ever have to witness such a process again). When your bear is stuffed, hearted, and sewn, you have the option to accessorize, choosing from a veritable Macy's of bear clothes, hats, shoes, jewelry, sunglasses, roller skates, and myriad other even-more-unlikely items. After all your bear has been through, it's only natural to want to buy him a present or two, but watch out—you can easily blow a hundred bucks getting your bear outfitted.

Our map of Downtown Disney, listing storefronts and restaurants, appears at left.

PART FIVE

DISNEYLAND PARK

ARRIVING *and* GETTING ORIENTED

IF YOU DRIVE, you will probably be directed to the parking garage on West Street near Ball Road. Parking costs $10 for cars, $12 for RVs, and $17 for buses. Be sure to make a note of your section, row, and space. A tram will transport you to a loading/unloading area connected to the entrance by a pedestrian corridor. Because security screening is conducted just before passing through the turnstiles, the lines to enter the park are often quite lengthy. Two entrance gates, 14 and 19, are blocked by trees situated in the entrance plaza about ten feet from the security checkpoint. The trees inhibit the formation of a line in front of both of the obstructed gates. These gates (14 and 19) are staffed nonetheless and draw guests from adjacent lines 13 and 20. This significantly speeds up the entry process for guests waiting in lines 13 and 20. Our advice on arriving, therefore, is to join line 13 or 20. Of the two, 13 is usually shorter than 20. Stroller and wheelchair rentals are to the right just outside the turnstile. As you enter Main Street, City Hall is to your left, serving as the center for general information, lost and found, and entertainment information.

If you haven't been given a freebie Disneyland Park map by now, City Hall is the place to pick one up. Also pick up a *Times Guide*. This pamphlet contains the daily entertainment schedule for live shows, parades, fireworks, and other events and tells you where you can find the characters. If a *Times Guide* is not available for the day you visit (a very rare occurrence), the daily entertainment schedule will be included in the park map. The park map lists all the attractions, shops, and eateries and provides helpful information about first aid, baby care, assistance for the disabled, and more.

Notice on your map that Main Street ends at a central hub from which branch the entrances to four other sections of Disneyland:

Not to Be Missed at Disneyland Park

Adventureland Indiana Jones Adventure

Critter Country Splash Mountain

Frontierland Big Thunder Mountain Railroad | Golden Horseshoe Stage

New Orleans Square The Haunted Mansion | Pirates of the Caribbean

Tomorrowland *Finding Nemo* Submarine Voyage | *Honey, I Shrunk the Audience*
    Space Mountain

Live entertainment *Fantasmic!*

Adventureland, Frontierland, Fantasyland, and **Tomorrowland.** Two
other "lands," **New Orleans Square** and **Critter Country,** can be reached
through Adventureland and Frontierland. **Mickey's Toontown** is located
on the far side of the railroad tracks from It's a Small World in Fantasyland. **Sleeping Beauty Castle,** the entrance to Fantasyland, is a focal
landmark and the visual center of the park. The castle is a great place
to meet if your group decides to split up for any reason during the day,
and it can serve as an emergency meeting place if you are accidentally
separated. Keep in mind, however, that the castle covers a lot of territory, so be specific about *where* to meet at the castle. Also be forewarned that parades and live shows sometimes make it difficult to
access the entrance of the castle fronting the central hub.

STARTING THE TOUR

EVERYONE WILL SOON FIND his or her own favorite and not-
so-favorite attractions in Disneyland Park. Be open-minded and
adventuresome. Don't dismiss a particular ride or show as not being
for you until *after* you have tried it. Our personal experience as well
as our research indicates that each visitor is different in terms of
which Disney offerings he or she most enjoys. So don't miss seeing an
attraction because a friend from home didn't like it; that attraction
may turn out to be your favorite.

We do recommend that you take advantage of what Disney does
best—the fantasy adventures such as Indiana Jones Adventure and
The Haunted Mansion, and the audio-animatronic (talking robots,
that is) attractions such as Pirates of the Caribbean. Unless you have
almost unlimited time, don't burn a lot of daylight browsing through
the shops. Except for some special Disney souvenirs, you can find
much of the same merchandise elsewhere. Try to minimize the time
you spend on midway-type rides, as you've probably got an amusement
park, carnival, or state fair close to your hometown. Don't, however,
mistake rides like Splash Mountain and the Big Thunder Mountain
Railroad for amusement-park rides. They may be of the flume-ride or
the roller-coaster genre, but they represent pure Disney genius. Similarly, do not devote a lot of time to waiting in line for meals. Eat a

disneyland park

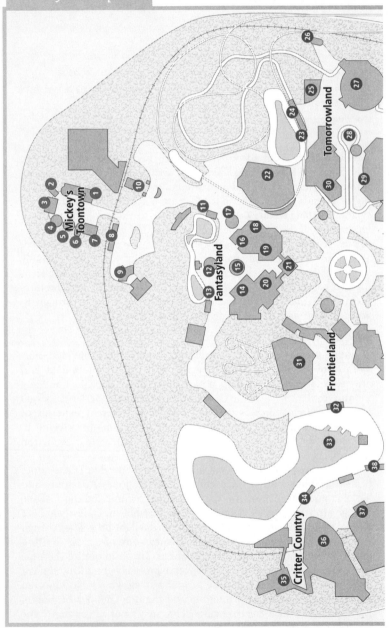

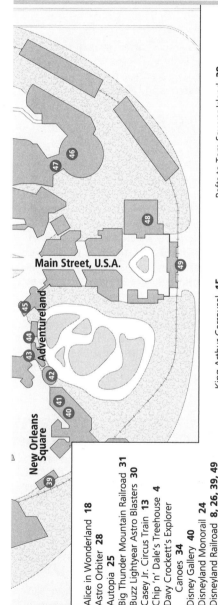

Main Street, U.S.A.

Adventureland

New Orleans Square

Rafts to Tom Sawyer Island **38**
Riverboat and Sailing Ship **32**
Roger Rabbit's Car Toon Spin **1**
Sleeping Beauty Castle **21**
Snow White's Scary Adventures **20**
Space Mountain **46**
Splash Mountain **36**
Star Tours **29**
Storybook Land Canal Boats **11**
Tarzan's Treehouse **42**
Tom Sawyer Island **33**

King Arthur Carrousel **15**
Mad Tea Party **17**
The Many Adventures of
   Winnie the Pooh **35**
Matterhorn Bobsleds **22**
Mickey's House **3**
Minnie's House **2**
Miss Daisy, Donald's Boat **6**
Mr. Toad's Wild Ride **16**
Peter Pan's Flight **19**
Pinocchio's Daring
   Journey **14**
Pirates of the
   Caribbean **41**

Alice in Wonderland **18**
Astro Orbiter **28**
Autopia **25**
Big Thunder Mountain Railroad **31**
Buzz Lightyear Astro Blasters **30**
Casey Jr. Circus Train **13**
Chip 'n' Dale's Treehouse **4**
Davy Crockett's Explorer
   Canoes **34**
Disney Gallery **40**
Disneyland Monorail **24**
Disneyland Railroad **8, 26, 39, 49**
Disneyland: The First 50 Years **48**
Dumbo the Flying Elephant **12**
Enchanted Tiki Room **45**
Fantasyland Theatre **9**
Finding Nemo Submarine
   Voyage **23**
Gadget's Go Coaster **5**
Goofy's Playhouse **7**
Haunted Mansion **37**
Honey, I Shrunk the Audience **47**
Indiana Jones Adventure **43**
Innoventions **27**
It's a Small World **10**
Jungle Cruise **44**

good early breakfast before you come, snack on vendor-sold foods during the touring day, or follow the suggestions for meals incorporated into the various touring plans presented.

ORGANIZATION OF PROFILES

WE HAVE GROUPED ATTRACTIONS into "lands," which are listed geographically—roughly clockwise from the entrance. The attraction profiles are listed alphabetically under their respective "lands" and are followed by comments on eateries and shops.

MAIN STREET, *U.S.A.*

THIS SECTION OF DISNEYLAND PARK is where you'll begin and end your visit. We have already mentioned that assistance and information are available at City Hall. The Disneyland Railroad stops at the Main Street Station, and you can board here for a grand circle tour of the park, or you can get off the train in New Orleans Square, Mickey's Toontown/Fantasyland, or Tomorrowland.

Main Street is an idealized version of a turn-of-the-20th-century American small-town street. Many visitors are surprised to discover that all the buildings are real, not elaborate props. Attention to detail here is exceptional—interiors, furnishings, and fixtures conform to the period. As with any real Main Street, the Disney version is essentially a collection of shops and eating places, with a city hall, a fire station, and an old-time cinema. A mixed-media attraction combines static exhibits recalling the life of Walt Disney with a patriotic remembrance of Abraham Lincoln. Horse-drawn trolleys, fire engines, and horseless carriages give rides along Main Street and transport visitors to the central hub (properly known as the Central Plaza).

Disneyland Railroad ★★★

APPEAL BY AGE	PRESCHOOL ★★★★	GRADE SCHOOL ★★★	TEENS ★★
YOUNG ADULTS ★★★½	OVER 30 ★★★½		SENIORS ★★★½

Type of attraction Scenic railroad ride around the park's perimeter; also transportation to New Orleans Square, Mickey's Toontown, Fantasyland, and Tomorrowland. **Scope and scale** Major attraction. **When to go** After 11 a.m. or when you need transportation. **Special comments** The Main Street and Mickey's Toontown/Fantasyland stations are usually the least-congested boarding points. **Duration of ride** About 20 minutes for a complete circuit. **Average wait in line per 100 people ahead of you** 8 minutes. **Assumes** 3 trains operating. **Loading speed** Fast.

Thumbs Up for the Whole Family

DESCRIPTION AND COMMENTS A transportation ride that blends an eclectic variety of sights and experiences with an energy-saving way of getting around the park. In addition to providing a glimpse of all the lands except Adventureland, the train passes through the Grand Canyon Diorama (between

Main Street Services

Most of the park's service facilities are centered in the Main Street section, including the following:

Baby Center/Baby Care Needs At the central hub end of Main Street

Banking Services/Currency Exchange At City Hall at the Railroad Station end of Main Street

Disneyland and Local Attraction Information City Hall building

First Aid First Aid Center two doors from Plaza Inn at the central-hub end of Main Street

Live Entertainment and Parade Information City Hall Building at the Railroad Station end of Main Street

Lost Adults and Messages City Hall building

Lost and Found Lost and Found for the entire resort is located east of the entrance of Disney's California Adventure

Lost Children At the central-hub end of Main Street

Storage Lockers Down Main Street one block (as you walk toward the castle) and to the right

Wheelchair and Stroller Rental To the right of the main entrance before you pass through the turnstiles

Tomorrowland and Main Street), a three-dimensional replication of the canyon, complete with wildlife, as it appears from the southern rim. Another sight on the train circuit is Primeval World, a depiction of a pre-historic peat bog and rain forest populated by audio-animatronic (robotic) dinosaurs. Opened in 1966, Primeval World was a precursor to a similar presentation in the Universe of Energy pavilion at Epcot.

TOURING TIPS Save the train ride until after you have seen the featured attractions, or use it when you need transportation. If you have small children who are hell-bent to see Mickey first thing in the morning, you might consider taking the train to Mickey's Toontown (a half circuit) and visiting Mickey in his dressing room as soon as you enter the park. Many families find that this tactic puts the kids in a more receptive frame of mind for the other attractions. On busy days, lines form at the New Orleans Square and Tomorrowland stations, but rarely at the Main Street or Mickey's Toontown/Fantasyland stations.

Disneyland: The First 50 Years   ★★★½

APPEAL BY AGE	PRESCHOOL ★	GRADE SCHOOL ★★½	TEENS ★★½
YOUNG ADULTS ★★★	OVER 30 ★★★½	SENIORS ★★★½	

Type of attraction Exhibits and film detailing the history of Disneyland. **Scope and scale** Minor attraction. **When to go** Whenever you want. **Duration of film** 12 minutes.

Thumbs Up for the Whole Family

DESCRIPTION AND COMMENTS This attraction occupies the Main Street Opera House replacing *The Walt Disney Story*, featuring *Great Moments with Mr. Lincoln*. Part of the Disneyland 50th-birthday celebration, the combination film-exhibit continues to operate well past the end of the anniversary period. *Disneyland: The First 50 Years* features Walt Disney and Disneyland memorabilia, early design renderings of the park and of the attractions, and a specially made, nostalgic film about how Disneyland came to be. Following the film, guests view another exhibit showcasing "the Disneyland that never was," highlighting attractions and shows planned but never brought to fruition. The exhibit also offers a glimpse of Disneyland's future.

TOURING TIPS A lovely remembrance. Visit anytime.

Main Street Cinema ★★

APPEAL BY AGE	PRESCHOOL ★★½	GRADE SCHOOL ★★½	TEENS ★★½
YOUNG ADULTS ★★★½		OVER 30 ★★★½	SENIORS ★★★½

Type of attraction Vintage Disney cartoons. **Scope and scale** Diversion. **When to go** Whenever you want. **Special comments** Wonderful selection of old-time flicks. **Duration of presentation** Runs continuously. **Preshow entertainment** None. **Probable waiting time** No waiting.

DESCRIPTION AND COMMENTS Excellent old-time movies, including some vintage Disney cartoons. Because the movies are silent, six can be shown simultaneously. No seats; viewers stand.

TOURING TIPS Good place to get out of the sun or rain or to kill time while others in your group shop on Main Street. Fun, but not something you can't afford to miss.

The Walt Disney Story, featuring *Great Moments with Mr. Lincoln* ★★★½

APPEAL BY AGE	PRESCHOOL ★	GRADE SCHOOL ★★½	TEENS ★★½
YOUNG ADULTS ★★★		OVER 30 ★★★	SENIORS ★★★

Type of attraction Nostalgic exhibits documenting the Disney success story followed by an audio-animatronic patriotic presentation. **Scope and scale** Minor attraction. **When to go** During the hot, crowded period of the day. **Special comments**

Thumbs Up for the Whole Family

Disneyland: The First 50 Years replaced *The Walt Disney Story* and *Mr. Lincoln* during the Disneyland 50th-anniversary celebration that ended December 31, 2006. *Disneyland: The First 50 Years* continues its run, and it remains to be seen when or if *The Walt Disney Story* and *Mr. Lincoln* will return.

Duration of presentation 15 minutes including preshow. **Preshow entertainment** Disney exhibits. **Probable waiting time** Usually no wait.

DESCRIPTION AND COMMENTS A warm, well-presented remembrance of the man who started it all. Well worth seeing; especially touching for those old

enough to remember Walt Disney himself. The attraction consists of a museum of Disney memorabilia, including a re-creation of Walt's office. Especially interesting are displays illustrating the construction and evolution of Disneyland. Beyond the Disney memorabilia, guests are admitted to a large theater where *Great Moments with Mr. Lincoln* is presented. A patriotic performance, *Great Moments* features an extremely lifelike and sophisticated audio-animatronic Abe Lincoln delivering the Gettysburg Address.

The Walt Disney Story and *Mr. Lincoln* were pulled out of the lineup for half of 2001, supposedly for a substantial revision and upgrade. Unfortunately, Walt and Abe were caught in a corporate Disney budget cut and some of the more ambitious plans for the attraction were scrapped. There's a lot of new Disney memorabilia in the new rendition, and the set surrounding *Mr. Lincoln* has been improved. In the revised presentation, Civil War photographer Mathew Brady photographs a young Union private before he goes to war. After the shoot, Brady takes the soldier along for an appointment with Lincoln. The presentation is primarily auditory. Wireless earphones make the story unfold three-dimensionally around you. Sounds of scissors, a fly, and Lincoln whispering in your ear are reproduced so realistically that it's almost impossible to differentiate from the real thing. Following the story of Brady, Lincoln, and the private, an audio-animatronic Lincoln delivers the Gettysburg Address.

TOURING TIPS You usually do not have to wait long for this show, so see it during the busy times of day when lines are long elsewhere or as you are leaving the park.

Transportation Rides

DESCRIPTION AND COMMENTS Trolleys, buses, and the like that add color to Main Street.

TOURING TIPS Will save you a walk to the central hub. Not worth waiting in line for.

MAIN STREET EATERIES AND SHOPS

DESCRIPTION AND COMMENTS Snacks, food, and specialty or souvenir shopping in a nostalgic, happy setting. Incidentally, the **Emporium** on Main Street and the **Star Trader** in Tomorrowland are the two best places for finding Disney trademark souvenirs.

TOURING TIPS The shops are fun, but the merchandise can be found elsewhere (except for certain Disney-trademark souvenirs). If seeing the park attractions is your objective, save the Main Street eateries and shops until the end of the day. If shopping is your objective, you will find the shops most crowded during the noon hour and near closing time. Remember, Main Street sometimes opens a half-hour earlier and usually closes a half-hour to an hour later than the rest of Disneyland Park.

ADVENTURELAND

ADVENTURELAND IS THE FIRST "LAND" to the left of Main Street and embodies an African-safari motif. Since the opening of the Indiana Jones Adventure, the narrow thoroughfares of Adventureland have been mobbed, making pedestrian traffic difficult.

Enchanted Tiki Room ★★★

APPEAL BY AGE	PRESCHOOL ★★½	GRADE SCHOOL ★★★	TEENS ★★
YOUNG ADULTS ★★★	OVER 30 ★★★		SENIORS ★★★

Type of attraction Audio-animatronic Pacific Island musical show. **Scope and scale** Minor attraction. **When to go** Before 11 a.m. and after 6 p.m. **Special comments** Very, very unusual. **Duration of presentation** 14½ minutes. **Preshow entertainment** Talking totem poles. **Probable waiting time** 11 minutes.

Dark   Loud

DESCRIPTION AND COMMENTS An unusual sit-down theater performance in which more than 200 birds, flowers, and tiki-god statues sing and whistle through a musical program.

TOURING TIPS One of the more bizarre of the Disneyland Park entertainments and rarely very crowded. We like it in the late afternoon, when we can especially appreciate sitting for a bit in an air-conditioned theater.

A reader from Cookeville, Tennessee, took exception to the rating for preschoolers and wrote:

I know that visitor reactions vary widely, but the [Enchanted Tiki Room] was our toddler's favorite attraction. We nearly omitted it because of the rating for preschoolers.

Indiana Jones Adventure (FASTPASS) ★★★★½

APPEAL BY AGE	PRESCHOOL ★★	GRADE SCHOOL ★★★★½	TEENS ★★★★½
YOUNG ADULTS ★★★★½	OVER 30 ★★★★½		SENIORS ★★★½

Type of ride Motion-simulator dark ride. **Scope and scale** Super-headliner. **When to go** Before 9:30 a.m. or use FASTPASS. **Special comments** Not to be missed; children must be 46" tall to ride; switching off available (see page 152). **Duration of ride** 3 minutes and 20 seconds. **Average wait in line per 100 people ahead of you** 3 minutes. **Assumes** Full-capacity operation with 18-second dispatch interval. **Loading speed** Fast.

Dark   Motion Sickness   Loud   Scary   Rough

DESCRIPTION AND COMMENTS This is a combination track ride and motion simulator. You ride a military troop-transport vehicle; in addition to moving along its path, the vehicle bucks and pitches (the simulator part) in sync with the visuals and special effects. Though the plot is complicated and not altogether clear, the bottom line is that if you look into the Forbidden Eye, you're in big trouble. The Forbidden Eye, of course, stands out like Rush Limbaugh in a diaper, and *everybody* stares at it. The rest of the ride consists of a mad race to escape the temple as it collapses around you. In the process, you encounter snakes, spiders, lava pits, rats, swinging bridges, and the house-sized granite bowling ball that everyone remembers from *Raiders of the Lost Ark.*

The Indiana Jones ride is a Disney masterpiece—nonstop action from beginning to end with brilliant visual effects. Elaborate even by Disney standards, the attraction provides a level of detail and variety of action that make use of the entire Imagineering arsenal of high-tech gimmickry. Combining a setting as rich as Pirates of the Caribbean with a ride that rivals Star Tours, Indiana Jones is a powerhouse.

Sophisticated in its electronic and computer applications, Indiana Jones purports to offer a different experience on each ride. According to the designers, there are veritable menus of special effects that the computer can mix and match. In practice, however, we could not see much difference from ride to ride. There are, no doubt, subtle variations, but the ride is so wild and frenetic that it's hard to apprehend subtlety. Between explosions and falling rocks your poor fried brain simply does not register nuance. If you ride twice and your date says, "The rat on the beam winked at me that time," it's probably a good idea to get away from Disneyland for a while.

The adventure begins in the queue, which sometimes extends out the entrance of the attraction and over the bridge leading to Adventureland! When you ultimately work your way into the attraction area, you find yourself at the site of an archaeology expedition with the Temple of Doom entrance beckoning only 50 feet away. After crossing a wooden bridge, you finally step into the temple. The good news is that you are out of the California sun. The bad news is that you have just entered Indiana Jones's indoor queuing area, a system of tunnels and passageways extending to within 50 yards of the Santa Monica pier.

Fortunately, the queuing area is interesting. You wind through caves, down the interior corridors of the temple, and into subterranean rotundas where the archaeologists have been hard at work. Along the way there are various surprises, as well as a succession of homilies etched in an "ancient" language on the temple walls. During our first visit we decoded the messages with feverish intensity, hoping to find one that translated to "restrooms." Trust us on this one: do *not* chug down Diet Cokes before you get in line for this attraction.

If you are dazed from spending what seems like half of your life in this line and are not up to deciphering the Disney hieroglyphics, not to worry. You will eventually stumble into a chamber where a short movie will explain the plot. From there it's back into the maze and finally on to the loading area. The ride itself is memorable. If you ride with a full bladder, it's absolutely unforgettable.

TOURING TIPS Indiana Jones stays fairly mobbed all day. Try to ride during the first hour the park is open or use FASTPASS. Another alternative, if you don't mind riding alone, is to take advantage of the singles line. Guests from the singles lines are tapped, one at a time, to fill any odd seats remaining in the ride vehicles before they are dispatched. Generally the wait for guests in the singles line is about one-third that of guests in the regular queue. Be forewarned that the singles line at Indiana Jones (the only singles line at Disneyland Park) is a bit of a maze, requiring you to negotiate your way up the exit ramp, up one elevator, across a walkway over the track, then down another elevator to the loading area.

During the first hour or so the park is open, Indiana Jones cast members often employ a line management technique known as "stacking." Simply stated, they allow the line for Indiana Jones to form outside of the attraction, leaving the cavernous inside queuing area virtually empty. Guests, of course, assume that the attraction is packed to the gills and that the outside line is overflow. Naturally, this discourages guests from getting in line. The reality is that the wait is not nearly as bad as it looks, and that it is probably as short as it will be all day. If you arrive in the park early and the Indiana Jones line appears huge, have the rest of your party get in line while you enter Indiana Jones *through the attraction exit* and check out the inside queue. If it is empty or sparsely populated, stacking is being practiced. Join your party in line and enjoy the attraction; your wait will be comparatively short. If the inside queue is bumper to bumper, try Indiana Jones later or use FASTPASS or the singles line. Stacking is also sometimes practiced during the hour just before the park closes.

There is one other thing you should know. Indiana Jones, because it is high-tech, breaks down a lot. The Disney people will announce that the ride is broken but usually will not estimate how long repairs will take. From our experience, most glitches are resolved in approximately 15 to 30 minutes, and probably the best advice is to stick it out.

If you miss Indiana Jones in the early morning and the FASTPASSes are all gone, use the singles line or try again during a parade or *Fantasmic!*, or during the hour before the park closes. Regarding the latter, the Disney folks will usually admit to the attraction anyone in line at closing time. During a recent visit to Indiana Jones, Disneyland Park closed at 7 p.m. We hopped in the line for Indiana Jones at 6:45 p.m. and actually got on the ride at 7:30 p.m.

Though the Indiana Jones ride is wild and jerky, it is primarily distinguished by its visual impact and realistic special effects. Thus, we encourage the over-50 crowd to give it a chance: we think you'll like it. As for children, most find the ride extremely intense and action-packed but not particularly frightening. We encountered very few children who met the 46-inch minimum-height requirement who were in any way intimidated.

Jungle Cruise ★★★

APPEAL BY AGE	PRESCHOOL ★★★★	GRADE SCHOOL ★★★★	TEENS ★★★
YOUNG ADULTS ★★★		OVER 30 ★★★½	SENIORS ★★★½

Type of ride A Disney outdoor-boat-ride adventure. **Scope and scale** Major attraction. **When to go** Before 10 a.m. or after 6 p.m. **Special comments** A Disney standard. **Duration of ride** 7½ minutes. **Average wait in line per 100 people ahead of you** 3½ minutes. **Assumes** 10 boats operating. **Loading speed** Moderate to slow.

DESCRIPTION AND COMMENTS A boat ride through jungle waterways. Passengers encounter elephants, lions, hostile natives, and a menacing hippo. A long-enduring Disney favorite with the boatman's spiel adding measurably to the fun. The ride was shortened in 1995 when

Thumbs Up for the Whole Family

Indiana Jones (next door) commandeered part of the Jungle Cruise's acreage. On the bright side, the Jungle Cruise was spruced up with a nifty new entrance building and queuing area.

As more technologically advanced attractions have been added to the park over the years, the Jungle Cruise has, by comparison, lost some of its luster. Though still a good attraction, it offers few thrills and no surprises for Disneyland Park veterans, many of whom can rattle off the ride's narration right along with the guide. For park first-timers, however, the Jungle Cruise continues to delight.

TOURING TIPS This ride loads slowly, and long lines form as the park fills. To compound problems, guests exiting Indiana Jones tend to head for the Jungle Cruise. Go early, or during a parade or a performance of *Fantasmic!* Be forewarned that the Jungle Cruise has an especially deceptive line: just when you think you are about to board, you are shunted into yet another queuing maze (not visible outside the ride). Regardless how short the line *looks* when you approach the Jungle Cruise, inquire about the length of the wait—at least you will know what you are getting into.

Tarzan's Treehouse ★★★

APPEAL BY AGE	PRESCHOOL ★★★★	GRADE SCHOOL ★★★★	TEENS ★★★
YOUNG ADULTS ★★★		OVER 30 ★★★	SENIORS ★★★

Type of attraction Walk-through treehouse exhibit. **Scope and scale** Minor attraction. **When to go** Before 11 a.m. and after 5 p.m. **Special comments** Requires climbing a lot of stairs; a very creative exhibit. **Duration of tour** 8–12 minutes. **Average wait in line per 100 people ahead of you** 7 minutes. **Assumes** Normal staffing. **Loading speed** Does not apply.

DESCRIPTION AND COMMENTS Inspired by Disney's 1999 animated film *Tarzan*, Tarzan's Treehouse replaced the venerable Swiss Family Treehouse that had been an Adventureland icon for 37 years. To enter the new attraction, you climb a rustic staircase and cross a suspension bridge. From there, as they say, it's all downhill. Pages from Jane's sketchbook scattered about tell the Tarzan story and provide insights to the various rooms and levels of the treehouse. At the base of the tree is an interactive play area where characters from Disney's *Tarzan* drop in for photos and autographs.

Thumbs Up for the Whole Family

TOURING TIPS A self-guided, walk-through tour that involves a lot of climbing up and down stairs but with no ropes or ladders or anything fancy. People stopping during the walk-through to look extra-long or to rest sometimes create bottlenecks that slow crowd flow. We recommend visiting this attraction in the late afternoon or early evening if you are on a one-day tour schedule.

ADVENTURELAND EATERIES AND SHOPS

DESCRIPTION AND COMMENTS With only one counter-service restaurant, a fruit stand, and a juice bar, pickings are a little slim in Adventureland. If you find yourself hungry in Adventureland, you will find a much better selection of food in nearby New Orleans Square, Frontierland, or on Main Street.

The shops in Adventureland are set up like an African bazaar and feature safari clothing, tribal crafts, and Disney stuff. If you are on a tight schedule, skip the shops or try them on your second day.

NEW ORLEANS SQUARE

ACCESSIBLE VIA ADVENTURELAND AND FRONTIERLAND, New Orleans Square is one of three lands that do not emanate from the central hub. The architecture and setting are Caribbean colonial, like New Orleans itself, with exceptional attention to detail.

Disneyland Railroad

DESCRIPTION AND COMMENTS The Disneyland Railroad stops in New Orleans Square on its circle tour around the park. See the description of the Disneyland Railroad under Main Street, U.S.A., for additional details regarding the sights en route.

TOURING TIPS This is a pleasant and feet-saving way to commute to Mickey's Toontown/Fantasyland, Tomorrowland, or Main Street. Be advised, however, that the New Orleans Square station is usually the most congested.

The Haunted Mansion ★★★★

APPEAL BY AGE	PRESCHOOL *varies*	GRADE SCHOOL ★★★★½	TEENS ★★★★
YOUNG ADULTS ★★★★	OVER 30 ★★★★		SENIORS ★★★★

Type of ride Indoor haunted-house ride. **Scope and scale** Major attraction. **When to go** Before 11:30 a.m. or after 6:30 p.m. **Special comments** Not to be missed; frightens some small children; some of Disneyland's best special effects. **Duration of ride** 5½-minute ride plus a 2-minute preshow. **Average wait in line per 100 people ahead of you** 2½ minutes. **Assumes** Both stretch rooms operating. **Loading speed** Fast.

DISNEY DISH WITH JIM HILL

"AND A GHOST WILL FOLLOW YOU HOME. . . ." Since The Haunted Mansion originally opened back in August 1969, the Ghost Host (as voiced by Disney legend Paul Frees) has been making the threat-promise that "a ghost will follow you home." Well, thanks to some new wireless technology, the Imagineers are finally making good on the Ghost Host's promise.

According to the current plan, guests will soon be able to use handheld devices like their cell phone or Nintendo DS to "capture" one of several ghosts that will be available for downloading inside of this ride. Then, once the guests return home, they'll be able to use this computer-generated spirit as an avatar on their computer. Mouse House managers hope this will encourage guests to "hurry back, hurry back."

Dark

Scary

DESCRIPTION AND COMMENTS With new characters (an ax-murdering bride), scenes, and effects added in 2006, The Haunted Mansion is a fun attraction more than a scary one. An ingenious preshow serves as a vehicle to deliver guests to the ride's boarding area, where they board "Doom Buggies" for a ride through the mansion's parlor, dining room, library, halls, and attic before descending to an uncommonly active graveyard. Disney employs almost every special effect in its repertoire in The Haunted Mansion, making it one of the most inventive and different of all Disney attractions. Be warned that some youngsters build a lot of anxiety concerning what they think they will see. The actual attraction scares almost nobody.

The Haunted Mansion is one of veteran *Unofficial Guide* writer Eve Zibart's favorite attractions. She warns:

Don't let the childishness of the old-fashioned Haunted Mansion put you off: this is one of the best attractions [in the park]. It's jam-packed with visual puns, special effects, hidden Mickeys, and really lovely Victorian-spooky sets. It's not scary, except in the sweetest of ways, but it will remind you of the days before ghost stories gave way to slasher flicks.

TOURING TIPS This would be more at home in Fantasyland, but no matter—it's Disney at its best: another not-to-be-missed attraction. Because The Haunted Mansion is in an especially high-traffic corridor (between Pirates of the Caribbean and Splash Mountain), it stays busy all day. Try to see The Haunted Mansion before 11:30 a.m., after 6:30 p.m., or while a parade is in progress. In the evening, crowds for *Fantasmic!* gather in front of The Haunted Mansion, making it very difficult to access.

Pirates of the Caribbean ★★★★

APPEAL BY AGE	PRESCHOOL ★★★	GRADE SCHOOL ★★★★½	TEENS ★★★★
YOUNG ADULTS ★★★★	OVER 30 ★★★★½		SENIORS ★★★★½

Type of ride A Disney indoor-adventure boat ride. **Scope and scale** Major attraction. **When to go** Before 11:30 a.m. or after 4:30 p.m. **Special comments** Frightens some small children; our pick as one of Disneyland's very best. **Duration of ride** Approximately 14 minutes. **Average wait in line per 100 people ahead of you** 3 minutes. **Assumes** 42 boats operating. **Loading speed** Fast.

Dark

Scary

Loud

DESCRIPTION AND COMMENTS Another boat ride, this time indoors, through a series of sets depicting a pirate raid on an island settlement, from the bombardment of the fortress to the debauchery that follows the victory. Pirates of the Caribbean was the target of a much-publicized political-correctness controversy relating to the objectification of women and the "boys will be boys" way in which the pirates' debauchery was depicted. Ultimately, Disney was pressured into revamping the attraction (though not much). More recently, the attraction underwent an extensive rehab that included the addition of characters (Jack Sparrow and Barbossa) from the three *Pirates of the Caribbean* movies.

TOURING TIPS Another not-to-be-missed attraction. Undoubtedly one of the most elaborate and imaginative attractions in Disneyland Park. Though engineered to move large crowds, this ride sometimes gets overwhelmingly busy in the early and midafternoon. Try to ride before noon or while a parade or *Fantasmic!* is in progress.

NEW ORLEANS SQUARE EATERIES AND SHOPS

DESCRIPTION AND COMMENTS Shops and restaurants in New Orleans Square impart a special realism to the setting. **The Blue Bayou** is to the left of the Pirates of the Caribbean exit. With its waterside, bayou-at-dusk setting, The Blue Bayou offers an exotic, romantic atmosphere equaled by few restaurants anywhere. Extensive changes in the New Orleans Square restaurants make them the park's premiere dining venues, with the widest variety of dining options available anywhere in the resort. The newly remodeled Blue Bayou, discussed above, has an extensive new menu and prices higher than a swamp cypress. Disney is repositioning The Blue Bayou as a fine-dining experience comparable to the Napa Rose restaurant at Disney's Grand Californian Hotel. **Café Orléans** has been transformed to a table-service restaurant, with a new kitchen and an entirely new menu featuring the popular Blue Bayou Monte Cristo sandwich; a meat-free Monte Cristo with Swiss, mozzarella, and double-cream Brie; a crab-salad sandwich; French onion soup; made-to-order crepes; and Mickey-shaped beignets. Diners can choose to eat indoors or on the patio. Priority Seating for the Blue Bayou and Café Orleans can be made 60 days in advance by calling the Disney Dine Line at ☎ 714-781-DINE.

Counter-service dining choices include the **French Market,** serving jambalaya and fried chicken, and the **Royal Street Veranda** specializing in gumbo and seafood chowder served in bread bowls, along with specialty coffees.

Possibly the most overlooked counter-service restaurant in the park is **La Petite Pâtisserie.** Consisting of only two modest serving windows midblock on Royal Street, it serves good desserts and coffee.

TOURING TIPS New Orleans Square offers the best dining in the park. If you have some extra time, treat yourself to a meal at The Blue Bayou. The food is excellent, and the atmosphere will knock you out.

CRITTER COUNTRY

CRITTER COUNTRY, SITUATED AT THE END of a cul-de-sac and accessible via New Orleans Square, sports a pioneer appearance not unlike that of Frontierland.

Davy Crockett's Explorer Canoes ★★★

APPEAL BY AGE	PRESCHOOL ★★★★	GRADE SCHOOL ★★★★	TEENS ★★★
YOUNG ADULTS ★★★		OVER 30 ★★★	SENIORS ★★★

Type of ride Scenic canoe ride. **Scope and scale** Minor attraction. **When to go** Before 11 a.m. **Special comments** Skip if the lines are long; closes at dusk. **Special comments** Most fun way to see Rivers of America. **Duration of ride** 8–10 minutes, depending on how fast you paddle. **Average wait in line per 100 people ahead of you** 12½ minutes. **Assumes** 6 canoes operating. **Loading speed** Slow.

DESCRIPTION AND COMMENTS Paddle-powered ride (you do the paddling) around Tom Sawyer Island and Fort Wilderness. Runs the same route with the same sights as the steamboat and the sailing ship. The canoes operate only on busier days and close at dusk. The sights are fun and the ride is a little different in that the patrons paddle the canoe. We think this is the most fun of any of the various river trips. Long lines from about 11 a.m. on reflect the popularity of this attraction.

TOURING TIPS The canoes represent one of four ways to see the same waterways. Since the canoes are slower in loading, we usually opt for the larger steamboat or sailing ship. If you are not up for a boat ride, a different view of the same sights can be had by hoofing around Tom Sawyer Island and Fort Wilderness. Try to ride before 11 a.m. or just before dusk. The canoes operate on selected days and seasonal periods only. If the canoes are a big deal to you, call ahead to make sure they are operating.

Splash Mountain (FASTPASS) ★★★★½

APPEAL BY AGE	PRESCHOOL †	GRADE SCHOOL ★★★★★	TEENS ★★★★★
YOUNG ADULTS ★★★★★		OVER 30 ★★★★½	SENIORS ★★★★½

† Many preschoolers are too short to meet the height requirement, while others are intimidated by watching the ride while standing in line. Of those preschoolers who actually ride, most give the attraction high marks; ★★★★.

Type of ride Water-flume adventure boat ride. **Scope and scale** Headliner. **When to go** Before 9:45 a.m. or use FASTPASS. **Special comments** A wet winner, not to be missed; children must be 40" tall to ride; those under 7 years of age must ride with an adult; switching off available (see page 152). **Duration of ride** About 10 minutes. **Average wait in line per 100 people ahead of you** 3½ minutes. **Assumes** Operation at full capacity. **Loading speed** Moderate.

Scary   Wet   Lose Things

DESCRIPTION AND COMMENTS Sporting new logs, Splash Mountain is a Disney-style amusement-park flume ride. The ride combines steep chutes with a variety of Disney's best special effects. Covering more than half a mile, the ride splashes through swamps, caves, and backwoods bayous before climaxing in a 52-foot plunge and Br'er Rabbit's triumphant return home. The entire ride is populated by more than 100 audio-animatronic characters, including Br'er Rabbit, Br'er Bear, and Br'er Fox, all regaling riders with songs, including "Zip-A-Dee-Doo-Dah."

TOURING TIPS This is the most popular ride in Disneyland Park for patrons of all ages—happy, exciting, and adventuresome all at once. Though eclipsed somewhat by the Indiana Jones attraction, Splash Mountain nevertheless builds crowds quickly during the morning, and waits of more than two hours are not uncommon once Disneyland Park fills up on a busy day. To avoid the crowds, arrive at the park before opening time and get in line at Splash Mountain no later than 40 minutes after Disneyland Park opens. Lines persist throughout the day until a few minutes before closing.

There are four ways to experience Splash Mountain without a long wait. The first is to be on hand when the park opens and to sprint over and get in line before anyone else. The second way is to allow the initial mob of Splash cadets to be processed through and to arrive at Splash Mountain about 20 to 40 minutes after the park opens or after riding *Finding Nemo* Submarine Voyage and/or Space Mountain. A third strategy is to get in line for Splash Mountain during a parade and/or a performance of *Fantasmic!* Be advised, however, that huge crowds gathering along the New Orleans Square and Frontierland waterfronts for *Fantasmic!* make getting to Splash Mountain very difficult (if not impossible) just before, during, and just after performances. Fourth, use FASTPASS.

A Suffolk, Virginia, mom contends that there are more important considerations than beating crowds:

The only recommendation I do have is to definitely wait to do Splash Mountain at the end of the day. We were seated in the front of the ride and needless to say we were drenched to the bone. If we had ridden the ride [first thing in

WARNING!
For Bouffants, Rug Wearers, and Elvis Impersonators
This Ride Will Muss Your 'Do

the morning] *according to your plan, I personally would have been miserable for the rest of the day. Parents, beware! It says you will get wet, not drowned.*

It is almost a certainty that you will get wet, and possibly drenched, riding Splash Mountain. If you visit on a cool day, you may want to carry a plastic garbage bag. By tearing holes in the bottom and sides, you can fashion a sack dress of sorts to keep you dry. Be sure to tuck the bag under your bottom. By the way, it doesn't matter whether you ride in front or back. You will get wet regardless. If you have a camera, either leave it with a nonriding member of your party or wrap it in a plastic bag.

DISNEY DISH WITH JIM HILL

YIKES! BEAR BUTTS AND T&A IN CRITTER COUNTRY Before any audio-animatronic figure can be installed in an attraction, the robot must go through a production phase known as "Test and Adjust," in which the new figure is run for hours on end, repeating over and over the same action it must perform every day.

Why do I mention this? Well, as you're floating through Splash Mountain and encounter Br'er Bear's butt sticking out of that hole in the honey tree, imagine the poor Imagineer who monitored this portly, fuzzy rump during its hours of testing.

One final word: This is not just a fancy flume ride; it is a full-blown Disney adventure. The scariest part by far is the big drop into the pool (visible from the sidewalk in front of Splash Mountain), and even this plunge looks worse than it really is. Despite reassurances, however, many children wig out after watching it from the sidewalk. A Grand Rapids, Michigan, mother recalls her kids' rather unique reaction:

We discovered after the fact that our children thought they would go under water after the five-story drop and tried to hold their breath throughout the ride in preparation. They were really too preoccupied to enjoy the clever Br'er Rabbit story.

Flash Mountain

Type of attraction Water-flume adventure strip show. **Scope and scale** Eye-popper. **When to go** Spring break, weekend nights. **Special comments** A liberating experience. **Author's rating** Author is too near-sighted to rate accurately. **Duration of presentation** About 2 seconds.

DESCRIPTION AND COMMENTS It was reported by the Associated Press that certain female Splash Mountain riders (though we're sure that male riders, not to be outdone, will soon follow their female compatriots in similar fashion) are behaving in a most un–Disney-like manner by "flinging their blouses open" as they plummet down the climactic plunge at the end of the ride. (Fully visible, we might add, to dozens of guests waiting in line in front of the attraction.)

Indeed, automatic cameras shooting souvenir photographs of participants have documented an astounding array of feminine anatomy in free-fall. The practice is apparently too spontaneous for Disneyland, which reports that it "has no plans at this time to change the theme of the attraction." Though, ever mindful of guest safety, management has concerns about "undue congestion" in front of the ride and the "possibility of guests catching cold." Disney also initiated what it calls its "nipple policy," which decrees that photos of offending guests shall be vaporized immediately. The policy applies to both men and women, so if you want to buy a souvenir pic, keep your shirt on. Cast members, however, some of whom had veritable scrapbooks of the floating strippers, are not unexpectedly irked by the policy.

TOURING TIPS   During spring break or weekend nights, spectators should stand on the walkway directly in front of Splash Mountain. Be sure to bring a sign denouncing such unchaste exhibitionist behavior, or, depending on your point of view, a camera with a telescopic lens. If you are a participant, you will have approximately two minutes following the big plunge to get yourself back together before you arrive at the unloading area.

The Many Adventures of Winnie the Pooh   ★★★½

APPEAL BY AGE	PRESCHOOL ★★★★½	GRADE SCHOOL ★★★★	TEENS ★★★
YOUNG ADULTS ★★★	OVER 30 ★★★		SENIORS ★★★

Type of ride Indoor track ride. Scope and scale Minor attraction. When to go Before 10 a.m. or in the 2 hours before closing. Special comments Critter Country's newest ride. Duration of ride About 3 minutes. Average wait in line per 100 people ahead of you 5 minutes. Loading speed Moderate.

DESCRIPTION AND COMMENTS   Opened in the summer of 2003, this addition to Critter Country replaced the alternately praised and maligned Country Bear

Thumbs Up for the Whole Family

Playhouse. Pooh is sunny, upbeat, and fun—more in the image of Peter Pan's Flight or Splash Mountain. You ride a "Hunny Pot" through the pages of a huge picture book into the Hundred Acre Wood, where you encounter Pooh, Piglet, Eeyore, Owl, Rabbit, Tigger, Kanga, and Roo as they contend with a blustery day. There's even a dream sequence with Heffalumps and Woozles, a favorite of this 30-something couple from Lexington, Massachusetts, who think Pooh has plenty to offer adults:

The attention to detail and special effects on this ride make it worth seeing even if you don't have children in your party. The Pooh dream sequence was great!

TOURING TIPS   Try to ride before 10 a.m., during a parade, or in the hours before closing. At extremely crowded times of year, Disney has been known to add Pooh to the FASTPASS lineup. Because of the ride's relatively small guest capacity, the daily allocation of FASTPASSes is usually distributed by 1 p.m. or so.

Critter Country Eateries and Shops

DESCRIPTION AND COMMENTS   Critter Country restaurants and shops offer the standard array of souvenirs and fast food. The main counter-service venue in Critter Country is the **Hungry Bear Restaurant,** which serves burgers, grilled chicken breasts, fried chicken tenders, and salads. Portions are large. Expect to pay $8 to $9 for a sandwich, fries, and drink. Children's meals featuring chicken tender strips are available for about $5 to $6. In keeping with the park's ongoing evaluation of menus, expect to see some new selections in Critter Country.

TOURING TIPS Even with the tremendous popularity of Splash Mountain, the restaurants in Critter Country remain good bets for avoiding the lunch and dinner rush. The Hungry Bear Restaurant, in addition, offers a spacious open deck with a great view of the New Orleans Square and Frontierland river activity. The **Harbour Galley,** a waterfront dockside eatery near the dock of the *Columbia,* serves McDonald's French fries.

FRONTIERLAND

FRONTIERLAND ADJOINS NEW ORLEANS SQUARE as you move clockwise around the park. The focus here is on the Old West, with log stockades and pioneer trappings. In addition to the attractions listed below, there is a small petting farm on the walkway to Fantasyland.

Big Thunder Mountain Railroad (FASTPASS) ★★★★

APPEAL BY AGE	PRESCHOOL ★★★	GRADE SCHOOL ★★★★	TEENS ★★★★
YOUNG ADULTS ★★★★		OVER 30 ★★★★	SENIORS ★★★

Type of ride Tame roller coaster with exciting special effects. **Scope and scale** Headliner. **When to go** Before 10:30 a.m. and after 6:30 p.m. or use FASTPASS. **Special comments** Great effects, though a relatively tame ride; children must be 40" tall to ride; those under age 7 must ride with an adult; switching off available (see page 152). **Duration of ride** 3½ minutes. **Average wait in line per 100 people ahead of you** 3 minutes. **Assumes** 5 trains operating. **Loading speed** Moderate to fast.

Scary

Rough

Lose Things

Motion Sickness

DESCRIPTION AND COMMENTS A roller-coaster ride through and around a Disney "mountain." The time is Gold Rush days, and the idea is that you are on a runaway mine train. Along with the usual thrills of a roller-coaster ride (about a five on a "scary scale" of ten), the ride showcases some first-rate examples of Disney creativity: lifelike scenes depicting a mining town, falling rocks, and an earthquake, all humorously animated.

TOURING TIPS A superb Disney experience, but not too wild a roller coaster. The emphasis here is much more on the sights than on the thrill of the ride itself. Regardless, it's a not-to-be-missed attraction.

As an example of how differently guests experience Disney attractions, consider this letter we received from a reader in Brookline, Massachusetts:

Being in the senior citizens' category and having limited time, my friend and I confined our activities to those attractions rated as four or five stars for seniors.

DISNEY DISH WITH JIM HILL

MEANWHILE, BACK AT THE RANCH . . . Big Thunder Ranch sits on the backside of Big Thunder Mountain Railroad along a quiet path that connects Fantasyland and Frontierland. In the past, the ranch has been used as a barbecue restaurant and as a petting farm. The Imagineers have a boxcar of plans for this relatively quiet corner of the park. Too many, in fact. Here are just a few of the ideas currently under consideration:

• A Woody's Roundup area, which would celebrate the cowboy toy from Pixar's popular *Toy Story* series. Preliminary plans call for a Bullseye the Horse–themed carousel, a Jessie the Cowgirl Tornado Twirl spinning attraction, and a dark ride that would be themed around this trio of characters.

• A *Lone Ranger* stunt show, which would be built around various characters and action scenes from Disney's upcoming big-screen western. Striving to introduce a whole new generation to the Masked Man and his faithful Indian companion, the film will reunite the writers, producer, and director of the hugely successful *Pirates of the Caribbean* series.

• Geyser Mountain, a brand-new thrill ride that would use the technology developed for *The Twilight Zone* Tower of Terror, only this time around, instead of dropping down an elevator shaft, you'd be propelled high in the air as your ride vehicle is blasted with a water jet from a super-geyser!

Because of your recommendation and because you listed it as "not to be missed," we waited for one hour to board the Big Thunder Mountain Railroad, which you rated a "5" on a scary scale of "10." After living through 3 ½ minutes of pure terror, I will rate that attraction a "15" on a scary scale of "10." We were so busy holding on and screaming and even praying for our safety that we did not see any falling rocks, a mining town, or an earthquake. In our opinion the Big Thunder Mountain Railroad should not be recommended for seniors or preschool children.

A woman from New England discovered that there's more to consider about Big Thunder than being scared:

Big Thunder Mountain Railroad was rated "5" on the scary scale. I won't say it warranted a higher scare rating, but it was much higher on the lose-your-lunch meter. One more sharp turn and the kids in front of me would have needed a dip in Splash Mountain!

Frontierland Shootin' Exposition ★★

APPEAL BY AGE	PRESCHOOL ★★½	GRADE SCHOOL ★★★½	TEENS ★★★½
YOUNG ADULTS ★★★	OVER 30 ★★★		SENIORS ★★★

Type of attraction Electronic shooting gallery. **Scope and scale** Diversion. **When to go** Whenever convenient. **Special comments** Not included in your admission; costs extra; a very nifty shooting gallery.

DESCRIPTION AND COMMENTS A very elaborate electronic shooting gallery that costs 50¢ to play. One of the few attractions in Disneyland Park not included in the admission pass.

TOURING TIPS Good fun for those who like to shoot, but definitely not a place to blow time if you are on a tight schedule. Try it on your second day if time allows.

Golden Horseshoe Stage   ★★★★½

APPEAL BY AGE   PRESCHOOL ★★★   GRADE SCHOOL ★★★★   TEENS ★★★★½
YOUNG ADULTS ★★★★½   OVER 30 ★★★★½   SENIORS ★★★★½

Type of attraction Western dance-hall stage show. **Scope and scale** Minor attraction. **When to go** Catch a show and lunch at the same time. **Special comments** Delightfully zany show; food is available. **Duration of presentation** 30 minutes.

DESCRIPTION AND COMMENTS The Golden Horse-shoe has always offered a decent show, hearty sandwiches, and a nice air-conditioned respite from the sun. A couple of years back, however, either intentionally or accidentally, Disney signed up an act so good that it turned

Thumbs Up for the Whole Family

the humble venue into one of the best attractions in either park. The new talent, the unfortunately named Billy Hill and the Hillbillies, consists of a quartet of master bluegrass fiddlers who also happen to be born comics. The show is double-over funny, zany, and totally engaging. And did we mention the fiddling is phenomenal? At the end of the show, we noticed something we've never seen at any Disney stage production—the audience refused to leave. Instead, they stood clapping and cheering like at a rock concert, trying to bring back the performers for an encore. They stayed at it so long that the fiddlers were forced to return and take a second bow (though they didn't perform another song). Still the audience lingered, departing only reluctantly after many minutes. If Disney has the good sense to hold on to this act, we rate the Golden Horseshoe ★★★★½ and classify it as not to be missed.

TOURING TIPS The Golden Horseshoe has changed its reservations system to first-come, first-served seating. Performance times are listed in the daily *Times Guide*. We recommend taking in a show and having lunch at the same time. Portions are big enough for kids to split. Be forewarned that guests seated on the first floor are likely to be conscripted into the show.

Mark Twain Riverboat   ★★★

APPEAL BY AGE   PRESCHOOL ★★★   GRADE SCHOOL ★★★   TEENS ★★½
YOUNG ADULTS ★★★   OVER 30 ★★★   SENIORS ★★★

Type of ride Scenic boat ride. **Scope and scale** Minor attraction. **When to go** Between 11 a.m. and 5 p.m. **Special comments** Provides an excellent vantage point; suspends operation at dusk. **Duration of ride** About 14 minutes. **Average wait to board** 10 minutes. **Assumes** Normal operations. **Loading method** En masse.

DESCRIPTION AND COMMENTS Large-capacity paddle-wheel riverboat that navigates the waters around Tom Sawyer Island and Fort Wilderness.

Thumbs Up for the Whole Family

A beautiful craft, the riverboat provides a lofty perch from which to see Frontierland and New Orleans Square.

TOURING TIPS One of two regularly operating boat rides that survey the same real estate. Since the Explorer Canoes are slower in loading, we think the riverboat makes more efficient use of touring time. If you are not in the mood for a boat ride, many of the same sights can be seen by hiking around Tom Sawyer Island and Fort Wilderness.

Sailing Ship *Columbia*   ★★★½

APPEAL BY AGE   PRESCHOOL ★★★★   GRADE SCHOOL ★★★½   TEENS ★★★
YOUNG ADULTS   ★★★½   OVER 30   ★★★   SENIORS   ★★★

Type of ride Scenic boat ride. **Scope and scale** Minor attraction. **When to go** Between 11 a.m. and 5 p.m. **Special comments** Pirates on extremely busy days; a stunning piece of workmanship. **Duration of ride** About 14 minutes. **Average wait to board** 10 minutes. **Assumes** Normal operations. **Loading method** En masse.

DESCRIPTION AND COMMENTS The *Columbia* is a stunning replica of a three-masted 18th-century merchant ship. Both its above and below decks are open to visitors, with below decks outfitted to depict the life and work environment of the ship's crew in 1787. The *Columbia* operates only on busier days and runs the same route as the canoes, keelboats, and the riverboat. As with the other river craft, the *Columbia* suspends operations at dusk.

Thumbs Up for the Whole Family

An Oregon reader, who liked the *Columbia* but had some problems with its officers, wrote:

It is truly a beautiful ship and would have been a pleasant ride but for the incessant jabbering of the "captain." A little humorous banter is always appreciated, but we were ready to strangle this guy. We went below deck for awhile to get away from him, and would recommend to others to do this, even with a more restrained captain, as it is a little museum complete with outfitted bunks and other sailing paraphernalia.

TOURING TIPS The *Columbia,* along with the *Mark Twain* Riverboat, provides a short-wait, high-carrying-capacity alternative for cruising the Rivers of America. We found the beautifully crafted *Columbia* by far the most aesthetically pleasing and historically interesting of any of the three choices of boat rides on the Rivers of America.

If you have time to be choosy, ride aboard the *Columbia*. After boarding, while waiting for the cruise to begin, tour below deck. Once the ride begins, come topside and stroll the deck, taking in the beauty and complexity of the rigging.

The *Columbia* does not usually require a long wait, which makes it a good bet during the crowded afternoon hours.

Pirate's Lair on Tom Sawyer Island   ★★★

APPEAL BY AGE PRESCHOOL ★★★★★   GRADE SCHOOL ★★★★★   TEENS ★★★½
YOUNG ADULTS   ★★★   OVER 30   ★★★   SENIORS   ★★★

Type of attraction Walk-through exhibit and rustic playground. **Scope and scale** Minor attraction. **When to go** Midmorning through late afternoon. **Special comments** The place for rambunctious kids; closes at dusk.

DESCRIPTION AND COMMENTS   Pirate's Lair on Tom Sawyer Island manages to impart something of a sense of isolation from the rest of the park. It has hills to climb, a cave and a treehouse to explore, tipsy bridges to cross, paths to follow, and a "rock-climbing" play area. It's a delight for adults but a godsend for children who have been in tow all day.

As an aside, a mother of four from Duncan, South Carolina, found Tom Sawyer Island as much a refuge as an attraction, writing:

I do have one tip for parents. In the afternoon, when the crowds were at their peak, the weather was hottest, and the kids started lagging behind, our organization began to suffer. We then retreated over to Tom Sawyer Island, which proved to be a true haven. My husband and I found a secluded bench and regrouped. Meanwhile, the kids were able to run freely in the shade. Afterwards, we were ready to tackle the park again refreshed and with direction once more.

Capitalizing on the successful *Pirates of the Caribbean* movies, Disney restyled Tom Sawyer Island as a "Pirate's Lair" in 2007. Though it's still a children's adventure playground, the island now has sets from the films such as William Turner's blacksmith shop, and story artifacts like Elizabeth Swann's love letters tucked into every nook and cranny. Included in the makeover are a number of special effects and gadgets. Kids exploring the caverns of Dead Man's Grotto will encounter spooky voices, ghostly apparitions, and buried treasure. Elsewhere, a sunken chest can be discovered by operating a hoist.

Evidently, you can't have a pirate's lair without a bunch of gore. A pop-up head and moving skeletal arm are just the beginning. There's also a "bone cage," and our favorite, a treasure chest containing Davy Jones's beating heart. If your child doesn't have a playmate, don't worry. There's usually a gang of itinerant pirates on hand to administer the "pirate oath" and, somewhat incongruously, lead sing-alongs. A couple times a day, there is an "interactive" brawl involving sword fights and cannon battles. Tom Sawyer Island is an improbable and logistically ill-suited venue for live entertainment, so don't be surprised if the brawl has moved to the mainland or gone the way of the dodo by the time of your visit.

TOURING TIPS   Pirate's Lair on Tom Sawyer Island is not one of Disneyland Park's more celebrated attractions, but it's certainly one of the most well done. Attention to detail is excellent and kids particularly revel in its adventuresome atmosphere. We think it's a must for families with children ages 5 to 15. If your party has only adults, visit the island on your second day, or stop by on your first day if you have seen the attractions you most wanted to see. We like the island from about noon until the island closes at dusk. Access is by raft from Frontierland, and you may have to stand in line to board both coming and going. Two or three rafts operate simultaneously, however, and the round trip is usually pretty time efficient. Tom Sawyer Island takes about 35 minutes or so to see, but many children could spend a whole day.

Raft to and from Tom Sawyer Island

Type of ride Transportation ride to Tom Sawyer Island. **Scope and scale** Minor attraction. **Special comments** Same information applies to return trip. **Duration of ride** A little over a minute one way. **Average wait in line per 100 people ahead of you** 4½ minutes. **Assumes** 3 rafts operating. **Loading speed** Moderate.

FRONTIERLAND EATERIES AND SHOPS

DESCRIPTION AND COMMENTS More specialty and souvenir shopping await visitors in Frontierland. One of our favorite restaurants in the park is **Rancho del Zocalo.** Good Mexican fare is available as you would expect, but the Rancho also serves the best barbecue chicken, ribs, and beef in the park. The restaurant is located across from the entrance of Big Thunder Mountain. Prices are in the $9-to-$11 range.

We also like the **River Belle Terrace** (roast chicken, pasta, salad). With prices ranging from $8 to $12 per person for a meal and a drink, all four Frontierland eateries are somewhat more expensive than Disney's fast-food burgers and hot dogs. Children's meals, running about $6, are available at all four restaurants.

TOURING TIPS Most guests do not know that the Golden Horseshoe serves food until they stop by for a show. This means that the Golden Horseshoe goes virtually unnoticed by the lunch crowd between shows.

FANTASYLAND

TRULY AN ENCHANTING PLACE, spread gracefully like a miniature alpine village beneath the towers of Sleeping Beauty Castle, Fantasyland is the heart of the park.

Alice in Wonderland ★★★

APPEAL BY AGE	PRESCHOOL ★★★½		GRADE SCHOOL ★★★½
TEENS ★★★	YOUNG ADULTS ★★★	OVER 30 ★★★	SENIORS ★★★

Type of ride Track ride in the dark. **Scope and scale** Minor attraction. **When to go** Before 11 a.m. or after 5 p.m. **Special comments** Good characterization and story line; do not confuse with Mad Tea Party ride. **Duration of ride** Almost 4 minutes. **Average wait in line per 100 people ahead of you** 12 minutes. **Assumes** 16 cars operating. **Loading speed** Slow.

Dark

DESCRIPTION AND COMMENTS This attraction recalls the story of *Alice in Wonderland* with some nice surprises and colorful effects. Guests ride nifty caterpillar cars in this Disney spookhouse adaptation. Though not a spring chicken, Alice is a third-generation Disney dark ride with more vibrant, evocative, and three-dimensional sets and characters than Pinocchio's Daring Journey or Mr. Toad's Wild Ride.

TOURING TIPS This is a very well-done ride in the best Disney tradition, with familiar characters, good effects, and a theme you can follow. Unfortunately, it loads very slowly.

Casey Jr. Circus Train ★★½

APPEAL BY AGE	PRESCHOOL ★★★★	GRADE SCHOOL ★★★
TEENS ★½	YOUNG ADULTS ★★★ OVER 30 ★★★	SENIORS ★★★

Type of ride Miniature-train ride. **Scope and scale** Minor attraction. **When to go** Before 11 a.m. or after 5 p.m. **Special comments** A quiet, scenic ride. **Duration of ride** A little more than 3 minutes. **Average wait in line per 100 people ahead of you** 12 minutes. **Assumes** 2 trains operating. **Loading speed** Slow.

DESCRIPTION AND COMMENTS A long-standing attraction and a pet project of Walt Disney, Casey Jr. circulates through a landscape of miniature towns, farms, and lakes. There are some stunning bonsai specimens visible from this ride, as well as some of the most manicured landscaping you are ever likely to see.

TOURING TIPS This ride covers the same sights as the Storybook Land Canal Boats but does it faster and with less of a wait. Accommodations for adults, however, are less than optimal on this ride, with some passengers having to squeeze into diminutive caged cars (after all, it is a circus train). If you do not have children in your party, you can enjoy the same sights more comfortably by riding the Storybook Land Canal Boats.

Disneyland Railroad

DESCRIPTION AND COMMENTS The Disneyland Railroad stops in Fantasyland/ Mickey's Toontown on its circuit around the park. The station is located to the left of It's a Small World, next to the Fantasyland Theatre. From this usually uncrowded boarding point, transportation is available to Tomorrowland, Main Street, and New Orleans Square.

Dumbo the Flying Elephant ★★★½

APPEAL BY AGE	PRESCHOOL ★★★★★	GRADE SCHOOL ★★★½
TEENS ★★	YOUNG ADULTS ★½ OVER 30 ★½	SENIORS ★½

Type of ride Disneyfied midway ride. **Scope and scale** Minor attraction. **When to go** Before 10 a.m. or during late evening parades, fireworks, and *Fantasmic!* performances. **Special comments** An attractive children's ride. **Duration of ride** 1 minute and 40 seconds. **Average wait in line per 100 people ahead of you** 12 minutes. **Assumes** Normal staffing. **Loading speed** Slow.

DESCRIPTION AND COMMENTS A nice, tame, happy children's ride based on the lovable Disney flying elephant. An upgraded rendition of a ride that can be found at state fairs and amusement parks across the country. Shortcomings notwithstanding, Dumbo is the favorite Disneyland Park attraction of most preschoolers. A lot of readers take us to task for lumping Dumbo in with state-fair midway rides. These comments from a reader in Armdale, Nova Scotia, are representative:

I think you have acquired a jaded attitude. I know [Dumbo] is not for everybody, but when we took our oldest child (then just 4), the sign at the end of the line said there would be a 90-minute wait. He knew and he didn't care, and he and I stood in the hot afternoon sun for 90 blissful minutes waiting for his 90-second flight. Anything that a 4-year-old would wait for that long and that patiently must be pretty special.

TOURING TIPS This is a slow-loading ride that we recommend you bypass unless you are on a very relaxed touring schedule. If your kids are excited about Dumbo, try to get them on the ride before 10 a.m., during the parades and *Fantasmic!,* or just before the park closes. Also, consider this advice from an Arlington, Virginia, mom:

Grown-ups beware! Dumbo is really a tight fit with one adult and two kids. My kids threw me out of their Dumbo and I had to sit in a Dumbo all by myself. Pretty embarrassing, and my husband got lots of pictures.

It's a Small World ★★★

APPEAL BY AGE	PRESCHOOL ★★★★★	GRADE SCHOOL ★★★½	TEENS ★★½
YOUNG ADULTS ★★★		OVER 30 ★★★	SENIORS ★★★½

Type of ride World brotherhood–themed indoor boat ride. **Scope and scale** Major attraction. **When to go** Anytime except after a parade. **Special comments** A pleasant change of pace. **Duration of ride** 14 minutes. **Average wait in line per 100 people ahead of you** 2½ minutes. **Assumes** Busy conditions with 56 boats operating. **Loading speed** Fast.

Thumbs Up for the Whole Family

DESCRIPTION AND COMMENTS A happy and upbeat attraction with a world-brotherhood theme and a catchy tune that will roll around in your head for weeks. Small boats convey visitors on a tour around the world, with singing and dancing dolls showcasing the dress and culture of each nation.

Almost everyone enjoys It's a Small World (well, there are those jaded folks who are put off by the dolls' homogeneous appearance, especially in light of the diversity theme), but it stands, along with the *Enchanted Tiki Room,* as an attraction that some could take or leave but that others consider one of

the real masterpieces of Disneyland Park. In any event, a woman from Holbrook, New York, wrote with this devilish suggestion for improvement:

Small World would be much better if each person got a few softballs on the way in!

A mom from Castleton, Vermont, added this:

It's a Small World at Fantasyland was like a pit stop in the Twilight Zone. They were very slow unloading the boats, and we were stuck in a line of about six boats waiting to get out while the endless chanting of that song grated on my nerves. I told my husband I was going to swim for it just to escape one more chorus.

TOURING TIPS Totally renovated and upgraded, It's a Small World is a fast-loading ride that's usually a good bet during the busier times of the day. The boats are moved along by water pressure, which increases as boats are added. Thus, the more boats in service when you ride (up to a maximum total of 60), the shorter the duration of the ride (and wait).

King Arthur Carrousel ★★★

**APPEAL BY AGE   PRESCHOOL ★★★★   GRADE SCHOOL ★★½   TEENS ★★
YOUNG ADULTS ★★½   OVER 30 ★★★   SENIORS ★★★**

Type of ride Merry-go-round. **Scope and scale** Minor attraction. **When to go** Before 11:30 a.m. or after 5 p.m. **Special comments** A showpiece carousel; adults enjoy the beauty and nostalgia of this ride. **Duration of ride** A little more than 2 minutes. **Average wait in line per 100 people ahead of you** 8 minutes. **Assumes** Normal staffing. **Loading speed** Slow.

DESCRIPTION AND COMMENTS A merry-go-round to be sure, but certainly one of the most elaborate and beautiful you will ever see, especially when lit at night.

TOURING TIPS Unless there are small children in your party, we suggest you appreciate this ride from the sidelines. If your children insist on riding, try to get them on before 11:30 a.m. or after 5 p.m. While nice to look at, the carrousel loads and unloads very slowly.

Mad Tea Party ★★

**APPEAL BY AGE   PRESCHOOL ★★★½   GRADE SCHOOL ★★★★   TEENS ★★★★
YOUNG ADULTS ★★★   OVER 30 ★★   SENIORS ★★**

Type of ride Midway-type spinning ride. **Scope and scale** Minor attraction. **When to go** Before 11 a.m. and after 5 p.m. **Special comments** You can make the teacups spin faster by turning the wheel in the center of the cup; fun but not worth the wait. **Duration of ride** 1½ minutes. **Average wait in line per 100 people ahead of you** 8 minutes. **Assumes** Normal staffing. **Loading speed** Slow.

DESCRIPTION AND COMMENTS Well done in the Disney style, but still just an amusement-park ride. *Alice in Wonderland*'s Mad Hatter provides the theme and patrons whirl around feverishly in big teacups. A rendition of this ride, sans Disney characters, can be found at every local carnival and fair.

TOURING TIPS This ride, aside from not being particularly special, loads notoriously slowly. Skip it on a busy schedule if the kids will let you. Ride in the morning of your second day if your schedule is more relaxed. A warning for parents who have not given this ride much thought: teenagers like nothing better than to lure an adult onto the teacups and then turn the wheel in the middle (which makes the cup spin faster) until the adults are plastered against the side of the cup and are on the verge of throwing up. Unless your life's ambition is to be the test subject in a human centrifuge, do not even consider getting on this ride with anyone younger than 21 years of age.

Matterhorn Bobsleds ★★★

APPEAL BY AGE	PRESCHOOL †	GRADE SCHOOL ★★★★	TEENS ★★★★
YOUNG ADULTS ★★★★		OVER 30 ★★★★	SENIORS ★★★

† Some preschoolers loved Matterhorn Bobsleds; others were frightened.

Type of ride Roller coaster. **Scope and scale** Major attraction. **When to go** During the first 90 minutes the park is open or during the hour before it closes. **Special comments** Fun ride but not too scary; 35" minimum-height requirement. **Duration of ride** 2½ minutes. **Average wait in line per 100 people ahead of you** 13 minutes. **Assumes** Both tracks operating with 10 sleds per track with 23-second dispatch intervals. **Loading speed** Moderate.

Scary

Rough

Lose Things

Motion Sickness

DESCRIPTION AND COMMENTS The Matterhorn is the most distinctive landmark on the Disneyland scene, visible from almost anywhere in the park. Updated and renovated in 1995, the Matterhorn maintains its popularity and long lines year in and year out. The Matterhorn Bobsleds is a roller-coaster ride with an alpine motif. On the scary scale, the ride ranks about six on a scale of ten (a little less intimidating than Space Mountain). The special effects cannot compare to Space Mountain, but they do afford a few surprises.

TOURING TIPS Lines for the Matterhorn form as soon as the gates open and persist throughout the day. Ride first thing in the morning or just before the park closes. If you are a roller-coaster person, ride Space Mountain and then hurry over and hop on the Matterhorn. If roller coasters are not the end-all for you, we recommend choosing one of the other coasters or saving one for a second day.

One of the things we like about the Matterhorn is that the entire queuing area is visible. This makes the lines look more oppressive than they actually are (causing newly arrived guests to bypass the attraction) and also provides an opportunity to closely approximate the time of your wait. If the line extending toward Tomorrowland reaches a point across from the Kodak Photo Spot, your wait to ride the Matterhorn Bobsleds will be about 16 minutes.

Mr. Toad's Wild Ride ★★½

APPEAL BY AGE	PRESCHOOL ★★★½	GRADE SCHOOL ★★★½	TEENS ★★★½
YOUNG ADULTS ★★★		OVER 30 ★★★	SENIORS ★★★

Type of ride Track ride in the dark. **Scope and scale** Minor attraction. **When to go** Before 11 a.m. **Special comments** Past its prime. **Duration of ride** Almost 2 minutes. **Average wait in line per 100 people ahead of you** 9 minutes. **Assumes** 12 cars operating. **Loading speed** Slow.

Dark

DESCRIPTION AND COMMENTS Mr. Toad is a twisting, curving ride in the dark that passes two-dimensional sets and props. There are a couple of clever effects, but basically it's at the technological basement of the Disney attraction mix. Its sister attraction at Walt Disney World was scrapped in 1999.

TOURING TIPS Not a great but certainly a popular attraction. Lines build early in the day and never let up. Catch Mr. Toad before 11 a.m.

Peter Pan's Flight ★★★★

APPEAL BY AGE	PRESCHOOL ★★★★	GRADE SCHOOL ★★★★	TEENS ★★★½
YOUNG ADULTS ★★★★		OVER 30 ★★★★	SENIORS ★★★★

Type of ride Indoor fantasy-adventure ride. **Scope and scale** Minor attraction. **When to go** Before 10 a.m. and after 6 p.m. **Special comments** Happy and mellow. **Duration of ride** Just over 2 minutes. **Average wait in line per 100 people ahead of you** 11 minutes. **Assumes** 13 ships operating. **Loading speed** Slow.

DESCRIPTION AND COMMENTS Although it is not considered one of Disneyland Park's major attractions, Peter Pan's Flight is superbly designed and absolutely delightful, with a happy theme, a reunion with some unforgettable Disney characters, beautiful effects, and charming

Thumbs Up for the Whole Family

music. Tiny pirate ships suspended from an overhead track launch you from Wendy's window to fly over nighttime London and on to Never Land and an encounter with Captain Hook, Mr. Smee, and the ubiquitous crocodile.

TOURING TIPS Though not a major feature of Disneyland Park, we nevertheless classify it as the best attraction in Fantasyland. Try to ride before 10 a.m. or after 6 p.m., during the afternoon or evening parade(s), or during a performance of *Fantasmic!* Peter Pan at Walt Disney World is a FASTPASS attraction and should be here as well.

Pinocchio's Daring Journey ★★

APPEAL BY AGE	PRESCHOOL ★★★	GRADE SCHOOL ★★★	TEENS ★★½
YOUNG ADULTS ★★½		OVER 30 ★★½	SENIORS ★★½

Type of ride Track ride in the dark. **Scope and scale** Minor attraction. **When to go** Before 11:30 a.m. and after 4:30 p.m. **Special comments** A big letdown. **Duration of ride** Almost 3 minutes. **Average wait in line per 100 people ahead of you** 8 minutes. **Assumes** 15 cars operating. **Loading speed** Slow.

Dark

DESCRIPTION AND COMMENTS This is another twisting, curving track ride in the dark, this time tracing the adventures of Pinocchio as he tries to find his way home. The action is hard to follow, and it lacks continuity. Although the sets are three-dimensional and more visually compelling than, say, Mr. Toad, the story line is dull and fails to engage the guest. Definitely the least interesting of the Fantasyland dark rides.

TOURING TIPS　The word must be out about Pinocchio, because the lines are seldom very long. Still, you will encounter the longest waits between 11:30 a.m. and 4:30 p.m.

Sleeping Beauty Castle

DESCRIPTION AND COMMENTS　Disneyland Park's most famous icon, Sleeping Beauty Castle is at the heart of Disneyland. The castle serves as a stage for any number of shows and special events.

Snow White's Scary Adventures ★★★

APPEAL BY AGE	PRESCHOOL ★★★	GRADE SCHOOL ★★★	TEENS ★★½
YOUNG ADULTS ★★★	OVER 30 ★★★		SENIORS ★★★

Type of ride Track ride in the dark. **Scope and scale** Minor attraction. **When to go** Before 11 a.m. and after 5 p.m. **Special comments** Quite intimidating for preschoolers; worth seeing if the wait is not long. **Duration of ride** Almost 2 minutes. **Average wait in line per 100 people ahead of you** 9 minutes. **Assumes** 10 cars operating. **Loading speed** Slow.

Dark

Scary

DESCRIPTION AND COMMENTS　Here, you ride in a mining car in the dark through a series of sets drawn from *Snow White and the Seven Dwarfs*. The attraction has a *Perils of Pauline* flavor and features Snow White (whom you never see) as she narrowly escapes harm at the hands of the wicked witch. The action and effects are a cut above Mr. Toad's Wild Ride but not as good as Peter Pan's Flight.

TOURING TIPS　Enjoyable but not particularly compelling. Experience it if the lines are not too long or on a second-day visit. Ride before 11 a.m. or after 5 p.m. if possible. Also, don't take the "scary" part too seriously. The witch looks mean, but most kids take her in stride. Or maybe not. A mother from Knoxville, Tennessee, commented:

The outside looks cute and fluffy, but inside, the evil witch just keeps coming at you. My 5-year-old, who rode Space Mountain three times [and took other scary rides] right in stride, was near panic when our car stopped unexpectedly twice during Snow White. [After Snow White] my 6-year-old niece spent a lot of time asking, "Will a witch will jump out at you?" before other rides. So I suggest that you explain a little more what this ride is about. It's tough on preschoolers who are expecting forest animals and dwarfs.

In point of fact, we receive more mail from parents about this ride than about all other Disneyland Park attractions combined. The bottom line is that it really punches the buttons of the 6-and-under crowd, when other more traditionally scary rides don't. Many kids, once frightened by Snow White's Scary Adventures, balk at trying any other attractions that go into the dark, regardless how benign.

Storybook Land Canal Boats ★★★

APPEAL BY AGE	PRESCHOOL ★★★		GRADE SCHOOL ★★½		TEENS ★★½
YOUNG ADULTS ★★★½		OVER 30 ★★★½		SENIORS ★★★½	

Type of ride Scenic boat ride. **Scope and scale** Minor attraction. **When to go** Before 10:30 a.m. and after 5:30 p.m. **Special comments** Pretty, tranquil, and serene. **Duration of ride** 9½ minutes. **Average wait in line per 100 people ahead of you** 16 minutes. **Assumes** 7 boats operating. **Loading speed** Slow.

DESCRIPTION AND COMMENTS Guide-operated boats wind along canals situated beneath the same miniature landscapes visible from the Casey Jr. Circus Train. This ride, offering stellar examples of bonsai cultivation, selective pruning, and minia-turization, is a must for landscape gardening enthusiasts. The landscapes include scenes from more recent Disney features, in addition to those from such classics as *The Wind in the Willows* and *The Three Little Pigs.*

Thumbs Up for the Whole Family

TOURING TIPS The boats are much more comfortable than the train; the view of the miniatures is better; and the pace is more leisurely. On the down-side, the lines are long, and if not long, definitely slow moving. The ride itself also takes a lot of time. Our recommendation is to ride Casey Jr. if you have children or are in a hurry. Take the boat if your party is all adults or your pace is more leisurely. If you ride the canal boats, try to get on before 10:30 a.m.

Fantasyland Theatre–Disney Princess Fantasy Faire

DESCRIPTION AND COMMENTS Originally installed as a teen nightspot called Videopolis, this venue has been converted into a sophisticated amphithe-ater where concerts and elaborate stage shows are performed according to the daily entertainment schedule. Better productions that have played the Fantasyland Theatre stage include *Beauty and the Beast Live, Snow White,* and *The Spirit of Pocahontas,* all musical stage adaptations of the respective Disney animated features. In 2007, adding fuel to the fire of little girls' infatuation with Disney princesses, an elaborate, interactive meet-and-greet called the Princess Fantasy Faire was installed. Here, little

---

DISNEY DISH WITH JIM HILL

PIDDLER ON THE ROOF The Imagineers used all sorts of tricks when they were building Disneyland's Storybook Land Canal Boat ride, even going so far as to find miniature redwoods to plant along the riverbank so the trees would match the scale of the tiny houses that line the canal. One fellow, looking for a way to make a miniature church roof look old and weathered, really went above and beyond the call of duty. Research revealed that urine has an extremely corrosive effect on metal—so guess how this Imagineer finished every lunch hour?

ones can meet princesses, participate in a crafts project, join in a combination stage show and coronation, listen to a princess read a story, and, of course, shop for princess duds and other regalia. The usual Disneyland queue must be endured to meet and be photographed with the duty princess on the Disney Princess Royal Walk, but no lines are required for the other activities and events. The coronation ceremony is a stage show involving several princesses with help from the children. Performed several times daily, showtimes are listed in the *Times Guide*. Kids learn dance steps and courtly gestures before the ceremony and cap the coronation with a May pole dance. This last is clearly something that most kids have never seen and that typically leaves them dumbfounded. There's great photos to be had, however, as the kids circle in conflicting directions tying the May pole in knots. Princess Storytelling is likewise scheduled in the *Times Guide*. It too is billed as interactive, but children's participation in the less than 10-minute event is minimal to nonexistent.

TOURING TIPS   Little girls love the Princess Fantasy Faire, as do boys age 6 and under. The best way to take in the whole thing is to arrive about ten minutes in advance of a coronation and then stay after the show for crafts, princess meet and greet, and storytelling. Incidentally, you won't believe how many of the kids come in costume. If you do everything you'll spend about an hour not counting shopping time. If the Fantasyland Theatre resumes staging full-blown musical productions, you'll want to work them into your touring itinerary. Most of the shows produced here are first-rate and definitely worth your time. On busy days, many guests arrive 45 to 60 minutes in advance to get good seats. Because the shows tend to be less than a half-hour in duration, however, it is no hardship to watch the show standing, and standing room is usually available up to five minutes before showtime. In the summer, evening performances are more comfortable.

FANTASYLAND EATERIES AND SHOPS

DESCRIPTION AND COMMENTS   Fantasyland offers the most attractions of any of the "lands" and the fewest places to eat. With the exception of the **Village Haus** counter-service restaurant, most of the food service in Fantasyland is supplied by street vendors. Add the daylong congestion to the scenario, and Fantasyland ties with Mickey's Toontown as the best place in the park *not* to eat. If you are hungry, it's much easier to troop over to Frontierland, New Orleans Square, or even back to Main Street than to grab a bite in Fantasyland. Plus, the Village Haus, the only full-scale eatery in Fantasyland, specializes in burgers, pizza, and the like—that is, nothing distinctive, different, or worth the hassle. If you are in the Fantasyland/Toontown area and feeling hungry, the smart move is to go for the bratwurst, knockwurst, or cinnamon crisps at the **Enchanted Cottage** counter-service restaurant. The Enchanted Cottage is part of the Fantasyland Theatre complex and is largely overlooked except when guests are gathering before a show.

TOURING TIPS Fast food is anything but in Fantasyland, and shopping is ho-hum. Don't bother with the shops unless souvenirs are a big priority.

MICKEY'S TOONTOWN

MICKEY'S TOONTOWN IS SITUATED across the Disneyland Railroad tracks from Fantasyland. Its entrance is a tunnel that opens into Fantasyland just to the left of It's a Small World. As its name suggests, Toontown is a fanciful representation of the wacky cartoon community where all of the Disney characters live. Mickey's Toontown was inspired by the Disney animated feature *Who Framed Roger Rabbit?*, in which humans were able to enter the world of cartoon characters.

Mickey's Toontown consists of a colorful collection of miniature buildings, all executed in exaggerated cartoon style with rounded edges and brilliant colors. Among the buildings are Mickey's and Minnie's houses, both open to inspection inside and out.

In addition to being the place where guests can be certain of finding Disney characters at any time during the day, this newest land also serves as an elaborate interactive playground where it's OK for the kids to run, climb, and let off steam.

Mickey's Toontown is rendered with masterful attention to artistic humor and detail. The colorful buildings each have a story to tell or a gag to visit upon an unsuspecting guest. There is an explosion at the Fireworks Factory every minute or so, always unannounced. Across the street, the sidewalk is littered with crates containing strange contents addressed to exotic destinations. If you pry open the top of one of the crates (easy to do), the crate will emit a noise consistent with its contents. A box of "train parts," for example, broadcasts the sound of a racing locomotive when you lift the top.

Everywhere in Mickey's Toontown are subtleties and absurdities to delight the imagination. Next to Goofy's Playhouse is a Goofy-shaped impact crater marking the spot where he missed his swimming pool while high diving. A sign in front of the local garage declares, "If we can't fix it, we won't."

While adults will enjoy the imaginative charm of Mickey's Toontown, it will quickly become apparent that there is not much for them to do there. Most of the attractions in Mickey's Toontown are for kids, specifically smaller children. Attractions open to adults include a dark ride drawn from *Who Framed Roger Rabbit?* (sort of a high-tech rendition of Mr. Toad's Wild Ride) and a diminutive roller coaster.

In many ways, Mickey's Toontown is a designer playground, a fanciful cousin to Tom Sawyer Island in Frontierland. What distinguishes Mickey's Toontown is that the play areas are specially designed for smaller children; it's much cleaner than Tom Sawyer Island (that is, no dirt—though this does not guarantee a dirt-free child upon leaving the area). Finally, in the noblest Disney tradition, you must wait in line for virtually everything.

Also, be forewarned that Mickey's Toontown is not very large, especially in comparison with neighboring Fantasyland. A tolerable crowd in most of the other lands will seem like Times Square on New Year's Eve in Mickey's Toontown. Couple this congestion with the unfortunate fact that none of the attractions in Mickey's Toontown are engineered to handle huge crowds, and you come face-to-face with possibly the most attractive traffic jam the Disney folks have ever created. Our advice is to see Mickey's Toontown earlier in the day, before 11 a.m., or in the evening while the parades and *Fantasmic!* are going on.

Chip 'n' Dale's Treehouse ★★

APPEAL BY AGE	PRESCHOOL ★★★★		GRADE SCHOOL ★★★½
TEENS –	YOUNG ADULTS –	OVER 30 –	SENIORS –

Type of ride Imaginative children's play area. **Scope and scale** Diversion. **When to go** Before 10:30 a.m. or after 5:30 p.m. **Special comments** Good exercise for the small fry. **Duration of play** Varies.

DESCRIPTION AND COMMENTS The play area consists of a treehouse with slides.

TOURING TIPS Located in the most remote corner of Mickey's Toontown and obscured by the crowd waiting to ride the roller coaster next door, the Treehouse is frequently overlooked. Of all the attractions in Mickey's Toontown, this is the easiest one to get the kids into without much of a wait. Most any child who can fit is allowed to rummage around in the Treehouse.

Disneyland Railroad

DESCRIPTION AND COMMENTS Mickey's Toontown and Fantasyland share a station on the Disneyland Railroad's route around the perimeter of the park. Usually the wait to board is short.

Gadget's Go Coaster ★★

APPEAL BY AGE	PRESCHOOL ★★★★		GRADE SCHOOL ★★★½
TEENS ★★½	YOUNG ADULTS ★★½	OVER 30 ★★½	SENIORS ★★

Type of ride Small roller coaster. **Scope and scale** Minor attraction. **When to go** Before 10:30 a.m., during the parades and *Fantasmic!* in the evening, or just before the park closes. **Special comments** Great for little ones but not worth the wait for adults; minimum-height requirement of 35". **Duration of ride** About 50 seconds. **Average wait in line per 100 people ahead of you** 10 minutes. **Assumes** Normal staffing. **Loading speed** Slow.

Rough   Lose Things

DESCRIPTION AND COMMENTS Gadget's Go Coaster is a very small roller coaster, the idea of which is that you are miniaturized and riding around in an acorn shell. The ride itself is pretty zippy, but it is over so quickly you hardly know you've been anywhere. In fact, of the 52 seconds the ride is in motion, 32 seconds are consumed in exiting the loading area, being ratcheted up the first hill, and braking into the off-loading area. The actual time you spend careening around the track is a whopping 20 seconds.

TOURING TIPS Because the cars of this dinky roller coaster are too small for most adults, there is a fair amount of whiplashing for taller people. Add to that the small carrying capacity of the ride (the track is too short for more than one train to operate) and you have a real engineering brain fart. Unfortunately, the ride is visually appealing. All the kids want to ride, subjecting the whole family to incarceration in a line whose movement can only be discerned by time-lapse photography. Our recommendation to parties touring without children: skip Gadget's Go Coaster. If there are children in your group, you've got a problem.

Goofy's Playhouse ★★½

APPEAL BY AGE	PRESCHOOL ★★★★		GRADE SCHOOL ★★★★
TEENS –	YOUNG ADULTS –	OVER 30 –	SENIORS –

Type of attraction A whimsical children's play area. **Scope and scale** Diversion. **When to go** Anytime.

DESCRIPTION AND COMMENTS Goofy's Playhouse is a small but nicely themed play area for the under-6 set. Usually not crowded, the playhouse is a pleasant place to let preschoolers ramble and parents relax while older sibs enjoy more adventurous attractions..

TOURING TIPS There's not a lot of shade, so early in the day or late in the day work best.

Mickey's House ★★★

APPEAL BY AGE	PRESCHOOL ★★★★★	GRADE SCHOOL ★★★★½	TEENS ★★★½
YOUNG ADULTS ★★★½		OVER 30 ★★★½	SENIORS ★★★½

Type of attraction Walk-through tour of Mickey's House and Movie Barn, ending with a personal visit with Mickey. **Scope and scale** Minor attraction and character-greeting opportunity. **When to go** Before 10:30 a.m. and after 5:30 p.m. **Special comments** Well done. **Duration of attraction** 15–30 minutes (depending on the crowd). **Average wait in line per 100 people ahead of you** 20 minutes. **Assumes** Normal staffing. **Touring speed** Slow.

DESCRIPTION AND COMMENTS Mickey's House is the starting point of a self-guided tour that winds through the famous mouse's house, into his backyard and past Pluto's doghouse, and then into Mickey's Movie Barn. This last stop harks back to the so-called "barn" studio where Walt Disney created a number of the earlier Mickey Mouse cartoons. Once in the Movie Barn, guests watch vintage Disney cartoons while awaiting admittance to Mickey's Dressing Room.

In small groups of one or two families, guests are ultimately conducted into the dressing room where Mickey awaits to pose for photos and sign autographs. The visit is not lengthy (two to four minutes), but there is adequate time for all of the children to hug, poke, and admire the star.

TOURING TIPS The cynical observer will discern immediately that Mickey's House, backyard, Movie Barn, and so on are no more than a cleverly devised queuing area designed to deliver guests to Mickey's Dressing

Room for the Mouse Encounter. For those with some vestige of child in their personalities, however, the preamble serves to heighten anticipation while providing the opportunity to get to know the corporate symbol on a more personal level. Mickey's House is well conceived and contains a lot of Disney memorabilia. You will notice that children touch everything as they proceed through the house, hoping to find some artifact that is not welded or riveted into the set (an especially tenacious child during one of our visits was actually able to rip a couple of books from a bookcase).

Meeting Mickey and touring his house are best done during the first two hours the park is open or, alternatively, in the evening during *Fantasmic!* performances. If meeting Mickey is at the top of your child's list, you might consider taking the Disneyland Railroad from Main Street to the Toontown/Fantasyland station as soon as you enter the park. Some children are so obsessed with seeing Mickey that they cannot enjoy anything else until they get Mickey in the rearview mirror.

Minnie's House ★★½

APPEAL BY AGE	PRESCHOOL ★★★★	GRADE SCHOOL ★★★½	TEENS ★★½
YOUNG ADULTS ★★½	OVER 30 ★★½		SENIORS ★★½

Type of attraction Walk-through exhibit. **Scope and scale** Minor attraction and character-greeting opportunity. **When to go** Before 11:30 a.m. and after 4:30 p.m. **Special comments** OK but not great. **Duration of tour** About 10 minutes. **Average wait in line per 100 people ahead of you** 12 minutes. **Touring speed** Slow.

DESCRIPTION AND COMMENTS Minnie's House consists of a self-guided tour through the various rooms and backyard of Mickey Mouse's main squeeze. Similar to Mickey's House, only predictably more feminine, Minnie's House likewise showcases some fun Disney memorabilia. Among the highlights of the short tour are the fanciful appliances in Minnie's kitchen. Like Mickey, Minnie is usually present to receive guests.

TOURING TIPS The main difference between Mickey's House and Minnie's House is that Minnie's House cannot accommodate as many guests. See Minnie early and before Mickey to avoid waiting outdoors in a long queue. Be advised that neither Mickey nor Minnie is available during parades.

Miss Daisy, Donald's Boat ★★

APPEAL BY AGE	PRESCHOOL ★★★★	GRADE SCHOOL ★★★½	TEENS –
YOUNG ADULTS –	OVER 30 –		SENIORS –

Type of attraction Creative play area with a boat theme. **Scope and scale** Diversion. **When to go** Before 10:30 a.m. and after 4:30 p.m. **Special comments** Designer play area. **Duration of play** Varies. **Average wait in line per 100 people ahead of you** Usually no waiting.

DESCRIPTION AND COMMENTS Another children's play area, this time with a tugboat theme. Children can climb nets, ring bells, survey Toontown from the captain's bridge, and scoot down slides. The idea is that Donald Duck (who, as everyone knows, lives in Duckburg) is visiting Toontown.

TOURING TIPS Kids more or less wander on and off of the *Miss Daisy,* and usually there is not any sort of organized line or queuing area. Enjoy this play area at your leisure and stay as long as you like.

Roger Rabbit's Car Toon Spin (FASTPASS)   ★★★

APPEAL BY AGE	PRESCHOOL ★★★	GRADE SCHOOL ★★★★	TEENS ★★★½
YOUNG ADULTS ★★★½		OVER 30 ★★★½	SENIORS ★★★½

Type of ride Track ride in the dark. **Scope and scale** Major attraction. **When to go** Before 10:30 a.m. and after 6:30 p.m. **Special comments** Ride with your kids, if you can stomach it. **Duration of ride** A little more than 3 minutes. **Average wait in line per 100 people ahead of you** 7 minutes. **Assumes** Full-capacity operation. **Loading speed** Moderate.

Dark   Rough   Motion Sickness

DESCRIPTION AND COMMENTS A so-called dark ride where guests become part of a cartoon plot. The idea is that you are renting a taxicab for a tour of Toontown. As soon as your cab gets under way, however, weasels throw a slippery glop (known as "dip") on the road, sending the cab into a more or less uncontrollable spin. This spinning continues as the cab passes through a variety of sets populated by cartoon and audio-animatronic characters and punctuated by simulated explosions. As a child of the 1960s put it, "It was like combining Mr. Toad's Wild Ride with the Mad Tea Party while tripping on LSD."

The main problem with the Car Toon Spin is that, because of the spinning, you are often pointed in the wrong direction to appreciate (or even see) many of the better visual effects. Furthermore, the story line is loose. The attraction lacks the continuity and humor of Splash Mountain or the suspense of The Haunted Mansion or Snow White's Scary Adventures.

A reader from Milford, Michigan, echoed our sentiments, lamenting:

The most disappointing ride to me was Roger Rabbit's Car Toon Spin. I stood 45 minutes for a fun-house ride and the wheel was so difficult to operate that I spent most of my time trying to steer the bloody car and missed the point of the ride.

TOURING TIPS The ride is popular for its novelty, and it is one of the few Mickey's Toontown attractions that parents (with strong stomachs) can enjoy with their children. Because the ride stays fairly thronged with people all day long, ride before 10:30 a.m., during parades and *Fantasmic!,* or in the hour before the park closes. Otherwise, use FASTPASS.

The spinning, incidentally, can be controlled by the guests. If you don't want to spin, you don't have to. If you do elect to spin, you still will not be able to approach the eye-popping speed attainable on the teacups at the Mad Tea Party. Sluggish spinning aside, our advice for those who are at all susceptible to motion sickness is not to get near this ride if you are touring with anyone under 21 years of age.

CHARACTER WATCHING

DESCRIPTION AND COMMENTS If you want to see characters, Mickey's Toontown is the place to go. In addition to Mickey, who receives guests all day
(except during parades) in his dressing room, and Minnie, who enter-
tains in her house, you are also likely to see Goofy and Pluto in front of
Toontown Hall and bump into such august personages as Daisy, Roger
Rabbit, and a host of others lurking around the streets. It would be a rare
event to visit Toontown without bumping into a few characters. From
time to time, horns sound and whistles blow atop the Toontown City
Hall, followed by a fanfare rendition of the Mickey Mouse Club theme
song. This indicates, as a mom from Texas explained to us, that "some
characters are fixin' to come out." And there you have it.

TOONTOWN EATERIES AND SHOPS

DESCRIPTION AND COMMENTS Food service in Mickey's Toontown is limited to
drinks, snacks, hot dogs, frozen yogurt, and pizza. The **Gag Factory,** which
sells Disney souvenirs, is one of the park's more entertaining shopping
venues. Even if you do not buy anything, the place is fun to walk through.

TOMORROWLAND

TOMORROWLAND IS A FUTURISTIC MIX of rides and experiences
that relates to technological development and what life will be like in
the years to come.

An exhaustive renovation of Tomorrowland was begun in 1996 and
completed in 2000. Before the renovation, Tomorrowland's 40-year-old
buildings more resembled 1970s motel architecture than anyone's vision
of the future. Tomorrowland's renovated design is more enduring,
reflecting a nostalgic vision of the future as imagined by dreamers and
scientists in the 1920s and 1930s. Frozen in time, Tomorrowland con-
jures up visions of Buck Rogers (whom nobody under 50 remembers),
fanciful mechanical rockets, and metallic cities spread beneath towering obelisks. Disney refers to the Tomorrowland as the "Future That
Never Was." *Newsweek* has dubbed it "retro-future."

Astro Orbiter ★★

APPEAL BY AGE	PRESCHOOL ★★★★	GRADE SCHOOL ★★★½	TEENS ★★★
YOUNG	ADULTS ★★	OVER 30 ★	SENIORS ★

Type of ride Very mild midway-type thrill ride. **Scope and scale** Minor attraction.
When to go Before 10 a.m. or during the hour before the park closes. **Special
comments** Not worth the wait. **Duration of ride** 1½ minutes. **Average wait in
line per 100 people ahead of you** 13 minutes. **Assumes** Normal staffing. **Loading speed** Slow.

Motion Sickness

DESCRIPTION AND COMMENTS Though the look is different and the
attraction has been relocated at the central-hub entrance to
Tomorrowland, the new Astro Orbiter ride is essentially a
makeover of the old Rocket Jets—that is, a visually appealing

midway-type ride involving small rockets that rotate on arms around a central axis. Be aware that the Astro Orbiter flies higher and faster than Dumbo and that it frightens some small children. The ride also apparently messes with certain adults, as a mother from Israel attests:

I think your assessment of the Rocket Jets [Astro Orbiter] as "very mild" is way off. I was able to sit through all the "Mountains" and the "Tours" . . . without my stomach reacting even a little, but after the Rocket Jets [Astro Orbiter], I thought I would be finished for the rest of the day. Very quickly I realized that my only chance for survival was to pick a point on the toe of my shoe and stare at it (and certainly not lift my eyes out of the "jet") until the ride was over. My 4-year-old was my copilot; she loved the ride (go figure), and she had us up high the whole time. It was a nightmare—people should be forewarned.

TOURING TIPS Astro Orbiter is essentially the same ride as the old Rocket Jets: slow to load and expendable on any schedule. If you want to take a preschooler on this ride, place your child in the seat first and then sit down yourself.

Buzz Lightyear Astro Blasters (FASTPASS) ★★★★

APPEAL BY AGE PRESCHOOL ★★★ GRADE SCHOOL ★★★★½ TEENS ★★★★½
YOUNG ADULTS ★★★★½ OVER 30 ★★★★½ SENIORS ★★★★

Type of ride Space-travel interactive dark ride. **Scope and scale** Major attraction. **When to go** Before 10:30 a.m. or after 6 p.m. **Special comments** A real winner! **Duration of ride** About 4½ minutes. **Average wait in line per 100 people ahead of you** 3 minutes. **Loading speed** Fast.

DESCRIPTION AND COMMENTS This attraction is based on the space-commando character of Buzz Lightyear from the film *Toy Story*. The marginal story line has you and Buzz Lightyear trying to save the universe from the evil Emperor Zurg. The indoor ride is interactive to the extent that

Thumbs Up for the Whole Family

you can spin your car and shoot simulated "laser cannons" at Zurg and his minions.

A similar attraction at the Magic Kingdom at Walt Disney World opened with little fanfare in 1998 but immediately became one of the most popular attractions in the park. The Disneyland version, situated across from Star Tours, is much the same except for one high-tech twist: folks at home can play along with guests on the ride in real time via the Internet. Through Web-cam technology, guests on the attraction are virtually paired up with Internet partners.

Praise for Buzz Lightyear is almost universal. This comment from a Massachusetts couple is typical:

Buzz Lightyear was the surprise hit of our trip! My husband and I enjoyed competing for the best score so much that we went on this ride several times during our stay. Definitely a must, especially when there's no wait.

TOURING TIPS Each car is equipped with two laser cannons and a score-keeping display. Each scorekeeping display is independent, so you can compete with your riding partner. A joy stick allows you to spin the car to line up the various targets. Each time you pull the trigger you'll release a red laser beam that you can see hitting or missing the target. Most folks' first ride is occupied with learning how to use the equipment (fire off individual shots as opposed to keeping the trigger depressed) and figuring out how the targets work. The next ride (as with certain potato chips, one is not enough), you'll surprise yourself by how much better you do. *Unofficial* readers are unanimous in their praise of Buzz Lightyear. Some guests, in fact, spend several hours on the attraction, riding again and again. See Buzz Lightyear after riding Space Mountain first thing in the morning or use FASTPASS.

Disneyland Monorail System ★★★

APPEAL BY AGE	PRESCHOOL ★★★	GRADE SCHOOL ★★★	TEENS ★★★
YOUNG ADULTS ★★★		OVER 30 ★★★	SENIORS ★★

Type of ride Scenic transportation. **Scope and scale** Major attraction. **When to go** During the hot, crowded period of the day (11:30 a.m.–5 p.m.). **Special comments** Nice relaxing ride with some interesting views of the park; take the monorail to Downtown Disney for lunch. **Duration of ride** 12–15 minutes round-trip. **Average wait in line per 100 people ahead of you** 10 minutes. **Assumes** 3 monorails operating. **Loading speed** Moderate to fast.

DESCRIPTION AND COMMENTS The monorail is a futuristic transportation ride that affords the only practical opportunity for escaping the park during the crowded lunch period and early afternoon. Boarding at the Tomorrowland monorail station, you can commute to the Disneyland Resort hotels and Downtown Disney complex, where it's possible to have a nice lunch without fighting the crowds. For those not interested in lunch, the monorail provides a tranquil trip with a nice view of Downtown Disney, Disney's California Adventure theme park, Fantasyland, and Tomorrowland.

TOURING TIPS We recommend using the monorail to commute to Downtown Disney for a quiet, relaxing lunch away from the crowds and the heat. If you only want to experience the ride, go whenever you wish; the wait to board is usually 15 to 25 minutes except in the 2 hours before closing. Also note that you must disembark and then queue up to reboard at Downtown Disney.

Disneyland Railroad

DESCRIPTION AND COMMENTS The Disneyland Railroad makes a regular stop at the Tomorrowland Railroad Station. For additional details about the railroad see the Disneyland Railroad write-up in the Main Street, U.S.A. section.

TOURING TIPS This station becomes fairly crowded on busy days. If you are interested primarily in getting there, it may be quicker to walk.

Finding Nemo Submarine Voyage ★★★★

APPEAL BY AGE	PRESCHOOL ★★★★½	GRADE SCHOOL ★★★★½
TEENS ★★★★ YOUNG ADULTS ★★★★	OVER 30 ★★★★	SENIORS ★★★★

Type of attraction Simulated submarine ride. **Scope and scale** Super-headliner.
When to go First hour the park is open. **Duration of ride** 13½ minutes. **Average
wait in line per 100 people ahead of you** 7½ minutes. **Loading speed** Slow to
Moderate. Assumes all 8 subs are operating.

DESCRIPTION AND COMMENTS *Finding Nemo* Submarine Voyage utilizes the
lagoon abandoned by a previous submarine
attraction that last sailed almost a decade
ago. The new voyage is based on the story
line of the hit Disney/Pixar animated feature
Finding Nemo. Here you board a submarine in
a loading area situated below the Disneyland
monorail station in Tomorrowland. After a quick lap of the open-air
lagoon, the sub passes through a waterfall and inside to follow the
general *Finding Nemo* story. The track is slightly longer than in the former attraction, but the lagoon is now smaller (the original waterfall
entrance has been moved forward by about 200 feet). Special effects
center around a combination of traditional audio-animatronics and,
once you're inside the dark interior of the building, what appear to be
rear-projection screens, under water, at a distance of three to ten feet
from the sub's windows. Encased in rock and shipwrecks, the screens
are very natural looking and allow the animated characters to appear
three-dimensionally in the undersea world. Other elements include
traveling through a minefield, a sea of jellyfish (very cool), and entering
the mouth of a whale. The volcano eruption has been retained but is
vastly improved from the previous incarnation. Another improvement
is the onboard sound system, which allows the story to "travel" from
front to back of the sub, and the visual experience is different depending on what seat you're in. Fans of the old sub ride should keep an eye
out for the goofy-looking sea serpent now artfully camouflaged at the
end of the ride.

Thumbs Up for the Whole Family

The attraction is terrific and rates at or close to five stars for all age
groups. You don't have to be a Nemo fan to be impressed by the scale
and effects. It's not fast-paced but, rather, leisurely in the way that
Pirates of the Caribbean is.

TOURING TIPS *Finding Nemo* Submarine Voyage is a complete theatrical and
technical success but in many ways an engineering failure. By lengthening
the duration of the voyage from 8 minutes to more than 13 minutes, by
failing to provide adequate loading facilities, and by being slowed down
due to a technical dispatching constraint, the Imagineers have reduced
the attraction's capacity to about 900 guests per hour, a shockingly small
capacity for a super-headliner attraction. Further, owing to the low carrying capacity, the subs are not a good candidate for FASTPASS (all FAST-
PASSes would be gone before noon). The bottom line is that the Submarine
Voyage is the most difficult attraction in the park to experience without a
long wait in line, and by long we mean 1 to 2½ hours.

The Submarine Voyage is usually among the Tomorrowland attractions open for early entry on Monday, Tuesday, Thursday, and Saturday.

Disneyland Resort hotel guests and guests holding advance purchase Park Hopper Tickets of three or more days (see page 20) are eligible for early entry. If you qualify, line up at the turnstiles at least 30 minutes before the early-entry period begins. When you're admitted to the park, crank over to the subs as fast as your feet and the Disney folks will allow. If you're not eligible for early entry, your only hope of avoiding a long wait is to be one of the first through the turnstiles on a non-early-entry day (currently on a Wednesday, Friday, or Sunday) and to ride the subs first thing.

The subs stay jammed all day and are affected very little by parades and other live-entertainment offerings that usually draw crowds away from the attractions. The lines diminish slightly as park-closing time approaches, especially when the park is open until 9 p.m. or later. As of this writing, Disney has been keeping the attraction open after the park closes to accommodate everyone still waiting in line at closing time.

Claustrophobes may not be comfortable with the experience, even though the sub doesn't actually submerge (we saw one 30-ish woman who started hyperventilating before the sub left the dock). Children may be scared of the same thing, or of the encounter with sharks (they keep their distance). The sharks here are a bit less menacing than in the movie, but we wouldn't be surprised if they get toned down some.

The bright-yellow subs, revived from the previous attraction, have been reengineered with electric power to minimize noise and pollution. The old subs seated 38 passengers; another pair of seats now sprouts below the feet of the captain, making 40 total, each with its own window. It's not easy to get 40 aboard, however, because the seats are narrow and a few guests take up two. Ideally, large guests should aim to be in one of the four seats at the front or back, but this may be difficult to negotiate. Wheelchair-bound guests or those who can't get down the spiral staircase into the sub can view the experience from a special topside viewing room (seats about six able-bodied persons plus two wheelchairs). With the exception of one small animated effect, the visual is identical (perhaps faster), but despite a large monitor the creatures appear smaller than when viewing them through a real porthole.

If there's a silver lining attached to the long queues for the Submarine Voyage, it's that it draws a lot of guests away from other Disneyland favorites such as Splash Mountain, Space Mountain, and Indiana Jones Adventure. (For an in-depth discussion of queuing strategies for this attraction, see page 272.)

Honey, I Shrunk the Audience   ★★★★½

APPEAL BY AGE PRESCHOOL ★★★½ GRADE SCHOOL ★★★★½ TEENS ★★★★½
YOUNG ADULTS ★★★★   OVER 30 ★★★★   SENIORS ★★★★½

Type of attraction 3-D film with special effects. **Scope and scale** Headliner. **When to go** Before 11 a.m. or during the late afternoon and evening. **Special comments** An absolute hoot! Not to be missed; routinely freaks out kids age 8 and under. **Duration of presentation** Approximately 17 minutes. **Preshow entertainment** 8 minutes. **Probable waiting time** 12 minutes (at suggested times).

Loud   Scary

DESCRIPTION AND COMMENTS *Honey, I Shrunk the Audience* is a 3-D offshoot of Disney's feature film, *Honey, I Shrunk the Kids. Honey, I Shrunk the Audience* features a stupefying array of special effects, including simulated explosions, smoke, fiber optics, lights, water spray, and even moving seats. Clever, frenetic, and uproarious, *Honey, I Shrunk the Audience* is, in our opinion, the best theater attraction in the Disney repertoire. We rate it as not to be missed.

TOURING TIPS The audio level is earsplitting in this theater. Small children are sometimes frightened by the sound volume, and many adults report that the loud soundtrack is distracting and even uncomfortable. While *Honey, I Shrunk the Audience* is a huge hit, it overwhelms children as old as 7 or 8. A dad from Lexington, South Carolina, writes:

Honey, I Shrunk the Audience is too intense for kids. Our 4-year-old took off his [3-D] glasses five minutes into the movie. Because of this experience, he would not wear the glasses in the Muppet movie.

An Arizona mom agrees, offering this report:

Our 3- and 4-year-olds loved all the rides. They giggled through Thunder Mountain three times, squealed with delight on Splash Mountain, thought Space Mountain was the coolest, and begged to ride Star Tours over and over. They even "fought ghosts" at The Haunted Mansion. But Honey, I Shrunk the Audience *dissolved them into sobbing, shaking, terrified preschoolers.*

Honey, I Shrunk the Audience is an exceptionally popular attraction. Try to work the production into your touring schedule before 11 a.m. or in the late afternoon or evening. The theater is large, so don't be intimidated if the line is long. Finally, try to avoid seats in the first several rows. If you are too close to the screen, the 3-D images do not focus properly.

Innoventions ★★★

APPEAL BY AGE	PRESCHOOL ★½	GRADE SCHOOL ★★★	TEENS ★★★★
YOUNG ADULTS ★★★★	OVER 30 ★★★		SENIORS ★★★

Type of attraction Multifaceted attraction featuring static and hands-on exhibits relating to products and technologies of the near future. **Scope and scale** Major diversion. **When to go** On your second day or after you have seen all the major attractions. **Special comments** Most exhibits demand time and participation to be rewarding; not much gained here by a quick walk-through; very commercial, but well presented.

DESCRIPTION AND COMMENTS Innoventions is housed in the large circular building last occupied by the audio-animatronic musical *America Sings*. Modeled after a similar attraction at Epcot in Walt Disney World, Innoventions was part of the 1996–2000 Tomorrowland renovation. The attraction consists of a huge, busy collection of industry-sponsored walk-through, hands-on exhibits. Dynamic, interactive, and forward looking, Innoventions most closely resembles a high-tech trade show. Featured products provide guests with a preview of consumer and industrial goods of the near future. Electronics, communications, and entertainment technologies, as you would expect, play a prominent role. Exhibits, many of which change each year, demonstrate such products as virtual-reality games, high-definition TV, voice-activated appliances, and various CD-ROM applications, among others. There are several major exhibit areas, each sponsored by a different manufacturer or research lab. The emphasis in the respective exhibits is on the effect of the product or technology on daily living. One of the exhibits drawing the most interest is a demonstration by Honda of ASIMO, the world's most advanced humanoid robot. ASIMO has two arms and two hands, allowing him to reach for things, switch lights on and off, and do the hokey pokey (just kidding).

TOURING TIPS Guests display a wide range of reactions to the many Innoventions exhibits. We can only suggest that you form your own opinion. In terms of touring strategy, we recommend you spend time at Innoventions on your second day. If you have only one day, visit sometime during the evening if you have the time and endurance. Be warned, however, that many Innoventions exhibits are technical in nature and may not be compatible with your mood or level of energy toward the end of a long day. Also be advised that you cannot get much of anything out of a quick walk-through of Innoventions; you have to invest a little time to understand what is going on. Finally, and predictably, teens, computer-savvy younger adults, and other electronic game buffs will enjoy Innoventions more than the average guest.

Space Mountain (FASTPASS) ★★★★½

| APPEAL BY AGE | PRESCHOOL † | GRADE SCHOOL ★★★★ | TEENS ★★★★½ |
| YOUNG ADULTS ★★★★½ | | OVER 30 ★★★★ | SENIORS † |

† Sample sizes were too small to derive ratings.

Type of attraction Roller coaster in the dark. **Scope and scale** Super-headliner. **When to go** Right after the park opens or use FASTPASS. **Special comments** Much improved. **Duration of ride** 2 minutes and 45 seconds. **Average wait in line per 100 people ahead of you** 3½ minutes. **Loading speed** Moderate.

Dark

Scary

Rough

Motion Sickness

Lose Things

DESCRIPTION AND COMMENTS After operating continuously for more than 25 years, Space Mountain was shut down in 2003 for a total rehab, including replacement of the track system. Disneyland Park's most popular attraction reopened in July 2005 with new ride vehicles, a new soundtrack, redesigned queuing and preshow areas, enhanced special effects (especially on launch and reentering the atmosphere), a revised narrative, and a very, very smooth ride. Retained, of course, is the essential theme of high-speed interstellar travel, or as more simply stated by a Space Mountain fan, "being flung around in the dark."

The most surprising thing about the new Space Mountain is its aesthetic beauty. No, we're not kidding. The vistas of the solar system and the stars, the distant galaxies, and passing comets are intoxicating and very realistic. Because you cannot see the ride's infrastructure, Space Mountain is no longer simply a roller coaster in a dimly lighted building with some Buck Rogers planets and meteors projected on the ceiling. Now that you can't see the track or anticipate where your vehicle will go, your eyes are free to feast on the rich visuals.

TOURING TIPS Space Mountain was the park's most popular attraction before it shut down for renovation. Now, answering the pent-up demand and high expectations of its many faithful, it is even more popular. Experience it immediately after the park opens or use FASTPASS.

Starcade

DESCRIPTION AND COMMENTS Starcade is nothing more or less than a large electronic-games arcade. The pièce de résistance is the Sega jet-combat simulator game—players actually roll upside down in the course of play. Though the game is expensive—$4 for about 2 minutes of play—many teens and young adults regard it as the highlight of their Disneyland day.

TOURING TIPS Enjoy your time in the area with a pocket full of quarters.

Star Tours ★★★★

Type of attraction Space-flight simulation ride. **Scope and scale** Major attraction. **When to go** Before 10 a.m. **Special comments** A blast; not to be missed; frightens many small children; expectant mothers are also advised against riding; minimum-height requirement of 40". **Duration of ride** Approximately 7 minutes. **Average wait in line per 100 people ahead of you** 6 minutes. **Assumes** 4 simulators operating. **Loading speed** Moderate.

Scary   Rough   Motion Sickness

DESCRIPTION AND COMMENTS The attraction consists of a ride in a flight simulator modeled after those used for training pilots and astronauts. Guests, supposedly on a little vacation outing in space, are piloted by a "droid" (short for android, aka humanoid, aka robot) on his first flight with real passengers. Mayhem ensues almost immediately as scenery flashes by at supersonic speed and the simulator bucks and pitches. You could swear you are moving at light speed. After several minutes of this, the droid somehow gets the spacecraft landed, and you discover you're grinning from ear to ear.

TOURING TIPS After many years, this ride still draws large crowds. Try to ride before 11 a.m. or after 4:30 p.m.

Be aware that the crowds in Tomorrowland are larger on cold or rainy days, when many guests skip Splash Mountain (a water-flume ride in Critter Country). Also, note that children must be at least 40 inches tall and 3 years of age to ride Star Tours.

Tomorrowland Autopia (FASTPASS) ★

APPEAL BY AGE	PRESCHOOL ★★★½		GRADE SCHOOL ★★★
TEENS ★	YOUNG ADULTS ½	OVER 30 ½	SENIORS ½

Type of ride Drive-'em-yourself miniature cars. **Scope and scale** Minor attraction. **When to go** Before 10 a.m. and after 5 p.m. or use FASTPASS. **Special comments** Boring for adults; great for preschoolers. **Duration of ride** Approximately 4½ minutes. **Average wait in line per 100 people ahead of you** 6 minutes. **Assumes** 35 cars operating on each track. **Loading speed** Slow.

Loud

DESCRIPTION AND COMMENTS An elaborate miniature freeway with gasoline-powered cars that will travel at speeds of up to seven miles an hour. The attraction design, with its sleek cars, auto noises, highway signs, and even an "off-road" section, is quite alluring. In fact, however, the cars poke along on a track that leaves the driver with little to do. Pretty ho-hum for most adults and teenagers. Of those children who would enjoy the ride, many are excluded by the requirement that drivers be 52 inches tall.

TOURING TIPS This ride is appealing to the eye but definitely expendable on a schedule for adults. Preschoolers, however, love it. If your preschooler is too short to drive, ride along and allow him or her to steer (the car runs on a guide rail) while you work the foot pedal.

A mom from North Billerica, Massachusetts, writes:

I was truly amazed by the number of adults in the line. Please emphasize to your readers that these cars travel on a guided path and are not a whole lot of fun. The only reason I could think of for adults to be in line was an insane desire to go on absolutely every ride. The other feature about the cars is that they tend to pile up at the end, so it takes almost as long to get off as it did to get on. Parents riding with their preschoolers should keep the car going as slow as it can without stalling. This prolongs the preschooler's joy and decreases the time you will have to wait at the end.

TOMORROWLAND EATERIES

DESCRIPTION AND COMMENTS **Redd Rocket's Pizza Port** in the old Mission to Mars building serves pizza, pasta, garlic bread, and salad. The ancient **Tomorrowland Terrace** features burgers, salads, and chicken nuggets.

LIVE ENTERTAINMENT *and* SPECIAL EVENTS

LIVE ENTERTAINMENT IN THE FORM OF BANDS, Disney character appearances, parades, singing and dancing, and ceremonies further enliven and add color to Disneyland Park on a daily basis. For specific information about what's happening on the day you visit, check the daily entertainment schedule in the *Times Guide*. Be forewarned, however, that if you are on a tight schedule, it is impossible to both see the park's featured attractions and take in the numerous and varied live performances offered. In our One-day Touring Plans, starting on page 274, we exclude the live performances in favor of seeing as much of the park as time permits. This is a considered tactical decision based on the fact that the parades and *Fantasmic!*, Disneyland Park's river spectacular, siphon crowds away from the more popular rides, thus shortening waiting lines.

The color and pageantry of live events around the park are an integral part of the Disneyland Park entertainment mix and a persuasive argument for second-day touring. Though live entertainment is varied, plentiful, and nearly continuous throughout the day, several productions are preeminent.

Fantasmic!

Loud

Scary

DESCRIPTION AND COMMENTS *Fantasmic!* is a mixed-media show presented one or more times each evening the park is open late (10 p.m. or later). Staged at the end of Tom Sawyer Island opposite the Frontierland and New Orleans Square waterfronts, *Fantasmic!* is far and away the most extraordinary and ambitious outdoor spectacle ever attempted in any theme park. Starring Mickey Mouse in his role as the sorcerer's apprentice from *Fantasia,* the production uses lasers, images projected on a shroud of mist, fireworks, lighting effects, and music in combinations so stunning you can scarcely believe what you have seen.

The Smith family from East Wimple stakes out their viewing spot for Fantasmic!

The plot is simple: good versus evil. The story gets lost in all the special effects at times, but no matter—it is the spectacle, not the story line, that is so overpowering. While *beautiful, stunning,* and *powerful* are words that immediately come to mind, they fail to convey the uniqueness of this presentation. It could be argued, with some validity, that *Fantasmic!* alone is worth the price of Disneyland Park admission. Needless to say, we rate *Fantasmic!* as not to be missed.

TOURING TIPS It is not easy to see *Fantasmic!* For the first show particularly, guests begin staking out prime viewing spots along the edge of the New Orleans Square and Frontierland waterfronts as much as four hours in advance. Similarly, good vantage points on raised walkways and terraces are also grabbed up early on. A mom from Lummi Island, Washington, dismantled her Disney stroller to make a nest:

We used the snap-off cover on the rental stroller to sit on during Fantasmic! *since the ground was really cold.*

Along similar lines, a middle-aged New York man wrote, saying:

Your excellent guidebook also served as a seat cushion while seated on the ground waiting for the show to begin. Make future editions thicker for greater comfort.

The best seats in the house are at the water's edge. For adults, it is really not necessary to have an unobstructed view of the staging area because most of the action is high above the crowd. Children standing in the closely packed crowd, however, are able to catch only bits and pieces of the presentation.

Probably the most painless strategy for seeing *Fantasmic!* is to attend the second show or the seasonally available third show. Usually, the second performance follows the first performance by about an hour and a half. If you let the crowd for the first show clear out and then take up your position, you should be able to find a good vantage point. The evening parade, which winds through Fantasyland and down Main Street, often runs concurrently with *Fantasmic!* for the first and second shows of the evening, essentially splitting the crowd between the two events. At the second *Fantasmic!* and second parade, however, there are fewer people in the park and viewing conditions are less crowded.

Rain and wind conditions sometimes cause *Fantasmic!* to be canceled. Unfortunately, Disney officials usually do not make a final decision about whether to proceed or cancel until just before showtime. We have seen guests wrapped in ponchos sit stoically in rain or drizzle for more than an hour with no assurance that their patience and sacrifice would be rewarded. Unless you can find a covered viewing spot, we do not recommend staking out vantage points on rainy or especially windy nights. On nights like these, pursue your own agenda until ten minutes or so before showtime, and then head to the waterfront to see what happens.

You can view *Fantasmic!* from a private viewing area located near the Tom Sawyer Island Raft Dock. If you want to be one of the elite, call

☎ 714-781-4400 at 8 a.m. exactly 30 days in advance. The price for the dock viewing area runs $59 for adults and children. A dessert box is included.

Finally, make sure to hang on to children during *Fantasmic!* and to give them explicit instructions for regrouping in the event you are separated. Be especially vigilant when the crowd disperses after the show.

PARADES

DISNEY THEME PARKS ARE FAMOUS THE WORLD OVER for their parades. On days when the park closes early, there is an afternoon parade. On days when the park closes late (10 p.m. to 1 a.m.), there are always evening parades, and often an afternoon parade as well.

The parades are full-blown Disney productions with some combination of floats, huge inflated balloons of the characters, marching bands, old-time vehicles, dancers, and, of course, literally dozens of costumed Disney characters. Themes for the parades vary from time to time, and special holiday parades are always produced for Christmas and Easter.

Parades always draw thousands of guests from the attraction lines. We recommend, therefore, watching from the departure point. With this strategy you can enjoy the parade, and then while the parade is continuing on its route, take advantage of the diminished lines at the attractions. Watching a parade that begins in Fantasyland from Small World Mall affords the greatest mobility in terms of accessing other areas of the park when the parade has passed.

Main Street is the most crowded area from which to watch a parade when it begins at Town Square. The opposite is true when the parade begins in Fantasyland. The upper platform of the Main Street train station affords the best viewing perspective along the route. The best time to get a position on the platform is when the parade begins in Fantasyland. When this happens, good spots on the platform are available right up to the time the parade begins. When you are at the end of the parade route, you can assume it will take the parade 15 to 18 minutes to get to you.

Keep an eye on your children during parades and give them explicit instructions for regrouping in the event you get separated. Children constantly jockey for better viewing positions. A few wiggles this way and a few wiggles the other, and presto, they are lost in the crowd. Finally, be especially vigilant when the crowd starts dispersing after the parade. Thousands of people suddenly strike out in different directions, creating a perfect situation for losing a child or two.

LIVE ENTERTAINMENT THROUGHOUT THE PARK

PARADES AND *FANTASMIC!* MAKE UP only a part of the daily live-entertainment offerings at Disneyland Park. The following is an incomplete list of other performances and events that are scheduled with some regularity and that require no reservations.

disneyland parade route

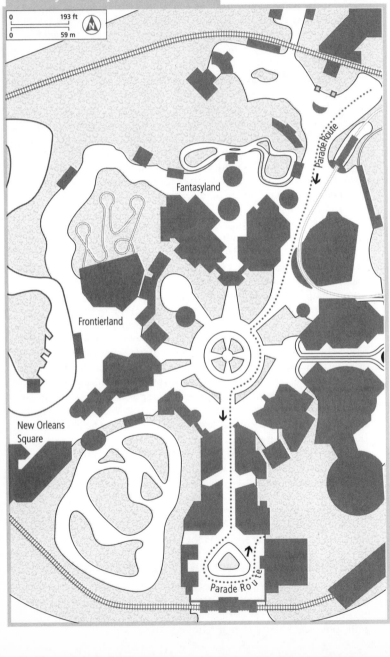

Parade of Dreams

For Disneyland's 50th-anniversary celebration, Disney launched a stunning parade called *Parade of Dreams*. Consisting of eight megafloats and just about every Disney character you've ever heard of, it's possibly the most stunning Disney parade ever. Each float has a different dream-related theme, such as Dreams of Imagination (Alice in Wonderland float) and Dreams of Adventure (*Lion King* float). Ringed by dancers, Disney characters, and various performers, the floats are both immense and elaborate. At three locations—Small World Mall, the central hub, and Main Street Town Square—each three-float segment of the parade stops and performs a two-minute show. If you station yourself at one of these viewing areas, you'll see all of the shows. However, if you're positioned elsewhere along the parade route you'll only see the parade in passing. *Parade of Dreams* is perhaps the most nostalgic and sentimental Disney parade ever produced. Parents will relive moments from their own childhoods as well as from those of their children.

Though *Parade of Dreams* has lights, it is really designed to be a daytime spectacle. Most days it runs at 3 p.m. and 7 p.m., with the first parade starting at Small World Mall and ending at Main Street Town Square. The later parade flows in the opposite direction.

FANTASYLAND THEATRE The park's premier venue for full-fledged musical productions starring the Disney characters. Also the home of the Disney Princess Fantasy Faire (see page 243). See the *Times Guide* for showtimes.

GOLDEN HORSESHOE VARIETY SHOW A Western saloon–style show alternates with a "hillbilly" show at the Golden Horseshoe stage in Frontierland. Check the *Times Guide* for showtimes.

JEDI TRAINING ACADEMY Staged at the Tomorrowland Terrace, the Jedi Training Academy recruits 30 young volunteers and trains them to fight with a light sword (looks like a huge illuminated Popsicle). Just when the training ends, Darth Vader and Darth Maul arrive with their Death Star troops and the young recruits join battle. The whole thing lasts about 25 minutes, and all volunteers are awarded a Jedi Training Academy diploma. It's a great photo op for parents and a major hoot for everyone else. To be chosen to participate, arrive early and seat your child in the first couple of rows surrounding the stage. showtimes are listed in the daily *Times Guide*.

PLAZA GARDENS This tented venue, located just beyond the central hub and to the left of the castle, hosts visiting high school and university bands, as well as swing dance bands.

STREET ENTERTAINMENT Various bands, singers, comics, and strolling musicians entertain in spontaneous (that is, unscheduled) street

264 PART 5 DISNEYLAND PARK

performances throughout the park. Musical styles include banjo, Dixieland, steel drum, marching, and fife and drum.

DISNEY ROCK GROUPS High-energy Disney rock groups perform seasonally in Tomorrowland according to the *Times Guide*.

RETREAT CEREMONY Daily at around dusk in Town Square, a small band and honor guard lower the flag and release a flock of white homing pigeons.

FIREWORKS REMEMBER . . . DREAMS COME TRUE Tinker Bell kicks off this sentimental fireworks spectacle with a new, zany flight path that makes you wonder what she's on besides pixie dust. *Remember . . . Dreams Come True* is the most elaborate and ambitious fireworks program in the park's history. Fireworks are seamlessly integrated with the voices of Walt Disney and dozens of Disney characters in the story of how the dream of Disneyland came true. Theme music from each of the park's lands as well as from Disney classic films combine to create a surprisingly moving production.

The show consists of five "acts," as Disney describes them. Julie Andrews's introduction leads to several famous Disney characters sharing their dreams. Then comes Tinker Bell's loopy flight followed by Walt Disney telling the story of his Disneyland dream. Finally Tink reappears for the heart-tugging finale, called "Wishes Everlasting." Each act is naturally accompanied by an Armageddon of fireworks, including some custom patterns created expressly for this production.

unofficial **TIP**
If you plan to leave the park after the fireworks, the second-floor platform of the Main Street train station affords one of the best views you'll find.

Without a doubt, the central hub is the best vantage point for watching *Remember . . . Dreams Come True*. Unfortunately, every guest in the park won't fit in the hub at the same time. The next-best positions are any open (that is, not canopied by trees) spots facing Sleeping Beauty Castle, followed by any open spot without something really big, like a Disney mountain, in the way. Concerning the latter, you'll be able to see the fireworks fine but will miss Tinker Bell.

SWORD IN THE STONE CEREMONY An audience-participation ceremony based on the Disney animated feature of the same name. Merlin the Magician selects youngsters from the audience to test their courage and strength by removing the sword Excalibur from the stone. Staged each day near King Arthur Carrousel according to the schedule in the *Times Guide*.

DISNEY CHARACTER APPEARANCES Disney characters appear at random throughout the park but are routinely present in Mickey's Toontown, Fantasyland, and on Main Street. A greeting area featuring Aladdin and Jasmine is located at Aladdin's Oasis in Adventureland (see the *Times Guide*). Disney princesses are on call daily at the Fantasyland Theatre (see 243). If you like your princesses wet, you can

visit Ariel, the Little Mermaid, at Triton's Garden off the path connecting the Matterhorn to the central hub.

DISNEY CHARACTER BREAKFASTS AND DINNERS Disney characters join guests for breakfast each morning until 11 a.m. at the **Plaza Inn** on Main Street, **Storyteller's Café** at the Grand Californian Hotel, and **PCH Grill** at Paradise Pier Hotel. Disney characters also join guests for breakfast and dinner at **Goofy's Kitchen** at the Disneyland Hotel, and **Ariel's Grotto** in California Adventure Park serves character meals with Ariel and friends.

UNHERALDED TREASURES *at* DISNEYLAND PARK

UNHERALDED TREASURES ARE SPECIAL FEATURES found in all of the Disney theme parks and add texture, context, beauty, depth, and subtlety to your visit. Generally speaking, Unheralded Treasures are nice surprises that should be accorded a little time. They are the proverbial Disney roses you should stop to smell. Lani Teshima, *Unofficial Guide* friend and writer for **www.mouseplanet.com,** knows them all. Her list follows.

TREASURE: Snow White's Grotto and Wishing Well

LOCATION: The front right of Sleeping Beauty Castle

A SLOW STROLL AROUND THE SLEEPING BEAUTY CASTLE can be romantic, but sitting quietly to its right is Snow White's Grotto and Wishing Well. If you stop for a few moments, you can hear the voice of Snow White singing "I'm Wishing" in the area. The grotto includes a trickling waterfall framing statues of Snow White and the Seven Dwarfs, placed on three tiers in such a way as to make Snow White appear to be off in the distance in an optical illusion that masks the fact that her statue is the same height as those of the dwarfs. Next to the grotto is a wishing well, where you can toss a coin and make a wish. The area is usually quiet and secluded, even on the most crowded days, making it a popular spot for smitten men to propose to their brides-to-be.

TREASURE: Disneyland Railroad

LOCATION: Stations in Main Street, U.S.A.; New Orleans Square; Fantasyland; and Tomorrowland

AFTER A LONG DAY, THE DISNEYLAND RAILROAD offers a nice way to get from one end of the park to another. But trains held a special place in Walt Disney's heart, and the railroad offers much more than just a ride back to the park gates. Pause and turn around before you enter Main Street station for a beautiful view of the entire length of Main Street, U.S.A. Inside the station, you can enjoy looking at model trains and other little exhibits. If you get off at the New Orleans Square station, stop and listen—that beeping sound you hear is Walt Disney's 1955 Disneyland park opening speech in land-line telegraphic code. And don't forget to ride from Tomorrowland back to Main Street so you can enjoy an unexpected treat: two large indoor dioramas inside the train tunnel, one depicting the Grand Canyon and another depicting a primeval world, complete with large-scale dinosaurs!

TREASURE: Windows on Main Street

LOCATION: Main Street, U.S.A.

EVER WONDER IF THE NAMES ON ALL THOSE WINDOWS on Main Street mean anything? Like guardian angels looking over everyone who walks through the park, these are the names of very special people who have had a profound influence on the park in some way. The names are also often associated with "professions" related to what they used to do when they worked for Disney. For example, the inscription for a window dedicated to the person who designed Disneyland's waterways reads, "Decorative Fountains and Watercolor by Fred Joerger." Disneyland still occasionally bestows this window honor in official dedication ceremonies in the park.

TREASURE: Frontierland Shooting Gallery

LOCATION: Frontierland

SMACK IN THE MIDDLE OF FRONTIERLAND is the shooting gallery where cowpokes can close an eye and squeeze the trigger to try to get their target to ping, ting, move, or light up. Don't discount the Frontierland Shooting Gallery as just another arcade gimmick. Everything about this well-themed attraction is dusty and rustic—except for the laser-powered guns, which are both safer and cause less wear on the targets—and about the only things missing are blowing tumbleweeds and Clint Eastwood.

TREASURE: Edible Plants

LOCATION: Tomorrowland

DON'T BE SO SURE THAT ALL YOU CAN FIND in Disneyland is junk food. The Disney theme parks are known for their magnificent landscaping, but did you know that many of the plants in Tomorrowland are edible, emphasizing the practicality of a future where the garden plants do double duty as your vegetable garden? For example, the entryway to Tomorrowland is lined with orange trees, and the bushes along the walkways are planted with leafy vegetables like lettuce, kale, and rhubarb, as well as herbs like sage, chives, and basil.

TREASURE: Carnation Plaza

LOCATION: Central Hub

IF YOU STILL HAVE ENERGY LEFT at the end of a long Saturday at Disneyland, did you know you don't even have to leave the park to put on your dancin' shoes? Near Frontierland at the castle-end of Main Street is Carnation Plaza, where every Saturday (and also on Fridays in the summer), swingers can dance the night away. Even if you're too tired to dance, you might catch some guys in crazy zoot-suit getups or seasoned veterans twirling in their poodle skirts.

TREASURE: Flag Retreat Ceremony

LOCATION: Main Street Square

EVERYDAY IN THE AFTERNOON, the Disneyland Band marches to the front of Main Street to performs a number of Americana tunes. Park security guards then lower the American flag as the band plays "The Star-Spangled Banner" in this very respectful ceremony. Though this 20-minute event (including the band's march down Main Street) has been happening for years, it has enjoyed a larger audience in recent years because of its patriotic feel.

TREASURE: *Partners* Statue

INSERT: Central Hub

AT THE CASTLE-END OF MAIN STREET, in the center of the circular hub, is a bronze statue of Walt Disney holding the hand of Mickey Mouse. With his right hand, Walt points outward to the park as if to say, "Look at this wonderful place." The statue, simply called *Partners,* pays homage to the two original ambassadors of Disneyland. If you stand in front of the statue, you can get a nice shot of it with Sleeping Beauty Castle in the background. The spot is encircled by a stone bench, and it's a great place to meet should your family decide to split off to visit different lands. There's more bronze in the area, too; smaller statues of other popular Disney figures like Dumbo, Goofy, and Pluto form a ring around this little garden oasis in the middle of the park.

TRAFFIC PATTERNS *at* DISNEYLAND PARK

WHEN WE BEGAN OUR RESEARCH on Disneyland, we were very interested in traffic patterns throughout the park, specifically these issues:

1. WHAT ATTRACTIONS AND WHICH SECTIONS OF THE PARK DO VISITORS HEAD FOR WHEN THEY FIRST ARRIVE? When guests are admitted to the various lands, the flow of people to Tomorrowland (Space Mountain, Buzz Lightyear, and *Finding Nemo* Submarine Voyage) is heaviest. The next most crowded land is Fantasyland, though the crowds are distributed over a large number of attractions. Critter Country is likewise crowded with its small area and only two attractions (Splash Mountain and Pooh). Adventureland, Frontierland, and New Orleans Square fill more slowly, with Mickey's Toontown not really coming alive until later in the morning. As the park fills, visitors appear to head for specific favored attractions that they wish to ride before the lines get long. This, more than any other factor, determines traffic patterns in the mornings and accounts for the relatively equal distribution of visitors throughout Disneyland.

ATTRACTIONS HEAVILY ATTENDED IN EARLY MORNING	
Adventureland	Indiana Jones Adventure
	Jungle Cruise
Critter Country	The Many Adventures of Winnie the Pooh
	Splash Mountain
Fantasyland	Dumbo the Flying Elephant
	Matterhorn Bobsleds
Tomorrowland	Buzz Lightyear Astro Blasters
	Finding Nemo Submarine Voyage
	Space Mountain
	Star Tours

2. HOW LONG DOES IT TAKE FOR THE PARK TO REACH PEAK CAPACITY FOR A GIVEN DAY? HOW ARE THE VISITORS DISPERSED THROUGHOUT THE PARK? There is a surge of "early birds" who arrive before or around opening time but are quickly dispersed throughout the empty park. After the initial onslaught is absorbed, there is a bit of a lull that lasts until about an hour after opening. Following the lull, the park is inundated with arriving guests for about two hours, peaking between 10 and 11 a.m. Guests continue to arrive in a steady but diminishing stream until around 2 p.m.

Sampled lines reached their longest length between noon and 3 p.m., indicating more arrivals than departures in the early afternoon. For general touring purposes, most attractions develop substantial lines between 9:30 and 11 a.m. In the early morning, Tomorrowland, Critter Country, and Fantasyland fill up first. By late morning and into early afternoon, attendance is fairly equally distributed throughout all of the "lands." Mickey's Toontown, because it is comparatively small, stays mobbed from about 11:30 a.m. on. By midafternoon, however, we noted a concentration of visitors in Fantasyland, New Orleans Square, and Adventureland, and a slight decrease of visitors in Tomorrowland.

In the late afternoon and early evening, attendance continues to be more heavily distributed in Tomorrowland, Critter Country, and Fantasyland. Though Space Mountain, Buzz Lightyear, Splash Mountain, Winnie the Pooh, and especially *Finding Nemo* Submarine Voyage remain inundated throughout the day, most of the other attractions in Tomorrowland and Critter Country have reasonable lines. In New Orleans Square, The Haunted Mansion, Pirates of the Caribbean, and the multitudes returning from nearby Critter Country keep traffic brisk. Frontierland and Adventureland (except for the Indiana Jones ride) become less congested as the afternoon and evening progress.

3. HOW DO MOST VISITORS GO ABOUT TOURING THE PARK? IS THERE A DIFFERENCE IN THE TOURING BEHAVIOR OF FIRST-TIME VISITORS AND REPEAT VISITORS? Many first-time visitors accompany friends or relatives who are familiar with Disneyland and who guide their tour. These tours sometimes do and sometimes do not proceed in an orderly (clockwise or counterclockwise) touring sequence. First-time visitors without personal touring guidance tend to be more orderly in their touring. Many first-time visitors, however, are drawn to Sleeping Beauty Castle on entering the park and thus commence their rotation from Fantasyland. Repeat visitors usually proceed directly to their favorite attractions or to whatever is new.

4. WHAT EFFECT DO SPECIAL EVENTS SUCH AS PARADES, FIREWORKS, AND *FANTASMIC!* HAVE ON TRAFFIC PATTERNS? Special events such as parades, fireworks, and *Fantasmic!* pull substantial numbers of visitors from the lines for rides, especially when *Fantasmic!* and a parade are staged at the same time. Unfortunately, however, the left hand taketh what the right hand giveth. A parade and *Fantasmic!* kicking off simultaneously snarls traffic flow throughout Disneyland so much that guests find themselves captive wherever they are. Attraction lines in Tomorrowland, Mickey's Toontown, Adventureland, and Fantasyland (behind the castle) diminish dramatically, making Space Mountain,

Buzz Lightyear, Star Tours, the Jungle Cruise, Indiana Jones Adventure, Peter Pan's Flight, and Snow White's Scary Adventures particularly good choices during the evening festivities. The remainder of the park (Critter Country, New Orleans Square, Frontierland, Main Street) is so congested with guests viewing the parade and *Fantasmic!* that it's almost impossible to move.

5. WHAT ARE THE TRAFFIC PATTERNS NEAR TO AND AT CLOSING TIME?
On our sample days, which were recorded in and out of season, park departures outnumbered arrivals beginning in midafternoon, with a substantial number of guests leaving after the afternoon parade. Additional numbers of visitors departed during the late afternoon as the dinner hour approached. When the park closed early, there were steady departures during the two hours preceding closing, with a mass exodus of remaining visitors at closing time.

When the park closed late, departures were distributed throughout the evening hours, with waves of departures following the evening parade(s), fireworks, and *Fantasmic!* performances. Though departures increased exponentially as closing time approached, a huge throng was still on hand when the park finally shut down. The balloon effect of this last throng at the end of the day generally overwhelmed the shops on Main Street, the parking lot, trams, and the hotel shuttles, and the exits onto adjoining Anaheim streets. In the hour before closing in the lands other than Main Street, touring conditions were normally uncrowded except at the Indiana Jones attraction in Adventureland and Splash Mountain in Critter Country.

DISNEYLAND PARK TOURING PLANS

THE DISNEYLAND PARK TOURING PLANS are step-by-step plans for seeing as much as possible with a minimum of time wasted standing in line. They are designed to assist you in avoiding crowds and bottlenecks on days of moderate-to-heavy attendance. On days of lighter attendance (see "Selecting the Time of Year for Your Visit," page 22), the plans will still save you time but will not be as critical to successful touring.

Choosing the Right Touring Plan
Six different touring plans are presented:

- One-day Touring Plan for Adults
- Author's Select One-day Touring Plan
- Dumbo-or-Die-in-a-Day Touring Plan for Adults with Small Children
- Two-day Touring Plan for Adults with Small Children
- Two-day Touring Plan A for Daytime Touring or for When the Park Closes Early (before 8 p.m.)

- Two-day Touring Plan B for Morning and Evening Touring or for When the Park Is Open Late (after 8 p.m.)

If you have two days to spend at Disneyland Park, the two-day touring plans are by far the most relaxed and efficient. Two-day Touring Plan A takes advantage of early-morning touring, when lines are short and the park has not yet filled with guests. This plan works well all year and is particularly recommended for days when Disneyland Park closes before 8 p.m. On the other hand, Two-day Touring Plan B combines the efficiencies of early-morning touring on the first day with the splendor of Disneyland Park at night on the second day. This plan is perfect for guests who wish to sample both the attractions and the special magic of Disneyland Park after dark, including *Fantasmic!,* parades, and fireworks. The Two-day Touring Plan for Adults with Small Children spreads the experience over two more-relaxed days and incorporates more attractions that both children and parents will enjoy.

If you have only one day but wish to see as much as possible, use the One-day Touring Plan for Adults. This plan will pack as much into a single day as is humanly possible, but it is pretty exhausting. If you prefer a more relaxed visit, try the Author's Select One-day Touring Plan. This plan features the best Disneyland Park has to offer (in the author's opinion), eliminating some of the less impressive attractions.

If you have small children, you may want to use the Dumbo-or-Die-in-a-Day Touring Plan for Adults with Small Children. This plan includes most of the children's rides in Fantasyland and Mickey's Toontown, and omits roller-coaster rides and other attractions that small children cannot ride (because of Disney's age and height requirements), as well as rides and shows that are frightening for small children. Because this plan calls for adults to sacrifice many of the better Disney attractions, it is not recommended unless you are touring Disneyland Park primarily for the benefit of your children. In essence, you pretty much stand around, sweat, wipe noses, pay for stuff, and watch the children have fun. It's great.

An alternative (to the Dumbo Plan) would be to use the One-day Touring Plan for Adults, or the Author's Select One-day Touring Plan, and take advantage of "switching off," a technique whereby children accompany adults to the loading area of rides with age and height requirements, but do not actually ride (see page 152). Switching off allows adults to enjoy the wilder rides while keeping the whole group together.

Park-opening Procedures

Your progress and success during your first hour of touring will be affected by the particular opening procedure the Disney people use that day.

A. All guests are held at the turnstiles until the park opens (which may or may not be at the official opening time). On admittance, all "lands" are open. If this is the case on the day you visit, blow right past Main Street and head for the first attraction on whatever touring plan you are following.

B. Guests are admitted to Main Street a half hour to an hour before the remaining "lands" open. Access to the other lands is blocked by a rope barrier at the central hub end of Main Street on these days. On admittance, move to the rope barrier and stake out a position as follows:

(1) If you are going to Indiana Jones or Splash Mountain first, take up a position in front of the Plaza Pavilion restaurant at the central-hub end of Main Street on the left. Wait next to the rope barrier blocking the walkway to Adventureland. When the rest of the park opens (and the rope drops), proceed quickly to Adventureland for Indiana Jones, or Critter Country by way of Adventureland and New Orleans Square for Splash Mountain.

(2) If you are going to *Finding Nemo* Submarine Voyage or Space Mountain first, wait on the right at the central-hub end of Main Street. When the rope drops at opening time, bear right and zip into Tomorrowland.

(3) If you are going to Fantasyland or Frontierland first, proceed to the end of Main Street and line up at the rope right of center.

(4) If you are going to Mickey's Toontown first, ascend to the platform of the Main Street Station of the Disneyland Railroad and board the first train of the day. Ride half a circuit, disembarking at the Fantasyland/Toontown Station. The train pulls out of the Main Street Station at the same time the rope is dropped at the central-hub end of Main Street.

Clip-out Touring Plans

For your convenience, we have prepared outline versions of all the touring plans presented in this guide. These pocket outlines present the same touring itineraries as the detailed touring plans, but with vastly abbreviated directions. First, select the touring plan that is most appropriate for your party, and then familiarize yourself with the detailed version of the plan. Once you understand how the touring plan works, clip out the pocket-outline version of your selected plan from the back of this guide and carry it with you as a quick reference when you visit the theme park.

THE CHALLENGE OF
FINDING NEMO SUBMARINE VOYAGE

BECAUSE IT'S NEW (AND BECAUSE IT'S GOOD), *Finding Nemo* Submarine Voyage stays mobbed all day except for the first few minutes after opening. To compound the problem, the subs have a small hourly carrying capacity, load slowly, and are not a FASTPASS attraction.

If you have early-entry privileges, arrive at the entrance 35 minutes before the early-entry period begins and sprint to the subs as soon as the park opens. If you don't have early-entry privileges, your only hope of avoiding a long wait is to be among the first through the turnstiles on a non-early-entry day (Wednesday, Friday, or Sunday) and zip straight to the subs. Unfortunately, this is not as straight-forward as it appears. To be among the first through the turnstiles, you'll need to arrive at the park, admission in hand, at least 35 minutes (preferably 45) minutes before opening.

Line up in front of Gate 13 even if it is unmanned. As opening time approaches, Gate 13 and adjacent gates 11 and 12 will all be staffed and have shorter queues than the other gates. Once you get through the turnstiles, hustle as fast as possible to the subs. In tests during the summer of 2007, the subs were posting a 40-minute wait by 10 minutes after park opening; by 15 minutes after park opening, the wait was already 90 minutes. Your goal, therefore, should be to arrive at the subs no later than 6 minutes after opening. But even if you are one the first to arrive at the subs, it will take 25 to 40 minutes to board, ride, and disembark. By this time, long lines will have formed at Space Mountain and other popular attractions.

If you have a very speedy person in your party, he or she can break away from the rest of the group on entering the park and race to Space Mountain to obtain FASTPASSes for everybody. After obtaining FASTPASSes, he or she rejoins you in line at *Finding Nemo.* Because the entire queue for the subs is in the open, locating and rejoining the rest of the group is usually simple.

The better solution is to tour Disneyland Park on two non-early-entry mornings, catching *Nemo,* the Matterhorn Bobsleds, Space Mountain, and Buzz Lightyear one morning and Splash Mountain, Big Thunder Mountain, Peter Pan's Flight, and Indiana Jones on the other. Because non-early-entry days alternate with early-entry ones, this two-morning plan requires at least three days at Disneyland Resort—usually two non-early-entry days at Disneyland Park and a visit to DCA on the day in between.

If you only have one day to devote to Disneyland Park and you want to ride the subs, doing so first thing after the park opens is the only sane approach; as noted above, however, the price of a short wait for *Finding Nemo* is longer waits at the other big attractions. Given the incredible challenge of the subs, you might decide that they're are not worth the effort. If you reach this conclusion, simply skip the touring plan for *Finding Nemo* Submarine Voyage.

In our touring plans, we assume that experiencing the subs is one of your touring priorities. Consequently, we list *Finding Nemo* as the first attraction on the itineraries. If the subs are not a big deal for you, simply skip them and continue with the touring plans.

PRELIMINARY INSTRUCTIONS FOR ALL DISNEYLAND PARK TOURING PLANS

ON DAYS OF MODERATE to heavy attendance, follow the touring plans exactly, deviating only when you do not wish to experience a listed show or ride. For instance, the touring plan may direct you to go next to Big Thunder Mountain, a roller-coaster ride. If you do not like roller coasters, simply skip that step and proceed to the next.

1. Buy your admission in advance (see "Admission Options" on page 20).
2. Call ☎ 714-781-7290 the day before you go for the official opening time.
3. Become familiar with the park-opening procedures (described on page 87), and read over the touring plan of your choice so that you will have a basic understanding of what you are likely to encounter as you enter the park.

DISNEYLAND PARK ONE-DAY TOURING PLAN FOR ADULTS

FOR Adults without small children.

ASSUMES Willingness to experience all major rides (including roller coasters) and shows.

Be forewarned that this plan requires a lot of walking and some backtracking; this is necessary to avoid long waits in line. A little extra walking coupled with some hustle in the morning will save you two to three hours of standing in line. Also be aware that you might not complete the tour. How far you get will depend on the size of your group, how quickly you move from ride to ride, how many times you pause for rest or food, how quickly the park fills, and what time the park closes.

ABOUT EARLY ENTRY If you are eligible for early entry, arrive at the turnstiles 30 minutes before the early-entry period begins on Monday, Tuesday, Thursday, or Friday (days subject to change) with admission in hand. Upon admission to the park experience: (1) *Finding Nemo* Submarine Voyage; (2) Space Mountain; (3) Buzz Lightyear; (4) Matterhorn Bobsleds; and (5) Peter Pan's Flight, in that order. If you're not able to enjoy all of the above during the early-entry hour, see as many as you can. When the park opens to the general public, continue the sequence until you've experienced all five. At that point, join the touring plan at Step 10 and proceed from there.

If you are not eligible for early entry, use the following plan on a non-early-entry day (currently Wednesday, Friday, or Sunday). Do not attempt to use the plan on an early-entry day—Disneyland Park will be packed with early-entry guests before you even make it past the turnstiles. If you wish to tour on an early-entry day but are not eligible for early entry, visit DCA (which does not participate in the early program) and save Disneyland Park for a non-early-entry day.

Note: The success of the touring plan hinges on your entering the park when it first opens.

1. Arrive at the park, admission in hand, at least 40 minutes before opening. Line up at Gate 13.
2. Once you get through the turnstiles, entrust all your admission passes to one very speedy person.

3. Dispatch the person with the passes to Space Mountain to obtain FASTPASSes.

4. Everyone else, hurry as quickly as possible to *Finding Nemo* Submarine Voyage.

5. The person who obtains the Space Mountain FASTPASSes rejoins the group in line at *Finding Nemo*. Enjoy the subs.

6. After the subs, ride the nearby Matterhorn Bobsleds if they're on your priority list.

7. Proceed to Fantasyland via the entrance next to the Mad Tea Party. Experience Peter Pan's Flight.

8. Return to Tomorrowland via the central hub and ride Buzz Lightyear.

9. Ride Space Mountain using your FASTPASSes.

10. Exit Space Mountain and turn left toward the central hub. Enter Frontierland and ride Big Thunder Mountain Railroad.

11. Keeping the waterfront on your right, head for Critter Country and Splash Mountain. Obtain FASTPASSes.

12. Also in Critter Country, experience the Many Adventures of Winnie the Pooh.

13. From Critter Country, head to Adventureland. Ride Indiana Jones.

14. Exit Indiana Jones to the right and take the Jungle Cruise. If you're a Disneyland veteran and don't care about the Jungle Cruise, skip to Step 15.

15. Continue to New Orleans Square and experience Pirates of the Caribbean.

16. Also in New Orleans Square, tour The Haunted Mansion.

17. Feel free at this time to grab a bite to eat if you're hungry. Now's also a good time to look over the *Times Guide* handout for live entertainment offerings. Whatever else, don't miss the show at the Golden Horseshoe Saloon in Frontierland.

18. In nearby Frontierland, ride either the Sailing Ship *Columbia* or the *Mark Twain* Riverboat.

19. Ride Splash Mountain using your FASTPASSes.

20. Return to Adventureland and see the show at the *Enchanted Tiki Room*.

21. Nearby, explore Tarzan's Treehouse.

22. Cross the central hub and return to Tomorrowland. Ride Star Tours if the wait isn't prohibitive.

23. Also in Tomorrowland, see *Honey, I Shrunk the Audience*.

24. Take the Disneyland Railroad from the Tomorrowland Station to the Fantasyland/Mickey's Toontown Station.

25. Exit the station to the left and pass under the railroad bridge to Mickey's Toontown. Though imaginative and colorful, Toontown is primarily for small children and expendable for most adults.

26. Pass back under the railroad bridge and bear left to It's a Small World, and ride.

27. While in Fantasyland sample any rides you missed earlier.
28. Check the *Times Guide* for parades, fireworks, and *Fantasmic!* Work these shows into the remainder of your day as time and energy allow.
29. Backtrack to pick up any attractions you may have missed earlier.
30. Continue to tour, saving Main Street for last. If you have any oomph left, see *Disneyland: The First 50 Years* (or *The Walt Disney Story–Great Moments with Mr. Lincoln*) on your way out of the park.

AUTHOR'S SELECT DISNEYLAND PARK ONE-DAY TOURING PLAN

FOR Adults touring without small children.

ASSUMES Willingness to experience all major rides (including roller coasters) and shows.

This touring plan is selective and includes only those attractions that, in the author's opinion, represent the best Disneyland Park has to offer.

Be forewarned that this plan requires a lot of walking and some backtracking; this is necessary to avoid long waits in line. A little extra walking coupled with some hustle in the morning will save you two to three hours standing in line. Note that you might not complete this tour. How far you get will depend on the size of your group, how quickly you move from ride to ride, how many times you pause for rest or food, how quickly the park fills, and what time the park closes. With a little zip and some luck, it is possible to complete the touring plan even on a busy day when the park closes early.

ABOUT EARLY ENTRY If you are eligible for early entry, arrive at the turnstiles 30 minutes before the early-entry period begins on Monday, Tuesday, Thursday, or Friday (days subject to change) with admission in hand. Upon admission to the park experience: (1) *Finding Nemo* Submarine Voyage; (2) Space Mountain; (3) Buzz Lightyear; (4) Matterhorn Bobsleds; and (5) Peter Pan's Flight, in that order. If you're not able to enjoy all of the above during the early-entry hour, see as many as you can. When the park opens to the general public, continue the sequence until you've experienced all five. At that point, join the touring plan at Step 7 and proceed from there.

If you are not eligible for early entry, use the following plan on a non-early-entry day (currently Wednesday, Friday, or Sunday). Do not attempt to use the plan on an early-entry day—Disneyland Park will be packed with early-entry guests before you even make it past the turnstiles. If you wish to tour on an early-entry day but are not eligible for early entry, visit DCA (which does not participate in the early program) and save Disneyland Park for a non-early-entry day.

Note: The success of the touring plan hinges on your entering the park when it first opens.

1. Arrive at the park, admission in hand, at least 40 minutes before opening. Line up at Gate 13.

2. Once you get through the turnstiles, entrust all your admission passes to one very fast person.

3. Dispatch the person with the passes to Space Mountain to obtain FASTPASSes.

4. Everyone else, high-tail it to *Finding Nemo* Submarine Voyage.

5. The person who obtains the Space Mountain FASTPASSes rejoins the group in line at *Finding Nemo.* Enjoy the subs.

6. After the subs, ride the nearby Matterhorn Bobsleds if they're on your priority list.

7. Proceed to Fantasyland via the entrance next to the Mad Tea Party. Experience Peter Pan's Flight.

8. Return to Tomorrowland via the central hub and ride Buzz Lightyear.

9. Ride Space Mountain using your FASTPASSes.

10. Exit Space Mountain and turn left toward the central hub. Enter Frontierland and ride Big Thunder Mountain Railroad.

11. Keeping the waterfront on your right, head for Critter Country and Splash Mountain. Obtain FASTPASSes.

12. Also in Critter Country, experience the Many Adventures of Winnie the Pooh.

13. From Critter Country, head to Adventureland. Ride Indiana Jones.

14. Continue to New Orleans Square and experience Pirates of the Caribbean.

15. Also in New Orleans Square, tour The Haunted Mansion.

16. Feel free at this time to grab a bite to eat if you're hungry. Now's also a good time to look over the *Times Guide* handout for live entertainment offerings. Whatever else, don't miss the show at the Golden Horseshoe Saloon in Frontierland.

17. In nearby Frontierland, ride either the Sailing Ship *Columbia* or the *Mark Twain* Riverboat.

18. Ride Splash Mountain using your FASTPASSes.

19. Cross the central hub and return to Tomorrowland. Ride Star Tours if the wait isn't prohibitive.

20. Also in Tomorrowland, see *Honey, I Shrunk the Audience.*

21. Take the Disneyland Railroad from the Tomorrowland Station to the Fantasyland/Mickey's Toontown Station.

22. Exit the station to the left and pass under the railroad bridge to Mickey's Toontown. Though imaginative and colorful, Toontown is primarily for small children and expendable for most adults.

23. Pass back under the railroad bridge and bear left to It's A Small World. Ride.

24. Check the *Times Guide* for parades, fireworks, and *Fantasmic!* Work these shows into the remainder of your day as time and energy allow.

25. Backtrack to pick up any attractions you may have missed earlier.

26. Continue to tour, saving Main Street for last. If you have any oomph

left, see *Disneyland: The First 50 Years* (or *The Walt Disney Story–Great Moments with Mr. Lincoln*) on your way out of the park.

DUMBO-OR-DIE-IN-A-DAY TOURING PLAN FOR ADULTS WITH SMALL CHILDREN

FOR Parents with children under age 7 who feel compelled to devote every waking moment to the pleasure and entertainment of their small children, and rich people who are paying someone else to take their children to the theme park.

ASSUMES Periodic stops for rest, restrooms, and refreshment.

The name of this touring plan notwithstanding, this itinerary is not a joke. Regardless of whether you are loving, guilty, masochistic, truly selfless, insane, or saintly, this touring plan will provide a small child with about as perfect a day as is possible at Disneyland Park.

This touring plan represents a concession to those adults who are determined, even if it kills them, to give their small children the ultimate Disneyland Park experience. The plan addresses the preferences, needs, and desires of small children to the virtual exclusion of those of adults or older siblings. If you left the kids with a sitter yesterday, or wouldn't let little Marvin eat barbecue for breakfast, this is the perfect plan for expiating your guilt. This is also a wonderful plan if you are paying a sitter, nanny, or chauffeur to take your children to Disneyland Park.

If this description has intimidated you somewhat or if you have concluded that your day at Disneyland Park is as important as your children's, use the One-day Touring Plan for Adults, making use of the switching-off option (see page 152) at those attractions that impose height or age restrictions.

Because the children's attractions in Disneyland Park are the most poorly engineered in terms of handling large crowds, the following touring plan is the least efficient of the six plans we present. It represents the best way, however, to experience most of the child-oriented attractions in one day if that is what you are determined to do. We do not make recommendations in this plan for meals. If you can, try to hustle along as quickly as is comfortable until about noon. After noon, it won't make much difference if you stop to eat or take it a little easier.

ABOUT EARLY ENTRY Do not attempt to use the plan on an early-entry day if you're not eligible for early entry—Disneyland Park will be packed with early-entry guests before you even make it past the turnstiles. If you wish to tour on an early-entry day but are not eligible for early entry, visit DCA (which does not participate in the early program) and save Disneyland Park for a non-early-entry day.

If you are eligible for early entry, experience *Finding Nemo* Submarine Voyage first thing and then ride Alice in Wonderland, Dumbo, and Peter Pan's Flight in that order. At the end of the early-entry hour, pick up the touring plan at Step 7.

Note: The success of this touring plan hinges on your being among the first to enter the park when it opens.

1. Arrive 40 minutes before the official opening time with your admission in hand.

2. Line up in front of Gate 13.

3. When you are admitted to the park, hurry to Tomorrowland and ride *Finding Nemo* Submarine Voyage. If your children are preschoolers, you might consider starting with the next step.

4. After the subs, keep the submarine lagoon on your right and proceed past the Matterhorn to Alice In Wonderland. Ride.

5. Exit to the left and continue in Fantasyland to Dumbo.

6. After Dumbo, experience Peter Pan's Flight.

7. Also in Fantasyland, ride the Storybook Land Canal Boats, or alternatively Casey Jr. Circus Train. Both attractions cover the same real estate.

8. In Fantasyland, ride the Mad Tea Party.

9. Next, head toward It's a Small World in the far corner of Fantasyland. Bypassing the ride for the moment, cross under the Disneyland Railroad tracks into Mickey's Toontown.

10. In Mickey's Toontown, try Roger Rabbit's Car Toon Spin if your children are plucky. Do not use FASTPASS unless the wait exceeds 30 minutes.

11. In Mickey's Toontown, ride Gadget's Go Coaster.

12. While in Mickey's Toontown, let off some steam in Goofy's Playhouse.

13. Tour Mickey's House and visit Mickey in his dressing room.

14. After seeing Mickey, turn right to enjoy Chip 'n' Dale's Treehouse.

15. Go to the far side of Mickey's House and tour Minnie's House.

16. Round out your visit to Mickey's Toontown with an inspection of Donald's Boat tied up next to Goofy's Playhouse.

17. Depart Toontown. Take the Disneyland Railroad from the Fantasyland/ Toontown station to New Orleans Square. Walk if you have a stroller that does not collapse.

18. Bear left on exiting the train station and follow the waterfront to Critter Country. Experience Winnie the Pooh.

19. Return to New Orleans Square and see Pirates of the Caribbean. If your children were frightened by Roger Rabbit's Car Toon Spin in Mickey's Toontown, skip ahead to Step 21.

20. Go left on leaving Pirates of the Caribbean to experience The Haunted Mansion. If your children were not frightened at Pirates of the Caribbean, they will do fine at The Haunted Mansion.

21. Go down to the waterfront and take a raft to Tom Sawyer Island. Allow the kids plenty of time to explore.

22. Catch the Disneyland Railroad at the New Orleans Square station and return to the Fantasyland/Toontown station.

23. In Fantasyland, ride It's a Small World.

24. Visit the Disney Princess Fantasy Faire at the Fantasyland Theatre to the left of the Fantasyland Railroad Station.

25. Return to the heart of Fantasyland and ride the King Arthur Carrousel.

26. In Fantasyland, also ride Pinocchio's Daring Journey if the wait does not exceed 15 minutes. Otherwise, skip ahead to Step 27.

27. Exit Pinocchio to your left and head to Frontierland.

28. In Frontierland, ride the *Mark Twain* Riverboat or the Sailing Ship *Columbia,* whichever departs first.

29 Leave Frontierland and go to Adventureland. Explore Tarzan's Treehouse if the wait is less than 15 minutes. Otherwise, skip ahead to Step 30.

30. In Adventureland, see the *Enchanted Tiki Room* show.

31. Leave Adventureland, cross the central hub, and enter Tomorrowland via the path that runs along the right side (as you face it from the central hub) of the Matterhorn.

32. In Tomorrowland, obtain a FASTPASS for Autopia.

33. Check your *Times Guide* for parades and live performances. The Jedi Training Academy at the Tomorrowland Terrace is particularly worthwhile.

34. In Tomorrowland, take the Disneyland monorail for a round-trip ride (you must disembark and reboard at Downtown Disney).

35. While in Tomorrowland, ride Autopia using your FASTPASS.

36. As soon as your return window for Autopia begins, obtain a FASTPASS for Buzz Lightyear. Your can do this either before or after riding Autopia.

37. This concludes the touring plan. Use any time remaining to revisit favorite attractions, see attractions that were not included in the touring plan, or visit attractions you skipped because the lines were too long. Also, consult your daily entertainment schedule for parades, Fantasyland Theatre productions, or other live entertainment that might interest you. As you drag your battered and exhausted family out of the park at the end of the day, bear in mind that it was you who decided to cram all this stuff into one day. We just tried to help you get organized.

DISNEYLAND PARK TWO-DAY TOURING PLAN FOR ADULTS WITH SMALL CHILDREN

FOR Parents with children under age 7 who wish to spread their Disneyland Park visit over two days.

ASSUMES Frequent stops for rest, restrooms, and refreshments.

This touring plan represents a compromise between the observed tastes of adults and the observed tastes of younger children. Included in this touring plan are many of the midway-type rides that your children may have the opportunity to experience (although in less exotic surroundings) at local fairs and amusement parks. These rides at Disneyland Park often require long waits in line, and they consume valuable touring time that could be better spent experiencing the many rides and shows found only at a Disney theme park and which best demonstrate the Disney genius. This touring plan is heavily weighted toward the tastes of younger children. If you want to balance it a bit, try working out a compromise with your kids to forgo some of the carnival-type rides (Mad Tea Party, Dumbo, King Arthur Carrousel, Gadget's Go Coaster) or such rides as the Tomorrowland Autopia.

Another alternative is to use one of the other Two-day Touring Plans and take advantage of "switching off" (see page 152). This technique allows small children to be admitted to rides such as Space Mountain, Indiana Jones, Big Thunder Mountain Railroad, and Splash Mountain. The children wait in the loading area as their parents ride one at a time; the nonriding parent waits with the children.

TIMING The following Two-day Touring Plan takes advantage of early-morning touring. On each day you should complete the structured part of the plan by 3 p.m. or so. We highly recommend returning to your hotel by midafternoon for a nap and an early dinner. If the park is open in the evening, come back to the park by 7:30 or 8 p.m. for the evening parade, fireworks, and *Fantasmic!*

ABOUT EARLY ENTRY Do not attempt to use the plan on early-entry days if you're not eligible for early entry—Disneyland Park will be packed with early-entry guests before you even make it past the turnstiles. Do Day One of the plan on a non-early-entry day. The next day will be an early-entry day, so visit DCA on that day (DCA does not participate in the early program). Come back to Disneyland Park on the following non-early-entry day and proceed with Day Two.

If you are eligible for early entry, experience *Finding Nemo* Submarine Voyage first thing and then ride Alice in Wonderland, Dumbo, and Peter Pan's Flight in that order. At the end of the early-entry hour, begin the touring plan, skipping any attractions called for in the touring plan that you experienced during early entry.

Note: Because the needs of small children are so varied, we have not built specific instructions for eating into the touring plan. Simply stop for refreshments or a meal when you feel the urge. For best results, however, try to keep moving in the morning. In the afternoon, you can eat, rest often, and adjust the pace to your liking.

DAY ONE

1. Arrive 30 to 40 minutes before the official opening time with your admission in hand.
2. Line up in front of Gate 13.
3. When you are admitted to the park, move quickly to the far end of Main Street. If there is no rope barrier, continue without stopping to Critter Country and Splash Mountain.
4. Ride Splash Mountain, taking advantage of the switching-off option if your children are too young or too short to ride.
5. While in Critter Country, ride The Many Adventures of Winnie the Pooh.

6. Backtrack to New Orleans Square and experience the Haunted Mansion. If your children seem intimidated by the prospect of The Haunted Mansion, skip ahead to Step 8.

7. After The Haunted Mansion, turn right and try Pirates of the Caribbean.

8. Bear right into Adventureland. Ride the Jungle Cruise.

9. Exit the Jungle Cruise to the left. Ride Indiana Jones, also in Adventureland.

10. Exit to the left (back toward The Haunted Mansion) and go to the Frontierland/New Orleans Square Station. Take the Disneyland Railroad one stop to the Fantasyland/Toontown Station.

11. Cross under the Disneyland Railroad tracks into Mickey's Toontown.

12. In Mickey's Toontown, try Roger Rabbit's Car Toon Spin if your children are plucky and have strong stomachs. Obtain FASTPASSes if the wait exceeds 30 minutes.

13. In Mickey's Toontown, ride Gadget's Go Coaster.

14. While in Mickey's Toontown, let off some steam in Goofy's Playhouse.

15. Tour Mickey's House and visit Mickey in his dressing room.

16. After seeing Mickey, turn right to enjoy Chip 'n' Dale's Treehouse.

17. Go to the far side of Mickey's House and tour Minnie's House.

18. Round out your visit to Mickey's Toontown with an inspection of Donald's Boat tied up next to Goofy's Playhouse.

19. Depart Mickey's Toontown the same way you entered, bearing left after you pass under the railroad tracks. Proceed to It's a Small World and ride.

20. Visit the Disney Princess Fantasy Faire at the Fantasyland Theatre to the left of the Fantasyland Railroad Station.

21. Next, return to the Fantasyland/Toontown Station. Take the Disneyland Railroad all the way around the park (back to Toontown), then stay on for one more stop and disembark in Tomorrowland. If you have a stroller that cannot go on the train, make a complete circuit on the train without the stroller and then walk from Toontown to Tomorrowland.

22. In Tomorrowland, obtain a FASTPASS for Autopia.

23. Also in Tomorrowland, enjoy a performance of *Honey, I Shrunk the Audience* (see the Small-child Fright-potential Chart on pages 144–147).

24. After the performance, take the monorail for a round trip.

25. Return with your FASTPASS to ride Autopia.

26. This concludes the touring plan for Day One. Use any time remaining to revisit favorite attractions, see attractions that were not included in the touring plan, or visit attractions you skipped because the lines were too long. Also, consult your daily entertainment schedule for parades, Fantasyland Theatre productions, or other live entertainment that might interest you. If the park is open in the evening, consider going back to your hotel for a nap and dinner and returning after 7 p.m. for a parade and *Fantasmic!*

DAY TWO

1. Arrive at the park, admission in hand, at least 40 minutes before opening. Line up at Gate 13.

2. If members of your party want to ride Space Mountain, entrust all your admission passes to one very fast person once you get through the turnstiles.

3. Dispatch the person with the passes to Space Mountain to obtain FASTPASSes.

4. Everyone else, proceed posthaste to *Finding Nemo* Submarine Voyage.

5. The person who obtains the Space Mountain FASTPASSes rejoins the group in line at *Finding Nemo.* Enjoy the subs.

6. After the subs, ride the nearby Matterhorn Bobsleds if they're on your priority list.

7. Head to Fantasyland via the central hub. Ride Dumbo if the wait is tolerable.

8. Backtracking toward the castle, ride Peter Pan's Flight.

9. Exiting Peter Pan to the right, ride Mr. Toad's Wild Ride.

10. Exit Mr. Toad to the right and bear right around the corner to Alice in Wonderland. Ride.

11. After Alice in Wonderland, try the Mad Tea Party next door.

12. Next, ride the Storybook Land Canal Boats, across the walk from the Mad Tea Party.

13. Bear right after the Canal Boats and return to the center of Fantasyland by the castle. Ride the King Arthur Carrousel.

14. Across from King Arthur Carrousel, experience Pinocchio's Daring Journey (we recommend skipping the nearby Snow White's Scary Adventures).

15. Exit Pinocchio to your left, leave Fantasyland, and go into Frontierland.

16. If you want, ride Big Thunder Mountain, taking advantage of the switching-off option. Use FASTPASS if the wait exceeds 30 minutes.

17. Take a cruise on the *Mark Twain* Riverboat or the Sailing Ship *Columbia,* whichever departs first.

18. Keeping the waterfront on your right, proceed to the rafts for transportation to Tom Sawyer Island. Allow the children to explore the island.

19. Leave Frontierland and pass through New Orleans Square into Adventureland. Explore Tarzan's Treehouse.

20. See the *Enchanted Tiki Room* show, also in Adventureland.

21. Return to Tomorrowland and ride Buzz Lightyear.

22. Ride Space Mountain using your FASTPASSes. Take advantage of switching off if you have children too young or too short to ride.

23. Also in Tomorrowland, ride Star Tours.

24. This concludes the touring plan for Day Two. Use any time remaining to revisit favorite attractions, see attractions that were not included in the touring plan, or visit attractions you skipped because the lines were

too long. Also, consult your daily entertainment schedule for parades, Fantasyland Theatre productions, or other live entertainment that might interest you. If the park is open in the evening, consider going back to your hotel for a nap and dinner and returning after 7 p.m. for a parade and *Fantasmic!*

DISNEYLAND PARK TWO-DAY TOURING PLAN A, FOR DAYTIME TOURING OR FOR WHEN THE PARK CLOSES EARLY

FOR Parties wishing to spread their Disneyland Park visit over two days and parties preferring to tour in the morning.

ASSUMES Willingness to experience all major rides (including roller coasters) and shows.

TIMING The following Two-day Touring Plan takes advantage of early-morning touring and is the most efficient of all the touring plans for comprehensive touring with the least time lost waiting in line. On each day you should complete the structured part of the plan by 3 p.m. or so. If you are visiting Disneyland Park during a period of the year when the park is open late (after 8 p.m.), you might prefer our Two-day Touring Plan B, which offers morning touring on one day and late afternoon and evening touring on the other day. Another highly recommended option is to return to your hotel around midafternoon for a well-deserved nap and an early dinner, and to come back to the park by 7:30 or 8 p.m. for the evening parade, fireworks, and live entertainment.

ABOUT EARLY ENTRY Do not attempt to use the plan on early-entry days if you're not eligible for early entry—Disneyland Park will be packed with early-entry guests before you even make it past the turnstiles. Do Day One of the plan on a non-early-entry day. The next day will be an early-entry day, so visit DCA on that day (DCA does not participate in the early program). Come back to Disneyland Park on the following non-early-entry day and proceed with Day Two.

If you're eligible for early entry, experience (1) *Finding Nemo* Submarine Voyage; (2) Space Mountain; (3) Buzz Lightyear; (4) Matterhorn Bobsleds; and (5) Peter Pan's Flight, in that order. If you're not able to enjoy all of the above during the early-entry hour, see as many as you can. When the park opens to the general public, continue the sequence until you've experienced all five. At that point, begin the touring plan, skipping any attraction you've already seen.

DAY ONE

1. Arrive at the park, admission in hand, at least 40 minutes before opening. Line up at Gate 13.

2. If members of your party want to ride Space Mountain, entrust all your admission passes to one person who can fly like the wind.

3. Dispatch the person with the passes to Space Mountain to obtain FASTPASSes.

4. Everyone else, hurry as fast as possible to *Finding Nemo* Submarine Voyage.

5. The person who obtains the Space Mountain FASTPASSes rejoins the group in line at *Finding Nemo*. Enjoy the subs.

6. After the subs, ride the nearby Matterhorn Bobsleds if they're on your priority list.

7. Proceed to Fantasyland via the entrance next to the Mad Tea Party. Experience Peter Pan's Flight.

8. Also in Fantasyland, ride the Storybook Land Canal Boats.

9. In Fantasyland, experience Mr. Toad's Wild Ride.

10. Still in Fantasyland, ride Snow White's Scary Adventures.

11. Next door to the left, ride Pinocchio's Daring Journey.

12. Return to Tomorrowland. Ride Space Mountain using your FASTPASSes.

13. Also in Tomorrowland, ride Buzz Lightyear.

14. Proceed to Frontierland and ride Big Thunder Mountain Railroad. Get a FASTPASS and return later to ride if the wait exceeds 25 minutes.

15. If you are hungry, try Rancho del Zocalo, across from the entrance to Big Thunder Mountain Railroad.

16. While in Frontierland, ride the *Mark Twain* Riverboat or the Sailing Ship *Columbia* (whichever departs first).

    Note: At this point, check your *Times Guide* daily entertainment schedule to see if there are any parades, fireworks, or live performances that interest you. Make note of the times and alter the touring plan accordingly. Because you've already seen all of the attractions for Day One that cause bottlenecks and have big lines, an interruption of the touring plan here will not cause you any problems. Simply pick up where you left off before the parade or show.

17. While in Frontierland, take a raft to Tom Sawyer Island.

18. After you return to the mainland, proceed through New Orleans Square to Adventureland. Tour Tarzan's Treehouse.

19. Exit to your right and see the *Enchanted Tiki Room* show.

20. Return to Main Street via the central hub. See *Disneyland: The First 50 Years.*

21. This concludes Day One of the touring plan. If you have any energy left, backtrack to pick up attractions you would like to ride again or may have missed or bypassed because the lines were too long. Check out any parades or live performances that interest you. Alternatively, return to your hotel and fall, exhausted, into bed.

DAY TWO

1. Arrive 30 to 40 minutes before the official opening time with your admission in hand.

2. Line up in front of Gate 13.

3. After passing through the turnstiles, continue to the end of Main Street, U.S.A. If there is no rope barrier, move as fast as you can to Adventureland and ride Indiana Jones.

4. Exit Indiana Jones to the left and pass through New Orleans Square to Critter Country. Ride Splash Mountain.

5. While in Critter Country, ride the Many Adventures of Winnie the Pooh.

6. After you ride Winnie the Pooh, leave Critter Country and return to Adventureland. Ride the Jungle Cruise.

7. Exit the Jungle Cruise to the left and go to New Orleans Square. Ride Pirates of the Caribbean.

8. While in New Orleans Square, experience The Haunted Mansion.

9. Returning to New Orleans Square, take the Disneyland Railroad to the Mickey's Toontown/Fantasyland Station, one stop down the line.

10. After you get off the train, bear to your left and cross under the railroad tracks to Mickey's Toontown.

11. In Mickey's Toontown, ride Roger Rabbit's Car Toon Spin. If the wait is prohibitive, obtain a FASTPASS and ride later.

12. If you have children in your party, tour Mickey's House and visit Mickey in his dressing room. Do the same at Minnie's House.

13. Leave Mickey's Toontown the same way you entered. Bear left after passing under the tracks and ride It's a Small World.

14. Passing between the lagoon and the Matterhorn, proceed to Tomorrow-land. The loading platform for the monorail is built over the docks for the lagoon. An escalator takes you up to the monorail loading area. If you are hungry, consider getting off the monorail at Downtown Disney for lunch (don't forget to have your hand stamped for reentry).

15. Return to Tomorrowland on the monorail. In Tomorrowland, see *Honey, I Shrunk the Audience.*

16. Also in Tomorrowland, ride Star Tours.

17. This concludes the touring plan. Revisit your favorite attractions, or try any rides and shows you may have missed. Check your daily entertain-ment schedule for parades or live performances that interest you.

DISNEYLAND PARK TWO-DAY TOURING PLAN B, FOR MORNING AND EVENING TOURING OR FOR WHEN THE PARK IS OPEN LATE

FOR Parties who want to enjoy Disneyland Park at different times of day, including evenings and early mornings.

ASSUMES Willingness to experience all major rides (including roller coasters) and shows.

TIMING This Two-day Touring Plan is for those visiting Disneyland Park on days when the park is open late (after 8 p.m.). The plan offers morning touring on one day and late afternoon and evening touring on the other day. If the park closes early, or if you prefer to do all of your touring during the morning and early afternoon, use the Two-day Touring Plan A, for Daytime Touring or for When the Park Closes Early.

ABOUT EARLY ENTRY If you are not eligible for early entry, do not try to use Day One of the plan on an early-entry day—Disneyland Park will be packed with early-entry guests before you even make it past the turnstiles.

If you're eligible for early entry and want to use Day One of the plan on an early-entry day, experience (1) *Finding Nemo* Submarine Voyage; (2) Space Mountain; (3) Buzz Lightyear; (4) Matterhorn Bobsleds; and (5) Peter Pan's Flight, in that order.   If you're not able to enjoy all of the above during the early-entry hour, see as many as you can. When the park opens to the general public, continue the sequence until you've experienced all five. At that point, begin the touring plan, skipping any attractions you've already seen.

DAY ONE

1. Arrive at the park, admission in hand, at least 30 minutes before opening. Line up at Gate 13.
2. If members of your party want to ride Space Mountain, entrust all your admission passes to your fastest person once you get through the turnstiles.
3. Dispatch the person with the passes to Space Mountain to obtain FASTPASSes.
4. Everyone else, hurry as fast as possible to *Finding Nemo* Submarine Voyage.
5. The person who obtains the Space Mountain FASTPASSes rejoins the group in line at *Finding Nemo.* Enjoy the subs.
6. After the subs, ride the nearby Matterhorn Bobsleds if they're on your priority list.
7. Proceed to Fantasyland via the entrance next to the Mad Tea Party. Experience Peter Pan's Flight.
8. Return to Tomorrowland via the central hub and ride Buzz Lightyear.
9. Ride Space Mountain using your FASTPASSes.
10. Exit Space Mountain and turn left toward the central hub. Enter Frontierland and ride Big Thunder Mountain Railroad.
11. Keeping the waterfront on your right, head for Critter Country and Splash Mountain. Obtain FASTPASSes.
12. Also in Critter County, experience the Many Adventures of Winnie the Pooh.
13. From Critter Country, head to Adventureland. Ride Indiana Jones.
14. Continue to New Orleans Square and experience Pirates of the Caribbean.
15. Also in New Orleans Square, tour The Haunted Mansion.

16. Feel free at this time to grab a bite to eat if you're hungry. Now's also a good time to look over the *Times Guide* handout for live-entertainment offerings. Whatever else, don't miss the show at the Golden Horseshoe Saloon in Frontierland.

17. In nearby Frontierland, ride either the Sailing Ship *Columbia* or the *Mark Twain* Riverboat.

18. Ride Splash Mountain using your FASTPASSes.

19. Continue to tour, saving Main Street for last. If you're not completely pooped, see *Disneyland: The First 50 Years* (or *The Walt Disney Story–Great Moments with Mr. Lincoln*) on your way out of the park.

20. This concludes the touring plan for Day One.

DAY TWO

1. Eat an early dinner and arrive at the park about 5:30 or 6 p.m.

2. Go to Adventureland and explore Tarzan's Treehouse.

3. Nearby, catch the show in the *Enchanted Tiki Room*.

4. Cross the central hub to Tomorrowland. Ride Star Tours if the wait isn't prohibitive.

5. Also in Tomorrowland, see *Honey, I Shrunk the Audience*.

6. Take the Disneyland Railroad from the Tomorrowland Station to the Fantasyland/Mickey's Toontown Station.

7. Exit the station to the left and pass under the railroad bridge to Mickey's Toontown. Though imaginative and colorful, Toontown is primarily for small children and expendable for most adults. Ride Roger Rabbit's Car Toon Spin if the wait is tolerable.

8. Pass back under the railroad bridge and bear left to It's a Small World. Ride.

9. Check the *Times Guide* for parades, fireworks, and *Fantasmic!* Work these shows into the remainder of your day as time and energy allow.

10. This concludes Day Two of the touring plan. Backtrack to pick up any attractions you may have missed earlier. Grab a bite to eat.

PART SIX

DISNEY'S CALIFORNIA ADVENTURE

A BRAVE NEW PARK

THE WALT DISNEY COMPANY'S newest American theme park, Disney's California Adventure, held its grand opening on February 8, 2001. Already known as DCA among Disneyphiles, the park is a bouquet of contradictions conceived in Fantasyland, starved in utero by corporate Disney, and born into a hostile environment of Disneyland loyalists who believe they've been handed a second-rate theme park. The park is new but full of old technology. Its parts are stunningly beautiful, yet come together awkwardly, failing to compose a handsome whole. And perhaps most lamentable of all, the California theme is impotent by virtue of being all-encompassing.

The history of the park is another of those convoluted tales found only in Robert Ludlum novels and corporate Disney. Southern California Disney fans began clamoring for a second theme park shortly after Epcot opened at Walt Disney World in 1982. Although there was some element of support within the Walt Disney Company, the Disney loyal had to content themselves with rumors and half-promises for two decades while they watched new Disney parks go up in Tokyo, Paris, and Florida. For years, Disney teasingly floated the "Westcot" concept, a California version of Epcot that was always just about to break ground. Whether it was a matter of procrastination or simply pursuing better opportunities elsewhere, the Walt Disney Company sat on the sidelines while the sleepy community of Anaheim became a sprawling city and property values skyrocketed. By the time Disney emerged from its Westcot fantasy and began to get serious about a second California park, the price tag—not to mention the complexity of integrating such a development into a mature city—was mind-boggling.

Westcot had been billed as a $2- to $3-billion, 100-plus-acre project, so that was what the Disney faithful were expecting when Disney's

disney's california adventure

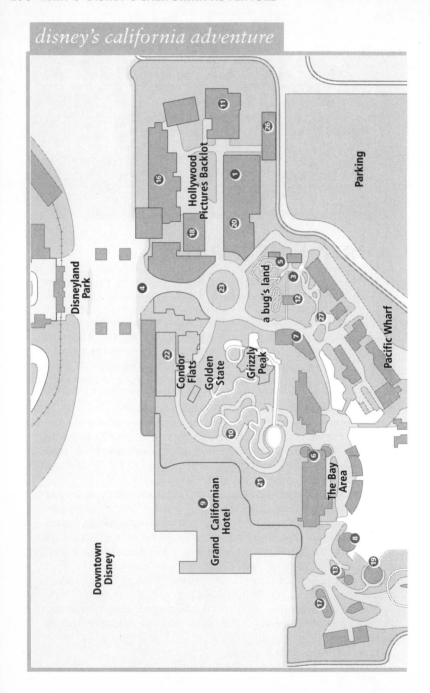

Parking

Disneyland Park

Hollywood Pictures Backlot

a bug's land

Pacific Wharf

Condor Flats

Golden State

Grizzly Peak

The Bay Area

Grand Californian Hotel

Downtown Disney

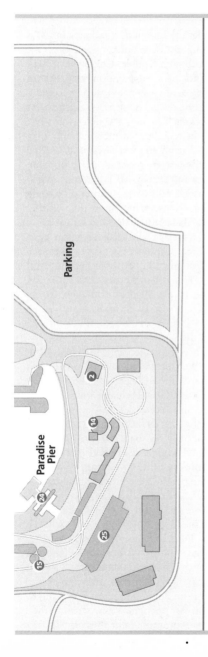

Paradise Pier

Parking

1. Animation Building
2. California Screamin'
3. Demonstration Farm
4. Entrance
5. Flik's Fun Fair
6. Golden Dreams
7. Golden Vine Winery
8. Golden Zephyr
9. Grand Californian Hotel

10. Grizzly River Run
11. Hyperion Theater
12. It's Tough to Be a Bug!
13. Jumpin' Jellyfish
14. King Triton's Carousel
15. Maliboomer
16. Monsters, Inc.: Mike and Sulley to the Rescue
17. Mulholland Madness

18. Muppet Vision 3-D
19. Orange Stinger
20. Playhouse Disney
21. Redwood Creek Challenge Trail
22. Soarin' over California
23. Sunshine Plaza (central hub)
24. Sun Wheel

25. Toy Story Mania
26. The Twilight Zone Tower of Terror
27. Ugly Bug Ball

California Adventure was announced. What they got was a park that cost $1.4 billion (slashed from an original budget of about $2.1 billion), built on 55 acres including a sizable carve-out for the Grand Californian Hotel. It's quite a small park by modern theme-park standards, but $1.4 billion, when lavished on 55 acres, ought to buy a pretty good park.

Then there's the park's theme. Although flexible, California Adventure comes off like a default setting, lacking in imagination, weak in concept, and without intrinsic appeal, especially when you stop to consider that two-thirds of Disneyland guests come from Southern California. As further grist for the mill, there's precious little new technology at work in Disney's newest theme park. Of the headliner attractions, only two, Soarin' over California, a simulator ride, and *Toy Story* Mania, a "virtual dark ride," break new ground. All the rest are recycled, albeit popular, attractions from the Animal Kingdom and Disney-MGM Studios. When you move to the smaller-statured second half of the attraction batting order, it gets worse. Most of these attractions are little more than off-the-shelf midway rides spruced up with a Disney story line and facade.

From a competitive perspective, Disney's California Adventure is an underwhelming shot at Disney's three Southern California competitors. The Hollywood section of DCA takes a hopeful poke at Universal Studios Hollywood, while Paradise Pier offers midway rides à la Six Flags Magic Mountain. Finally, the whole California theme has for years been the eminent domain of Knott's Berry Farm. In short, there's not much originality in DCA, only Disney's now-redundant mantra that "whatever they can do, we can do better."

Finally, after more than seven years of basically being in denial about Disney's California Adventure, the Walt Disney Company now seems willing to admit that this theme park (which only pulls in about a third of Disneyland's attendance annually) needs some help. To address DCA's problems, the Mouse is poised to spend some serious money on an extreme makeover. Over the next ten years, as much as $10 billion will be spent on Disneyland Resort, with the lion's share going to DCA.

Starting at the park entrance, the Imagineers are looking to work their magic on DCA. They'll be pouring on the theming, enhancing detail wherever they can, and adding three new e-ticket attractions, all with an eye toward eventually making California Adventure a worthy companion for its sister theme park across the plaza.

Imagineering and the Disneyland Entertainment staff will be pulling out the stops to transform DCA into a must-see park. This means everything from adding a Vegas-quality water show to Paradise Lagoon (to begin nightly performances in late 2008 or early 2009) to reworking entire areas of the theme park so that they celebrate particular Pixar films. Speaking of which, the Pixar characters are going to play a very big part in DCA's revival. For openers, a new street parade will begin rolling through California Adventure later this year, featuring characters from every Pixar film ever produced.

Mind you, the rest of the Disneyland Resort will also be experiencing its own plussing up. Look for Downtown Disney to increase in size, adding at least five new shops, clubs, and restaurants to its line-up. Likewise, the Disneyland Hotel will experience a face-lift as festive new furnishings and the most up-to-date amenities are folded into the 58-year-old resort. There's also at least one new hotel on the drawing boards, plus a Disney Vacation Club property. According to the rumor mill, there might even be a third theme park in the works, possibly to be built on the Disneyland employee parking lot.

Meanwhile, as the Disneyholics churn up cyberspace debating DCA's theme and worrying whether the budget for the makeover will be torpedoed like the budget for the original park was, the rest of us will have some fun enjoying the park that is.

ARRIVING *and*
GETTING ORIENTED

THE ENTRANCE TO Disney's California Adventure faces the entrance to Disneyland Park across a palm-shaded pedestrian plaza called the **Esplanade.** If you arrive by tram from one of the Disney parking lots, you'll disembark at the Esplanade. Facing east toward Harbor Boulevard, Disneyland Park will be on your left and DCA will be on your right. In the Esplanade are ticket booths, the group sales office, and resort information.

Seen from overhead, Disney's California Adventure is roughly arrayed in a fan shape around the park's central visual icon, **Grizzly Peak.** At ground level, however, the park's layout is not so obvious. From the Esplanade you pass through huge block letters spelling "California," and through the turnstiles. To your left and right you'll find guest services, as well as some shops and eateries. Among the shops is **Greetings from California,** offering the park's largest selection of Disney-trademark merchandise. A second shop of note, **Engine-Ears Toys,** selling upscale toys, creates the impression of stepping into a model-train layout. To your right you'll find stroller and wheelchair rental, lockers, restrooms, an ATM, and phones.

After passing under a whimsical representation of the Golden Gate Bridge, you arrive at the park's central hub. The hub area, **Sunshine Plaza,** is dominated by a fountain fronting an arresting metal sculpture of the sun. In addition to serving as a point of departure for the various themed areas, Sunshine Plaza one of the best places in the park to encounter the Disney characters. With the fountain and golden sun in the background, it's a great photo op.

"Lands" at DCA are called "districts," and there are four of them. A left turn at the hub leads you to the **Hollywood Pictures Backlot** district of the park, celebrating California's history as the film capital of the

Not to Be Missed at Disney's California Adventure

Golden State	**Grizzly River Run**
	Soarin' over California
Hollywood Studios Backlot	**Hyperion Theater**
	Muppet Vision 3-D
	The Twilight Zone **Tower of Terror**
a bug's land	*It's Tough to Be a Bug!*
Paradise Pier	**California Screamin'**
	Toy Story **Mania (opens 2008)**

world. The **Golden State** district of the park is to the right or straight. Golden State is a somewhat amorphous combination of separate themed areas that showcase California's architecture, agriculture, industry, history, and natural resources. Within the Golden State district, you'll find **Condor Flats** by taking the first right as you approach the hub. **Grizzly Peak** will likewise be to your right, though you must walk two-thirds of the way around the mountain to reach its attractions. The remaining two Golden State themed areas, **The Bay Area** and the **Pacific Wharf,** are situated along a kidney-shaped lake and can be accessed by following the walkway emanating from the hub at seven o'clock and winding around Grizzly Peak. A third district, **a bug's land,** is situated opposite the **Golden Vine Winery** and can be reached by taking the same route. The fourth district, **Paradise Pier,** recalls seaside amusement parks of the first half of the 20th century. It is situated in the southwest corner of the park, across the lake from The Bay Area.

Park-opening Procedures

Guests are usually held at the turnstiles until official opening time. On especially busy days, guests are admitted to Golden Gateway and Condor Flats 30 minutes before official opening time. Be aware that DCA usually opens at 10 a.m., one or two hours later than Disneyland Park.

HOLLYWOOD PICTURES BACKLOT

HOLLYWOOD PICTURES BACKLOT OFFERS attractions and shopping inspired by California's (and Disney's) contribution to television and the cinema. Visually, the district is themed as a studio back lot with sets, including an urban street scene, soundstages, and a central street with shops and restaurants that depict Hollywood's golden age.

Disney Animation ★★★½

What it is Behind-the-scenes look at Disney animation. **Scope and scale** Major attraction. **When to go** Anytime. **Special comments** Quite amusing, though not very educational. **Duration of experience** 35–55 minutes. **Probable waiting time** 5 minutes.

DESCRIPTION AND COMMENTS The Disney Animation building houses a total of ten shows, galleries, and interactive exhibits that collectively provide a sort of crash course in animation. Moving from room to room and exhibit to exhibit, you follow the Disney animation process from concept to finished film, with a peek at each of the steps along the way. Throughout, you are surrounded by animation, and sometimes it's even projected above your head and under your feet!

Thumbs Up for the Whole Family

Because DCA's Animation building is not an actual working studio, the attraction does not showcase artists at work on real features, and the interactive exhibits are more whimsical than educational. In one, for example, you can insert your voice into a cartoon character. You get the idea. It takes 40 to 55 minutes to do all the interactive stuff and see everything. Best of the Disney Animation lineup is *Turtle Talk with Crush,* featuring the 152-year-old sea turtle from the Disney/Pixar film *Finding Nemo.* Originally developed for the Seas pavilion at Epcot, *Turtle Talk with Crush is* the first attraction incorporating the technology of real-time animation. Here, Crush answers questions, jokes, and makes conversation with guests in real time. The animation is brilliant, and guests of all ages list *Crush* as their favorite Animation-building feature.

TOURING TIPS On entering the Animation building, you'll step into a lobby where signs mark the entrances of the various exhibits. Sorcerer's Workshop is an interactive exhibit where you can act and sing with various cartoon scenes through a touch-screen computer interface. The Animation Academy, hosted by a Disney cartoonist, teaches you how to draw a Disney character. Both provide a good foundation on the animation process and will enhance your appreciation of the other exhibits. Save Turtle Talk with Crush for last. You probably won't experience much of a wait for the Disney Animation offerings except on weekends and holidays. Even then, the Animation building clears out considerably by late afternoon.

Hyperion Theater ★★★★

What it is Venue for live shows. **Scope and scale** Major attraction. **When to go** After experiencing DCA's rides. **Special comments** Great venue, not to be missed. **Duration of experience** 45 minutes. **Probable waiting time** 30 minutes.

Thumbs Up for the Whole Family

DESCRIPTION AND COMMENTS This 2,000-seat theater is DCA's premier venue for live productions, many of which are based on Disney animated films and feature Disney characters. Shows exhibit Broadway quality in every sense, except duration of the presentation, and alone are arguably worth the price of theme-park admission. *Disney's Aladdin: A Musical Spectacular,* was the Hyperion Theater's feature show in 2006 and may well continue into 2007 or longer. A breezy stage version of the Aladdin story, it's by far the theater's most accomplished production to date. In the evening, the Hyperion is often used as a stage for separate-admission concerts and special events.

TOURING TIPS The lavish productions hosted by the Hyperion Theater are rightly very popular and commonly sell out on busier days. Presentations are described, and showtimes listed, in the park *Times Guide.* The theater is multilevel. Though all seats provide a good line of sight, we recommend sitting on the ground level relatively close to the entrance doors (if possible) to facilitate an easy exit after the performance. Finally, be forewarned that the sound volume for Hyperion Theater productions would give heavy-metal rock concerts a good run for the money.

Monsters, Inc.: Mike and Sulley to the Rescue ★★★½

APPEAL BY AGE	PRESCHOOL ★★½	GRADE SCHOOL ★★★★	TEENS ★★★½
YOUNG ADULTS ★★★½		OVER 30 ★★★½	SENIORS ★★★

Type of attraction Dark ride. Scope and scale Major attraction. When to go Before 11 a.m. Special comments Disney's best dark ride in years. Duration of ride 3¾ minutes. Average wait in line per 100 people ahead of you 4 minutes. Loading speed Moderate.

Dark

DESCRIPTION AND COMMENTS Based on characters and the story from the Disney/Pixar film *Monsters, Inc.,* the ride takes you through childphobic Monstropolis as Mike and Sulley try to return baby Boo safely to her bedroom. If you haven't seen the film, the story line won't make much sense. In a nutshell, a human baby gets loose in a sort of parallel universe populated largely by amusing monsters. Good monsters Mike and Sulley try to return Boo to her home before the bad monsters get their hands on her.

The Disney Imagineers did a very good job on the *Monsters, Inc.* ride, re-creating the humor, characters, and setting of the film in great detail. The section of the attraction where you ride through the door warehouse with all of its lifts and conveyors is truly inspired. Special effects are first-rate, and there are lots of subtle and not-so-subtle jokes worked into the whole experience. As in the Tower of Terror, you'll have to ride several times to catch them all.

TOURING TIPS The attraction is very popular. It should be a FASTPASS attraction but it isn't. Try to ride the first hour the park is open, during a parade, or during the last hour before closing. Because it's near several theater attractions it's subject to experiencing a sudden deluge of guests when the theaters disgorge their audiences.

Monsters, Inc. is an iffy attraction for preschoolers: some love it and some are frightened. Increase your odds for a positive experience by exposing your little ones to the movie before leaving home.

Muppet Vision 3-D ★★★★½

APPEAL BY AGE	PRESCHOOL ★★★★	GRADE SCHOOL ★★★★½	TEENS ★★★★
YOUNG ADULTS ★★★★½		OVER 30 ★★★★½	SENIORS ★★★★½

What it is 3-D movie featuring the Muppets. **Scope and scale** Major attraction. **When to go** Before noon or after 4 p.m. **Special comments** Must see; 3-D effects and loud noises frighten many preschoolers. **Duration of presentation** 17 minutes. **Probable waiting time** 20 minutes.

DESCRIPTION AND COMMENTS *Muppet Vision 3-D* provides a total sensory experience, with wild 3-D action augmented by auditory, visual, and tactile special effects. If you're tired and hot, this zany presentation will make you feel brand new.

Thumbs Up for the Whole Family

TOURING TIPS Although extremely popular, this attraction handles crowds exceedingly well. Your wait should not last longer than 20 minutes except on days when the park is jam-packed. Special effects and loud noises may frighten some preschoolers.

Playhouse Disney—Live on Stage! ★★★★

APPEAL BY AGE	PRESCHOOL ★★★★★	GRADE SCHOOL ★★★	TEENS ★★
YOUNG ADULTS ★★★		OVER 30 ★★	SENIORS ★★★

What it is Live show for children. **Scope and scale** Minor attraction. **When to go** Per the daily entertainment schedule. **Special comments** A must for families with preschoolers; audience sits on the floor. **Duration of presentation** 20 minutes. **Probable waiting time** 10 minutes.

DESCRIPTION AND COMMENTS The show features characters from the Disney Channel's *Jo Jo's Circus, Bear in the Big Blue House,* and *Stanley.* A simple plot serves as the platform for singing, dancing, some great puppetry, and a great deal of audience participation. The characters, who ooze love and goodness, rally throngs of tots and preschoolers to sing and dance with them. The jumping, squirming, and high-stepping is facilitated by having the audience sit on the floor so that children can spontaneously erupt into motion when the mood strikes. Even for adults without kids, it's a treat to watch the tykes rev up. If you have a younger child in your party, all the better: just stand back and let the video roll.

For preschoolers, *Playhouse Disney* will be the highlight of their day, as a Thomasville, North Carolina, mom attests:

Playhouse Disney was fantastic! My 3-year-old loved it. The children danced, sang, and had a great time.

TOURING TIPS The show is headquartered in what was formerly the ABC Soap Opera Bistro restaurant to the right of the entrance to the Hollywood Studios District. Because the tykes just can't get enough, it has become a hot ticket. Show up at least 20 minutes before showtime. Once inside, pick a spot on the floor and take a breather until the performance begins.

The Twilight Zone Tower of Terror (FASTPASS) ★★★★★

APPEAL BY AGE   PRESCHOOL ★★★   GRADE SCHOOL ★★★★★   TEENS ★★★★★
YOUNG ADULTS ★★★★★   OVER 30 ★★★★★   SENIORS ★★★★½

What it is Sci-fi-theme indoor thrill ride. **Scope and scale** Super-headliner. **When to go** The first 30 minutes the park is open. **Special comments** DCA's best attraction; not to be missed; must be 40" tall to ride; switching-off option offered (page 152). **Duration of ride** About 4 minutes plus preshow. **Average wait in line per 100 people ahead of you** 4 minutes. **Assumes** All elevators operating. **Loading speed** Moderate.

Dark

Scary

Rough

Lose Things

Motion Sickness

DESCRIPTION AND COMMENTS
The Twilight Zone Tower of Terror, which opened in the spring of 2004, is a new species of Disney thrill ride, though it borrows elements of The Haunted Mansion at Disneyland Park. The story is that you're touring a once-famous Hollywood hotel gone to ruin. As at Star Tours, the queuing area integrates guests into the adventure as they pass through the hotel's once-opulent public rooms. From the lobby, guests are escorted into the hotel's library, where Rod Serling, speaking on an old black-and-white television, greets the guests and introduces the plot.

The Tower of Terror is a whopper at 13-plus stories tall. It breaks tradition in terms of visually isolating themed areas. The entire park is visible from the top, but you have to look quick!

The ride vehicle, one of the hotel's service elevators, takes guests to see the haunted hostelry. The tour begins innocuously, but at about the fifth floor things get pretty weird. You have entered the Twilight Zone. Guests are subjected to a full range of special effects as they encounter unexpected horrors and optical illusions. The climax of the adventure occurs when the elevator reaches the 13th floor and the cable snaps.

The big question before DCA's Tower of Terror opened was how will it compare to the Walt Disney World version. As it turns out, the attractions are very similar but definitely not clones. The adventure begins the same way—you pass through the hotel lobby and into the library for the preshow. Following the preshow, you enter the boarding area. Once you're on the elevator, however, the two attractions part company. In the Disney World version, the elevator stops at a couple of floors to reveal some eerie visuals, but then actually moves out of the shaft onto one of the floors. The effects during this brief sojourn are remarkable, and more remarkable still is that you don't know that you've reentered the shaft until the elevator speeds skyward. In the DCA Tower of Terror the elevator never leaves the shaft. The visuals and special effects are equally compelling, but there's never that feeling of disorientation that distinguishes the Florida attraction. The DCA Tower of Terror is more straightforward, therefore, and consequently a little less mysterious. Once the elevator-dropping ensues, both versions are about the same. Regardless which version you try, however, you won't be disappointed.

The Tower has great potential for terrifying young children and rattling more mature visitors. If you have teenagers in your party, use them as experimental probes—if they report back that they really, really liked it, run as fast as you can in the opposite direction. Seriously, avoid assuming this attraction isn't for you. A senior from the United Kingdom tried the Tower of Terror and liked it very much, writing:

I was thankful I read your review of the Tower of Terror, or I would certainly have avoided it. As you say, it is so full of magnificent detail that it is worth riding, even if you don't fancy the drops involved.

TOURING TIPS This one ride is worth your admission to DCA. Because of its height, the tower is a veritable beacon, visible from outside the park and luring curious guests as soon as they enter. Because of the attraction's popularity with schoolkids, teens, and young adults, you can count on a footrace to get there when the park opens. For the foreseeable future, expect the tower to be mobbed most of the day.

To access the Tower of Terror, bear left from the park entrance into the Hollywood Pictures Backlot. Continue straight to the Hyperion Theater and then turn right. To save time, when you enter the library waiting area, stand in the far back corner across from the door where you entered and at the opposite end of the room from the TV. When the doors to the loading area open, you'll be one of the first admitted.

GOLDEN STATE

THIS DISTRICT CELEBRATES California's cultural, musical, natural, and industrial diversity. The centerpiece of the district is Grizzly Peak— one of the subdistricts within Golden State and yet another of Disney's famed "mountains" (with "Boulder Bear" at its summit). Surrounding Grizzly Peak are **The Bay Area, Golden Vine Winery, Condor Flats,** and **Pacific Wharf.** We've grouped those with attractions below.

THE BAY AREA

CURIOUSLY, IN DCA'S GOLDEN STATE the landmark chosen to represent the Bay Area is the Palace of Fine Arts built for the 1915 Panama Pacific International Expo. Inside you'll find artists and craftsmen busy at their trade, and, of course, ready to sell their creations. The themed area's only attraction is the film *Golden Dreams*.

Golden Dreams ★★★½

APPEAL BY AGE	PRESCHOOL ★★½	GRADE SCHOOL ★★★★	TEENS ★★★
YOUNG ADULTS ★★★½		OVER 30 ★★★★	SENIORS ★★★★

What it is Film about the history of California. **Scope and scale** Major attraction. **When to go** After experiencing the rides, the Muppets, and the bugs. **Special comments** A moving presentation. **Duration of presentation** 17 minutes. **Probable waiting time** 15 minutes.

DESCRIPTION AND COMMENTS Narrated by Whoopi Goldberg, *Golden Dreams* is a nostalgic film about the history of California, recognizing the many different races, ethnicities, and people who contributed to the state's settlement and development. Originally designed to be a multimedia production with moving sets and animatronics similar to *American Adventure* at Epcot, the attraction was hammered by budget cuts and ultimately premiered with only a small (for Disney) arsenal of special effects.

Thumbs Up for the Whole Family

A little heavy on schmaltz (which we *Unofficials* kinda like), *Golden Dreams* is a very sweet brotherhood-of-man flick. For once, Disney refrained from rewriting or overly sanitizing the historic content, and there's enough lightheartedness and humor to make the presentation fun. Because this is a kaleidoscopic overview, it's debatable how much you'll learn about California's past, but you'll nonetheless appreciate (at least we did) the film's uplifting message.

TOURING TIPS *Golden Dreams*'s isolated location makes it a good choice for midday touring. Check it out after the rides, the Muppets, and the bugs. *Golden Dreams* was designed to run continuous back-to-back performances. On slow days, however, only a few shows a day are scheduled, and showtimes, unfortunately, are not listed in the handout park map. To determine performance times, it's necessary to actually go to the theater and eyeball an inconspicuous little sign.

CONDOR FLATS

SITUATED JUST TO THE RIGHT of the central hub, Condor Flats pays homage to California aviation. The pedestrian walkway is marked like a runway, and all of the buildings look like airplane hangars. Condor Flats is the home of one of the park's super-headliner attractions, **Soarin' over California.**

Soarin' over California (FASTPASS) ★★★★½

APPEAL BY AGE	PRESCHOOL –	GRADE SCHOOL ★★★★★	TEENS ★★★★½
YOUNG ADULTS ★★★★★		OVER 30 ★★★★★	SENIORS ★★★★

What it is Flight-simulation ride. **Scope and scale** Super-headliner. **When to go** The first 30 minutes the park is open, or use FASTPASS. **Special comments** The park's best ride; may induce motion sickness; 40" minimum-height requirement; switching off available (see page 152). **Duration of ride** 4½ minutes. **Loading speed** Moderate.

DESCRIPTION AND COMMENTS Once you enter the main theater, you're secured in a seat not unlike the ones used on inverted roller coasters (in which the coaster is suspended from above). Once

Thumbs Up for the Whole Family

everyone is in place, the floor drops away and you are suspended with your legs dangling. Thus hung out to dry, you embark on a hang-glider tour of California with IMAX-quality images projected below you, and with the simulator moving your seat in sync with the movie. The IMAX images are well chosen and slap-dab beautiful. Special effects include wind, sound, and even olfactory stimulation. The ride itself is thrilling but perfectly smooth, exciting, and relaxing simultaneously. We think Soarin' over California is a must-see for guests of any age who meet the 40-inch minimum-height requirement. And yes, seniors we interviewed were crazy about it.

TOURING TIPS   Aside from being a true technological innovation, Soarin' over California also happens to be located near the entrance of the park, thus ensuring heavy traffic all day. It should be your very first attraction in the morning, or, alternatively, use FASTPASS. If you are among the first through the turnstiles at park opening, sprint to Soarin' over California as fast as your little feet can carry you. If you arrive later and elect to use FASTPASS, obtain your FASTPASS before noon. Later than noon you're likely to get a return period in the hour before the park closes, or worse, find that the day's supply of FASTPASSes is gone. If both Soarin' over California and the Tower of Terror are on your itinerary, sprint to Soarin' the moment the park opens and ride. Next, proceed to the Tower of Terror and obtain a FASTPASS (FASTPASS kiosks open the same time as the attraction). With Tower of Terror FASTPASS in hand, continue to the next attraction on your itinerary.

GOLDEN VINE WINERY

THIS DIMINUTIVE WINERY situated at the base of Grizzly Peak and across from a bug's land is the smallest of the Golden State themed areas. It would be a stretch to call it an attraction, much less a themed area.

Golden Vine Winery   ★★★

APPEAL BY AGE	PRESCHOOL –	GRADE SCHOOL ★ ½	TEENS ★★ ½
YOUNG ADULTS ★★★		OVER 30 ★★★	SENIORS ★★★

What it is Infomercial and exhibit about California wines. **Scope and scale** Minor attraction/exhibit. **When to go** Anytime. **Special comments** Quite informative. **Duration of film** 7½ minutes. **Probable waiting time** 15 minutes for film.

DESCRIPTION AND COMMENTS   This Mission-style complex, squeezed into the side of Grizzly Peak, offers a demonstration vineyard and a short film that is basically an infomercial about winemaking. The rest of the facility, predictably, is occupied by shops, a tasting room, and a restaurant.

TOURING TIPS   Save the winery for the end of the day. If there's much of a wait to see the film, leave it for another visit.

GRIZZLY PEAK

GRIZZLY PEAK, a huge mountain shaped like the head of a bear, is home to **Grizzly River Run,** a white-water raft ride, and the **Redwood Creek Challenge Trail,** an outdoor playground for children that resembles an obstacle course.

Grizzly River Run (FASTPASS) ★★★★½

| APPEAL BY AGE | PRESCHOOL – | GRADE SCHOOL ★★★★½ | TEENS ★★★★½ |
| YOUNG ADULTS ★★★★½ | | OVER 30 ★★★★½ | SENIORS ★★★★½ |

What it is White-water raft ride. **Scope and scale** Super-headliner. **When to go** First hour the park is open, or use FASTPASS. **Special comments** Not to be missed; you are guaranteed to get wet, and possibly soaked; 42" minimum-height requirement. **Duration of ride** 5½ minutes. **Average wait in line per 100 people ahead of you** 5 minutes. **Loading speed** Moderate.

Scary   Wet   Rough   Lose Things

DESCRIPTION AND COMMENTS White-water raft rides have been a hot-weather favorite of theme-park patrons for almost 20 years. The ride consists of an unguided trip down a man-made river in a circular rubber raft, with a platform mounted on top seating six to eight people. The raft essentially floats free in the current and is washed downstream through rapids and waves. Because the river is fairly wide with numerous currents, eddies, and obstacles, there is no telling exactly where the raft will go. Thus, each trip is different and unpredictable. The rafts are circular and a little smaller than those used on most rides of the genre. Because the current can buffet the smaller rafts more effectively, the ride is wilder and wetter.

What distinguishes Grizzly River Run from other theme-park raft rides is Disney's trademark attention to visual detail. Where many raft rides essentially plunge down a concrete ditch, Grizzly River Run winds around and through Grizzly Peak, the park's foremost visual icon, with the great rock bear at the summit. Featuring a 50-foot climb and two drops—including a 22-footer where the raft spins as it descends—the ride flows into dark caverns and along the mountain's precipitous side before looping over itself just before the final plunge.

When Disney opened the Kali River Rapids raft ride at the Animal Kingdom theme park at Walt Disney World, it was roundly criticized (and rightly so) for being a weenie ride. Well, we're here to tell you that Disney learned its lesson. Grizzly River Run is a heart-thumper, one of the best of its genre anywhere. And at five-and-a-half minutes from load to unload, it's also one of the longest. The visuals are outstanding, and the ride is about as good as it gets on a man-made river. While it's true that theme-park raft rides have been around a long time, Grizzly River Run has set a new standard, one we don't expect to be equaled for some time.

TOURING TIPS This attraction is hugely popular, especially on hot summer days. Ride the first hour the park is open, after 4:30 p.m., or use FASTPASS. Make no mistake, you will certainly get wet on this ride. Our recommendation is to wear shorts to the park and bring along a jumbo-sized trash bag, as well as a smaller plastic bag. Before boarding the raft, take off your socks and punch a hole in your jumbo bag for your head. Though you can also cut holes for your arms, you will probably stay drier with your arms inside the bag. Use the smaller plastic bag to wrap around your shoes. If you are worried about mussing your hairdo, bring a third bag for your head.

A Shaker Heights, Ohio, family who adopted our garbage-bag attire, however, discovered that staying dry on a similar attraction at Walt Disney World is not without social consequences:

I must tell you that the Disney cast members and the other people in our raft looked at us like we had just beamed down from Mars. Plus, we didn't cut arm holes in our trash bags because we thought we'd stay drier. Only problem was once we sat down we couldn't fasten our seat belts. The Disney person was quite put out and asked sarcastically whether we needed wet suits and snorkels. After a lot of wiggling and adjusting and helping each other we finally got belted in and off we went looking like sacks of fertilizer with little heads perched on top. It was very embarrassing, but I must admit that we stayed nice and dry.

If you forget your plastic bag, ponchos are available at the adjacent Rushin' River Outfitters.

Redwood Creek Challenge Trail and *Magic of Brother Bear* Show   ★★★½

APPEAL BY AGE   PRESCHOOL ★★★★   GRADE SCHOOL ★★★★★   TEENS ★★
YOUNG   ADULTS   ★★   OVER 30   ★★   SENIORS   ★★

What it is Elaborate playground and obstacle course. **Scope and scale** Minor attraction. **When to go** Anytime. **Special comments** Very well done; 42" minimum-height requirement. **Duration of experience** About 20 minutes, though some kids could stay all day.

DESCRIPTION AND COMMENTS   An elaborate maze of rope bridges, log towers, and a cave, the Redwood Creek Challenge Trail is a scout-camp combination of elements from Tarzan's Treehouse and Tom Sawyer Island. Built into and around Grizzly Peak, the Challenge Trail has eye-popping appeal for young adventurers.

The *Magic of Brother Bear* is a sweet children's show about nature, starring the characters Koda and Kenai from the *Brother Bear* film. The show is pretty corny, but the kids eat it up. There's enough subtle humor to keep adults chuckling, but the real attraction is watching the younger children interact with the characters. The signage to the tiny amphitheater is nonexistent. To get there, enter the Redwood Creek Challenge Trail and descend the steps on the front left. At the bottom, turn left to the amphitheater.

TOURING TIPS   The largest of several children's play areas in the park, and the only one that is dry (for the most part) and relatively shady, the Challenge Trail is the perfect place to let your kids cut loose for a while. Though the Challenge Trail will be crowded, you should not have to wait to get in. Experience it after checking out the better rides and shows. Be aware, however, that the playground is quite large, and that you will not be able to keep your children in sight unless you tag along with them.

A **BUG'S LAND**

THIS DISTRICT IS DISNEY'S RESPONSE to complaints that DCA lacked appeal for younger children. a bug's land incorporates the vestiges of Bountiful Valley Farm, celebrating California's agribusiness, into a bug's-eye world of giant objects, children's rides, and the *It's Tough to Be a Bug!* attraction.

Bountiful Valley Demonstration Farm ★★

APPEAL BY AGE	PRESCHOOL ★★★	GRADE SCHOOL ★★	TEENS ★½
YOUNG ADULTS ★★	OVER 30 ★★		SENIORS ★★½

What it is Farming exhibit and playground. **Scope and scale** Minor attraction–exhibit. **When to go** Anytime. **Special comments** A bit anemic. **Touring time** About 10 minutes for a comprehensive look.

DESCRIPTION AND COMMENTS This area features demonstration crops, including an orange grove. Sponsored by Caterpillar, the farm includes an exhibit tracing the evolution of land cultivation from primitive methods to today's wonderful, large Caterpillar tractors. Other features include the opportunity to sit on a Caterpillar tractor, to see a Caterpillar skid-steer loader, and, of course, to purchase "select Caterpillar merchandise and toys." (Give us a break.) There's also a kid's water-maze play area fashioned from leaking irrigation pipes and sprinklers (we promise we're not making this up).

TOURING TIPS Check out the farm at your leisure and try not to step on the radishes. If you buy a tractor, have it sent to Package Pick-up to be retrieved when you leave the park.

Flik's Fun Fair ★★★½

APPEAL BY AGE	PRESCHOOL ★★★★½	GRADE SCHOOL ★★★½
TEENS –	YOUNG ADULTS –	OVER 30 –	SENIORS –

What it is Children's rides and play areas. **Scope and scale** Minor attraction. **When to go** Before 11:30 a.m. for the rides; anytime for the play areas. **Special comments** Preschool heaven. **Touring time** About 50 minutes for a comprehensive visit.

DESCRIPTION AND COMMENTS Flik's Fun Fair is a children's park as seen through the eyes of an insect. Children can wander among 20-foot-tall blades of grass, tunnel-sized garden hoses, an enormous anthill, and the like. Kiddie rides include Flik's Flyers, with a balloon-ride theme; a drive-it-yourself car ride called Tuck and Roll's Drive 'Em Buggies; Heimlich's Chew Chew Train, a miniature-train ride; and a mini–Mad Tea Party ride titled Francis's Ladybug Boogie, where you can spin your own "ladybug."

TOURING TIPS Though they're colorful and magnetically alluring to the under-8 crowd, all of the rides are low capacity, slow loading, and ridiculously brief. Our advice is to ride them sequentially before 11 a.m. if you visit on a weekend or during the summer. The play areas, of course, can be enjoyed anytime, but then you're faced with the prospect of the kids caterwauling to get on the rides.

Following is the relevant data on the kiddie rides (note that waiting times are per 50 people ahead of you as opposed to the usual 100 people):

HEIMLICH'S CHEW CHEW TRAIN (train ride)

Special comments Adults as well as children can ride

Ride time Almost 2 minutes

Average wait in line per 50 people ahead of you 5 minutes

TUCK AND ROLL'S DRIVE 'EM BUGGIES (bumper cars)

Special comments Adults as well as children can ride. Cars are much slower than on normal bumper-car rides.

Ride time Almost 2 minutes

Average wait in line per 50 people ahead of you 12 minutes

FLIK'S FLYERS (suspended "baskets" swing around a central axis)

Ride time Almost 1½ minutes

Average wait in line per 50 people ahead of you 6 minutes

FRANCIS'S LADYBUG BOOGIE (adaptation of the Mad Tea Party)

Ride time 1 minute

Average wait in line per 50 people ahead of you 8 minutes

It's Tough to Be a Bug! ★★★★

| APPEAL BY AGE | PRESCHOOL ★★★★ | GRADE SCHOOL ★★★★½ | TEENS ★★★★½ |
| YOUNG ADULTS ★★★★½ | OVER 30 ★★★★½ | | SENIORS ★★★★½ |

What it is 3-D movie. **Scope and scale** Major attraction. **When to go** After experiencing DCA's better rides. **Special comments** 3-D effects and loud noises frighten many preschoolers. **Duration of presentation** 8½ minutes. **Probable waiting time** 20 minutes.

Loud

Scary

Dark

DESCRIPTION AND COMMENTS *It's Tough to Be a Bug!* is an uproarious 3-D film about the difficulties of being a very small creature and features some of the characters from the Disney/Pixar film *a bug's life. It's Tough to Be a Bug!* is similar to *Honey, I Shrunk the Audience* at Disneyland Park in that it combines a 3-D film with an arsenal of tactile and visual special effects. In our view, the special effects are a bit overdone and the film somewhat disjointed. Even so, we rate the *Bug* as not to be missed.

TOURING TIPS Because it's situated in one of the sleepier themed areas, *Bug* is not usually under attack from the hordes until late morning. This should make *It's Tough to Be a Bug!* the easiest of the park's top attractions to see.

Be advised that *It's Tough to Be a Bug!* is very intense and that the special effects will do a number on young children as well as anyone who is squeamish about insects. Check out the following comments from readers who saw *It's Tough to Be a Bug!* at Walt Disney World. First, from a mother of two from Mobile, Alabama:

It's Tough to Be a Bug! *was too intense for any kids. Our boys are 5 and 7, and they were scared to death. They love bugs, and they hated this movie. All of the kids in the theater were screaming and crying. I felt like a terrible mother for taking them into this movie. It is billed as a bug movie for kids, but nothing about it is for kids.*

But a Williamsville, New York, woman had it even worse:

We almost lost the girls to any further Disney magic due to the 3-D movie It's Tough to Be a Bug! *It was their first Disney experience, and almost their last. The story line was nebulous and difficult to follow—all they were aware of was the torture of sitting in a darkened theater being overrun with bugs. Total chaos, the likes of which I've never experienced, was breaking out around us. The 11-year-old refused to talk for 20 minutes after the fiasco, and the 3½-year-old wanted to go home—not back to the hotel, but home.*

Most readers, however, loved the *Bugs*, including this mom from Brentwood, Tennessee:

Comments from your readers make It's Tough to Be a Bug! *sound worse than* Alien Encounter. *It's not. It's intense like* Honey, I Shrunk the Audience *but mostly funny. The bugs are cartoonlike instead of realistic and icky, so I can't understand what all the fuss is about. Disney has conditioned us to think of rodents as cute, so kids think nothing of walking up to a mouse the size of a portable toilet but go nuts over some cartoon bugs. Get a grip!*

Ugly Bug Ball ★★★½

APPEAL BY AGE	PRESCHOOL ★★★★	GRADE SCHOOL ★★★★	TEENS ★★
YOUNG ADULTS ★★★		OVER 30 ★★★	SENIORS ★★★

What it is Musical stage show about insects. **Scope and scale** Minor attraction. **When to go** Anytime as per the daily entertainment schedule. **Special comments** A very pleasant surprise. **Duration of presentation** 17 minutes plus autographing session.

DESCRIPTION AND COMMENTS Madame Butterfly offers dancing lessons to prepare the insects and kids for the gala *Ugly Bug Ball* while a curmudgeonly spider gets in the way. Dances the kids learn include the Heimlich Maneuver and the Tarantula Tango. A very clever and witty show, the *Ugly Bug Ball* is as much fun for adults as for kids. In fact, we recommend it to adults without children in their party.

TOURING TIPS The tiny outdoor theater with bench seats is located between the demonstration gardens and Bountiful Valley Farmers Market counter-service restaurant. Shade is limited.

PARADISE PIER

WRAPPED AROUND THE SOUTHERN SHORE of the kidney-shaped lake, Paradise Pier is Disney's version of a seaside amusement park from the first five decades of the 20th century. It covers about one-third of Disney's California Adventure and contains around half of the attractions. Paradise Pier's presence at DCA is ironic, and in a perverse way it brings the story of Walt Disney and Disneyland full circle. Walt, you see, created Disneyland Park as an alternative to parks such as this; parks with a carnival atmosphere, simple midway rides, carny games, and amply available wine, beer, and liquor. Amazingly, corporate

Disney has made just such a place the centerpiece of Disneyland's sister park, slaughtering in effect one of the last of Walt's sacred cows. Fancy names and window dressing aside, what you'll find on Paradise Pier is a merry-go-round, a Ferris wheel, a roller coaster, a wild mouse, carny games (stacked against you), and beer.

California Screamin' (FASTPASS) ★★★★

APPEAL BY AGE	PRESCHOOL –	GRADE SCHOOL ★★★★★	TEENS ★★★★½
YOUNG ADULTS ★★★★		OVER 30 ★★★★	SENIORS †

† *The number of riding seniors surveyed was too small to derive a rating.*

What it is Big, bad roller coaster. **Scope and scale** Super-headliner. **When to go** Ride first thing in the morning, or use FASTPASS. **Special comments** Long and smooth; may induce motion sickness; 48" minimum-height requirement; switching off available (see page 152). **Duration of ride** 2½ minutes. **Loading speed** Moderate to fast.

Scary   Motion Sickness   Lose Things

DESCRIPTION AND COMMENTS This apparently antiquated wooden monster is actually a modern steel coaster, and at 6,800 feet, the second longest in the United States. California Screamin' gets off to a 0-to-55-mph start by launching you up the first hill like a jet fighter plane off the deck of a carrier (albeit with different technology). From here you will experience tight turns followed by a second launch sending you over the crest of a 110-foot hill with a 107-foot drop on the far side. Next, you bank and complete an elliptical loop inside the giant Mickey head visible all over the park. A diving turn followed by a series of camelbacks brings you back to the station. Speakers play a synchronized soundtrack complete with recorded canned screaming.

We were impressed by the length of the course and the smoothness of the ride. From beginning to end, the ride is about 2½ minutes, with 2 minutes of actual ride time. En route the coaster slows enough on curves and on transition hills to let you take in the nice view. On the scary-o-meter, Screamin' is certainly worse than Space Mountain but doesn't really compare with some of the steel coasters at nearby Magic Mountain. What Screamin' loses in fright potential, however, it makes up in variety. Along its course, Disney has placed every known curve, hill, dip, and loop in roller-coaster design.

TOURING TIPS California Screamin' is a serious coaster, a coaster that makes Space Mountain look like Dumbo. Secure any hats, cameras, eyeglasses,

WARNING!
For Bouffants, Rug Wearers, and Elvis Impersonators
This Ride Will Muss Your 'Do

or anything else that might be ripped from your person during the ride. Stay away completely if you're prone to motion sickness.

Engineered to run several trains at once, California Screamin' does a better job than any roller coaster we've seen at handling crowds, at least when the attraction is running at full capacity. Recently, presumably because of maintenance and staffing problems, several trains were side-tracked. This turned a well-designed coaster into a mammoth bottleneck. The coaster was sometimes shut down two or more times a day for technical problems. Early in the morning, however, it's usually easy to get two or three rides under your belt in about 15 minutes. Ride in the first hour the park is open or use FASTPASS.

Golden Zephyr ★★

APPEAL BY AGE	PRESCHOOL ★★★½		GRADE SCHOOL ★★★½
TEENS ★★	YOUNG ADULTS ★½	OVER 30 ★½	SENIORS ★½

What it is Zephyrs spinning around a central tower. **Scope and scale** Minor attraction. **When to go** The first 90 minutes the park is open or just before closing. **Special comments** Totally redundant; can't operate on breezy days. **Duration of ride** About 2½ minutes. **Loading speed** Slow.

Motion Sickness

DESCRIPTION AND COMMENTS First, a zephyr is a term often associated with blimps. On this attraction, the zephyrs look like open-cockpit rockets. In any event, each zephyr holds about a dozen guests and spins around a central axis with enough centrifugal force to lay the zephyr partially on its side. As it turns out, the Golden Zephyrs are very touchy, as zephyrs go: they can't fly in a wind exceeding about 5 mph. Needless to say, the attraction is shut down much of the time.

TOURING TIPS A colorful, beautiful attraction, it is another slow-loading cycle ride. Go during the first hour and a half the park is open or be prepared for a long wait.

Jumpin' Jellyfish ★★

APPEAL BY AGE	PRESCHOOL ★★★		GRADE SCHOOL ★★★
TEENS ★½	YOUNG ADULTS ★★	OVER 30 ★★	SENIORS ★★

What it is Parachute ride. **Scope and scale** Minor attraction. **When to go** The first 90 minutes the park is open or just before closing. **Special comments** All sizzle, no meat; can't operate on breezy days; 40" minimum-height requirement. **Duration of ride** About 45 seconds. **Loading speed** Slow.

DESCRIPTION AND COMMENTS On this ride, you're raised on a cable to the top of the tower and then released to gently parachute back to earth. Mostly a children's ride, Jumpin' Jellyfish is paradoxically off-limits to those who would most enjoy it because of its 40-inch minimum-height restriction. For adults, the attraction is a real snore. Oops, make that a real bore—the paltry 45 seconds duration of the ride is not long enough to fall asleep.

TOURING TIPS The Jellyfish, so called because of a floating jellyfish's resemblance to an open parachute, is another slow-loading ride of very low capacity. Get on early in the morning or be prepared for a long wait.

King Triton's Carousel   ★★★

APPEAL BY AGE	PRESCHOOL ★★★★		GRADE SCHOOL ★★★
TEENS –	YOUNG ADULTS –	OVER 30 –	SENIORS –

What it is Merry-go-round. **Scope and scale** Minor attraction. **When to go** Before noon. **Special comments** Beautimus. **Duration of ride** A little less than 2 minutes. **Loading speed** Slow.

DESCRIPTION AND COMMENTS   On this elaborate and stunningly crafted carousel, dolphins, sea horses, seals, and the like replace the standard prancing horses.

TOURING TIPS   Worth a look even if there are no children in your party. If you have kids who want to ride, try to get them on before noon.

Maliboomer   ★★½

APPEAL BY AGE	PRESCHOOL –	GRADE SCHOOL ★★★½	TEENS ★★★★
YOUNG ADULTS ★★★½		OVER 30 ★★★	SENIORS †

† The number of riding seniors surveyed was too small to derive a rating.

What it is Vertical launch and free-fall thrill ride. **Scope and scale** Major attraction. **When to go** The first hour the park's open. **Special comments** Overrated; may induce motion sickness; 52" minimum-height requirement; switching off available (see page 152). **Duration of ride** 50 seconds. **Loading speed** Slow.

Scary

Motion Sickness

Lose Things

DESCRIPTION AND COMMENTS   Maliboomer consists of three towers that are easy to recognize since they're the tallest structures in the park. It's themed to resemble a giant rendition of the midway test-of-strength booth where you try to ring a bell high atop a pole by hitting a plate on the ground with a sledgehammer. When you hit the plate, a metal projectile is launched vertically up the shaft toward the bell. Well, on this attraction, you take the place of the metal projectile and are launched up the tower and allowed to free-fall during part of your trip back toward the ground. Naturally, this might leave you feeling like your own bell's been rung.

   As it turns out, Maliboomer looks much scarier than it actually is. The launch speed is really quite civilized, though everyone screams for appearance's sake. In fact, there's so much high-decibel screaming on this attraction that Disney installed clear plastic "scream guards" to prevent all the hollering from being broadcast across Anaheim (we kid you not). If the launch is so-so, the free-fall wins the big-weenie award. The only full-fledged adrenaline rush comes from waiting anxiously to be launched. In short, there's not enough bite for a real thrill-ride enthusiast to justify the wait. If you've never experienced similar attractions at other parks, however, Maliboomer will provide a gentle introduction to the genre.

TOURING TIPS   Though great fun for those with strong stomachs, this type of ride is an infamously slow loader. Try to ride during the first hour the park is open. Bins are provided to store purses, glasses, and other loose items while you ride. If the wait is long, split up your group and use the singles line.

Mulholland Madness (FASTPASS) ★★★

APPEAL BY AGE	PRESCHOOL †	GRADE SCHOOL ★★★½	TEENS ★★★½
YOUNG ADULTS ★★★		OVER 30 ★★★	SENIORS †

† The number of riding preschoolers and seniors surveyed was too small to derive a rating.

What it is Disney version of a wild (or mad) mouse ride. **Scope and scale** Major attraction. **When to go** During the first hour the park's open. **Special comments** Space Mountain with the lights on; may induce motion sickness; 42" minimum-height requirement; switching off available (see page 152). **Duration of ride** About 1½ minutes. **Loading speed** Slow to moderate.

Scary

Motion Sickness

Lose Things

DESCRIPTION AND COMMENTS Themed as a wild drive on the California freeways, Mulholland Madness is a designer wild mouse (sometimes also called "mad mouse"). If you're not familiar with the genre, it's a small, convoluted roller coaster where the track dips and turns unexpectedly, presumably reminding its inventor of a mouse tearing through a maze. To define it more in Disney terms, the ride is similar to Space Mountain, only outdoors and therefore in the light. Mulholland Madness is an off-the-shelf midway ride in which Disney has invested next to nothing in spiffing up. In other words, fun but nothing special.

TOURING TIPS A fun ride, but also a slow-loading one, and one that breaks down frequently. Ride during the first hour the park is open or use FASTPASS.

Orange Stinger ★★★

APPEAL BY AGE	PRESCHOOL ★★★	GRADE SCHOOL ★★★	TEENS ★½
YOUNG ADULTS ★★★		OVER 30 ★★	SENIORS ★★

What it is Swings rotating around a central tower. **Scope and scale** Minor attraction. **When to go** The first 90 minutes the park is open or just before closing. **Special comments** Simple but fun; 48" minimum-height requirement. **Duration of ride** Less than 1½ minutes. **Loading speed** Slow.

Motion Sickness

Lose Things

DESCRIPTION AND COMMENTS On the Orange Stinger, you ride swings that look like giant bees. The bees swing in a circle around a central tower and inside of what looks like a partially peeled orange. Ride junkies state that the Orange Stinger has good "foot chop," which essentially means that your feet come very close to the enclosing orange. In addition to the foot chop, the ride is augmented by loud buzzing (really!). In the scary department, it's a wilder ride than Dumbo, but foot chop and frenetic buzzing notwithstanding, the Orange Stinger is still just swings going in circles. Lamentably, the 48-inch minimum-height restriction precludes from riding those who would most enjoy the attraction.

TOURING TIPS This is a fun and visually appealing ride, but it's also one that loads slowly and occasions long waits unless you wrangle your bee during the first hour or so the park is open. Be aware that it's possible for the swing chairs to collide when the ride comes to a stop—the author once picked up a nice bruise when an empty swing smacked him during touchdown.

Sun Wheel ★★

APPEAL BY AGE	PRESCHOOL ★★★		GRADE SCHOOL ★★★
TEENS ★★½	YOUNG ADULTS ★★½	OVER 30 ★★½	SENIORS ★★

What it is Ferris wheel. **Scope and scale** Major attraction. **When to go** The first 90 minutes the park is open or just before closing. **Special comments** The world's largest chicken coop; may induce motion sickness. **Duration of ride** 2 minutes. **Loading speed** Slow.

DESCRIPTION AND COMMENTS Higher than the Matterhorn attraction at Disneyland Park, this whopper of a Ferris wheel tops out at 150 feet. Absolutely spectacular in appearance, with an enormous sun emblem in the middle of its wheel, the aptly named Sun Wheel offers stunning views in all directions. Unfortunately, however, the view is severely compromised by the steel mesh that completely encloses the passenger compartment. In essence, Disney has created the world's largest revolving chicken coop. As concerns the ride itself, some of the passenger buckets move laterally from side to side across the Sun Wheel in addition to rotating around with the wheel. Because it feels like your bucket has become unattached from the main structure, this lateral movement can be a little disconcerting if you aren't expecting it.

TOURING TIPS Ferris wheels are the most slow loading of all cycle rides. Thus, we were very curious to see how the loading and unloading of the Sun Wheel is engineered. The Sun Wheel has a platform that allows three compartments to be loaded at once. The lateral sliding buckets are loaded from the two outside platforms, while the stationary compartments are loaded from the middle platform. Loading the entire wheel takes about six and a half minutes, following which the Sun Wheel rotates for a two-minute ride. And speaking of the ride, the Sun Wheel rotates so slowly that the wonderful rising and falling sensations of the garden-variety Ferris wheel are completely absent. For our money, the Sun Wheel is beautiful to behold but terribly boring to ride. If you decide to give it a whirl, ride the first hour the park is open or in the hour before the park closes.

S.S. Rustworthy ★★★

APPEAL BY AGE	PRESCHOOL ★★★	GRADE SCHOOL ★★★	TEENS –
YOUNG ADULTS –		OVER 30 –	SENIORS –

What it is Wet play area. **Scope and scale** Minor attraction. **When to go** Anytime. **Special comments** Small but effective; children will get drenched.

DESCRIPTION AND COMMENTS A rusty shipwreck (supposedly on the bottom of the sea) surrounded by giant starfish, clams, and other sea creatures, as well as by fountains that randomly erupt, squirt, and spray. Children pretend to avoid being squirted while contriving to get as wet as possible without drowning.

TOURING TIPS Your kids will want to cavort on the S.S. *Rustworthy* even if the weather is cool. Be prepared to set some limits—or, alternatively, to carry some dry clothes.

Toy Story Mania *(opens 2008)* (FASTPASS)

APPEAL BY AGE   NOT OPEN AT PRESS TIME

What it is 3-D ride-through indoor shooting gallery. Scope and scale Headliner. When to go Before 10:30 a.m., after 6 p.m., or use FASTPASS. Duration of ride About 4½ minutes. Average wait in line per 100 people ahead of you 3 minutes. Loading speed Fast.

DESCRIPTION AND COMMENTS *Toy Story* Mania ushers in a whole new generation of Disney attractions: "virtual dark rides". Since Disneyland opened in 1955, ride vehicles have moved past two- and three-dimensional sets often populated by audio-animatronic (AA) figures. Designed by the Imagineers and constructed by skilled craftsmen, these amazingly detailed sets and robotic figures literally defined the Disney creative genius in attractions such as Pirates of the Caribbean, The Haunted Mansion, and Peter Pan's Flight. Now for *Toy Story* Mania, the elaborate sets and endearing AA characters are gone. Imagine long corridors, totally empty, covered with reflective material. There's almost nothing there . . . until you put on your special 3-D glasses. Instantly, the corridor is full and brimming with color, action, and activity thanks to projected computer-generated images.

Conceptually, *Toy Story* Mania is an interactive shooting gallery much like Buzz Lightyear, except that your ride vehicle passes through a totally virtual midway with booths offering such games as ring toss, dart throwing, and ball throwing. You use a cannon on your ride vehicle to play as you move along from booth to booth. Unlike the laser guns in Buzz Lightyear, however, the *Toy Story* Mania cannons take advantage of the digital-image technology to toss rings, shoot balls, and even throw eggs and pies. Each game booth is manned by a *Toy Story* character, including Woody, Buzz Lightyear, Hamm, Bo-Peep, and the Little Green Men, who are right there beside you in 3-D glory cheering you on. In addition to the 3-D imagery, you also experience various smells, vehicle motion, wind, and water spray. The ride begins with a training round to familiarize you with your cannon and the nature of the games and then continues on through a number of "real" games where you compete with your riding mate. The technology has the ability to self-adjust the level of difficulty according to each player's ability so that every rider is both challenged and has a positive experience.

Finally, and also of note, a new generation of "living character" AA figures will be introduced in the preshow queuing area of *Toy Story* Mania. A six-foot-tall Mr. Potato Head breaks new ground for an AA character by interacting with and talking to guests in real time (similar to *Turtle Talk with Crush*).

TOURING TIPS *Toy Story* Mania will be very popular. Because it's in Paradise Pier, at the far end of the park, we don't expect it to become mobbed until 90 minutes or so after the park opens. If you love this kind of attraction and want to ride multiple times without much wait, morning is the time. Later in the day, use FASTPASS.

PARADES *and*
LIVE ENTERTAINMENT

AFTERNOON AND EVENING PARADES The afternoon parade has been usurped during the Disneyland anniversary celebration by the Block Party Bash described below. The evening parade is a reincarnation of the Main Street Electrical Parade from Disneyland Park.

The good news is that both the Block Party Bash and evening parades are good shows. The afternoon event makes up in color and enthusiasm what it lacks in coherence. And the evening Electrical Parade? Well, it's been a surefire winner for decades, featuring billions of itty-bitty lights, lots of floats, and a battalion of Disney characters. The parade route runs from a gate to the left of the Pizza Oom Mow Mow restaurant at Paradise Pier, through The Bay Area, around a bug's land side of Grizzly Peak, and on to Sunshine Plaza, where it takes a lap around the fountain and then disappears backstage near *Playhouse Disney*. On days when the crowds are light, any place along the parade route will suffice. On days of heavy attendance, try to score a viewing spot on the elevated courtyard or steps of the Golden Vine Winery.

A new parade based on Pixar movies and Pixar characters is in the works and is expected to debut in late 2007 or early 2008. The new parade is the first installment of an overall effort to put DCA on a more equal footing with Disneyland Park, which attracts almost three times as many guests as DCA.

The parade route jams pedestrian traffic throughout the park, essentially trapping you in place until the parade passes. If you don't intend to watch the parade, get situated wherever you want to be before it starts. Disney cast members will be able to tell you in which direction the parade will run.

HIGH SCHOOL MUSICAL PEP RALLY We can't fault Disney for trying to cash in on the success of *High School Musical,* an original movie premiered on the Disney Channel in 2006. The kids who sing and dance their way through a 20-minute recap of the film's major musical numbers do an outstanding job. With little dialogue and stage props that consists of nothing more than basketball shaped balloons and cheesy "Go Wildcats!" banners, Disney's not given them much to work with. You can't fault the cast's enthusiasm, energy, and volume, however. They'll either set your toe a-tappin' or give you a major migraine. Children will miss the actual stars from the film, while adults will wonder what the school's feeding these kids to eliminate all traces of teen angst and raging hormones.

BLOCK PARTY BASH This street festivity is DCA's main event in the Disneyland 50th-anniversary celebration. The Bash consists of highly orchestrated "spontaneous" street parties that erupt around the park. Each party includes music (some live), dancing, and novel street entertainment. Featuring 26 characters from the Disney/Pixar films *Toy Story, Monsters, Inc., a bug's life,* and *The Incredibles,* the Block Party Bash is three parts interactive show and one part parade. Usually starting at Paradise Pier with the improbable gang of green army men, giant marching orange highway cones, alphabet blocks (the "block" party part), 60 dancers, 16 acrobats, 12 pairs of "jumping" stilts, three large floats, and the Pixar characters, the Bash stops for three 11-minute shows along its route. Each time it cranks up, pretty much everyone within 50 yards is sucked into the merriment (when's the last time you danced with a highway cone?). Of the three performance stops, Golden State, across from Paradise Pier, and Sunshine Plaza, near the park's entrance, offer the best viewing and most elbowroom. The third stop is at the entrance to a bug's land.

HYPERION THEATER A state-of-the-art theater that hosts the best of DCA's live shows as well as special concerts and events. Check the daily entertainment schedule in the handout park map to see what's playing and for showtimes.

HOLLYWOOD BACKLOT STAGE This open-air stage features small productions and Disney characters. One of our favorite venues in the park.

PACIFIC WHARF STAGE A small outdoor stage that features live rock, country, and pop. Check the daily entertainment schedule for acts.

"THE MAGIC OF BROTHER BEAR" TOTEM CEREMONY Storytelling at the Redwood Creek Challenge Trail across from Grizzly Mountain.

STREET ENTERTAINMENT Mobile rock bands (on flatbed trailers and woody wagons), acrobats, and comedy sketches on the Hollywood Pictures Backlot are part of the scheduled street entertainment. Unlike at Disneyland Park where street entertainers appear on a more or less impromptu basis, most of DCA's street acts operate according to a specific performance schedule listed on the park *Times Guide.*

DISNEY CHARACTERS Character appearances are listed in the daily entertainment schedule. In addition, Flik and Atta can usually be found at a bug's land, Chip 'n' Dale hang out around the Redwood Challenge Trail, Cruella De Vil makes appearances in the Hollywood Pictures Backlot, and Ariel's Grotto restaurant at Paradise Pier offers character dining featuring Captain Mickey and friends.

Although Disney's California Adventure is only a few years old, it already has a few unheralded treasures; read on for details.

UNHERALDED TREASURES
at DCA

TREASURE: Golden Zephyr "Train"

LOCATION: Just inside the main entrance

DISNEY'S CALIFORNIA ADVENTURE might lack a railroad that runs its perimeter, but you can enjoy a replica of an observation car from the famous *California Zephyr* to the right as you enter the park. The train houses part of Engine-Ear Toys, Baker's Field Bakery, and Bur-r-r Bank Ice Cream; the outdoor seating area is themed to look like a train station. Take a peek inside, even if you don't plan to eat. *California Zephyr* memorabilia of all types decorates the walls and harks back to a time when people traveled cross-country on these exciting trains with the famous observation domes.

TREASURE: Cove Bar

LOCATION: On the bridge to Paradise Pier

ARIEL'S GROTTO IS A FIXED-PRICE character-meal restaurant on the span connecting Paradise Pier to the Golden State area. Instead of heading downstairs to the restaurant from the entrance, though, go around the walkway. There, you'll find the Cove Bar, where you can enjoy a full-service bar and a small selection of food. For some, the thought of a cocktail at the end of a long day might be enticement enough; but this is a good spot even for teetotalers—it's one of the best places to enjoy the view. It's a bit too sunny during the day, but as the sun sets and the evening lights come on, the Cove turns into a mellow hideaway where you can enjoy a beautiful view of Paradise Pier. In the background, you hear music, laughter, and the occasional sounds of a roller coaster. You look out and see the small waves lapping against the pier that houses a brightly lit carousel—enough to make you forget you're sitting in the middle of a completely artificial environment.

TREASURE: Redwood Creek Challenge Trail

LOCATION: Opposite Grizzly Peak

MAYBE A VISIT TO A THEME PARK was your kid's idea, and you prefer going on a quiet walk in the woods or enjoying a hike in a national park. If you just want to take a break from the hectic rush of a trip to DCA, hop over to the Redwood Creek Challenge Trail. Looking at the park map, you probably assume this is just a playground designed for little kids, but the area is actually a good representation of a wilderness park. OK, so you don't really need to bring your bird-watching book, but there are various nooks and crannies, as well as a few "ranger buildings" that are very well themed (down to the wildlife books on the shelves). You could easily spend a portion of your day just enjoying the decidedly rustic feel of Redwood Creek.

TRAFFIC PATTERNS *at* DISNEY'S CALIFORNIA ADVENTURE

ONE OF THE PROBLEMS Disney had at DCA early on was that there was no traffic to create patterns. Attendance figures were far less than projected, though guests on hand did stack up daily at Soarin' over California and Grizzly River Run. On the relatively few crowded days (mostly weekends), the park didn't handle crowds particularly well. If Disney's gate projections had panned out, the park would have been in gridlock much of the time. The year 2006 was better, thanks primarily to *The Twilight Zone* Tower of Terror.

If you happen to hit DCA on a day of high attendance, here's what to expect. A high percentage of the early morning arrivals will beat feet directly to the Tower of Terror and/or Soarin' over California and then continue (on warmer days) to Grizzly River Run. When the Tower of Terror opened in 2004 it instantly became the park's biggest draw and relieved much of the pressure on Soarin' over California and Grizzly River Run. Other than the Tower of Terror and *Monsters, Inc.,* the Hollywood Pictures Backlot is deserted, as are Golden State Winery, Pacific Wharf, a bug's land, and The Bay Area until midmorning. As the lines build at Tower, Soarin', and Grizzly, and as guests begin opting for FASTPASSes at these attractions, the crowd begins working its way into Paradise Pier. California Screamin' sees its share of traffic as locals in the know arrive to beat the crowd at the coaster and at the slow-loading cycle rides at Paradise Pier. By late morning on a busy day, you'll find sizable lines at most of DCA's rides. By noon or earlier, the ride queues are substantial and the crowds redistribute to the park's shows. *Playhouse Disney, Muppet Vision,* and the Hyperion Theater each draw good-sized crowds. By 2 p.m., the whole park is fairly socked in with guests, and even minor attractions and displays like the sourdough-bread and tortilla-baking demonstrations build lines. Park departures increase significantly after 3 p.m., with lots of Park Hopper and Annual Passport holders heading over to Disneyland Park. By the dinner hour, crowds at DCA have thinned appreciably. As closing time approaches, long lines are found only premier attractions. During our research visits, there was no daily capstone event at DCA comparable to *Fantasmic!* and the fireworks at Disneyland Park. When DCA offers a capstone event, the bulk of the evening crowd departs at the end of the show. During our visits, the largest wave of departing guests occurred after the Electrical Parade. Just before closing, crowd levels are thin except, of course, at Soarin' over California and the Tower of Terror.

CALIFORNIA ADVENTURE ONE-DAY TOURING PLAN

Before You Go

1. Buy your admission in advance (see page 20).
2. Call ☎ 714-781-7290 the day before visiting for official opening time.

At the Park

This touring plan assumes a willingness to experience all rides and shows. If the plan calls for you to experience an attraction that does not interest you, simply skip it and proceed with the plan. Height and age requirements apply to many attractions. If you have children who are not eligible to ride, avail yourself of the switching-off option. This touring plan includes most of the amusement park rides on Paradise Pier. If you're short on time or wish to allocate more of the day to DCA's theatrical attractions, consider forgoing a few of the slow-loading rides. Because DCA doesn't participate in the early-entry program, crowds are smaller at DCA on Monday, Tuesday, Thursday, and Saturday when Disneyland Park is running early entry.

1. Arrive at the entrance turnstiles with admission in hand 30 minutes before official opening time.
2. After entering the park, bear right to Condor Flats. Ride Soarin'. Do not use FASTPASS.
3. Retracing your steps toward the park entrance, enter the Hollywood Studios Backlot and proceed to the Tower of Terror. Obtain FAST-PASSes. The FASTPASSes will be honored from the beginning of the return window until park closing.
4. In the Hollywood Studios Backlot, ride *Monsters, Inc.: Mike and Sulley to the Rescue.*
5. Proceed back through Condor Flats and beyond to the Grizzly River Run. Either ride or obtain a FASTPASS. Usually Grizzly River Run's FASTPASS machines are not hooked up to the park's FASTPASS system. This means that you will be issued a FASTPASS even though you're currently holding one for the Tower of Terror.
6. Continue on to the California Screamin' roller coaster on the far side of the lake in the Paradise Pier section of the park. Ride. Feel free to ride the coaster a second or third time if the waiting times are short.
7. Bear left on exiting and continue around the lake to Mulholland Madness. Do not use FASTPASS.
8. A new headliner attraction, *Toy Story* Mania, opens at Paradise Pier in 2008. If it's open during your visit, ride now.
9. Across the plaza from Mulholland Madness, ride the Sun Wheel.

10. Backtracking with the lake on your right, proceed next to the Orange Stinger and ride.

11. Continuing back toward the roller coaster, ride the Golden Zephyr.

12. If your party includes small children, ride King Triton's Carousel.

13. Departing Paradise Pier, stop in the San Francisco area and check out the showtimes for *Golden Dreams,* starring Whoopi Goldberg. Interrupt the touring plan to return and see the show if it's on your to-do list.

14. You may remember from our coverage of FASTPASS that you can obtain a second FASTPASS anytime after the return window on your first FAST-PASS begins. So head back to Grizzly River Run if you elected to skip it earlier. Go ahead and ride if the wait is 30 minutes or less. Otherwise, obtain FASTPASSes.

15. Head back toward the lake and turn left, keeping Grizzly Peak on your left side. Proceed to a bug's land. See *It's Tough to Be a Bug!*

16. Also in a bug's land, try the kiddie rides at Flik's Fun Fair, if there are small children in your party. Check the *Times Guide* for scheduled performances of *Ugly Bug Ball.*

17. Turn right on exiting a bug's land and return to the Hollywood Studios Backlot. From this point on, feel free to interrupt the touring plan for lunch or a snack.

18. There are three excellent shows in the Hollywood Pictures Backlot district: *Playhouse Disney–Live on Stage!,* whatever the current show is at the Hyperion Theater, and *Muppet Vision 3-D. Muppet Vision 3-D* runs back-to-back shows all day, but the other presentations offer a limited number of performances with showtimes listed in the park *Times Guide.* The Hyperion Theater should be on everyone's itinerary. *Playhouse Disney–Live on Stage!* is an absolute must for families with children age 7 years and younger but is expendable for groups of adults or older children.

    What you want to do at this point, using the entertainment schedule in the *Times Guide,* is to work out a plan for seeing the shows that interest you. We suggest making the excellent Hyperion Theater production your top priority. Find the next scheduled performance and plan to be there, arriving 20 to 30 minutes before showtime. Between arriving early, getting seated, seeing the 40-minute show, and exiting, allocate about an hour and 15 minutes altogether for this activity.

    Once you determine the specific Hyperion Theater performance you'll attend (and know what time you have to be there and when you'll be done), you can develop a schedule for seeing the other presentations. As concerns the other shows, allocate 30 to 35 minutes for *Muppet Vision* and 45 to 55 minutes for *Playhouse Disney.* You don't have to worry about arriving early for the *Muppets* because the show runs con-tinuously back-to-back.

    If you have time gaps in your schedule (once you've gotten every-thing sorted out), you can use the gaps to tour the Animation building. If you have a big gap, say 45 minutes, you can use it to ride Tower of

Terror and Grizzly River Run utilizing the FASTPASSes you obtained earlier. Remember that the return window printed on the FASTPASS is only a preferred time. The FASTPASS is good from the beginning of the time window until park closing.

19. Return to Golden State and visit any of the minor attractions, including the film about winemaking at the winery, and tortilla- and bread-making demonstrations on Pacific Wharf. See *Golden Dreams* in the San Francisco area if you missed it before.

20. If you have children, let them take a crack at the Redwood Creek Challenge Trail near Grizzly River Run and the fountain playground nearby in Paradise Pier.

21. This concludes the touring plan. Check your daily entertainment schedule for parades, live performances, fireworks, and special events. Adjust the remainder of your visit accordingly. Drop by the Animation building in Hollywood on your way out of the park if you missed some of the exhibits earlier in the day.

PART SEVEN

UNIVERSAL STUDIOS HOLLYWOOD

UNIVERSAL STUDIOS HOLLYWOOD WAS THE FIRST film and television studio to turn part of its facility into a modern theme park. By integrating shows and rides with behind-the-scenes presentations on moviemaking, Universal Studios Hollywood created a new genre of theme park, stimulating in the process a number of clone and competitor parks. First came the Disney-MGM Studios at Walt Disney World, followed shortly by Universal Studios Florida, also near Orlando. Where Universal Studios Hollywood, however, evolved from an established film and television venue, its cross-country imitators were launched primarily as theme parks, albeit with some production capability on the side. Disney is also challenging Universal in California with Disney's California Adventure. Adjacent to Disneyland Park, DCA does not have production facilities, but one of its themed areas focuses on Hollywood and the movies.

Located just off US 101 north of Hollywood, Universal Studios operates on a scale and with a quality standard rivaled only by Disney, SeaWorld, and Busch Gardens parks. Unique among American theme parks for its topography, Universal Studios Hollywood is tucked on top of, below, and around a tall hill that in many states would pass for a mountain. The studios comprise an open-access area and a controlled-access area. The latter contains the working soundstages, back lot, wardrobe, scenery, prop shops, postproduction, and administration. Guests can visit the controlled-access area only by taking the Studio Tour. The open-access area, which contains the park's rides, shows, restaurants, and services, is divided into two sections. The main entrance provides access to the upper section, the Upper Lot, on top of the hill. Seven theater shows and one ride, as well as the loading area for the Studio Tour, are located in the Upper Lot. The Lower Lot, at the northeastern base of the hill, is accessible from the Upper Lot via escalators. There are two rides, two shows, and walk-through exhibits in the Lower Lot. All attractions, including rides, shows, tours, and exhibits, are fully profiled in the section "Universal Studios Hollywood Attractions."

The park offers all standard services and amenities, including stroller and wheelchair rental, lockers, diaper-changing and infant-nursing facilities, car assistance, and foreign-language assistance. Most of the park is accessible to disabled guests, and TDDs are available for the hearing impaired. Almost all services are in the Upper Lot, just inside the main entrance.

GATHERING INFORMATION

THE MAIN UNIVERSAL STUDIOS information number is ☎ 818-622-3801. Calling this number, however, often results in up to 20 minutes of holding time or about 7 minutes on hold followed by a disconnect. If you have problems, try calling ☎ 818-622-3735 or 818-622-3750. While Universal Studios' Web site at **www.universalstudioshollywood .com** is easy to navigate, obtaining information over the phone would try the patience of Buddha. For all three numbers listed, a recording recites the park's operating hours for every day of the month (!) before you are offered a menu from which to choose. To short-circuit the interminable operating-hours litany, dial 4.

WHAT MAKES UNIVERSAL STUDIOS HOLLYWOOD DIFFERENT

WHAT MAKES UNIVERSAL STUDIOS HOLLYWOOD different is that the attractions, with a couple of exceptions, are designed to minimize long waits in line. The centerpiece of the Universal Studios experience is the Studio Tour. While on the tram, you experience an earthquake, are attacked by the killer shark from *Jaws,* are grabbed by King Kong, and endure a simulated rain shower and a flash flood, among other things. In other parks, including Universal's sister park in Florida, each of these spectacles is presented as an individual attraction, and each has its own long queue. At Universal Studios Hollywood, by contrast, you suffer only one very manageable wait to board the tram and then experience all of these events as part of the tour.

In addition to the time savings and convenience provided by the tram tour, most of the live shows at Universal Studios Hollywood are performed in large theaters or stadiums. Instead of standing in line outside, guests are usually invited to enter the theater and wait in seated comfort for the production to begin.

TIMING *Your* VISIT

CROWDS ARE LARGEST IN THE SUMMER (Memorial Day through Labor Day) and during specific holiday periods during the rest of the year. Christmas Day through New Year's Day is extremely busy, as are Thanksgiving weekend, the week of Washington's birthday,

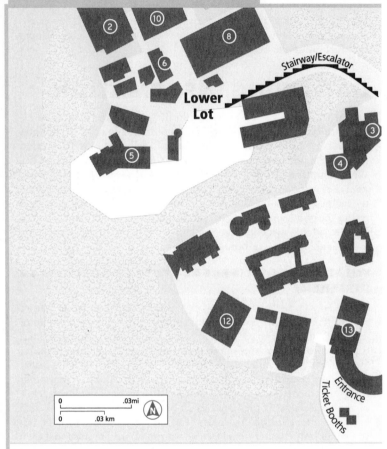

universal studios hollywood

Stairway/Escalator

Lower Lot

Entrance

Ticket Booths

0   .03mi
0   .03 km

1. *Back to the Future:* The Ride
2. *Backdraft*
3. *Fear Factor Live*
4. *Hollywood Animal Actors*
5. *Jurassic Park:* The Ride
6. *Lucy—A Tribute*
7. Nickelodeon Blast Zone
8. Revenge of the Mummy

spring break for schools and colleges, and the two weeks bracketing Easter. The least busy time is from after Thanksgiving weekend until the week before Christmas. The next slowest times are September through the weekend preceding Thanksgiving, January 4 through the first week of March, and the week following Easter to Memorial Day weekend.

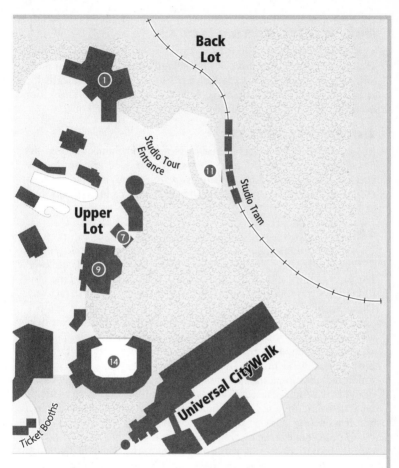

9. *Shrek 4-D*
10. Special Effects Stages
11. Studio Tour

12. *Terminator 2: 3-D*
13. Universal's House of Horrors
14. *Waterworld*

SELECTING THE DAY OF THE WEEK FOR YOUR VISIT

WEEKENDS ARE MORE CROWDED than weekdays year-round. Saturday is the busiest day. Sunday, particularly Sunday morning, is the best bet if you have to go on a weekend, but it is still extremely busy. During the summer, Friday is very busy; Monday, Wednesday, and Thursday are usually less so; Tuesday is normally the slowest of all.

During the off-season (September through May, holidays excepted), Tuesday is usually the least-crowded day, followed by Thursday.

HOW MUCH TIME TO ALLOCATE

ALTHOUGH THERE'S A LOT TO SEE and do at Universal Studios Hollywood, you can (unlike at Disneyland) complete a comprehensive tour in one day. If you follow our touring plan, which calls for being on hand at park opening, you should be able to check out everything by mid- to late afternoon, even on a crowded day.

ENDURANCE LEVELS

NEVER MIND that Universal Studios Hollywood claims to cover 400 acres; the area you will have to traverse on foot is considerably smaller. In fact, you will do much less walking and, miracle of miracles, much less standing in line at Universal Studios Hollywood than at Disneyland.

COST

ONE-DAY TICKETS ARE AVAILABLE for about $61 for adults, about $51 for children ages 3 to 9, and about $59 for seniors age 60 and over. For $119 (adults and children) you can obtain a Front of Line Pass that allows you to skip right to the front of the line at all attractions. Discounts in the neighborhood of 11% are often available if you buy your passes on the Universal Web site. Moreover, you can print tickets purchased on the Universal Web site and thereby eliminate any waiting associated with buying your admission at the park ticket kiosks. In 2007 Universal ran an on-line promotion that offered unlimited additional days admission for the remainder of the calendar year if you purchased a one-day pass at full price. Also available were discount coupons in Anaheim area brochure racks that offered $8 off a one-day pass for up to six people.

You can count on being able to see all you want in a single day, even during the busier times of year. In addition to the Web-site discounts, admission discounts are sometimes offered in area freebie publications available in hotels. Admission discounts are also periodically offered to AAA members. Vacation packages including lodging and park admission are available from Hilton and Sheraton hotels, both of which offer accommodations close to the studios.

For avid fans, Universal offers several annual passes ranging in cost from around $61 to $99. The main differences are free parking and no blackout dates with the pricier passes. For more information, see the Universal Web site or call ☎ 800-864-8377.

In a groundbreaking initiative, Universal Studios Hollywood became the first major theme park to offer a guaranteed rain check. If it rains more than one-eighth of an inch by 2 p.m., Universal will issue you a rain check good for 30 days.

THE SHUTTLE

UNIVERSAL OFFERS A SHUTTLE service from Anaheim to Universal Studios Hollywood. The service is free for guests who purchase their Universal admissions at **www.universalstudioshollywood.com.** Following confirmation of purchase, buyers are given a phone number for making shuttle reservations. The service picks up guests at their Anaheim hotel and returns them there at the end of the day.

ARRIVING *and* GETTING ORIENTED

MOST FOLKS ACCESS UNIVERSAL STUDIOS by taking US 101, also called the Hollywood Freeway, and following the signs to the park. If the freeway is gridlocked, you can also get to the Studios by taking Cahuenga Boulevard and then turning north toward Lankershim Boulevard. If you are coming from Burbank, take Barham Boulevard toward US 101, and then follow the signs.

Universal Studios has a big, multilevel parking garage at the top of the hill. Signs directing you to the garage are a bit confusing, so pay attention and stay to the far right when you come up the hill. Even after you have made it to the pay booth and shelled out $10 to park (and that's $15 if your RV is more than 15 feet long), it is still not exactly clear where you go next. Drive slowly, follow other cars proceeding from the pay booths, and avoid turns onto ramps marked "Exit." You may become a bit disoriented, but ultimately you will blunder into the garage. Once parked, make a note of your parking level and the location of your space.

Walk toward the opposite end of the garage from where you entered and exit into Universal CityWalk, a shopping, dining, and entertainment complex (no admission required) situated between the parking structure and the main entrance of the park. As an aside, CityWalk is much like Downtown Disney at Disneyland. Some of Universal's better restaurants and more interesting shops are at CityWalk, and it's so close to the theme-park entrance that you can conveniently pop out of the park to grab a bite (don't forget to have your hand stamped for reentry).

Universal Studios' ticket booths and turnstiles are about 100 yards from the main parking garage. If you need cash, an ATM is outside and to the right of the main entrance. There is also an ATM inside the park next to the Cartooniversal store. Nearby is a guest-services window. As you enter the park, be sure to pick up a park map and a daily entertainment schedule.

THE UPPER LOT

THE UPPER LOT IS ESSENTIALLY a large, amorphous pedestrian plaza. The freebie park map shows a number of street names such as

New York Street and Baker Street, and place names like Cape Cod and Moulin Rouge, but on foot these theme distinctions are largely lost and placement of buildings appears almost random. In other words, do not expect the sort of thematic integrity that you find at Disneyland.

Inside the main entrance, stroller and wheelchair rentals are on the right, as are rental lockers. Straight ahead is a TV Audience Ticket Booth, where you can obtain free tickets to join the audience for any TV shows that are taping during your visit (subject to availability).

Attractions in the Upper Lot are situated around the perimeter of the plaza. If you picture an imaginary clock with the main entrance at 6 o'clock, then *Hollywood Animal Actors* is at 10 o'clock, *Fear Factor Live* at 11 o'clock, Back to the Future: the Ride at 12 o'clock, the Studio Tour at 1 o'clock, *Shrek 4-D* at 3 o'clock, and *Waterworld* at 5 o'clock. Between *Fear Factor Live* and Back to the Future (11 and 12 o'clock) are the escalators and stairs that lead to the Lower Lot. The Upper Lot attractions are described in detail below.

THE LOWER LOT

THE LOWER LOT IS ACCESSIBLE ONLY via the escalators and stairs descending from the back left section of the Upper Lot. Configured roughly in the shape of the letter T, the Lower Lot is home to *Jurassic Park:* The Ride, currently one of the headliner attractions at Universal Studios Hollywood. As you step off the escalator, *Jurassic Park* is straight ahead. A hard right brings you to Revenge of the Mummy; moving down the stem of the T, *Lucy—A Tribute* is on your left—both are walk-through, interactive exhibits. At the base of the T are two theater attractions. To your left is *Backdraft,* and to your right, the Special Effects Stages. The Lower Lot attractions are described below, following the Upper Lot attractions.

UNIVERSAL STUDIOS HOLLYWOOD ATTRACTIONS

UPPER-LOT ATTRACTIONS

Back to the Future: **The Ride** ★★★★

APPEAL BY AGE	PRESCHOOL –	GRADE SCHOOL ★★★★	TEENS ★★★★
YOUNG ADULTS ★★★★		OVER 30 ★★★★	SENIORS ★★½

What it is Flight-simulator thrill ride. **Scope and scale** Super-headliner. **When to go** First thing in the morning. **Special comments** Not to be missed, if you have a strong stomach; very rough ride; may induce motion sickness; must be 40" tall to ride. **Duration of ride** 4½ minutes. **Loading speed** Moderate.

Dark

Scary

Rough

Loud

Motion Sickness

DESCRIPTION AND COMMENTS This attraction is history at Universal Studios Orlando and may be going the way of the dinosaur at the California park as well. On tap is a thrill ride based on, of all things, *The Simpsons*. (Can Bart be scarier than Biff?) Anyway, for the moment, guests in Doc Brown's lab get caught up in a high-speed chase through time that spans a million years. An extremely intense simulator ride, Back to the Future is similar to Star Tours at Disneyland Park, but it is much rougher and jerkier. Though the story line doesn't make much sense, the visual effects are wild and powerful. The vehicles (DeLorean time machines) in Back to the Future are much smaller than those of Star Tours, so the ride feels more personal and less like a group experience.

In a survey of tourists who had experienced simulator rides in Universal Studios and Disneyland Park, riders age 34 and under preferred *Back to the Future* to the Disney attraction by a 7:5 margin. Older riders, however, stated a 2:1 preference for Star Tours over *Back to the Future*. The remarks of a woman from Mount Holly, New Jersey, are typical:

Our favorite [overall] attraction was Back to the Future *at Universal. Comparing it to Star Tours, it was more realistic because the screen surrounds you.*

Most guests also find *Back to the Future* wilder than its Disney cousins. A Michigan woman writes:

Back to the Future *was off the charts on the scary-o-meter. It made Splash and Big Thunder Mountains seem like carnival kiddie rides.*

An English woman from Fleet Hants, who was tired of being jerked around, finally got mad:

The simulators were fun, but they do seem to go out of their way to jerk you about, and the Back to the Future one was SO jerky that it made me quite angry.

A man from Evansville, Indiana, reminds us that *Back to the Future* can humble even the most intrepid:

The Back to the Future *ride at Universal was very rough, and we are members of a roller-coaster club. We have seldom experienced such a rough ride and have ridden over 300 coasters. If it was too strong for us, we shudder to think about mere mortals.*

Because the height requirement on *Back to the Future* has been lowered from 46 inches to 40 inches, younger children are riding. Many of them require preparation. A Virginia mother suggests:

The 5-year-old was apprehensive about the ride, but he liked it a lot. We assured him ahead of time that 1) it's only a movie, and 2) the car doesn't actually go anywhere, just shakes around. This seemed to increase his ability to enjoy that ride (rather than taking all the fun out of it).

TOURING TIPS As soon as the park opens, ride Revenge of the Mummy and *Jurassic Park* in the Lower Lot and then return to the Upper Lot for *Back* *to the Future. Note:* Sitting in the rear seat of the car makes the ride more realistic.

Fear Factor Live ★★★

What it is Live version of the gross-out-stunt TV show on NBC. **Scope and scale** Headliner. **When to go** 6–8 shows daily; crowds are smallest at the first and second-to-last shows. **Special comments** Great fun if you love the TV show.

Yucky

DESCRIPTION AND COMMENTS In each show, park guests compete against each other in several extreme stunts. The stunts—like drinking bug smoothies, scaling tall walls, and swimming in a tank full of eels—were developed with help from the brains (?) behind the NBC television show *Fear Factor* and are no less creepy than the ones you see on TV.

The primary contestants, screened and chosen in advance, compete for prizes by performing three different elimination stunts. In between these stunts are two mini-stunts with contestants who are chosen from the audience.

If you don't want to be onstage, you can still play an interactive role in the audience by controlling cannons that blast contestants with water, air, and other such things (like hard rubber balls . . . ouch!). Prepare to be grossed out—parts of this show are not for the faint of heart or anyone with a weak stomach. Many of the stunts may be too intense for kids younger than 8.

TOURING TIPS Apparently, the odds are more in your favor for getting into Harvard than being chosen to appear on the TV version of *Fear Factor,* so if you've ever wanted a chance to test your mettle, the theme-park version may be your big chance. Participants for the physical stunts are chosen early in the morning outside the theater and sometimes between shows. The victims—er, contestants—for the ick-factor stunts, like the bug-smoothie drinking, are chosen directly from the audience. Sit close to the front and wave your hands like crazy when it comes time for selection.

Hollywood Animal Actors ★★★½

What it is Trained-animals stadium performance. **Scope and scale** Major attraction. **When to go** After you have experienced all rides. **Special comments** Warm and delightful. **Duration of presentation** 20 minutes. **Probable waiting time** 15 minutes.

Thumbs Up for the Whole Family

DESCRIPTION AND COMMENTS *Hollywood Animal Actors* features various critters, including some rescued from shelters, demonstrating behaviors that animals often perform in the making of motion pictures. The live presentation is punctuated by clips from films and television shows. Of course, the animals often exhibit an independence that frustrates their trainers while delighting the audience.

TOURING TIPS Presented five or more times daily, the program's schedule is in the daily entertainment guide. Go when it's convenient for you; queue about 15 minutes before showtime.

Nickelodeon Blast Zone ★★★★

APPEAL BY AGE	PRESCHOOL ★★★★	GRADE SCHOOL ★★★★	TEENS ★★★★
YOUNG ADULTS ★★★½		OVER 30 ★★★½	SENIORS ★★★½

What it is Elaborate interactive playground. **Scope and scale** Major attraction. **When to go** Anytime. **Special comments** Almost overwhelming. **Duration of experience** Either set limits up front or plan to stay all day.

Wet

DESCRIPTION AND COMMENTS The Nickelodeon Blast Zone is a Wal-Mart–sized themed area based on various Nickelodeon channel television shows. Within the Blast Zone are three interactive play areas.

The first play area, Wild Thornberrys Adventure Temple, is a jungle-themed, two-story enclosure containing some 25,000 foam balls. Children (of all ages) can throw or (using air cannons) shoot the balls at each other. To add to the mayhem, there's an orangutan statue that spits balls in all directions when irritated (not hard to do). The second area, Nickelodeon Splash, is also a two-story affair where the idea is to come as close as possible to drowning on dry land while fully clothed. There are geysers, water cannons, a rocket blasting water, and the periodic dumping of two 500-gallon water buckets (in case you're wondering, that's enough water to fill a 20- by 30-foot swimming pool). Some of the spewing, squirting, and dousing you can control yourself. Other soggy manifestations erupt periodically with little warning. Finally, there's the Nick Jr. Backyard, a playground for age 6 and under, featuring slides, cargo nets, a climbing pole, and other assorted equipment.

TOURING TIPS The Wild Thornberrys' foam-ball extravaganza and the splash zone can be enjoyed by mischievous guests of any age. The balls neither hurt when they hit nor get you wet. As for the water playground, it's hard to participate without getting pretty soaked. Stay away on colder days, and bring a change of clothes on warmer ones. Be forewarned that even the Nick Jr. Backyard toddler playground comes equipped with a set of little water jets.

The foam-ball palace and the drowning factory are both big places where you can lose sight of your kids in a hurry (or until they nail you with a foam ball or water cannon). Keeping an eye on your children at Nick Jr.'s, by contrast, is easy.

Shrek 4-D ★★★★

APPEAL BY AGE	PRESCHOOL ★★★★	GRADE SCHOOL ★★★★½	TEENS ★★★★½
YOUNG ADULTS ★★★★½		OVER 30 ★★★★½	SENIORS ★★★★

What it is 3-D theater show. **Scope and scale** Headliner. **When to go** The first hour the park is open or after 4 p.m. **Duration of show** About 20 minutes.

DESCRIPTION AND COMMENTS *Shrek 4-D* is based on characters from the hit movie *Shrek*. A preshow presents the villain from the movie, Lord Farquaad, as he appears on various screens to describe his posthumous plan to reclaim his lost bride, Princess Fiona, who married Shrek. The plan is posthumous since Lord Farquaad ostensibly died in the movie, and it's his ghost making the plans, but never mind. Guests then move into the main theater, don their 3-D glasses, and recline in seats equipped with "tactile transducers" and "pneumatic air propulsion and water spray nodules capable of both vertical and horizontal motion." As the 3-D film plays, guests are also subjected to smells relevant to the onscreen action (oh boy).

Technicalities aside, *Shrek* is a real winner. It's irreverent, frantic, laugh-out-loud funny, and iconoclastic. Concerning the latter, the film takes a good poke at Disney with Pinocchio, the Three Little Pigs, and Tinker Bell (among others) all sucked into the mayhem. The film quality and 3-D effects are great, and like the feature film, it's sweet without being sappy. Plus, in contrast to Disney's *Honey, I Shrunk the Audience* or *It's Tough to Be a Bug!*, *Shrek 4-D* doesn't generally frighten children under 7 years of age.

TOURING TIPS Universal claims they can move 2,400 guests an hour through *Shrek 4-D*. If true, that should keep things moving efficiently. Still, expect big crowds. Try to see *Shrek* before 11 a.m.

Studio Tour ★★★★½

APPEAL BY AGE	PRESCHOOL ★★★	GRADE SCHOOL ★★★★	TEENS ★★★★
YOUNG ADULTS ★★★★		OVER 30 ★★★★	SENIORS ★★★★

What it is Indoor-outdoor tram tour of soundstages and back lot. **Scope and scale** Headliner. **When to go** After experiencing the other rides. **Duration of ride** About 42 minutes. **Loading speed** Fast.

Scary

Loud

DESCRIPTION AND COMMENTS The Studio Tour is the centerpiece of Universal Studios Hollywood and, at 42 minutes, is one of the longest attractions in American theme parks. The tour departs from the tram tour boarding facility to the *right* of Back to the Future and down the escalator. (Please note that there is also an escalator to the left of *Back to the Future*, so don't get confused.)

The tour circulates through the various street scenes, lagoons, special-effects venues, and storage areas of Universal's back lot. The tram passes several soundstages where current films and television shows such as *CSI* and *Crossing Jordan* are in production and actually enters three soundstages where action inspired by *Earthquake*, *The Mummy*, and *King Kong* is presented. The Studio Tour was greatly improved in 2006 with a robotic car chase from *The Fast and the Furious: Tokyo Drift* and the addition of sets and film-making demonstrations from *King Kong* and *War of the Worlds*. Other famous sets visited include those from *Psycho*, *Jaws*, *Back to the Future*, and *The Grinch Who Stole Christmas*. A simulated flash flood, long a highlight of the tour, was enhanced by increasing the volume of water used.

Universal distributes some of the most indecipherable press releases in the entertainment business. Here's how they described the aforementioned robotic car chase:

Utilizing advanced robotics and state-of-the-cinematic-art computer-generated pre-visualization technology, the new tram feature will thrust guests into close-up range of the pulse-pounding, rubber-burning underground world of street racing. Robotic racers will dazzle guests with an awesome "in your face" display of explosive action via large scale remote control simulation, then surprise and enthrall with a dexterous automotive dance demonstration of intricate programming set to a hip-hop beat.

Now wouldn't you be willing to pay good money just to get a peek at whoever wrote that?

As a great enhancement, all trams are equipped with video monitors showing clips from actual movies that demonstrate how the various sets and soundstages were used in creating the films.

The great thing about the Studio Tour is that you see everything without leaving the tram—essentially experiencing four or five major attractions with only one wait.

TOURING TIPS Though the wait to board might appear long, do not be discouraged. Each tram carries several hundred people and departures are frequent, so the line moves quickly. We recommend taking the tram tour after experiencing the other rides plus the two theater-soundstage presentations on the Lower Lot.

Including your wait to board and the duration of the tour, you will easily invest an hour or more at this attraction. Remember to take a restroom break before queuing up. Though the ride as a whole is gentle, some segments may induce vertigo or motion sickness—especially "The Curse of the Mummy's Tomb," inspired by *The Mummy* and adapted from the old avalanche-effect section of the tour. Finally, be aware that several of the scenes may frighten small children.

Terminator 2: 3-D ★★★★★

APPEAL BY AGE	PRESCHOOL ★★★	GRADE SCHOOL ★★★★★	TEENS ★★★★★
YOUNG ADULTS ★★★★★		OVER 30 ★★★★★	SENIORS ★★★★

What it is 3-D thriller mixed-media presentation. **Scope and scale** Super-headliner. **When to go** Just after opening or after 4:30 p.m. **Special comments** Furiously paced high-tech experience; not to be missed; our favorite California attraction; very intense for some preschoolers and grade-schoolers. **Duration of presentation** 20 minutes, including an 8-minute preshow. **Probable waiting time** 20–40 minutes.

Dark   Loud   Scary

DESCRIPTION AND COMMENTS The Terminator "cop" from *Terminator 2* morphs to life and battles Arnold Schwarzenegger's T-100 cyborg character. For those who missed the *Terminator* flicks, here's the plot: A bad robot arrives from the future to kill a nice boy. Another bad robot (who has been reprogrammed to be good) pops up at the same time to save the boy. The bad robot chases the boy and the rehabilitated robot while menacing the audience in the process.

The attraction, like the films, is all action, and you really don't need to understand much. What's interesting is that it uses 3-D film and a theater full of sophisticated technology to integrate the real with the imaginary. Images seem to move in and out of the film, not only in the manner of traditional 3-D, but also in actuality. Remove your 3-D glasses momentarily and you'll see that the guy on the motorcycle is actually onstage.

We've watched this type of presentation evolve, pioneered by Disney's *Captain EO; Honey, I Shrunk the Audience;* and *Muppet Vision 3-D. Terminator 2: 3-D,* however, goes way beyond lasers, with moving theater seats, blasts of hot air, and spraying mist. It creates a multidimensional space that blurs the boundary between entertainment and reality. Is it seamless? Not quite, but it's close. We rank *Terminator 2: 3-D* as not to be missed and consider it the absolute best theme-park theater attraction in the United States. If *Terminator 2: 3-D* is the only attraction you see at Universal Studios Hollywood, you'll have received your money's worth.

TOURING TIPS The 700-seat theater changes audiences about every 19 minutes. Even so, because the show is very popular, expect to wait about 25 to 40 minutes. The attraction, opposite the Hollywood Globe Theater and behind the Universal House of Horrors, receives much traffic during the morning and early afternoon. By about 4 p.m., however, lines diminish somewhat. We recommend seeing the show first thing after the park opens or holding off until afternoon. If you can't stay until late afternoon, see the show first thing in the morning. Families with young children should know that the violence characteristic of the *Terminator* movies is largely absent from the attraction. It has suspense and action but not much blood and guts.

Universal House of Horrors ★★★

APPEAL BY AGE	PRESCHOOL –	GRADE SCHOOL ★★★	TEENS ★★★½
YOUNG ADULTS ★★★½		OVER 30 ★★★	SENIORS ★★½

What it is A fun-house–style walk-through of scenes based on classic Universal horror films, incorporating robotics, hydraulics, real people, smoke, and mirrors. **Scope and scale** Minor attraction. **When to go** Anytime. **Special comments** Not suitable for age 10 and under. **Duration of presentation** Varies. **Probable waiting time** 3–5 minutes.

Dark

Loud

Scary

DESCRIPTION AND COMMENTS This attraction is an extremely elaborate horror maze. It's quite similar to the walk-through "haunted houses" that spring up all over the country for Halloween. Basically, you walk in near darkness through the tight, winding corridors of Dracula's castle, occasionally coming upon a large set from the Van Helsing vampire-killing film (including a 50-foot bridge overlooking Frankenstein's monster while he enjoys a little electroshock therapy). As you pick your way through the dark, there are lots of gruesome sights, disorienting devices like mirrors, and worst of all, live people springing out of dark corners and cubby holes to startle you. This last factor makes the House of Horror a bad bet for kids under 10 years of age. If you don't like being startled but really want to see the attraction, follow some teenage or college girls through. The leaping, growling, menacing ghouls will expend lots of extra energy on the girls and be in a state of relative depletion when you pass through.

TOURING TIPS The Universal House of Horrors is located very near the main entrance to the park. It doesn't last long (as the length of the experience depends on how badly you want out), and it can be gotten out of the way quickly. The only time things slow down is when a herd of quests clogs the entrance right after the adjacent *Terminator 2: 3-D* show lets out.

Waterworld ★★★★

APPEAL BY AGE	PRESCHOOL ★★★	GRADE SCHOOL ★★★★	TEENS ★★★★
YOUNG ADULTS ★★★★		OVER 30 ★★★½	SENIORS ★★★½

What it is Arena show featuring simulated stunt-scene filming. **Scope and scale** Major attraction. **When to go** After experiencing all of the rides and the tram tour. **Special comments** Well done. **Duration of presentation** 15 minutes. **Probable waiting time** 15 minutes.

DESCRIPTION AND COMMENTS Drawn from the film *Waterworld*, this outdoor theater presentation features stunts and special effects performed on and around a small man-made lagoon. The action involves Jet Skis and various other craft, and of course, a lot of explosions and falling

Thumbs Up for the Whole Family

from high places into the water. Fast-paced and well adapted to the theater, the production is in many ways more compelling than the film that inspired it.

TOURING TIPS Wait until you have experienced all of the rides and the tram tour before checking out *Waterworld*. Because it is located near the main entrance, most performances are sold out. Arrive at the theater at least 15 minutes before the showtime listed in the daily entertainment schedule.

LOWER-LOT ATTRACTIONS

Backdraft ★★★★

APPEAL BY AGE	PRESCHOOL ★★★½	GRADE SCHOOL ★★★★	TEENS ★★★★
YOUNG ADULTS ★★★★		OVER 30 ★★★★	SENIORS ★★★★

What it is A multisequence mini-course on special effects. **Scope and scale** Major attraction. **When to go** After you have experienced all of the rides. **Special comments** Sugar-coated education. **Duration of presentation** About 14 minutes. **Probable waiting time** 20 minutes.

DESCRIPTION AND COMMENTS Guests move from theater to theater in this mini-course attraction. The presentation draws its inspiration from the movie *Backdraft*, which is about firefighters. Segments show the use of miniatures, demonstrate blue matte filming techniques, and discuss the precautions necessary for filming explosions and fire. The finale involves a "hot set" where a *Backdraft* scene involving a fire in a chemical warehouse is re-created. Consistently high-tech, the entire presentation is nicely organized, well paced, and unexpectedly informative. In addition to learning something about how movies are made, you will gain some insight into the origin of fires and how firefighters extinguish them.

TOURING TIPS See *Backdraft* after you've ridden all the rides on your must-see list.

Jurassic Park: **The Ride** ★★★★

APPEAL BY AGE	PRESCHOOL ★★★	GRADE SCHOOL ★★★½	TEENS ★★★½
YOUNG ADULTS ★★★★		OVER 30 ★★★★	SENIORS ★★★★

What it is Indoor-outdoor adventure ride based on the movie *Jurassic Park*. **Scope and scale** Super-headliner. **When to go** Before 10:30 a.m. **Special comments** 46" minimum-height requirement. **Duration of ride** 6 minutes. **Loading speed** Fast.

Scary

Rough

Wet

Lose Things

DESCRIPTION AND COMMENTS Guests board boats for a water tour of Jurassic Park. Everything is tranquil as the tour begins; the boat floats among large herbivorous dinosaurs such as *Brontosaurus* and *Stegosaurus*. Then word is received that some of the carnivores have escaped their enclosure, and the tour boat is accidentally diverted into Jurassic Park's water-treatment facility. Here the boat and its riders are menaced by an assortment of hungry meat-eaters led by the ubiquitous *T. rex*. At the climactic moment, the boat and its passengers escape by dropping over a waterfall.

Jurassic Park is impressive in its scale, but the number of dinosaurs is a little disappointing. The big herbivores are given short shrift to set up the plot for the carnivore encounter, which leads to floating around in what looks like a brewery. When the carnivores make their appearance, however, they definitely get your attention. The final drop down a three-story flume to safety is a dandy.

TOURING TIPS You can get very wet on this ride. Even before the boat leaves the dock you must sit in the puddles left by previous riders. Once the boat is under way, there's a little splashing but nothing major until the big drop at the end of the ride. When you hit the bottom, enough water will cascade into the boat to extinguish a three-alarm fire. Our recommendation is to bring along an extra-large plastic garbage bag and (cutting holes for your head and arms) wear it like a sack dress. If you forget to bring a garbage bag, you can purchase a Universal Studios poncho for about $8.

Young children must endure a double whammy on this ride. First, they are stalked by giant, salivating (sometimes spitting) reptiles, and then they are catapulted over the falls. Wait until your kids are fairly stalwart before you spring *Jurassic Park* on them.

Jurassic Park stays jammed most of the day. Ride early in the morning after Revenge of the Mummy.

Lucy—A Tribute ★★★

APPEAL BY AGE	PRESCHOOL ★	GRADE SCHOOL ★	TEENS ★★
YOUNG ADULTS ★★★		OVER 30 ★★★	SENIORS ★★★

What it is Walk-through tribute to Lucille Ball. **Scope and scale** Diversion. **When**

to go Anytime. **Special comments** A touching remembrance. **Duration of experience** About 10 minutes. **Probable waiting time** None.

DESCRIPTION AND COMMENTS   The life and career of comedienne Lucille Ball are spotlighted, with emphasis on her role as Lucy Ricardo in the long-running television series *I Love Lucy*. Well designed and informative, the exhibit succeeds admirably in recalling the talent and temperament of the beloved redhead.

TOURING TIPS   See Lucy during the hot, crowded midafternoon, or after you have seen all of the other Lower Lot attractions. Adults could easily stay 15 to 30 minutes. Children, however, get restless after a few minutes.

Revenge of the Mummy   ★★★★

APPEAL BY AGE	PRESCHOOL –	GRADE SCHOOL ★★★½	TEENS ★★★★½
YOUNG ADULTS ★★★★½		OVER 30 ★★★★	SENIORS ★★★½

What it is High-tech dark ride. **Scope and scale** Super-headliner. **When to go** The first hour the park is open or after 4 p.m. **Special comments** Wear your asbestos: hot! **Duration of ride** About 2½ minutes.

Dark

Scary

Rough

Lose Things

Motion Sickness

DESCRIPTION AND COMMENTS   Revenge of the Mummy replaced the now-closed *E.T.* attraction in spring 2004. It's kinda hard to wrap your mind around the actual attraction, but it pretty much lives up to the Universal press release, though the press release is generally incomprehensible. Here, quoting that press release, are some of the things you can look forward to: "authentic Egyptian catacombs; high-velocity show immersion system [we think this has something to do with very fast baptism]; magnet-propulsion launch wave system; a "Brain Fire" [!] that hovers [over you] with temperatures soaring to 2,000 degrees Fahrenheit; and canoptic jars containing grisly remains."

Of course the art of the press release is to create allure and excitement without actually spilling the beans. Actually, Revenge of the Mummy is an indoor dark ride based on the *Mummy* flicks, where guests fight off "deadly curses and vengeful creatures" while flying through Egyptian tombs and other spooky places on a high-tech roller coaster. The special effects are cutting-edge, integrating the best technology from such attractions as *Terminator 2: 3-D, Fear Factor,* and Back to the Future, with a propulsion system and visuals that are way cool.

The queuing area serves to establish the story line: You're in a group touring a set from the *Mummy* films when you enter a tomb where the fantasy world of film gives way to the real thing. Along the way you are warned about a possible curse. The visuals are rich and compelling as the queue makes its way to the loading area where you board a sort of clunky, Jeep-looking vehicle. The ride begins as a slow, very elaborate dark ride, passing through various chambers including one where flesh-eating scarab beetles descend on you. Suddenly your vehicle stops and then drops backward and rotates. Here's where the aforementioned "magnet-propulsion launch wave system" comes in. In more ordinary language, this means you're shot at high speed up the first hill of the roller-coaster part of the ride. We don't want to ruin your experience by divulging too much, but the coaster part of the ride offers its own panoply of surprises. We will tell you this, however: there are no barrel rolls or any upside-down stuff. And though it's a wild ride by anyone's definition, the emphasis remains as much on the visuals, robotics, and special effects as on the ride itself.

TOURING TIPS Revenge of the Mummy has a very low riders-per-hour capacity for the park's top draw. Your only prayer for a tolerable wait is to be on hand when the park opens and sprint immediately to the Mummy. If you can ride Space Mountain without getting sick, you should be fine on this. Switching off is available.

Special Effects Stages ★★★

APPEAL BY AGE	PRESCHOOL ★★½		GRADE SCHOOL ★★★		TEENS ★★★½
YOUNG ADULTS ★★★½		OVER 30 ★★★		SENIORS ★★★½	

What it is A three-part mini-course on special effects, filming action sequences, and sound effects. **Scope and scale** Major attraction. **When to go** Anytime. **Special comments** Predictable, but still interesting; may frighten young children. **Duration of presentation** 30 minutes. **Probable waiting time** 15 minutes.

DESCRIPTION AND COMMENTS Guests view a presentation on special effects, and audience members participate in a demonstration showing how actors are filmed against a blue or green screen in the studio, then superimposed onto film shot on location. Next, the audience is ushered to an adjoining stage to view a presentation on makeup and movie monsters. The final destination is a soundstage, in which the audience views and participates in a presentation on Foley art—aka sound effects—culminating in a movie scene based on the film *Shrek*.

TOURING TIPS This high-capacity attraction is in the most remote corner of the park, which usually means a short wait. The daily entertainment schedule lists the Special Effects Stages show as running continuously; it does not. It operates on a fixed performance schedule that is posted (as of this writing) nowhere except at the attraction.

UNIVERSAL STUDIOS HOLLYWOOD *for* YOUNG CHILDREN

WE DO NOT RECOMMEND Universal Studios Hollywood for preschoolers. Of 11 major attractions, all but 2 (*Hollywood Animal Actors* and *Shrek 4-D*) have the potential for flipping out sensitive little ones. See the Small-child Fright-potential Chart on page 338.

LIVE ENTERTAINMENT
at UNIVERSAL STUDIOS HOLLYWOOD

THE THEATER AND AMPHITHEATER ATTRACTIONS operate according to the entertainment schedule available with handout park maps. The number of daily performances of each show varies from as few as three a day during less busy times of year to as many as ten a day during the summer and holiday periods. Blues Brothers impersonators offer a high-energy show in the Upper Lot near the front entrance on weekends. The instrumental track is, unfortunately, prerecorded, but the show is a spirit lifter nonetheless. Also in the Upper Lot, look for the Doo Wop Singers belting out 1950s and 1960s harmonies near Mel's Diner.

DINING *at* UNIVERSAL STUDIOS HOLLYWOOD

THE COUNTER-SERVICE FOOD at Universal Studios runs the gamut from burgers and hot dogs to pizza, fried chicken, crepes, and Mexican specialties. We rank most selections marginally better than fast food. Prices are comparable to those at Disneyland.

If you are looking for full-service dining, try **Wolfgang Puck's Cafe, Cafe Tu Tu Tango,** or the **Hard Rock Cafe** in the Universal CityWalk just outside the park entrance. Our favorite in the park is the **Hollywood Grill** burger joint across from *Waterworld.* If you leave the park for lunch, be sure to have your hand stamped for reentry.

UNIVERSAL STUDIOS HOLLYWOOD ONE-DAY TOURING PLAN

THIS PLAN IS FOR GROUPS OF ALL SIZES and ages and includes thrill rides that may induce motion sickness or get you wet. If the plan calls for you to experience an attraction that does not interest you, proceed to the next step. The plan calls for minimal backtracking.

Before You Go

1. Call ☎ 818-622-3801 the day before your visit for the official opening time. If you can't get through, call ☎ 818-622-3735 or 818-622-3750. On all numbers, press 4 for a live attendant.

Universal Studios Hollywood Small-child Fright-potential Chart

Backdraft Intense re-creation of fire terrifies many preschoolers.

Back to the Future: **The Ride** Intense, rough thrill ride. Potentially terrifying for people of any age.

Fear Factor Live Gross, loud, and frenetic, the show can freak out guests of any age.

Hollywood Animal Actors Not frightening in any way.

Jurassic Park: **The Ride** Intense water-flume ride. Potentially terrifying for people of any age.

Nickelodeon Blast Zone Nature of the attraction encourages aggressive play. Getting soaked is a definite possibility at the Nickelodeon Splash section of the Zone.

Revenge of the Mummy Scares guests of all ages.

Shrek 4-D Special effects may frighten preschoolers.

Special Effects Stages Some intense special effects. Shows the bloody shower scene from *Psycho*.

Studio Tour Certain parts of the tour are too frightening and too intense for many preschoolers.

Terminator 2: 3-D Extremely intense and potentially frightening for visitors of any age.

Universal House of Horrors Frightens guests of all ages.

Waterworld Fighting, gunplay, and explosions may frighten children age 4 and under.

2. If you have young children in your party, consult the Universal Studios Hollywood Small-child Fright-potential Chart (above).

At the Park

1. On the day of your visit, eat breakfast and arrive at Universal Studios Hollywood 20 minutes before opening time. Park, buy your admission, and wait at the turnstiles. If you drive, you will save some time by dropping a member of your party off at the front entrance to purchase tickets while you park.

2. At the turnstile, ask an attendant whether any rides or shows are closed that day. Adjust the touring plan accordingly.

3. When the park opens, head for the back left section of the Upper Lot. Take the escalators to the Lower Lot and make a hard right to Revenge of the Mummy.

4. Exiting the Mummy, experience *Jurassic Park* across the plaza.

5. Skip the other Lower Lot attractions for now. Return to the Upper Lot, bearing left to *Back to the Future.* Ride.

6. Next see *Shrek 4-D,* also in the Upper Lot.

7. Head toward the park entrance, bearing right before the turnstile, to *Terminator 2: 3-D.* Note that *Terminator* sometimes runs back-to-back shows and at other times schedules shows at specific times as detailed in the daily entertainment schedule.

8. Our apologies for all the walking, but the walking saves a lot of time standing in line. Return to the Lower Lot and see *Backdraft* and the Special Effects Stages. Check the daily entertainment schedule for performance times before you make the long trek.

9. If you are a Lucille Ball fan, check out the tribute to Lucy before you depart the Lower Lot. Return to the Upper Lot.

10. Check your daily entertainment schedule for *Fear Factor Live, Waterworld,* and *Hollywood Animal Actors* showtimes. Plan the rest of your schedule around seeing these shows. Note that you should arrive at the theater 30 minutes before showtime for *Fear Factor* and *Waterworld* and 20 minutes before *Hollywood Animal Actors.*

11. With your show schedule in mind, decide when you'd like to eat lunch and when you'd like to take the Studio Tour. Allocate an hour and 10 minutes for the tour (counting the 45-minute tour, coming and going, and waiting to load).

12. If you have time to kill between stage shows, check out the Universal House of Horrors and the Blues Brothers show. If you have children 12 years and younger, try the Nickelodeon Blast Zone play area.

13. This concludes the touring plan. Spend the remainder of your day revisiting your favorite attractions or inspecting sets and street scenes you may have missed. Also, check your daily entertainment schedule for live performances that interest you.

APPENDIX

READERS' QUESTIONS *to* *the* AUTHOR

QUESTION:

When you do your research, are you admitted to the park for free? Do the Disney people know you are there?

ANSWER:

We pay the regular admission, and usually the Disney people do not know we are on site. Both in and out of Disneyland, we pay for our own meals and lodging.

QUESTION:

How often is the Unofficial Guide *revised?*

ANSWER:

We publish a new edition once a year but make corrections every time we go to press.

QUESTION:

I have an older edition of the Unofficial Guide. *How much of the information in it is still correct?*

ANSWER:

Veteran travel writers will acknowledge that 5 to 8% of the information in a guidebook is out of date by the time it comes off the press! Disneyland is always changing. If you are using an old edition of the *Unofficial Guide,* the descriptions of attractions existing when the guide was published should still be generally accurate. Many other things, however, particularly the touring plans and the hotel and restaurant reviews, change with every edition. Finally, and obviously, older editions of the *Unofficial Guide* do not include new attractions or developments.

QUESTION:

Do you write each new edition from scratch?

ANSWER:

We do not. With a destination the size of Disneyland, it's hard enough keeping up with what is new. Moreover, we put great effort into communicating the most salient and useful information in the clearest possible language. If an attraction or hotel has not changed, we are very reluctant to tinker with its coverage for the sake of freshening up the writing.

QUESTION:

Do you stay at Disneyland hotels? If not, where do you stay?

ANSWER:

We do stay at Disneyland-area hotels from time to time, usually after a renovation or management change. Since we began writing about Disneyland in 1984, we have stayed in more than 33 different properties in various locations around Anaheim.

QUESTION:

How many people have you interviewed or surveyed for your age-group ratings on the attractions?

ANSWER:

Since the publication of the first edition of the *Unofficial Guide* in 1985, we have interviewed or surveyed more than 13,650 Disneyland patrons. Even with such a large sample, however, we continue to have difficulty with certain age groups. Specifically, we love to hear from seniors concerning their experiences with Splash Mountain, Big Thunder Mountain Railroad, Space Mountain, the Matterhorn Bobsleds, Star Tours, Indiana Jones, and Disney's California Adventure attractions.

QUESTION:

How are your age-group ratings determined? I am 42 years old. During Star Tours, I was quite worried about hurting my back. If the senior-citizens rating is determined only by those brave enough to ride, it will skew the results.

ANSWER:

The reader makes a good point. Unfortunately, it's impossible to develop a rating unless the guest (of any age group) has actually experienced the attraction. So yes, all age-group ratings are derived exclusively from members of that age group who have experienced the attraction. Health problems, such as a bad back, however, can affect guests of any age, and Disney provides more-than-ample warnings on attractions that warrant such admonitions. But if you are in good health, our ratings will give you a sense of how much others your age enjoyed the attraction.

QUESTION:

I laughed at the "When to go" suggestions [for the attractions]. Too many were before 10 a.m. and after 5 p.m. What are we supposed to do between 10 a.m. and 5 p.m.?

ANSWER:

Our best advice is to go back to your hotel and take a nice nap. More in keeping with the spirit of your question, however, the attractions with the shortest waits between 10 a.m. and 5 p.m. are as follows:

DISNEYLAND PARK	DISNEY'S CALIFORNIA ADVENTURE
Enchanted Tiki Room	Boudin Bakery
Fantasyland Theatre	Bountiful Valley Farm
Innoventions	Disney Animation
It's a Small World	Golden Dreams
Mark Twain Riverboat	It's Tough to Be a Bug!
Sailing Ship Columbia	Mission Tortilla Factory
Tom Sawyer Island	Redwood Creek Challenge Trail
Disneyland: The First 50 Years	

QUESTION:

I have heard that when there are two lines to an attraction, the left line is faster. Is this true?

ANSWER:

In general, no. We have tested this theory many times and usually have not gained an advantage of even 90 seconds by getting in one line versus another. What *does* occasionally occur, however, is after a second line has *just been opened,* guests ignore the new line and persist in standing in the established line. As a rule of thumb, if you encounter a two-line waiting configuration with no barrier to entry for either and one of the lines is conspicuously less populated than the other, get in it.

AND FINALLY . . .

A reader from Raleigh, North Carolina, has an ax to grind:

Really annoying were the inconsiderate idiots taking flash pictures on the dark rides. ("Look, there's Captain Jack Sparrow!" *FLASH* "Ooh, look, there he is again!" *FLASH*) And that was with a disposable camera, like they're really going to get a good picture in the first place. I was really hoping Tigger would pop out and slap them.

ACCOMMODATIONS INDEX

RESTAURANT INDEX

SUBJECT INDEX

All attractions are listed alphabetically as well as by park or "land." California Adventure and Universal Studios Hollywood attractions are designated by (DCA) and (USH), respectively; all others are in Disneyland Park.

One-day Plan for Adults

Disneyland

1. Arrive at least 40 minutes before opening. Line up at Gate 13 and give all admission passes to one person.
2. Dispatch this person to Space Mountain to obtain FASTPASSes.
3. Everyone regroup in line and ride *Finding Nemo Submarine Voyage* (see page 272).
4. Ride the Matterhorn Bobsleds.
5. Go to Fantasyland and ride Peter Pan's Flight.
6. Return to Tomorrowland and ride Buzz Lightyear.
7. Ride Space Mountain using your FASTPASSes.
8. Enter Frontierland and ride Big Thunder Mountain Railroad.
9. Go to Critter Country and Splash Mountain. Obtain FASTPASSes.
10. Ride the Many Adventures of Winnie the Pooh.
11. Go to Adventureland and ride Indiana Jones.
12. Take the Jungle Cruise.
13. Go to New Orleans Square and experience Pirates of the Caribbean.
14. Tour The Haunted Mansion.

15. Have lunch and catch the show at the Golden Horseshoe Saloon in Frontierland.
16. In Frontierland, ride either the Sailing Ship *Columbia* or the *Mark Twain* Riverboat.
17. Ride Splash Mountain using your FASTPASSes.
18. Return to Adventureland and see the show at the *Enchanted Tiki Room*.
19. Explore Tarzan's Treehouse.
20. Return to Tomorrowland and ride Star Tours.
21. See *Honey, I Shrunk the Audience*.
22. Take Disneyland Railroad from the Tomorrowland Station to the Fantasyland Station.
23. Ride It's a Small World in Fantasyland.
24. Sample any rides you missed earlier.
25. Check the *Times Guide* for parades, fireworks, and *Fantasmic!*
26. Visit any attractions you may have missed earlier.
27. See *Disneyland: The First 50 Years* or *Great Moments with Mr. Lincoln.*

Author's Select One-day Plan

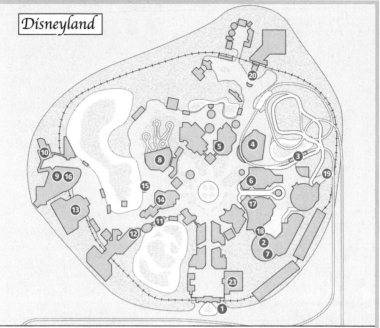

Disneyland

1. Arrive at the park at least 40 minutes before opening. Line up at Gate 13 and entrust all of your admission passes to one person.
2. Dispatch this person to Space Mountain to obtain FASTPASSes.
3. Regroup in line at *Finding Nemo* Submarine Voyage (see page 272).
4. Ride the Matterhorn Bobsleds.
5. Go to Fantasyland and ride Peter Pan's Flight.
6. Return to Tomorrowland and ride Buzz Lightyear.
7. Ride Space Mountain using your FASTPASSes.
8. Enter Frontierland and ride Big Thunder Mountain Railroad.
9. Head for Critter Country and Splash Mountain. Obtain FASTPASSes.
10. Ride the Many Adventures of Winnie the Pooh.
11. Head to Adventureland and ride Indiana Jones.
12. Continue to New Orleans Square and experience Pirates of the Caribbean.
13. Tour The Haunted Mansion.
14. Have lunch and see the show at the Golden Horseshoe Saloon in Frontierland.
15. Ride the Sailing Ship *Columbia* or the *Mark Twain* Riverboat.
16. Ride Splash Mountain using your FASTPASSes.
17. Return to Tomorrowland and ride Star Tours.
18. See *Honey, I Shrunk the Audience.*
19. Take Disneyland Railroad from Tomorrowland Station to Fantasyland Station.
20. In Fantasyland, ride It's A Small World.
21. Check the *Times Guide* for parades, fireworks, and *Fantasmic!*
22. Visit any attractions you may have missed earlier.
23. See *Disneyland: The First 50 Years* or *Great Moments with Mr. Lincoln.*

Dumbo-or-Die-in-a-Day Plan

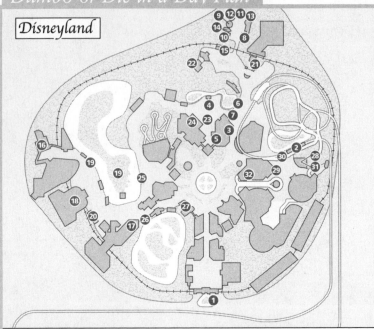

Disneyland

1. Arrive 40 minutes before the official opening time and line up in front of Gate 13.
2. Go to Tomorrowland and ride *Finding Nemo* Submarine Voyage.
3. Ride Alice In Wonderland.
4. Go to Fantasyland and ride Dumbo.
5. Ride Peter Pan's Flight.
6. Ride the Storybook Land Canal Boats or Casey Jr. Circus Train.
7. Ride the Mad Tea Party.
8. Go to Mickey's Toontown, try Roger Rabbit's Car Toon Spin.
9. Ride Gadget's Go Coaster.
10. Check out Goofy's Playhouse.
11. Tour Mickey's House and visit Mickey in his dressing room.
12. See Chip 'n' Dale's Treehouse.
13. Tour Minnie's House.
14. Check out Donald's Boat tied up next to Goofy's Playhouse.
15. Take Disneyland Railroad from Toontown Station to New Orleans Square.
16. Go to Critter Country and experience Winnie the Pooh.
17. Return to New Orleans Square and see Pirates of The Caribbean.
18. Experience the Haunted Mansion.
19. Take a raft to Tom Sawyer Island and explore.
20. Take Disneyland Railroad from New Orleans Square Station to Fantasyland.
21. In Fantasyland, ride It's a Small World.
22. Visit the Disney Princess Fantasy Faire at the Fantasyland Theatre.
23. Ride the King Arthur Carrousel.
24. Ride Pinocchio's Daring Journey.
25. Go to Frontierland and ride the *Mark Twain* Riverboat or the Sailing Ship *Columbia*.
26. Go to Adventureland and explore Tarzan's Treehouse.
27. See the *Enchanted Tiki Room* show.
28. Go to Tomorrowland and obtain a FASTPASS for Autopia.
29. Check out the Jedi Training Academy at the Tomorrowland Terrace.
30. Take the Disneyland monorail for a round-trip ride.
31. Ride Autopia using your FASTPASS.
32. Obtain a FASTPASS for Buzz Lightyear either before or after riding Autopia.
33. Revisit favorites or see other attractions you missed. Check your daily entertainment schedule for parades, Fantasyland Theatre productions, or other live entertainment.

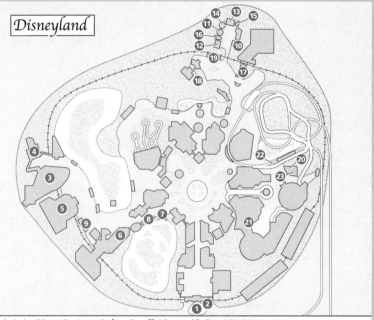

Two-day Plan for Adults with Children: Day One

Disneyland

1. Arrive 30 to 40 minutes before the official opening time.
2. Line up in front of Gate 13.
3. Go to Critter Country and ride Splash Mountain.
4. Ride The Many Adventures of Winnie the Pooh.
5. Head to New Orleans Square and experience The Haunted Mansion.
6. Ride Pirates of the Caribbean.
7. Go to Adventureland and ride the Jungle Cruise.
8. Ride Indiana Jones.
9. Go from the Frontierland/New Orleans Square Station to the Fantasyland/Toontown Station on the Disneyland Railroad.
10. In Mickey's Toontown, try Roger Rabbit's Car Toon Spin.
11. Ride Gadget's Go Coaster.
12. Let off some steam in Goofy's Playhouse.
13. Tour Mickey's House and visit Mickey in his dressing room.
14. Enjoy Chip 'n' Dale's Treehouse.
15. Tour Minnie's House.
16. Check out Donald's Boat, tied up next to Goofy's Playhouse.
17. Go to Fantasyland and ride It's a Small World.
18. Visit the Disney Princess Fantasy Faire at the Fantasyland Theatre.
19. Take the Disneyland Railroad to Tomorrowland.
20. In Tomorrowland, obtain a FASTPASS for Autopia.
21. Enjoy a performance of *Honey, I Shrunk the Audience*.
22. Take the monorail for a round trip.
23. Return with your FASTPASS to ride Autopia.
24. Revisit favorites or see other attractions you missed. Check your daily entertainment schedule for parades, Fantasyland Theatre productions, or other live entertainment that might interest you. Return after 7 p.m. for a parade and *Fantasmic!*

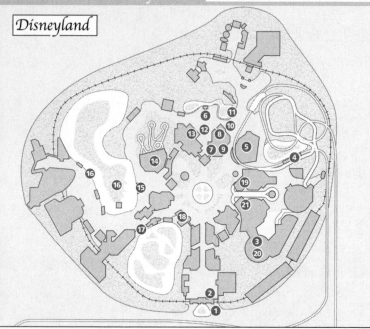

Two-day Plan for Adults with Children: Day Two

Disneyland

1. Arrive at the park at least 40 minutes before opening and line up at Gate 13.
2. Give all your admission passes to one person.
3. Dispatch the person with the passes to Space Mountain to obtain FASTPASSes.
4. Regroup in line at *Finding Nemo Submarine Voyage* (see page 272).
5. Ride the Matterhorn Bobsleds.
6. Go to Fantasyland and ride Dumbo.
7. Ride Peter Pan's Flight.
8. Ride Mr. Toad's Wild Ride.
9. Ride Alice in Wonderland.
10. Visit the Mad Tea Party.
11. Ride the Storybook Land Canal Boats.
12. Ride the King Arthur Carrousel.
13. Experience Pinocchio's Daring Journey.
14. Go to Frontierland and ride Big Thunder Mountain.

15. Cruise on the *Mark Twain* Riverboat or the Sailing Ship *Columbia*.
16. Explore Tom Sawyer Island.
17. Go to Adventureland and explore Tarzan's Treehouse.
18. See the *Enchanted Tiki Room* show.
19. Return to Tomorrowland and ride Buzz Lightyear.
20. Ride Space Mountain using your FASTPASSes (your FASTPASS will still be valid).
21. Ride Star Tours.
22. Revisit favorites or see attractions you missed. Check your daily entertainment schedule for parades, Fantasyland Theatre productions, or other live entertainment that might interest you. Return after 7 p.m. for a parade and *Fantasmic!*

Two-day Plan A: Day One

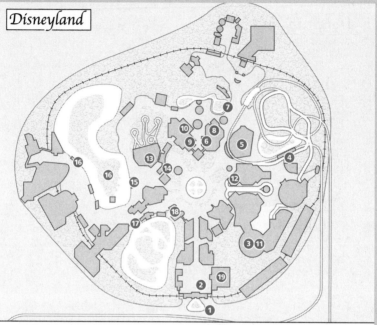

Disneyland

1. Arrive 40 minutes before opening and line up at Gate 13.
2. Give all of your admission passes to one person.
3. Dispatch this person to Space Mountain to obtain FASTPASSes.
4. Regroup in line at *Finding Nemo Submarine Voyage* (see page 272).
5. Ride the Matterhorn Bobsleds.
6. Go to Fantasyland and ride Peter Pan's Flight.
7. Ride the Storybook Land Canal Boats.
8. Ride Mr. Toad's Wild Ride.
9. Ride Snow White's Scary Adventures.
10. Ride Pinocchio's Daring Journey.
11. Return to Tomorrowland. Ride Space Mountain using your FASTPASS.
12. Ride Buzz Lightyear.
13. Go to Frontierland and ride Big Thunder Mountain Railroad.
14. Try Rancho del Zocalo for lunch.
15. In Frontierland, ride the *Mark Twain Riverboat* or the Sailing Ship *Columbia*.
16. Take a raft to Tom Sawyer Island.
17. Go to Adventureland and tour Tarzan's Treehouse.
18. See the *Enchanted Tiki Room* show.
19. Return to Main Street and see *Disneyland: The First 50 Years*.
20. Revisit favorites or see attractions you missed earlier. Check out any parades or live performances that interest you.

Two-day Plan A: Day Two

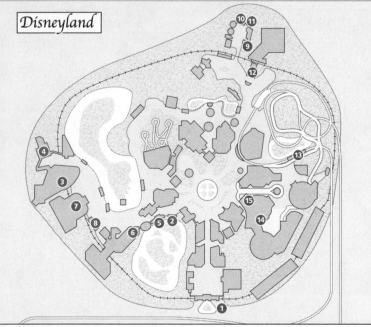

1. Arrive 40 minutes before the official opening time and line up in front of Gate 13.
2. Go to Adventureland and ride Indiana Jones.
3. Go to Critter Country and ride Splash Mountain.
4. Ride The Many Aventures of Winnie the Pooh.
5. Return to Adventureland and ride the Jungle Cruise.
6. Go to New Orleans Square and ride Pirates of the Caribbean.
7. Experience The Haunted Mansion.
8. Take the Disneyland Railroad to the Mickey's Toontown/Fantasyland Station.
9. Go to Mickey's Toontown and ride Roger Rabbit's Car Toon Spin.
10. Tour Mickey's House and visit Mickey in his dressing room.
11. Do the same at Minnie's House.
12. Go to Fantasyland and ride It's a Small World.
13. Go to Downtown Disney on the monorail for lunch. Have your hand stamped for reentry.
14. Return to Tomorrowland on the monorail and see *Honey, I Shrunk the Audience*.
15. Ride Star Tours.
16. Revisit your favorites or see any attractions you missed. Check your daily entertainment schedule for parades or live performances that interest you.

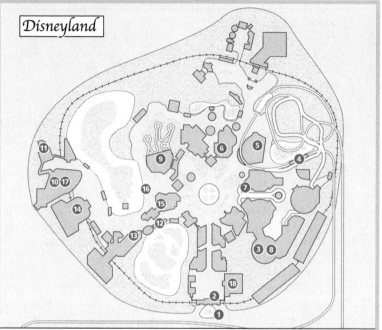

Disneyland

1. Arrive at the park at least 30 minutes before opening. Line up at Gate 13.
2. Give all of your admission passes to one person.
3. Dispatch this person to Space Mountain to obtain FASTPASSes.
4. Regroup in line at *Finding Nemo Submarine Voyage* (see page 272).
5. Ride the Matterhorn Bobsleds.
6. Go to Fantasyland and ride Peter Pan's Flight.
7. Return to Tomorrowland and ride Buzz Lightyear.
8. Ride Space Mountain using your FASTPASSes.
9. Go to Frontierland and ride Big Thunder Mountain Railroad.
10. Go to Critter Country and Splash Mountain. Obtain FASTPASSes.
11. Ride The Many Adventures of Winnie the Pooh.
12. Go to Adventureland and ride Indiana Jones.
13. Continue to New Orleans Square and experience Pirates of the Caribbean.
14. Tour The Haunted Mansion.
15. Have lunch and see the show at the Golden Horseshoe Saloon in Frontierland.
16. Ride either the Sailing Ship *Columbia* or the *Mark Twain* Riverboat.
17. Ride Splash Mountain using your FASTPASSes.
18. See *Disneyland: The First 50 Years* or *Great Moments with Mr. Lincoln*.

Two-day Plan B: Day Two

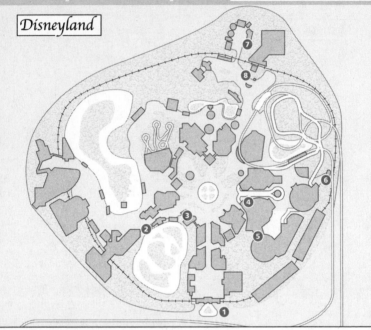

1. Eat an early dinner and arrive at the park about 5:30 or 6 p.m.
2. Go to Adventureland and explore Tarzan's Treehouse.
3. See the show in the *Enchanted Tiki Room.*
4. Go to Tomorowland and ride Star Tours.
5. See *Honey, I Shrunk the Audience.*
6. Take the Disneyland Railroad from the Tomorrowland Station to the Fantasyland/ Mickey's Toontown Station.
7. In Mickey's Toontown, ride Roger Rabbit's Car Toon Spin.
8. Go to Fantasyland and ride It's A Small World.
9. Check the *Times Guide* for parades, fireworks, and *Fantasmic!*
10. Pick up any attractions you may have missed earlier. Grab a bite to eat.

One-day Plan

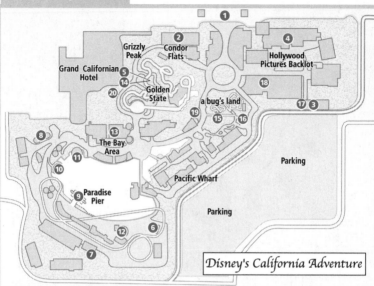

Disney's California Adventure

1. Arrive at the entrance 30 minutes before official opening time.
2. Ride Soarin' over California.
3. Go to the Hollywood Pictures Backlot and the Tower of Terror. Obtain FASTPASSes.
4. Ride *Monsters, Inc.*: Mike and Sulley to the Rescue.
5. Go to Grizzly River Run. Either ride or obtain a FASTPASS.
6. Ride the California Screamin' roller coaster in the Paradise Pier section of the park.
7. *Toy Story* Mania opens at Paradise Pier in 2008. If it's open, ride now.
8. Ride Mulholland Madness.
9. Ride the Sun Wheel.
10. Ride the Orange Stinger.
11. Ride the Golden Zephyr.
12. Ride King Triton's Carousel.
13. Stop in the San Francisco area and check out the showtimes for *Golden Dreams* starring Whoopi Goldberg.
14. Go to Grizzly River Run if you skipped it. Ride or obtain FASTPASSes.

15. Go to a bug's land. See *It's Tough to Be a Bug!*
16. Ride the kiddie rides at Flik's Fun Fair, and check the *Times Guide* for scheduled performances of *Ugly Bug Ball*.
17. Return to the Hollywood Pictures Backlot. Experience Tower of Terror and have lunch.
18. Check out *Playhouse Disney—Live on Stage!*, whatever the current show is at the Hyperion Theater, or *Muppet Vision 3-D*.
19. Return to Golden State and see the film about winemaking, tortilla- and bread-making demonstrations on Pacific Wharf, or *Golden Dreams* in San Francisco.
20. See the Redwood Creek Challenge and the fountain playground in Paradise Pier.
21. Check your daily entertainment schedule for parades, live performances, fireworks, and special events. View exhibits in the Animation building in Hollywood.

Universal Studios One-day Touring Plan

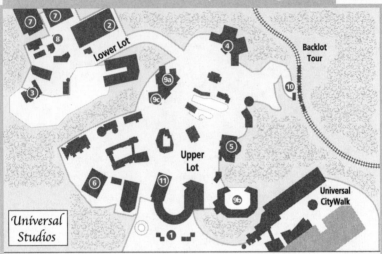

1. Arrive 20 minutes before opening time.
2. Go to Revenge of the Mummy.
3. Check out *Jurassic Park*.
4. Ride *Back to the Future*.
5. See *Shrek 4-D*.
6. See *Terminator 2: 3-D*.
7. Return to the Lower Lot and see Backdraft and the Special Effects Stages.
8. See the tribute to Lucy. Return to the Upper Lot.
9. Check your daily entertainment schedule for **a)** *Fear Factor Live,* **b)** *Waterworld,* and **c)** *Hollywood Animal Actors* showtimes.

10. Eat lunch and plan to take the Studio Tour. Allocate an hour and ten minutes for the tour.
11. Check out the Universal House of Horrors and the *Blues Brothers* show or try the Nickelodeon Blast Zone play area.
12. Revisit your favorites or see attractions you missed. Check your daily entertainment schedule for live performances that interest you.